DEVELOPING A SUSTAINABILITY MINDSET IN MANAGEMENT EDUCATION

With an expanding awareness of the challenges of sustainability, featured more in the daily news than in higher education textbooks, scholars and faculty have been called to connect their syllabi to the 'real world'. This book doesn't just offer the 'why'; it offers the 'how' through presenting the definition and model of the 'sustainability mindset' to help educators frame curricula to facilitate broad and deep systemic learning among current and future leaders.

A sustainability mindset is intended to help individuals analyze complex management challenges and generate truly innovative solutions. The sustainability mindset breaks away from traditional management disciplinary silos by integrating management ethics, entrepreneurship, environmental studies, systems thinking, self-awareness and spirituality within the dimensional contexts of thinking (knowledge), being (values) and doing (competency).

This book is aimed at professors, faculty members, instructors, teaching assistants, researchers and doctoral students in higher learning management education programs. Chapter contributors are all teaching professionals from programs around the world, who have been doing research and creating curricula, assessments, tools, and more for the students in their classes, and the book will be globally applicable.

Kerul Kassel is faculty at Fielding Graduate University, author of *The Thinking Executive's Guide to Sustainability* (Business Expert Press, 2014) and has been awarded year-on-year fellowships at Fielding's Institute for Social Innovation. Her work has appeared in peer-reviewed journals and conferences around the world.

Isabel Rimanoczy is Convener of the PRME Working Group on the Sustainability Mindset and author of *Big Bang Being: Developing the Sustainability Mindset* (2014) and *Stop Teaching* (2016). She is a Fellow of the Schumacher Institute and a Strategic Sustainability Adviser with One Planet Environmental Network.

'*Developing a Sustainability Mindset in Management Education* is relevant to students, educators, administrators, and leaders worldwide. It is a thoughtful, insightful, and purposeful book that breaks away from the traditional academic silos to allow educators to teach using systems thinking, self-awareness, and spirituality. The various authors present a re-conceptualization of education philosophies and objectives, new ways of developing a sustainability mindset in management students, and an opportunity to bring students into alignment with the United Nations' 2030 Sustainable Development Goals.'

Margaret A. Goralski, PhD, Coordinator Capstone Business Experiences & Assistant Professor of Strategy, Quinnipiac University, Connecticut, USA

'Over the last decade, business management has been involved in an active debate over several global problems facing humanity. At the center of the debate is the search for engaging leaders in the private sector to support the United Nations' Sustainable Development Goals and the United Nations' Principles for Responsible Management Education. Key to success in this direction is opening the mindset of business leaders to a holistic global view. *Developing a Sustainability Mindset in Management Education*, edited by two visionary researchers, focuses on the essential factor of developing this *weltanschauung* or world vision mindset, and offers both theoretical and practical methods. A remarkable collection of articles by like-minded and engaged researchers from around the world to help prepare leaders for dealing with common problems.'

Mehdi Majidi, Ph.D., University Professor and international consultant, Sustainable Socioeconomic Development

'The book calls for a holistic approach to management education that simultaneously addresses the "heads, hands and hearts" of future business leaders and the organizations they will create and/or work for. It also provides evidence and inspirational stories on how the possibility of developing the specific logos, pathos and ethos of sustainable mindset for the new role of business in society, sustainable development and responsible leadership could be turned into reality, both inside and outside the classroom.'

Milenko Gudić, Co-chair PRME Working Group on Poverty, a Challenge for Management Education; Founding Director, Refoment Consulting and Coaching, Belgrade Serbia

'Developing "The Sustainability Mindset", what an important idea! We, as a species, are in urgent need of learning for sustainability in order to become native again on this planet. Holistic educational approaches like the ones promoted by this book – learning to know, to do and to be – have enormous potential to foster such learning.'

Oliver Laasch, Ph.D., Founder of the Center for Responsible Management Education; Assistant Professor in Strategy, Nottingham University Business School

'If business education intends to foster global prosperity, then we must be more purposeful about developing the values, attitudes, and beliefs of our students. This book is about doing that. It informs and inspires by drawing on the ideas and experiences of pioneering professors from more than a dozen countries.'

Dan LeClair, Chief Operating Officer, AACSB

DEVELOPING A SUSTAINABILITY MINDSET IN MANAGEMENT EDUCATION

Edited by
Kerul Kassel and Isabel Rimanoczy

Routledge
Taylor & Francis Group

LONDON AND NEW YORK

First published 2018
by Routledge
2 Park Square, Milton Park, Abingdon, Oxon OX14 4RN

and by Routledge
711 Third Avenue, New York, NY 10017

Routledge is an imprint of the Taylor & Francis Group, an informa business

British Library Cataloguing-in-Publication Data
A catalogue record for this book is available from the British Library

Library of Congress Cataloging-in-Publication Data
Names: Kassel, Kerul, editor. | Rimanoczy, Isabel, 1956– editor.
Title: Developing a sustainability mindset in management education / edited by Kerul Kassel and Isabel Rimanoczy.
Description: Abingdon, Oxon ; New York, NY : Routledge, 2018. | Includes index.
Identifiers: LCCN 2017052838 | ISBN 9781783538171 (hbk) | ISBN 9781783537273 (pbk)
Subjects: LCSH: Business education. | Management. | Sustainability.
Classification: LCC HD30.4 .D47 2018 | DDC 658.0071—dc23
LC record available at https://lccn.loc.gov/2017052838

ISBN: 978-1-78353-817-1 (hbk)
ISBN: 978-1-78353-727-3 (pbk)
ISBN: 978-1-351-06334-0 (ebk)

Typeset in Bembo
by Apex CoVantage, LLC

CONTENTS

PART III
Integrating sustainability mindset in programmatic learning goals

FIGURES AND TABLES

Figures

Tables

CONTRIBUTING AUTHORS

Helen Akolgo-Azupogo is head of the Center for Cross-Cultural Ethics at Regentropfen College of Applied Science in Kansoe, Ghana. She is a graduate of the University of Development Studies in Tamale, where she worked on projects related to gender and public health issues. Akolgo-Azupogo also teaches and conducts research in the area of ethics and ethical decision-making at the Miller Institute for Transdisciplinary and Development Studies located in Bolgatanga, Ghana. She can be contacted at helen.azupogo@recas-ghana.com.

Janaina Franciscatto Audino is a Ph.D. Student at UNISINOS (University of Vale do Rio dos Sinos). She holds a Master's degree in Educational Management (2014), post-graduated on Management School (2011), graduated in Pedagogy (2002). Since 2010 she is the executive at Instituto JAMA, a family institute created in 2009 to direct the social investment of Jayme Sirotsky's family, supporting projects in the educational areas, social assistance, and culture. The Institute is a non-profit organization, qualified as an Organization of the Public Civil Society (OSCIP) and is located in the city of Porto Alegre, Rio Grande do Sul. Janaina has academic and professional experience in the areas of educational management and in the third sector, acting as a guest teacher in post-graduate courses. She can be contacted at janaina@institutojama.com.br.

Roland Bardy is Executive Professor at Florida Gulf Coast University's Lutgert College of Business, a retired executive from BASF, and Principal with Bardy Consult. He has more than 30 years' experience working with multinationals, and since his retirement in 1999 has lectured and consulted worldwide. His research interests are in leadership, ethics, and sustainability, and he can be contacted at r.bardy@t-online.de.

Janaína Pimenta Lemos Becker has a Ph.D. in Applied Linguistics from Universidade do Vale do Rio dos Sinos (UNISINOS), Brazil. She has been a professor at UNISINOS since 2005, dedicating herself to teaching at the undergraduate level and to academic management. At the undergraduate level, she teaches Portuguese Language in business administration courses, and she teaches Methods and Techniques of Education in the undergraduate course of Portuguese Language. Since 2013, she is also dedicated to academic management: she is coordinator of the undergraduate Major Program in Business Administration – Major in Management for Innovation and Leadership. She is an assistant professor at UNISINOS Business School, Brazil. Please contact Janaína at janainab@unisinos.br.

Janette Brunstein is a researcher and professor of the Stricto Sensu Post-Graduation Program in Business Administration from Presbyterian University Mackenzie. Her work is focused on education, learning, and development of competencies for sustainability academic and organizational environments. She is a leader of a research group, entitled Research and Foundation in Administration, which is supported by the National Counsel of Technological and Scientific Development (CNPq). She has more than ten years of academic experience, and during the last eight years, she has been coordinating some projects within the national ambit, supported by organs in furtherance of the Brazilian Government, which aims to insert the theme of sustainability into business administration courses. She is currently Professor and Researcher of Business Administration at Universidade Presbiteriana Mackenzie CCSA – Centro de Ciências Sociais e Aplicadas (Social SciencesApplied Centre) at Post-graduation Program Campus and can be reached at janette@mackenzie.br.

Javier Collado-Ruano is Titular Professor in the National University of Education in Ecuador. He holds a Ph.D. in Dissemination of Knowledge by the Federal University of Bahia (Brazil) and also a Ph.D. in Philosophy by the University of Salamanca (Spain). He has a master's degree in Sociology of Education by the University of Seville (Spain) and Graduation in History by the University of Valencia (Spain) with specialization in International Relations and Archeology by the University of Palermo (Italy). He is founder and director at *Global Education Magazine* (supported by UNESCO and UNHCR) and President at Education for Life NGO. He is also an Academic Member of the Big History Institute (Australia), an Academic Member at World Biomimetic Foundation (Spain), a Member of the editorial board at the *Journal of International Society of Philosophy and Cosmology* (Ukraine), an Advisory Board Member at Shreeranya Renewable India, Chief Advisor and Conferment of Fellowship Awards at PAN African Institute for Entrepreneurship and Community Development (Nigeria), and Education Advisor at Human Dignity and Humiliation Studies (USA). His research interests are transdisciplinary, biomimicry, sustainable development, global citizenship, e-learning, cultural anthropology, culture of peace, spirituality, emotional intelligence, sociology, democracy and governability, poverty eradication, human rights, philosophy, epistemology, arts, globalization, co-evolution, big history, complexity, and life. Javier welcomes readers to email him at Javier.collado@unae.edu.ec.

Silvia M. Russi De Domenico is a graduate in Chemical Engineering from the University of São Paulo (USP) in Brazil, and she holds master's and doctorate degrees in Business Administration at USP and Mackenzie Presbyterian University (UPM), respectively. She is currently lecturing and researching in the Graduate Programme in Business Administration at UPM. The focus of her work is on human values and practices within the environment of the organisation, stakeholder relationships, organisational change, and organising. She has professional work experience in organizational behaviour, strategic planning, and team development. She may be contacted at silviarussi@mackenzie.br.

Consuelo Garcia de la Torre has a Ph.D. in Management, HEC University of Montreal and an MBA in IAG of Louvain-la-Neuve University, Belgium. She is currently a full-time professor at the EGADE Business School, Tecnológico de Monterrey, in Mexico. She is a member of the Mexican National Research System (SNI 1) and a member and fellow of the Academy of Management. She represents the Mexico chapter of the International Network of Humanistic and Management. She is also part of the research group with strategic focus on social innovation in EGADE Business School. She has published articles regarding corporate social responsibility, ethics for higher education, humanistic and perspectives on international business management, and humanistic management in Latin America. Dr. Garcia de la Torre can be contacted at cogarcia@itesm.mx.

Colin Heaton is a visiting instructor in Sustainable Living at Maharishi University of Management. He has degrees in Education and in Environmental Policy. His teaching encourages students to explore the science and ethics of policy issues with open minds and to unlock the awesome creative potential of their minds. Dr. Heaton is available for inquiring readers at cheaton@mum.edu.

Dennis Heaton is Director of the Management Ph.D. programme at Maharishi University of Management (MUM) in Fairfield, Iowa, USA, which focuses on consciousness and sustainability. Dennis has explored the interface of psychological models from Western developmental psychology and Eastern models of higher states of consciousness, and he is a proponent of consciousness-based management education, which includes the transcendental meditation technique. He is a member of the PRME Working Group for the Sustainability Mindset. Dr. Heaton welcomes inquiries at dheaton@mum.edu.

amelia naim indrajaya is a researcher, writer, trainer, and motivator, and a faculty member of IPMI Business School, in Jakarta, Indonesia. She is also the founder of PT Rentang Gunaputra, a training and management consulting company. She has helped numerous companies in conducting their trainings, including Toyota,

Telkom, and Kimia Farma. She is also the Head of the Center for Sustainability Mindset and Social Responsibility (CSMSR) of IPMI International Business School. She obtained her doctoral degree from Strategic Management, Faculty of Economy and Business, Universitas Indonesia. Currently she teaches CSR Strategies, Managerial Communication and Good Corporate Governance at IPMI International Business School, Jakarta. She can be contacted at amelia.naim@ipmi.ac.id.

Kerul Kassel, Ph.D., is a faculty member at Fielding Graduate University, teaching in the Sustainability Leadership, Global Leadership, and Humane Workplace programs, and is the author of *The Thinking Executive's Guide to Sustainability* (Business Expert Press, 2014). She has been awarded year-on-year fellowships at Fielding's Institute for Social Innovation. Dr. Kassel holds a Ph.D. in Human and Organizational Systems and master's degrees in Human Development and Social Ecology. She is a Certified Sustainability Professional through the International Society of Sustainability Professionals, is a LEED Green Associate, and holds multiple professional coaching certifications. Her work has appeared in peer-reviewed journals and in conferences around the world. She is a member of the international Principles for Responsible Management Education (PRME) Working Group on the Sustainability Mindset, a program of the United Nations Global Compact. Her research agenda focuses on sustainable enterprise, business practices and education, and leadership for sustainability in organizations. She can be contacted at kkassel@fielding.edu.

Mario Vázquez Maguirre holds a Ph.D. (Business) from EGADE Business School, Tecnológico de Monterrey and an MSc (Economics and Public Policy) at EGAP, Tecnológico de Monterrey. He is currently a professor of entrepreneurship and corporate social responsibility at Universidad de Monterrey (UDEM). His primary research lines include social entrepreneurship, social enterprises and social development, humanistic management, and sustainability. He has worked in corporations such as BBVA and UPS, and he has served as consultant to small and medium-sized enterprises (SMEs) and non-governmental organisations (NGOs). He welcomes emails from readers at mario.vazquez@udem.edu.

Shelley F. Mitchell, Ph.D., is Professor of Management and Sustainability at Hult International Business School in Cambridge, Massachusetts, where she teaches Corporate Social Responsibility. Shelley completed her Ph.D. (2012) in Natural Resources and Environmental Studies as part of an interdisciplinary program between the Natural Resources and Earth Systems Science Graduate Program and the Paul College of Business and Economics at the University of New Hampshire (UNH), where she also earned her MBA (2002) with an emphasis in entrepreneurship. At UNH, she was an instructor and course coordinator for Introduction to Business and currently teaches Strategic Management and Business, Government, and Society courses. Prior to academia, Shelley worked in a variety of executive roles in the private, public, and non-profit sectors including as a startup co-founder, at New Hampshire Public Television, and at the Indianapolis Zoological Society. Her empirical research focuses on how small to medium-sized enterprises (SMEs) use innovation for ecological sustainability, strategy and sustainable business models, social enterprises and entrepreneurship, and sustainability in management education. In 2010, she was selected to participate in the first Oikos Foundation for Economy and Ecology Young Scholars Entrepreneurship Academy in Urnäsch, Switzerland. In 2016, Shelley was a co-recipient of the Junior Faculty Best Paper Award for the most significant contribution to management education from the MED division of the Academy of Management (AOM). She is also a frequent chair and organizer of professional development workshops and symposia at AOM. She can be emailed at shelley.mitchell@faculty.hult.edu.

Mary Grace Neville, a Fulbright Fellow and an associate professor of business, is a teacher-scholar at liberal arts colleges internationally and a practitioner of strategic change and organizational development. She earned her Ph.D. in Organizational Behavior from Case Western Reserve University, and her MBA degree at the Wharton School of Business. Neville is an emeritus faculty of Southwestern University in Texas, and currently full-time faculty at Al Akhawayn University in Morocco. Readers are encouraged to contact the author at marygrace.neville@gmail.com.

Alexander Tetteh Kwasi Nuer, Ph.D. is a lecturer (Agribusiness and Social Audit) with the Department of Agricultural Economics and Extension, University of Cape Coast, Ghana. He is also a pro bono faculty at College of Tropical Agriculture (KITA) Ghana, Apromase/Kumasi, Ghana. He obtained his MSc and Ph.D. studies from Wageningen University & Research, The Netherlands. His postdoctoral research was further pursued with the Agriculture Economics and Rural Policy Group of Wageningen University & Research, while he served as a postdoctoral researcher with ISSER-University of Ghana. He has conducted many sustainability-related studies in Zambia, Rwanda, Tanzania, and Ghana. He is a team leader and project coordinator with the College of Agriculture (KITA) in Ghana and also runs his consultancy Alamnyaki Social Initiative in Ghana. He can be reached at alexander.nuer@gmail.com.

Henrietta Onwuegbuzie, Ph.D., leads sessions in entrepreneurship on the MBA and Executive programmes at Lagos Business School (LBS), and is currently Academic Director for the Owner-Manager Programme and Project Director for the Impact Investing policy initiative at the Lagos Business School. She has an MSc (with honours) in Economics and Business Administration from the University of Navarre, Spain; an MBA from Lagos Business School; and a Ph.D. in Management (Entrepreneurship) from Lancaster University, UK. She welcomes inquiries on her work at honwuegbuzie@lbs.edu.ng.

Isabel Rimanoczy, Ed.D., has made it her life purpose to promote change accelerators. Aware of the complex challenges our planet (and us in it) are facing, she works alongside those who can make an impact on a greater scale. She is the convener of the PRME Sustainability Mindset Working Group, an international cohort of more than 75 academics from 67 universities on five continents promoting teaching for a paradigmatic shift. She is Global Academic Ambassador for *AIM2Flourish*, the international initiative to promote businesses as agents of world benefit by teaching 17 Sustainable Development Goals. She is the author of several books, including *BIG BANG BEING: Developing the Sustainability Mindset* and *Stop Teaching: Principles and Practices for Responsible Management Education*. Isabel has published more than 140 articles and book chapters and is a contributing blogger for the *Huffington Post*. She is the founder and director of *MINERVAS, Women Changing the World*, a nonprofit 501(c)3 organization that supports women making a difference. She earned her doctorate at Columbia University, has her MBA from Universidad de Palermo, and is a licensed psychologist from the Universidad de Buenos Aires. She encourages readers to contact her at www.IsabelRimanoczy.net.

Arthur Rubens is currently Professor of Management at Florida Gulf Coast University, Lutgert College of Business. He has more than 25 years of experience as an educator, administrator, and consultant, and he has taught classes in multiple countries. His research interests are in leadership, ethics, economic development and sustainability. He can be contacted at arubens@fgcu.edu.

Marta Fabiano Sambiase holds a bachelor's degree in Human Science from Universidade de São Paulo (USP) with a Specialist by Business School Fundação Getulio Vargas (FGV), and earned her master's and doctorate degrees in Business Administration from Universidade Presbiteriana Mackenzie in 2003 and 2009, respectively. She is currently a professor and researcher in Management, Strategy for Sustainability, Behavioural Strategy in Relations Dimensions, fundamentally at the Universidade Presbiteriana Mackenzie, CCSA – Centro de Ciências Sociais e Aplicadas (Social Sciences Applied Centre). She is available to be contacted at martasambiase@mackenzie.br.

Soraia Schutel has a Ph.D. in Management from the Federal University of Rio Grande do Sul (UFRGS), Brazil. As part of her Ph.D., she studied and developed her theses at HEC Montréal, Canada. She specialized in Social Psychology at the State University of St. Petersburg, Russia, and studied Leadership for Transition at Schumacher College, UK. Her research focuses on education for sustainability, transformative learning, and women and leadership. She has academic and professional experience in more than 25 countries. She is an assistant professor at Unisinos Business School, Brazil, and welcomes reader inquiries at sschutel@unisinos.br.

Radha R. Sharma, Ph.D., is Dean, Research, Centers of Excellence at Case Centre Raman Munjal (Hero MotoCorp) and Chair, Professor of Organizational Behavior in the Department of Human Behavior and Organizational Development. She is Editor of *Vision: A Journal of Business Perspective* (SAGE), Associate

Editor of *Frontiers in Psychology*, and located at the Management Development Institute, Mehrauli Road, Sukhrali Gurgaon, India. She can be reached at radha@mdi.ac.in or radhasharma308@gmail.com.

Karthyeni Sridaran has a rich cross-cultural international work experience, with more than 25 years in public, private, consulting, and academic sectors. Currently, she is engaged as an academic at the University of Melbourne teaching postgraduate and undergraduate subjects at the Department of Management, and she is also developing an MBA subject curriculum for the Kaplan Business School in Melbourne, Australia, where she lives. Her skills and competencies are in the increasingly important fields of conscious leadership, workplace wellness, positive psychology, and sustainable enterprise. As an academic for the last 17 years, she has been teaching and researching within a wide range of management disciplines, such as organizational wellness, international human resource management, organisational behaviour, managing People and organizations, managerial communications, conflict management and management competencies. Prior to her academic career, Karthyeni has worked and consulted in public, private and non-profit organisations in several countries, where she has developed a variety of customer and human relations initiatives. She is passionate and proactive in transforming individuals and groups in classroom and boardroom settings, with the ultimate aim of shifting mindsets toward a consciousness model of management and leadership.

Ijeoma Ugwanyi is currently a Doctor of Philosophy candidate in Management (Strategy/Entrepreneurship) at the City University of Hong Kong. Prior to this, she worked as a research assistant at the Lagos Business School, Pan-Atlantic University, where she assisted faculty in research projects with titles such as indigenous entrepreneurship, experiential learning in entrepreneurship, teaching ethics in entrepreneurship, inclusive growth, and sustainable development. These projects led to publications in book chapters, journals, and international conference proceedings. Her current research interests include entrepreneurship, international business, family business, strategic business models, emerging market dynamics, innovation and data analytics. She enjoys traveling and mentoring as pastimes.

Charlie Yang is Associate Professor in the Department of Management, MIS, and International Business at Southern Connecticut State University in Connecticut, USA. His current research interests are mindfulness and the sustainability mindset, storytelling/gossiping organizations, and the application of Darwinian evolutionary ideas in management and organization studies. He is also passionate about using meditation and arts in his teaching of management courses, such as Mindful Leadership and Creativity and Innovation. He can be reached at: Associate Professor, Department of Management, MIS, and International Business, Southern Connecticut State University, 205 School of Business Building, New Haven, CT 06515, USA YangC1@southernct.edu.

Angus W.H. Yip is a sustainability consultant specialising in Environmental, Social and Governance (ESG) reporting for listed companies. He is also Adjunct Associate Professor at Institute of China Business of the University of Hong Kong SPACE. Angus was a corporate banker, but he is passionate about sustainability, so he changed his career to sustainability by studying for a master's degree in Sustainability Leadership at the Cambridge Institute for Sustainability Leadership (CISL), at the University of Cambridge. He is now pursuing a Ph.D. degree at the University of Warwick, UK. Angus encourages readers to contact him at angus.yip@ teacher.hkuspace.hku.hk.

FOREWORD

Many people believe that there is a crisis today in management education. Born of the failures of management and leadership over the last few decades, as witnessed in the Global Financial Crisis of 2007–2008, which few foresaw and even fewer knew how to resolve, and the growing crisis of climate change, accompanied by a range of potential sustainability disasters and systemic inequality threatening social stability, among numerous other risks. The crisis in management and consequently in management education is also underpinned by charges of ethical, human rights, labor rights, and other violations of human dignity, evident in the numerous company crises and scandals that have taken place since the turn of the century.

At the same time, management education generally seems stuck in silos of disciplines and functional responsibilities with little capacity to integrate across these areas, despite pressing needs for a more holistic approach that takes into account the social and ecological problems facing the world. What Kassel and Rimanoczy have done with *Developing a Sustainability Mindset in Management Education* is to present a new vision for management education. That vision is grounded in three fundamental concepts – being, thinking, and doing – that frame the sustainability mindset and provide a framework for the chapters in this book. These three dimensions collectively constitute the sustainability mindset when integrated with four emerging content areas: a systems perspective, spiritual intelligence, an ecological worldview, and emotional intelligence. And, as the chapters in this book demonstrate, there are places around the world where experiments in management education demonstrate the feasibility of introducing such topics into the curriculum.

Still, such topics are too infrequently found in management education. But they will likely prove 'business central' in an uncertain, ecologically and socially challenged, digitally connected future unlike anything humans have dealt with in the past. In fact, the sustainability mindset is a systems-based approach to managing that fundamentally understands the deep interconnections of humans, thriving ecological systems that support the human project, and healthy societies within those ecosystems.

The premise of this forward-looking book is that the old functional and analytical approaches to management education, while important, are no longer sufficient for future leaders and managers to cope with the world they will actually face. Approaches need to be based in developing greater self- and other-awareness, as well as ecological sensitivity, and systems or holistic thinking, which the authors illustrate in grounded ways. The key insight is that simply understanding the disciplines and functional areas of management is not enough, because what the authors term 'being,' or awareness of assumptions and values that underpin knowledge, will be vital to coping successfully in the future. Emphasis only on costs and benefits and wealth maximization by companies, disregard for the effects of managerial decisions on stakeholders or nature, and even a narrow focus just on the company are ways of thinking – and being – in the world that no longer provide an adequate basis for decision making.

Future leaders need to understand not just what their businesses need to do internally and competitively to be successful, but equally importantly, how they fit into and affect their social and environmental contexts. That understanding combines the first two elements of the framework for this book – being and thinking (or the cognitive understanding needed to lead and manage well) – and links to the third element of doing. All management decisions integrally have ethical content that cannot be teased apart from the impacts of those decisions, for both good and ill. Through the types of programs described here, students can learn that many, if not most, business decisions have ecological, human, and sometimes societal consequences that need at the least to be mitigated and at best to be worked through so that any impacts are impermanent.

The sustainability mindset described throughout the book is a very different mindset from the traditional linear thinking taught in business schools. It is, in effect, a circular way of thinking that implies the very connectedness to the world around us that is needed and is fostered by the sustainability mindset. It implies that both self-awareness and reflectiveness are fundamental demands on tomorrow's leaders and managers. It implies a need for not just cognitive but also emotional maturity in our leaders and managers of the future. When combined with understanding of the sustainability implications of decisions, such self-awareness (being) means that the knowledge gained (thinking) can potentially result in actions (doing) that much better aligns businesses with the ecological and societal realities of the world.

The implications of this mindset shift for management education, as outlined in this book, are stunning. From linear, narrowly analytical, and functional thinking and learning, the curriculum needs to be much more expansive, encompassing individual (including spiritual), collective, societal, and ecological dimensions. Management students need to learn to think about regenerativity, interconnectedness, and interdependence, and about how their own behaviors and practices affect others and the world around them in ways not typically considered in management education programs. With these ideas as a backdrop, *Developing a Sustainability*

Mindset in Management Education provides a roadmap for the kinds of management education programs, curricula, and new ways of being, thinking, and doing that are much needed in our world.

Sandra Waddock
Galligan Chair of Strategy
Carroll School Scholar of Corporate Responsibility
Professor of Management
Boston College
Carroll School of Management
Chestnut Hill, MA 02467 USA

INTRODUCTION

About a decade ago, a number of ethical corporate scandals combined with environmental negative impacts of business practices led academics to question what we were teaching in our business schools. At a conference organized by the Fowler Center at Case Western Reserve University, in which "business as an agent of world benefit" was explored, exemplary leaders shared stories about innovative ways in which their organizations were trying to have a better impact on society or the environment. Why were there not more such leaders? What did we have to do differently in our management education? These questions prompted the creation of the Principles of Responsible Management Education (PRME) initiative. The same questions led Rimanoczy to study business leaders championing sustainability initiatives and Kassel to study how the value orientations of Fortune 1000 CEOs might relate to an organization's sustainability practices. The purpose of our studies was to identify what these leaders knew, what motivated them, and perhaps find ways to intentionally develop a new generation of sustainability-minded leaders.

A few years later, Rimanoczy's qualitative exploratory study provided data and elements that could be included into management and organizational change courses: the elements pertained to the domain of 'thinking' (knowledge) and 'being' (values), and were at the foundation of sustainability actions. She labeled this the 'sustainability mindset', a term that suggested a shift in how we traditionally interpreted information, how we analyzed options and made decisions. The elements of the sustainability mindset were converted into learning goals, and a course was designed to pilot how to develop them. The course was run at the graduate level as an elective, semester-long, three-credit program.

The transformational impact observed in the attitudes of the students, collected informally via feedback, postings and expressions of their paradigm shift, motivated Rimanoczy to invite colleagues from around the world to form a learning community on the so-called sustainability mindset, to share their own similar practices or approaches to develop a paradigm shift towards sustainability, or to adopt or adapt the components of the existing course that best suited their own context. In 2014, LEAP! was created, with the mission captured in the acronym: to Leverage resources, Expand awareness, Accelerate change and Partner.

This network has since become the PRME Working Group on the Sustainability Mindset, with more than 75 members from 67 institutions in 26 countries. The Working Group members meet virtually and face to face, participate in workshops, develop syllabi, write collaborative papers and visit each other's classes. During the first international meeting, attended by members from Indonesia, the Philippines, India, France, the UK, and the US, the question emerged: what exactly is the sustainability mindset? While there was a shared intuitive understanding that it was about ways of thinking and ways of being, it became apparent that we needed to review the existing literature in more depth with regard to the sustainability competencies, skills and attitudes in order to establish the different theoretical underpinnings, and develop a model that could be shared.

In 2016 the conceptual framework was presented at the Academy of Management International Conference in Anaheim, California, authored by three LEAP members: Kassel, Rimanoczy and Mitchell, winning the Management Education and Development Division's Junior Faculty Best Paper Award, for the most significant contribution to management education by a Junior Faculty authorship team.

This book is another step in the journey of the international Working Group, whose vision is to achieve the Sustainable Development Goals proclaimed by the United Nations Global Compact and adopted by the 193 member countries in 2015, by developing a sustainability mindset. With a growing number of members, broader cultural diversity and the multiplying sustainability practices being applied in higher education classrooms around the world, we thought it was time to share with a larger audience some of the experiences, practices and conceptual approaches related to the sustainability mindset and the impact that is being created.

As editors, we envision this edited work as a contribution to educators around the world, particularly in regard to developing a mindset that acts as a sustainability lens through which to analyze challenges, information and solutions. This book features conceptual frameworks, tools, exercises and practices for faculty members to use in their courses and programs to develop such a mindset.

This book is largely aimed at professors, faculty members, instructors, teaching assistants, researchers, doctoral students in higher-learning management education programs and practitioners. Our chapter contributors are scholars and academics with doctoral degrees from around the world who have been doing research and creating curricula, assessments, tools and more for the students in their classes, which makes the contents globally applicable. A substantial portion of the methods, tools and assessments described in these chapters will also have applicability for management practitioners wishing to help their clients or their organizational cultures to develop a sustainability mindset.

How this book is organized

The chapters in this book present theories, pedagogical approaches, exercises and activities that showcase different ways to develop a sustainability mindset, as well as examples of the impact of the mindset in action.

The chapters are grounded in literature relevant to their topics. They are rigorous in their construction and presentation, and they have been selected to be of practical value to educators who are passionate about developing an enhanced sustainability mindset in their students and in their schools. Our authors teach in management education programs around the world.

Part I offers several theoretical approaches that support a model for a sustainability mindset, with authors writing from the USA, Australia, Brazil, China, India, and Ecuador. Part II continues with examples from faculty who teach in programs in Brazil, Indonesia, Nigeria, The Netherlands, Zambia and Indonesia, and who are integrating curricular changes to their courses to support the development of a sustainability mindset in their students. Some of these changes emphasize in particular one or two dimensions of the tripartite model (knowing, being, doing), and others have intentionally redesigned their courses to balance all three. The chapter authors in Part III discuss how their programs integrate learning goals aimed at a sustainability mindset, not only for students, but for entire programs – and beyond. It is heartening to know that such holistic programs, melding head with heart and hands, have been developing and gaining traction in the USA, Mexico, Ghana, Morocco and farther afield.

We have organized the book to deliver inspiration and hope, as well as nuts and bolts (actual exercises, assignments, and projects) to faculty who may feel they are struggling alone to assimilate a more well-rounded and holistic approach to management education that embodies the triple bottom line systemically. A number of our authors have been in that position, searching for a means acceptable to their colleagues, supervisors, programs and administration to bring a longer time-frame, greater social equity, deeper environmental justice and spiritually grounded ethical considerations into not only management education but also management practices.

In Part I, the theoretical discussions begin with the foundational chapter on a sustainability mindset model by Kerul Kassel, Isabel Rimanoczy and Shelley Mitchell, intended to help educators frame curricula to facilitate broad and deep systemic learning. The model's purpose is to support current and future leaders in learning to analyze complex management challenges and generate truly innovative solutions. The authors suggest that the model breaks away from traditional management disciplinary silos by integrating management ethics, entrepreneurship, environmental studies, systems thinking, self-awareness and spirituality within the dimensional contexts of being (values), thinking (knowledge) and doing (competency). The chapter explores the model's dimensions and their content areas, reflecting on how educators are facilitating this mindset in the context of management education and leadership development.

Isabel Rimanoczy and Karthyeni Sridaran build on the notion of the *being dimension*, drawing comparisons from their research studies of US, Australian and Malaysian business leaders in which each's independent findings came to similar conclusions. The spiritual domain, their data implies, is a fundamental tacit dimension on which an inner mind-shift can accelerate external transformations for firms to address the ultimate need for human well-being in the world. Their chapter additionally describes tools and initiatives that build not only knowledge and skills but more importantly the values, will and vision to transform students into responsible corporate citizens of the future.

In bringing theory to bear on the relationship between values and management education for sustainability, Marta Sambiase, Janette Brunstein and Silva De Domenico utilize Schwartz and Bilsky's (1990) Theory of Basic Values, along with broader literature on values in business, and the United National Millennium Declaration to introduce elements they assert can contribute to sustainability mindset. They suggest ways to foster students' reflective practices that help them recognize and question the values underlying their responses to a given situation, creating disorienting dilemmas in the classroom that prompt them to consider how they feel and act in relation to a problem, why they select particular problem-solving strategies, and evaluating the premises and assumptions around the problem.

Employing motivational theory to assess decision making in Hong Kong's small and medium public enterprises (SMEs), Angus Yip suggests a way for management faculty to use such theory in case study development for management educators. The selected motivational theories apply at both individual and organizational levels, such that they can be adapted for general frameworks to cultivate students' sustainability mindset so as to bridge the mindset-behavior gap in the business context. After outlining the theory, particularly as it applies to stakeholder relations, the second segment of this chapter outlines a process for faculty to use to assist students in exploring motivational theory in management practice and its real-world impacts.

Next, Radha Sharma delves into the dimension of values, ethics and virtues and provides a paradigm for sustainable organizations and society leveraging traditional Western and Indian wisdom, exploring the concept of Eudaimonia, meaning human flourishing brought about by right actions. Imparting concern for others and a sense of responsibility towards various stakeholders, including the environment, are important in a globally connected, multicultural world, where socioeconomic and technological developments have shifted values, and in which spiritual teachings and religious values have taken a back seat. Exercises to make explicit the ethical considerations of management policy conclude this chapter.

A Cosmodern Education paradigm, in which interiority and a triple literacy of emotional, spiritual, ecological feeling/thinking/acting, aimed at identifying core patterns and issues (that are overlooked or unexplored in almost all educational programs and models), forms the evolution of pedagogy, as theorized by Javier Collado-Ruano, at Universidad Nacional de Educación in Ecuador. By combining many interior and exterior dimensions and types of intelligence, students (and society) can be more interconnected with each other and with the biosphere's needs, for a more resilient future that is in harmony with the coevolution of natural processes of nature, enacting the United Nations Sustainable Development Goals. Rather than simply transmitting knowledge and values, Cosmodern Education is a constructive, creative and transformative act.

Faculty who have been concerned about the values and siloed orientation of conventional management education, and have largely worked on their own, describe their efforts and suggestions in Part II to meld a systemic view of business, blending in social and environmental concerns and impacts in the courses they facilitate.

Expecting a 100% return at the end of the term on their school's $30 investment in the students' enterprise efforts, Henrietta Onwuegbuzie and Ijeoma Ugwuanyi describe the success of their social enterprise incubator project within an MBA entrepreneurship course at Lagos Business School in Nigeria. Their purpose is to have students experience, combining their own head, heart, and hands, how a social impact is compatible with business profitability, a divergence from the traditional dichotomy between profit-seeking businesses and socially sensitive ones. The authors also describe their additional curricular additions aimed at developing sustainability mindset in their students: the exercise of observing and analyzing businesses, which allows learning from reflective observation, use of case studies on entrepreneurs who intentionally seek to impact society through their businesses, and listening to such entrepreneurs share their journeys in person.

Standing for the concept of business as a force for good, Amelia Naim Indrajaya has incorporated several curricular innovations at Institut Pengembangan Manajemen Indonesia in Jakarta. A variety of student projects melded into a course titled "Outstanding Value: The Knowing, Being and Doing" offers students opportunities to explore their values and life purpose through examples, as well as brainstorming and experimenting with ways that enterprise can contribute to positive social and environmental impact, using the United Nations Sustainable Development Goals as a lens. The learning journey is designed to span from the micro to the macro, beginning with individual development, moving to team development, then focusing on total system development, and concluding with redefining the role of business.

Intercultural collaboration is the means through which Alex Nuer explores development of sustainability mindset in students from differing cultures. This chapter explores sustainability mindset elements in the context of research in which undergraduate students from The Netherlands and Zambia jointly conduct action research within dairy agriculture value chains in Zambia. The chapter highlights learning outcomes, new knowledge gained, and insights shared by students, based on cross-cultural perspectives in complex environments that have divergent values and thinking. Using capacity building in the area of joint development of field studies as boots-on-the-ground work, the chapter describes how it helped faculty and students to test, in a practical and applied manner, how their knowledge and experiences shape their worldview, appreciating both their own culture and gaining an appreciation for multicultural diversity.

Through his course on "Mindful Leadership" in the Department of Management at Southern Connecticut State University, Charlie Yang analyzes his students' meditation journals and their reflection essays on aesthetic appreciation, discusses the pedagogical implications of mindfulness and its practices for developing management students' practical wisdom. He proposes that mindfulness and its practices are not merely useful tools for stress reduction but also effective meaning-making practices that can be more actively adopted to cultivate management students' self-awareness, their sense of purpose and values, and social-emotional skills for the sake of more responsible management education.

The institutional innovations explored in Part III begin with what the authors term a transformative learning pedagogical approach, informed by participatory action research. At the USINOS Business School in Brazil, Soraia Schutel, Janaína Pimenta Lemos Becker and Janaina Franciscatto Audino have analyzed competencies developed by management students, finding that the students' worldviews were expanded as they acquired new values. Their social competencies, such as empathy, cooperation and critical thinking, increased significantly. Beyond the pedagogical impact on students, though, they emphasize the importance of an institutional culture that embraced innovation in its educational processes, and how this impacted their stakeholder relationships.

At the Universidad de Monterrey in Mexico, the "Drivers of Change" program was instituted by a hybrid of Catholic congregations and businesspeople from the region, with the purpose of providing comprehensive business management preparation to students under the premise that the realization of the individual is only possible through service to others. Mario Vázquez Maguirre and Consuelo Garcia de la Torre describe the eight-semester transversal program, in which students learn about both for-profit and non-governmental organizational management, speaking with practitioners who have both succeeded and failed, understanding theoretical concepts through service learning projects that are founded on the goal of community development.

Consciousness-Based Education (CBE) is a learning model that informs the Maharishi University of Management in Iowa, United States. Dennis and Colin Heaton describe how being, knowing and doing are handled in distinctive ways through this transdisciplinary learning model, in ways that contribute to the Systems Perspective, Spiritual Intelligence and Ecological Worldview content areas of the sustainability mindset. The CBE model highlights its own tripartite structure with the knower, the known and the process of knowing as a path toward holistically connecting different forms and types of knowledge, and to enhance a sense of oneness and interconnectedness that can be adapted to leadership and management practices in diverse organizations.

The institutional co-creation for sustainability by partnering with government, non-governmental organizations and business as the "fourth mission" of education is foundational to the new Regentropfen College of Applied Science in Kansoe, in Ghana's Upper East Region. Helen Akolgo-Azupogo, of Regentropfen College, with Roland Bardy and Arthur Rubens of Florida Gulf Coast University, describe how the region's stakeholders are engaged to provide the region with increased opportunities to improve their overall social and economic well-being.

Regentropfen's Center for Cross-Cultural Ethics and Sustainable Development, a sub-entity of the college, together with its Business and Career Development Center, are integral to the institutional design of managing a delicate balance of teaching, research and community outreach.

Envisioning business students as consumers of education shifts the frame of reference in Mary Grace Neville's research. In asking how to best prepare those students for a technologically, multicultural, geo-politically complex, and systemically challenged management world, she urges critical and ethical thinking skills and a robust set of relevant disciplines. These are central to a liberal arts approach, one which she urges, through the framework of a Capacity Map, as a format for business education. Her aim is the empowerment of business educators to better steward the future by shifting from an educational paradigm that prioritizes "individualistic training to a futuristic developmental mindset" so as to best navigate the rapidly shifting and increasingly challenging world of business and beyond.

All in all, through the colorful lenses of their particular cultures and contexts, a voice seems to emerge. One calling for a new approach to education: holistic, engaged, connecting information with values and purpose, and with one goal: the urgent betterment of our planetary experience.

ACKNOWLEDGEMENTS

This book has been an international labor of love. We would like to express our gratitude to all members of LEAP!, the PRME Working Group on the Sustainability Mindset, for their ongoing participation and for nurturing this movement towards a more integral way of thinking about the present and the future. Since its inception, in 2013, the LEAP! cohort has been exchanging ideas, resources, experiences and hesitations, which collectively led to a better practice. This book, with contributions of 23 colleagues from around the world, is a visible impact of this community.

We also appreciate the support from Jonas Haertle, Nikolai Ivanov and Florencia Librizzi at PRME, as well as our colleague Milenko Gudic, who mentored us in our initial stages.

To Rebecca Marsh, our deep-felt gratitude for listening to our project and understanding the value of sharing stories from around the world, with the world.

And to each contributor, we thank them for their patience, professionalism and academic rigor in pursuing this venture.

Kerul Kassel and Isabel Rimanoczy

PART I

Theoretical foundations for sustainability mindset in management education

1

A SUSTAINABILITY MINDSET MODEL FOR MANAGEMENT EDUCATION

Kerul Kassel, Isabel Rimanoczy and Shelley F. Mitchell

Introduction

The connections between climate-related events and social and economic impact have been increasingly featured in the media, and also addressed by corporations and educators. For too long, we have taken for granted the services rendered by the biosphere and the variety of negative social impacts incurred through management practices. There is also an expanded public awareness that it is impossible to engineer infinite growth and profit without attending to planetary and civilizational constraints. The disciplines of management and management education, traditionally anchored in the economist model of maximizing shareholder value and validating selfish behaviors (Hühn, 2013; Moosmayer, 2013), which are aware of their contribution to the problems, are in the process of revising educational approaches and content.

Management literature has long sought to provide an objective, empirical perspective. Yet the practice of management, and in particular management for sustainability, is within the realm of social science, complex (Lissack, 1999) and messy (Sayer, 2000). It presents paradoxes, ambiguities, uncertainty, lack of data and a welter of complex interconnected variables. Integrating the topic of sustainability into management education thus involves incorporating psychological, social, organizational, ecological, policy and other dimensions, from the micro to the macro levels.

In this foundational chapter we explore the current shortcomings in management education to develop a new generation of globally responsible leaders; we suggest what may be missing for a sustainability mindset; and we provide recommendations that can help educators in developing such aspects among current and future leaders. We first review related literature, then propose a definition and model. We explore the four content areas of systems perspectives, ecological worldview, spiritual intelligence and emotional intelligence, and their respective developmental goals of the proposed mindset, and finish by reflecting on how educators are facilitating this mindset in the context of management education and leadership development. In presenting the sustainability mindset concept, we introduce the dimensions as a type of phoropter to clearly focus on the being (values), thinking (knowledge) and doing (competency) in each of the four content areas. The dimensions, components and developmental areas we suggest as comprising sustainability mindset inform a broader, more complex understanding of management practices and their impact on the organization, community and broader world. Such a mindset, we believe, incorporates a more deeply ethical stance, a wider human, biospheric and chronological scope in consideration, and a more balanced approach to leadership and the use of power than much of the current management education curriculum is able or aims to instill in students.

By mindset we mean the lenses with which individuals view the world and their role/place in it, as well as underlying assumptions, beliefs and values that inform that lens. Yeager and Dweck (2012) posit that mindset is an implicit theory, core assumptions that are rarely made explicit which "create a framework for making predictions and judging the meaning of events in one's world" (p. 303). Building on this work, we posit a sustainability mindset as incorporating a systemic approach to understanding, one which goes beyond technical knowledge, in understanding the interconnections of a healthy ecosystem and a thriving society (Van Lopik, 2013, p. 108). In addition, a sustainability mindset is shaped by values and personal purpose.

What the authors found missing in management education to prepare students for a rapidly changing world was the goal of thinking, being and acting in new ways. The inadequacy of the dominant management maxims and their (unexamined) underlying assumptions and values, as well as the predominant focus on the cognitive aspects in education, motivated the authors of this chapter to describe a more integrated and holistic developmental goal: a sustainability mindset that represents a paradigmatic shift for traditional management education. Our contention is that the application (doing) of any learned theory (knowing) must be informed by awareness about the values, beliefs and assumptions underlying that knowledge, the perspectives of stakeholders, and be motivated from a personally held sense of purpose (being).

In the following sections we offer a brief review of trends in management and management education, including corporate social responsibility and related topic areas, and reflect on the need for a sustainability mindset in learning and education. We then offer a brief overview of the concepts of mindset and sustainability, followed by our definition of the sustainability mindset. We present the content areas, dimensions and components including the theoretical frameworks that support those dimensions, and propose a model for developing it, as well as a call for a paradigmatic shift in management education to meet the urgent demands of our time.

We conclude with suggested applications of the model for educators, as well as avenues of future research.

Trends in management and management education

With increasing attention on the social, environmental and economic impacts and injustices of management practices, management education has started to look for ways of connecting the traditional neo-liberal principles guiding capitalism with corporate social responsibility (CSR). Over the last several decades, management education has utilized management practice as a sometimes unquestioned source for forwarding management principles. For example, "doing well by doing good" has been introduced into courses of marketing or strategy, highlighting the opportunity of creating competitive advantage for the firm, instead of a systemic or ethical reason (Laszlo, 2008; Willard, 2002, 2005, 2009). This approach has been called "the business case for sustainability" (Salzmann, Ionescu-somers, & Steger, 2005). Reinhardt (2008) suggested viewing "environmental problems as business issues" with the decision criteria as whether resolving these issues will "deliver positive returns or . . . reduce risk" (p. 37). As such, corporate attention boils down to "when it *really* pays to be green" (p. 53), and "Far from being a soft issue grounded in emotions or ethics, sustainable development involves cold, rational business logic" (Magretta, 2008). Practicing CSR then becomes an obligation of the firm, rather than a strategic option, *only if* it enhances shareholder value (Tudway & Pascal, 2006).

A growing body of literature examines the underlying assumptions of this perspective. Among the earlier contributors are Post and Altman (1994), who suggested a tripartite model of compliance-based, market-driven and values-driven set of motivations for environmental management programs. In reviewing the history of CSR literature, Sison (2009) suggested a two-category typology, that of a liberal-minimalist mindset that emphasizes rights and freedom from the constraints of state intervention versus a civic/communitarian mindset that privileges duty and a "freedom to participate in social goods and decisions" (p. 235).

Other scholars have proposed frameworks of moral reciprocity versus financial performance orientation (Sharp & Zaidma, 2010) or have reconciled the extremes of utilitarian ethics against duty ethics, through a holistic "middle way" (Ketola, 2008) of virtue ethics, in which the motives, nature and history of an individual's or organization's behavior determine the presence or absence of virtue. A recent review of the CSR literature revealed that existing research exhibits a narrow research scope, a low degree of interdisciplinary integration, with a pointed emphasis on financial consequences and performance, and low consideration of managerial implications of climate change in management research (Linnenluecke & Griffiths, 2013).

More recently, business management schools have begun to evaluate their underlying assumptions in approaching education. In 2007, the United Nations–sponsored Principles for Responsible Management Education (UN-PRME) originated after the Global Forum for Business as Agent of World Benefit, hosted at the Weatherhead School of Management at Case Western Reserve University. Prompted by a reflection that a majority of corporate scandals had been led by alumni of U.S. business schools, UN-PRME is not only a set of principles, but is also a global engagement platform for academic institutions with the purpose of inspiring responsible management education, research and thought leadership (Forray, Leigh, & Kenworthy, 2015). With more than 663 university signatories, the Principles are intended to instill capabilities and values supporting the creation of sustainable value among management students, integrated into curriculum and research, and embedded through partnership and dialogue with industry, media, consumers, governments and other stakeholders. While some question the degree to which adhering to the Principles implies a real shift in the focus of management education away from the traditional goals of growth and profit, it is undoubtedly a major first step into a new direction.

Accreditation bodies are also mandating change (Wu, Huang, Kuo, & Wu, 2010). In 2013, in its update to standards for business schools, the Association to Advance Collegiate Schools of Business (AACSB) added social responsibility and sustainability to the first paragraph of their standards preamble. The organization also added these topics to the eligibility criteria in their core values and guiding principles and in the general skill areas and general business and management knowledge sections of their learning and teaching accreditation standards.

Management education shortcomings

A 2010 (Rimanoczy) study of sixteen business leaders championing sustainability initiatives indicated that the management education of the leaders interviewed had created a fragmented understanding of reality. This made it initially difficult for them to think of the interconnections between business and sustainability in the three realms of the triple bottom line: economic prosperity, environmental health and social well-being. This and other research points to the deficiency in management education for equipping students to address global challenges and develop an understanding of the complex interrelationships at play (Gintis & Khurana, 2007; Spitzeck, 2011). Furthermore, while ethics courses are present in many management education programs, they tend to explore theoretical frameworks and fail at examining the values and assumptions behind our collective or personal behaviors, including who, and what, matters in business decision-making (Adkins, Gentile, Ingols, & Trefalt, 2011).

The issue of whom and what to include determines focus and goals with regard to who benefits and who does not. When the objective is to maximize the return on investment, it leads to the disregard for consequences and impacts on other stakeholders (Freeman, Wicks, & Parmar, 2004). "Negative externalization" exemplifies the disconnection between the economic goals and the social and ecological viability, and the costs are carried, knowingly or unknowingly, by others who have not agreed to it. Yet, the organization does not exist in a vacuum. Its success is linked to the well-being and engagement of its employees, the strength of the communities within which it operates, the financial ability of its customers to afford its products, and the health of the biosphere in enhancing security to its operations (Kassel, 2014).

Time perspective is a cogent component, as well. Among the most highly prioritized management values is very short-term financial metrics. While quarterly performance, annual gains and exponential growth are rewarded, an emphasis on rapid and explosive growth in the near term has often had a negative impact when viewed over an extended span of time, whether that impact occurs within the organization or among its stakeholders. Damage to the long-term viability of the organization, its employees, vendors, resource base and customers occurs due to the pressure for more immediate results.

This can be traced to an either/or logic: either short term or long term; either command-and-control or chaos; either certainty or doubt; either profit or the environment. Yet, the economic system and its subsystem of industry cannot work at cross-purposes to the larger biospheric system on which it depends. The biosphere is the living planetary envelope within which all social and economic activity occurs. So how is the next generation prepared to address this reality? Some business schools include required or elective courses on sustainability and ethics. Some universities create Sustainability Centers that foster interdisciplinary connections and offer a variety of sustainability-related courses to students across-campus, offering certificates, minors or majors. The more progressive institutions seek to embed sustainability into their courses, albeit management education is still a domain lagging behind, filled with contradictions because of the traditional market-driven values (Pirson, op. cit.). Until the underlying assumptions and values motivating our behaviors are examined, at the most personal level, it may be difficult to create any paradigmatic shift (Scharmer & Hub, 2010).

What is a sustainability mindset?

The authors define the sustainability mindset as incorporating the dimensions of values (being), and knowledge (thinking), expressed in actions or competencies (doing):

> Sustainability mindset is a way of thinking and being that results from a broad understanding of the ecosystem's manifestations, from social sensitivity, as well as an introspective focus on one's personal values and higher self, and finds its expression in actions for the greater good of the whole.

By 'broad understanding of the ecosystem's manifestations' we refer to an appreciation of the interconnections between the different components of our ecosystem and the complexity of impacts our human behaviors have on the system (Capra, 1997). By 'social sensitivity' we refer to the empathic understanding of human interactions and interconnectedness. By 'introspective focus on the personal values' we refer to self-awareness of the espoused values and values in action (Argyris, 1987, p. 93) as they relate to our sustainable or unsustainable behaviors. By 'focus on the higher self' we refer to the inclusion of the spiritual dimension, and the consideration of purpose, meaning (Delbecq, 2008; Neal, 2008), and one-ness (Krishnan, 2008). Finally, by 'actions for the greater good of the whole' we refer not only to altruistic or philanthropic actions but also to entrepreneurial or business actions that include and serve all stakeholders' interests, including the planet and future generations

(Mackey & Sisodia, 2014; Porter & Kramer, 2011).This definition illustrates the complexity of the challenges, which call three perspectives: the individual, the social and the ecosystem, and also within the cognitive, emotional, psychological and spiritual realm.The point needs to be made that attitudes and mental inclinations are the result of many factors: experiences, information, values, emotions, beliefs, therefore reaching beyond the mere cognitive sphere.Yeager and Dweck (2012) posit that mindset is an implicit theory, core assumptions that are rarely made explicit which "create a framework for making predictions and judging the meaning of events in one's world" (p. 303). Mindset is related to the concepts of paradigm and worldview, and while it has a socially constructed root (Kearney, 1984; Kuhn & Hacking, 2012), it is also shaped by the personal experiences, purpose and character (Wong, 2012).

When faced with disorienting situations or crises, individuals and societies can undergo a crisis of worldview which "undermines the basic beliefs underlying the basic practice" (Fang, Kang, & Liu, 2004; Mezirow, 1994), thus prompting a transformation in their mindset. Humankind has begun to awaken to the interconnections among planet, people and prosperity, and is beginning to recognize that our alterations to the biosphere result in climate change, desertification and species loss, and how greater income disparity creates social unrest.As society undergoes fundamental changes, these changes trigger shifts in educational paradigms as well. Fang and colleagues summarize the trends in education as transitioning "from a closed system to an open one, from a bureaucratic approach to a team-based one, and from a student-screening focus to a learner-enabling one" (p. 299). They suggest that mindset indicators be based on measuring knowledge and its application to situations, affective attitudes toward scenarios and situations, and intentions of behaviors.

The sustainability mindset model: dimensions, content areas and elements

In considering mindset, it is just as important *what* leaders know, what they think and do, as *how* they think, their motivations for 'acting', and their particular way of being in the world, all of which informs their actions. Exploring not only behaviors but also the drivers of those behaviors can provide guidance on how to intentionally develop sustainability-minded leaders. As Schein (2015) points out, a better understanding of ecological worldviews as psychological drivers (why), plus leadership capacities as collaborator-in-chief (how) leads to deep sustainability initiatives (what) where we can act as sustainability leaders.

Theoretical foundations

Aside from a well-cited 1995 management theory paper by Gladwin, Kennelly, and Krause (1995), a review of management literature related to the topic of mindset and paradigms revealed a paucity of research or models, with the exception of the concept of global mindset or global leadership mindset. Using these and research from the nascent CSR field, as well as management education and ethics, we found some common patterns in the thinking, being and acting dimensions (see Figure 1.1).

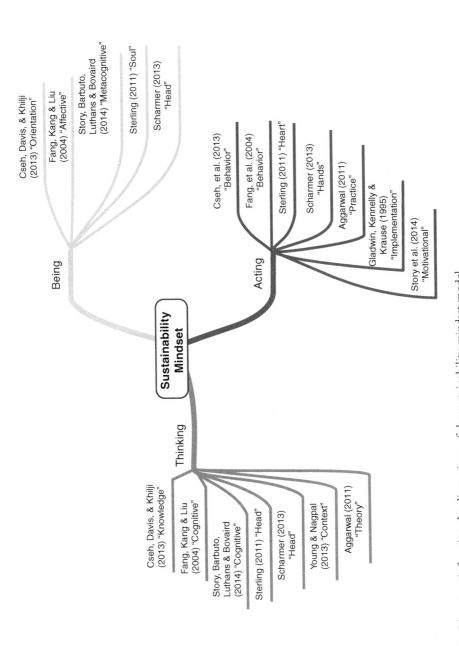

FIGURE 1.1 Literature informing the dimensions of the sustainability mindset model

Being

Cseh, Davis, & Khilji (2013) "Orientation"

Fang, Kang & Liu (2004) "Affective"

Story, Barbuto, Luthans & Bovaird (2014) "Metacognitive"

Sterling (2011) "Soul"

Scharmer (2013) "Head"

Acting

Cseh, et al. (2013) "Behavior"

Fang, et al. (2004) "Behavior"

Sterling (2011) "Heart"

Scharmer (2013) "Hands"

Aggarwal (2011) "Practice"

Gladwin, Kennelly & Krause (1995) "Implementation"

Story et al. (2014) "Motivational"

Sustainability Mindset

Thinking

Cseh, Davis, & Khilji (2013) "Knowledge"

Fang, Kang & Liu (2004) "Cognitive"

Story, Barbuto, Luthans & Bovaird (2014) "Cognitive"

Sterling (2011) "Head"

Scharmer (2013) "Head"

Young & Nagpal (2013) "Context"

Aggarwal (2011) "Theory"

With slightly different nuances, we found numerous references to these three 'dimensions'. The cognition, values and competencies appeared as knowledge, orientation and behavior (Cseh, Davis, & Khilji, 2013); cognitive, affective and behavioral (Fang et al., 2004); cognitive, metacognitive and motivational (Story, Barbuto, Luthans, & Bovaird, 2014); head, soul and heart (Sterling, 2011); head, heart and hands (Scharmer & Kaufer, 2013). Gladwin et al. (1995) also point to these dimensions through their suggested paradigmatic shifts: from exterior to interior and from concept to implementation. Although it is a bold statement to suggest that some degree of spiritual (not necessarily religious) awareness and practice plays a significant role in a sustainability mindset, a number of the scholars cited here point to exactly such a dimension. Sterling's (2011) approach to transformative learning for sustainability integrates innovative and systemic characteristics, as well as a spiritual component, referring to a paradigm change driven by epistemic learning (p. 25). While applied specifically to higher education, this conceptualization is the closest to the proposed sustainability mindset model, although it would require some adjustment for the purposes of development for practicing managers.

Some of the authors address systemic aspects, for example, Gladwin and colleagues (1995) suggest a sustaincentric approach that addresses flaws of both technocentric and ecocentric orientations. This approach incorporates many systemic elements, such as connectivity, inclusiveness, equity, self-organization and nature's capital, although it doesn't address the internal state of the leader, her mindfulness, self-awareness and deeper questions about purpose.

Fang et al. (2004) also refer to a systems approach through positing an open versus closed institutional system, and innovative approaches such as learner-centered versus student-centered, and team-oriented versus bureaucratic design, although the model does not address management education or practice specifically.

The dimensions of the global leadership mindset (GLM) management model proposed by Cseh et al. (2013) include systemic (p. 490) and innovative (p. 492) aspects. The GLM model contains components that strongly dovetail with the dimensions of thinking (knowledge), being (values) and doing (competencies): the thinking dimension includes sense-making, analysis, reasoning and judgment; the being dimension includes awareness, mindfulness, collaboration and openness; the doing dimension is "an enactment of orientation and knowledge" (Cseh et al., 2013, p. 491). Similar to the global mindset concept earlier proposed by Gupta and Govindarajan (2002), however, the GLM model fails to incorporate many of the social and environmental features of the sustainability mindset model. These two critical dimensions are required to address social justice and environmental challenges we face.

Designing a sustainability mindset model

The qualitative exploratory study conducted by one of the authors suggested not only the three dimensions of being, thinking and doing, which were validated in the literature, but also a number of elements within each dimension that were clustered into four content areas: systems perspective, spiritual intelligence, ecological worldview and emotional intelligence. An overview of management literature and other empirical studies focusing on sustainability motivations and behaviors, corporate social responsibility and triple-bottom-line approach led the authors to adjust and validate those content areas. These areas serve both as a model of sustainability mindset and as a guide for developing that mindset with students (see Collado-Ruano, Chapter 6 in this book).

It is recommended that to develop a sustainability mindset, the four content areas are enacted through collaborative and innovative action, via projects or initiatives that nurture the development of the four areas, and become the mindset in action (see also Schutel, Becker & Audino, Chapter 11; Vazquez Maguirre & Garcia de la Torre, Chapter 12; and Onwuegbuzie & Ugwuanyi, Chapter 7 in this book). (See Figure 1.2.)

The *systems perspective* content area is informed by an approach that takes into account that every individual, organization and industry are subsystems of the larger biosphere, interdependent with an array of economic, social and environmental subsystems. A *systems perspective* includes the needs and interests of these deeply intertwined subsystems, influencing research, analysis of data, strategy and decision making (Elkington, 1998; Hawken, Lovins, & Lovins, 2013; Kassel, 2014; Senge, 2008).

The *spiritual intelligence* content area refers to values, purpose, principles and a sense of one-ness (Cashman, 2008; Doppelt, 2012; Rimanoczy, 2010; Scharmer & Kaufer, 2013; Zohar, 2012). Spiritual intelligence is the capacity with which we address and solve problems of meaning and purpose: how we consider our actions and lives in a wider, richer, meaning-giving context, and the internal wisdom with which we can assess that one course of action or one life-path is more meaningful than another.

The *ecological worldview* content area incorporates specifically environmental conditions, trends and challenges from a global viewpoint, seeking to conserve or restore resources, mitigate harm and adapt to changing conditions. It addresses the interactions and impact between human and nature, and also between humans, in the sense of place within an ecological system (Goleman, 2009; Hawken, 1993; Kegan, 1982; Kohlberg, 1984; Nattras & Altomare, 1999; Perry, 1968).

The *emotional intelligence* content area speaks to the importance of self-scrutiny and introspection, understanding self and anchors of our identity, ability to maintain equanimity and resilience on the individual, team, organizational and even general social interaction level. (Goleman, 1995; Goleman, Boyatzis & McKee, 2002; Salovey, Mayer & Caruso, 2004; Senge, 2006).

Collaborative and innovative action refers to the sustainability mindset in action, both as a goal and as a learning process. The exploratory study with sustainability-minded leaders showed that as they stepped into action, they found collaboration and innovation essential to tackle the complex challenges with others and to invent new ways of operating that were less harmful (Rimanoczy, 2010). When developing a sustainability mindset with students, the inclusion of collaborative projects requiring innovation provide an experiential learning opportunity that feeds back into the four content areas, providing insights and opportunities to develop social sensitivity, ecoliteracy, self-awareness and to discover the satisfaction of meaningful work. In addition, individuals develop their skills to work in teams, and their self-confidence is enhanced as they see how they are able to become proactive, shaping a better world.

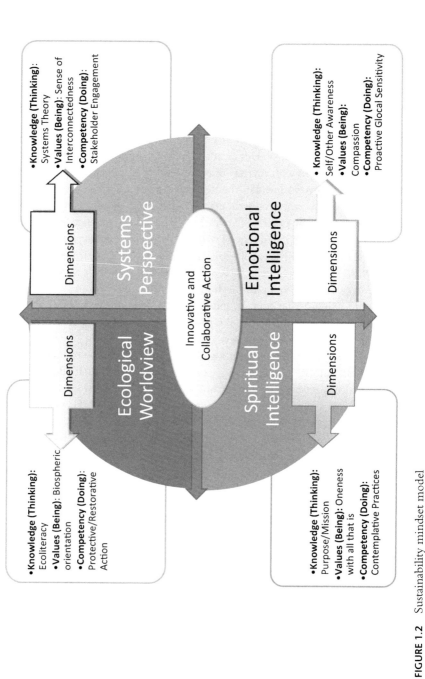

Knowledge (Thinking): Ecoliteracy
Values (Being): Biospheric orientation
Competency (Doing): Protective/Restorative Action

Knowledge (Thinking): Systems Theory
Values (Being): Sense of Interconnectedness
Competency (Doing): Stakeholder Engagement

Knowledge (Thinking): Purpose/Mission
Values (Being): Oneness with all that is
Competency (Doing): Contemplative Practices

Knowledge (Thinking): Self/Other Awareness
Values (Being): Compassion
Competency (Doing): Proactive Glocal Sensitivity

Dimensions

Ecological Worldview

Systems Perspective

Innovative and Collaborative Action

Spiritual Intelligence

Emotional Intelligence

FIGURE 1.2 Sustainability mindset model

CONTENT AREAS	DIMENSIONS		
	Knowledge (knowing, thinking)	Values (being)	Competencies (doing)
Ecological Worldview	Ecoliteracy	Biospheric	Protective/Restorative Action
Systemic Perspective	Systems theory	Sense of interconnectedness	Stakeholder engagement
Emotional Intelligence	Self/Other-awareness	Compassion	Proactive glocal sensitivity
Spiritual Intelligence	Purpose, Mission	Oneness with all that is	Contemplative Practices

FIGURE 1.3   Dimensions, content areas and themes

What does it look like, to develop the systemic perspective, an ecological world-view, emotional intelligence and spiritual intelligence? Based on the model, the authors developed a grid of specific contents that could provide guidance for educators who are interested in developing the sustainability mindset (see Figure 1.3).

This grid illustrates the way the authors analyzed each of the four content areas, through the lens of the thinking/being/doing dimensions. In the following section, we will describe the particular developmental elements that educators can focus on to develop a sustainability mindset, independently of the discipline they teach. Although this way of organizing the elements may be debatable, it is presented as a scaffolding to capture the multidimensional character of the sustainability mindset.

Content area: ecological worldview

The empirical study found that learning about the ecological challenges of the planet played a major motivational role in the leaders studied, particularly as the information became a trigger of emotional responses that in turn led them to act in restorative ways (Rimanoczy, 2010). This sequence of learning about the prob-lems, feeling sad, guilty, angry or concerned, and motivated to act was also found among students participating in a course to develop the sustainability mindset (Rimanoczy, 2014). Given the importance of this content area, which encompasses a broad understanding of the manifestations of ecosystems, we analyzed it through the lenses of the thinking, being and doing dimensions, to define how it could be developed. This brings together an awareness and appreciation of the intercon-nection between both abiotic and biotic attributes of ecosystems. It provides a basic conceptualization of how the natural world works and of the human interac-tion with the planet's natural ecosystems (Kreb, 2008). The Ecological Worldview content area includes the three dimensions of ecoliteracy (knowledge), biospheric orientation (values) and protective/restorative action (competency) as a way of illustrating the heart, hands and mind connection.

TABLE 1.1 Ecoliteracy

CONTENT AREAS	DIMENSIONS		
	Knowledge (knowing, thinking)	Values (being)	Competencies (doing)
Ecological Worldview	Ecoliteracy	Biospheric	Protective/restorative action
Systemic Perspective	Systems theory	Sense of interconnectedness	Stakeholder engagement
Emotional Intelligence	Self/other-awareness	Compassion	Proactive glocal sensitivity
Spiritual Intelligence	Purpose, mission	Oneness with all that is	Contemplative Practices

Ecoliteracy comprises the developmental element of the **knowledge** dimension in the ecological worldview content area. According to the Center for Ecoliteracy's 2015 Annual Report, the greatest challenge we face as a human race is to build and nurture sustainable communities designed in a way that businesses honor and cooperate with nature's inherent ability to sustain life. A first step toward this endeavor is an understanding of the principles of ecology: an ecological literacy that brings us closer to achieving the goal of sustainable communities. It is surprising how distanced management students are from the natural world that supports their life, and how little they know about the role and services nature provides. In one class where the students were asked what they need nature for, they mentioned mostly entertainment (vacations, walks in the park, kayaking). Furthermore, there is little awareness of where their food comes from and the negative impact on the environment of our consumption habits. The growing realization of the earth as a common home forms a compelling reason for creating a sustainable world for future generations as our common, and urgent, task (Capra & Mattei, 2015).

David W. Orr, a noted environmental educator, recommends that some part of the curriculum, from kindergarten through doctoral-level education, be dedicated to the study of natural systems in the manner in which we experience them. One example would be immersion in a particular component of the natural world, advancing to higher levels of disciplinary knowledge (Francis, 2011). In a basic experience of the natural world, we can understand how nature sustains life and nurtures a healthy community, while gaining an appreciation of how we feed ourselves and know the places where we live (a sense of place), work and learn. When compared to the emphasis placed on financial literacy for business majors, the sustainability mindset has *ecoliteracy* as a content area for learning and leadership in the 21st century. Schein (2015) lists eight social science disciplines, which are interrelated "ecological worldview traditions": deep ecology, eco-psychology, environmental sociology, social psychology, ecological economics, indigenous studies,

TABLE 1.2 Biospheric

CONTENT AREAS	DIMENSIONS		
	Knowledge (knowing, thinking)	Values (being)	Competencies (doing)
Ecological Worldview	Ecoliteracy	Biospheric	Protective/restorative action
Systemic Perspective	Systems theory	Sense of interconnectedness	Stakeholder engagement
Emotional Intelligence	Self/other-awareness	Compassion	Proactive glocal sensitivity
Spiritual Intelligence	Purpose, mission	Oneness with all that is	Contemplative Practices

integral ecology and developmental psychology. This multiple-lens approach can be integrated into the business curriculum to help students better understand broader implications of sustainability.

A way to integrate this developmental element into the classroom would be to explore the contents of ecoliteracy as linked to current events, in order for the students to experience in the real world the impacts of human actions on the social and ecological environment.

While the cognitive understanding of the ecology as the system where all our life unfolds is important, there is a deontological component motivating our behaviors that can be developed. We call this development element the **biospheric orientation**, which means placing importance on the earth's biosphere, which includes all of the planet's ecosystems. The biosphere is that portion of the earth in which living (biotic) organisms exist and interact with one another along with their non-living (abiotic) environment. Contrasting with a utilitarian viewpoint, this component of the sustainability mindset is about realizing and appreciating the innate worth of and the interdependence within this thin, life-supporting global membrane of air, water, soil and organisms. The interrelationship between humans and the natural world means we live in an integral ecology, one that could be explored by students participating in field trips or by hosting guest speakers.

Discovering this value can occur at a personal level, within a community and in a business or governmental enterprise. As such, a **biospheric orientation** can lead to responsible, sustainable and ethical behavior among leaders. As business leaders, understanding one's individual impact, as well as the business impact on the biosphere, will be critical for collaborative skills and strategic thinking in addressing social, economic and environmental challenges, such as water shortage, food scarcity or loss of biodiversity. The recently released 2030 United Nation's Sustainable Development Goals have set a high standard for businesses as key partners in taking a lead role in ending poverty, fighting inequality and injustice, and tackling climate change issues (www.undp.org). The United Nations Principles for Responsible Management Education (PRME) is another key driver of sustainability in management education. PRME signatories state their commitment to develop the capacity and values of students to work inclusively and sustainably in the global economy for responsible leadership. Several faculty use the principles of PRME as a curricular development lens and a number are integrating them into curricula. For example, Hult International Business School provides a visual overview of the proportion of compulsory courses where learning objectives include explicit reference to ethics, responsibility and sustainability across all programs offered by the school.

Upon closer examination of the economic, social, health and ecological pressures that business leaders need to address, there are three distinct and interconnected trends: (1) declining natural resources, (2) radical transparency provided by the internet and (3) increasing expectations by stakeholders. In combination, these trends have become major market forces that are redefining the way companies operate (Laszlo & Zhexembayeva, 2011). The intellectual understanding of these conditions will be a necessary foundation, but the emotional connection coming from a deep-felt biospheric orientation will propel action.

We propose the element *protective and restorative action* as the **competency** dimension of the Ecological Worldview content area. The first definition of sustainable development called for a development that meets the needs of the present without compromising the ability of future generations to meet their own needs (World Commission on Environment and Development, 1987).

Since then, however, there are few natural places left on the planet that have not been affected or degraded to some degree by human activities, and so any development that aims at sustainable living conditions calls for *protective and restorative action* to halt further degradation. The study of ecology teaches us that if one species goes extinct, the whole ecosystem is more fragile and is forced to adapt

TABLE 1.3 Protective/restorative action

CONTENT AREAS	DIMENSIONS		
	Knowledge (knowing, thinking)	Values (being)	Competencies (doing)
Ecological Worldview	Ecoliteracy	Biospheric	Protective/restorative action
Systemic Perspective	Systems theory	Sense of interconnectedness	Stakeholder engagement
Emotional Intelligence	Compassion	Self/other-awareness	Proactive glocal sensitivity
Spiritual Intelligence	Purpose, mission	Oneness with all that is	Contemplative Practices

accordingly, or fail (Eisenstein, 2013). For this reason, ***protective and restorative actions*** are paired. Ecological restoration is the process of trying to repair damage caused by humans and businesses to the dynamics of natural ecosystems. Examples include replanting forests, restoring grasslands or wetlands, and reclaiming urban industrial areas (brownfields) and old mining sites. Scientists, who study how natural ecosystems recover, are learning how to hasten repair operations using a variety of approaches. These include rehabilitation, replacement and creating artificial ecosystems, although restored ecosystems still differ from their original status.

The opportunity for students to see the impact of loss of biodiversity and to be involved in a restoration activity along with reflection on their experience brings a priceless experiential learning component to developing a sustainability mindset (Allen-Gil, Walker, Thomas, & Shevory, 2005; Beringer, Wright, & Malone, 2008; Kolb, 1984; Rimanoczy, 2016; Williams, & Brown, 2013). For example, offering hands-on learning opportunities to use the principles of permaculture as a teaching framework in the context of a business start-up can give students a broader overview of the applied areas of sustainability, waste reduction, renewable energy, green building, fair trade, life-cycle analysis, closed-loop systems, carbon/ecological footprints and other sustainable business practices (Kassel, 2014). There are also case studies on companies that have utilized innovation for ecological sustainability. The case method promotes strategic scenario thinking, as it creates an opportunity for students to handle a real-life situation they might encounter in a future management career.

Content area: systemic perspective

In an organizational context, a systemic perspective considers all of the behaviors of the firm as a whole, in relation to its operating environmental. From the broader perspective, commerce exists only relationally. It cannot function without the customers it serves, or without all of the people, materials and societal infrastructure in its supply, manufacture and distribution chain, or without the employees who convert physical or intellectual capital into products and services, or without the health of the economic system. A sustainability mindset understands that any business is a subsystem among other subsystems, embedded within larger systems (their industry, the economy, society, the earth's biosphere). The success of any business is inextricably intertwined with and dependent on the stability and longevity of those systems. The developmental elements in this dimension are characterized by developing an understanding of the systemic nature of the world, expanding a sensibility about how a separation between industry and planet are both illusory and counterproductive, and enhancing skills at collaborating innovatively with others (individual, teams, divisions, organizations, communities, even industries and nations) for a more widely shared set of positive outcomes.

The exploratory study indicated that sustainability-minded leaders analyzed data and made decisions using a both-and logic, cyclical flow and long-term thinking (Rimanoczy, 2010). These elements are all pertaining to ***systems theory*** and fall

TABLE 1.4 Systems theory

CONTENT AREAS	DIMENSIONS		
	Knowledge (knowing, thinking)	*Values (being)*	*Competencies (doing)*
Ecological Worldview	Ecoliteracy	Biospheric	Protective/restorative action
Systemic Perspective	Systems theory	Sense of interconnectedness	Stakeholder engagement
Emotional Intelligence	Self/other-awareness	Compassion	Proactive glocal sensitivity
Spiritual Intelligence	Purpose, mission	Oneness with all that is	Contemplative Practices

within the content area of Systemic Perspective in the **knowledge (thinking)** dimension, as presented by Boulding (1956), Capra (1997) and Meadows (2008). The developmental element of *both-and logic*, also called paradoxical thinking (Lewis, 2000), contrasts with binary, either/or thinking. When thinking with an either/or approach, the individual sides with one interpretation, clear and distinct opinions, and a right/wrong distinction, something that developmental psychologists classify as conventional thinking (Kohlberg, 1984). In contrast, the *both-and* logic invites one to accept paradox and contradictions as part of the complex world. This includes accepting a degree of chaos and uncertainty, gray zones, evolving circumstances, particularities and context, changing landscapes and transitions. It also suggests approaches to problems and solutions that are inclusive of different perspectives and needs of stakeholders, all characteristics of the post-conventional stages of development (Baron, & Cayer, 2011).

Considerations and decisions made using an either/or approach can be inflexible, limiting the options and, therefore, the opportunities. The ability to hold multiple perspectives simultaneously is an important leadership competency, and is particularly relevant in a stakeholder management context, whether inter- or intra-team, – organization, or – sector. One way to incorporate both-and logic is to analyze case studies or watch a media clip from a movie and then writing a report answering a set of questions based on ethical and environmental issues derived from the film to assess where either/or and both-and logic might have been used. The authors have kept alert to when the students presented radical views during class discussions that reflected their either/or thinking. They then used those 'just-in-time teachable moments' to highlight how the polarized thinking can limit our understanding. By developing both-and thinking in students, educators are not only equipping them for a more complex world but also helping them engage in more harmonious relationships with the environment and others.

Cyclical flow: Just as all forms of life experience a cyclical flow – birth, life, death – as an artifact of human life, the organizations we invent appear to be subject to the same rules (Kassel, 2014). Management education is built around logic and rational thinking, fact-based conclusions and hard data. Students are encouraged to clearly articulate cause-and-effect connections when analyzing a problem, laying out clear plans and strategies. Linear thinking is, however, insufficient to address complex challenges, and this applies particularly to sustainability. The idea of infinite growth, for example, is an economic construct that defies all laws of nature. Many scholars have long questioned the assumption of unlimited growth and the consequences of such a way of thinking in our collective behaviors (Drucker, 1994; Meadows, Meadows, Randers, & Behrens, 1972).

As we are increasingly faced with resource depletion, due to extraction or destruction, the idea of a post-growth or de-growth society becomes an interesting alternative for survival and sustainability (Muraca, 2012; Schneider, Kallis, & Martinez-Alier, 2010). Yet growth remains mostly an unquestioned value in our management education classrooms. Integrating the developmental element of cyclical flow thinking means understanding limits, considering relationships and the impact of varying contexts, finding patterns of behaviors, identifying multiple causes, even factoring in unknown variables, and paying attention to tendencies. For example, the authors invited students to work in small teams on a flipchart or whiteboard, with a focal problematic point (e.g., water scarcity, or shorter life cycle of our portable devices). Then they are asked to identify all the cycles that intervene, which may come from very different categories (e.g., changing our phone is related to carrier advertising, to new product development, to mining for materials, to disposal and accumulation (or reuse) of electronic waste, to pricing strategies, to social media, access to financing, etc.). In a second step, they are invited to consider planetary boundaries, patterns of behaviors, reinforcing loops, tendencies and values. The reflection is prompted then to discuss how systems operate in nature, where energy is clean, there is no waste and food is local. How do nature's solutions compare to human-technological ones? Because all human production is dependent on natural resources, leaders of tomorrow would benefit from incorporating the lens of a cyclical flow that guides the natural sciences, as they create strategies and make decisions.

Long-term thinking: In management education, students are sometimes invited to envision future scenarios, to identify opportunities and create strategies to explore them with the long term in mind, a way to integrate this developmental element. Yet, outside of the classroom our fast-paced civilization demands that individuals and organizations respond to what is seen as urgent. Urgency and short-term issues take priority over long-term considerations, without proper consideration of the implications and impacts of the choices.

Ironically, the 21st century is marked by the visible consequences of decisions made with insufficient consideration of the future beyond the quarter or year. Elkington (1998) predicted that time horizons will switch from a wide view of current circumstances informing knowledge to a longer perspective that uses the past as a lesson and the state of the future, generations ahead, as one of the most important considerations in decision making. With 'sustainability' (sustaining = maintaining existence) becoming a more widely recognized aspiration, educators will have a well-supported ground to discuss with the new generation ways to embed a long-term lens into their thinking habits.

The authors brought this aspect into the classroom discussion by inviting the students to write down some short-term decisions they had recently made, without pondering their long-term impact, and then the opposite. The discussion that followed was exploring how we tend to operate, what are the consequences we suffer from it, and how a long-term perspective could be included into our short-term thinking, if possible. Current events and case studies highlighting short- versus long-term decision making have been used to generate classroom discussions.

Empirical and conceptual studies about sustainability leadership characteristics have indicated the importance of a *sense of interconnectedness*, a developmental element which the authors place within the **values** (Being) dimension of the Systemic Perspective (Divecha & Brown, 2013; Rimanoczy, 2010). Systems theory points to units formed by and connected to subsystems, all while interlocked and inextricably embedded in larger interconnected systems (nations, governments, local communities and ecosystems) and subsystems (in the case of business: employees, vendors, customers, regulators, media, etc.). While understanding the connections is an act of cognition, we want to highlight the deontological aspects behind this act.

Cultures in the Western-Northern hemisphere have been moving towards individualization and differentiation, with a focus on uniqueness of products, services or personality. This places priority on values such as independence, autonomy, self-regulation, self-determination and advocacy to convince others of our personal perspective. These socially accepted values shape the identity of individuals, how they want to perceive themselves and thus it influences behavior.

In contrast, interconnectedness draws attention to *shared qualities* as opposed to differences, a realization that not a single being is independent, and that we all

TABLE 1.5 Sense of interconnectedness

CONTENT AREAS	DIMENSIONS		
	Knowledge (knowing, thinking)	Values (being)	Competencies (doing)
Ecological Worldview	Ecoliteracy	Biospheric	Protective/restorative action
Systemic Perspective	Systems theory	Sense of interconnectedness	Stakeholder engagement
Emotional Intelligence	Self/other-awareness Compassion	Compassion	Proactive glocal sensitivity
Spiritual Intelligence	Purpose, mission	Oneness with all that is	Contemplative Practices

depend on all other beings – whether human, animal or vegetal. Kurucz, Colbert and Marcus suggest that sustainability requires an epistemology that posits humans as connected, versus individualistic (2014, p. 439). From the perspective of human development, the movement from ego-centric to eco-centric is seen as an evolutionary step (Hutchison, 2016; Scharmer & Kaufer, 2013; Wilber, 2001, p. 239) that can prepare individuals to address the planetary challenges in more effective ways. Field trips to locations from which natural resources are sourced or effluents are disposed, especially where environmental degradation occurs through destroying a habitat to procure the resource, or where production has significantly impacted ecological or community health, is one way to embed this developmental element in a course. Examining corporate 'catastrophes' (Exxon *Valdez*; *Deepwater Horizon*; Union Carbide in Bophal; Rana factory collapse in Bangladesh) can also be used to highlight the consequences of short-term thinking. Deeply exploring a supply chain is another method that will aid in students' sense of interconnectedness.

Reflecting on how the Systemic Perspective is expressed in sustainable behaviors, the authors found that ***engagement with all relevant stakeholders*** was a key developmental element in the **competency** (doing) dimension. Traditionally, accounting methods have not taken into consideration externalities such as climate change, contaminated air and water, loss of soil and its fertility, damage to local cultures and communities, or even employee burnout. Firms are used to making decisions thinking with a narrow horizon, a small circle of shareholders or the most pressing stakeholders that may threaten organizational profit. However, with increasing levels of transparency, there is an augmented pressure to account for those externalities. Management educators staying within the traditional paradigm of the neo-liberal purpose of the firm (profit for the shareholders) will not only be failing their students but also exposing them to future liabilities as corporations will be held accountable for new responsibilities towards the stakeholders.

TABLE 1.6 Stakeholder engagement

CONTENT AREAS	DIMENSIONS		
	Knowledge (knowing, thinking)	Values (being)	Competencies (doing)
Ecological Worldview	Ecoliteracy	Biospheric	Protective/restorative action
Systemic Perspective	Systems theory	Sense of interconnectedness	Stakeholder engagement
Emotional Intelligence	Self/other-awareness Compassion	Compassion	Proactive glocal sensitivity
Spiritual Intelligence	Purpose, mission	Oneness with all that is	Contemplative Practices

This has been observed by Mezhei (2011), who calls for including more collaboration among stakeholders across the value chain in design and policy, and Young and Nagpal (2013), because of the need of understanding actors in the wider political landscape, engaging and building effective relationships with new kinds of external partners (pp. 496–497). The authors have created an exercise in the classroom where they asked the students to gather in trios and list all the stakeholders involved in them drinking their morning coffee. The importance of managing multiple stakeholder relationships, especially addressing their particular concerns, creating mutual sustainability interests based on these particular concerns, and empowering stakeholders to act as intermediaries for nature and sustainable development has been indicated as a key competency (Hörisch, Freeman, & Schaltegger, 2014).

Content area: emotional intelligence

Sustainability encompasses not only planet and prosperity but also people, and for many individuals realizing their personal contribution to the problems by scrutinizing their values and behaviors is the most compelling motivation to act. Several exploratory and empirical studies found that leaders who engaged with sustainability showed higher levels of self-awareness (Divecha & Brown, 2013; Rimanoczy, 2010; Schein, 2015; Visser & Courtice, 2011), indicating that skills at intra- and interpersonal relations are a vital component of the sustainability mindset.

Sustainability-related issues are complex, bringing into consideration many interrelated areas of knowledge, difficult challenges and wicked problems, in which a multitude of stakeholders have varying interests and levels of power and influence. For most people, reflection on these issues brings up a welter of emotions. Interaction within and among groups is often charged with tension and entrenched differences. In order to avoid overwhelm, gloom and conflict impasse, self-awareness is a core element that enables cooperation and mutual appreciation, facilitating individuals and groups to work through obstacles and complications.

TABLE 1.7 Self/other-awareness

	DIMENSIONS		
CONTENT AREAS	Knowledge (knowing, thinking)	Values (being)	Competencies (doing)
Ecological Worldview	Ecoliteracy	Biospheric	Protective/restorative action
Systemic Perspective	Systems theory	Sense of interconnectedness	Stakeholder engagement
Emotional Intelligence	Self/other-awareness Compassion	Compassion	Proactive glocal sensitivity
Spiritual Intelligence	Purpose, mission	Oneness with all that is	Contemplative Practices

We propose Goleman's (1998) definition of *self- and other-awareness*, "the ability to recognize and understand your moods, emotions, and drives, as well as their effect on others" (p. 88), as the developmental element of the **knowledge** dimension in this content area. The "ability to recognize" points to the cognitive capacity to parse out the content of our moods, emotions, rather than being driven by them by default. Default reactions form patterns, which we learn to recognize, first by reflection and analysis after the fact, and later developing the capacity to be present to how and when they are arising moment by moment. Journaling about situations in which the students have experienced tension, conflict or struggle within the context of a course content or a project is just one among many methods to develop this knowledge dimension of the emotional intelligence content area. Course exercises and program activities and projects can also be constructed that help uncover espoused values versus values in action, as they relate to individual habits and behaviors.

A valuable exercise to develop self- and other-awareness is prompting the students to identify what are their personal contributions to the planetary challenges. This exercise of self-scrutiny is a powerful way to uncover the personal assumptions, beliefs, motivations and identity anchors.

Discovering the personal contribution to the problems is cognitive exercises, accompanied with strong affects, such as guilt, despair, overwhelm, sadness and shock (Rimanoczy, 2010). These emotions are a foundation for the revision of the personal values and for the development of social sensitivity, empathy and compassion. We assert that *compassion* is a primary element of the **values** component. Although empathy is one of Goleman's components and appears related to compassion, his definition is more limited in scope: "the ability to understand the emotional makeup of other people and skill in treating people according to their emotional reactions" (1998, p. 95). By compassion, we mean not only understanding others' emotional makeup and reactions and responding accordingly but also a suspension of judgment of others and an

TABLE 1.8 Compassion

CONTENT AREAS	DIMENSIONS		
	Knowledge (knowing, thinking)	*Values (being)*	*Competencies (doing)*
Ecological Worldview	Ecoliteracy	Biospheric	Protective/restorative action
Systemic Perspective	Systems theory	Sense of interconnectedness	Stakeholder engagement
Emotional Intelligence	Self/other-awareness Compassion	Compassion	Proactive glocal sensitivity
Spiritual Intelligence	Purpose, mission	Oneness with all that is	Contemplative Practices

TABLE 1.9 Proactive glocal sensitivity

CONTENT AREAS	DIMENSIONS		
	Knowledge (knowing, thinking)	*Values (being)*	*Competencies (doing)*
Ecological Worldview	Ecoliteracy	Biospheric	Protective/restorative action
Systemic Perspective	Systems theory	Sense of interconnectedness	Stakeholder engagement
Emotional Intelligence	Self/other-awareness Compassion	Compassion	Proactive glocal sensitivity
Spiritual Intelligence	Purpose, mission	Oneness with all that is	Contemplative Practices

appreciation of both their strengths and limitations, which is deeper and more trust-building.

Curricular activities such as having students interview stakeholders, evaluating their own environmental or social footprint, or conducting participatory action research are ways to integrate this dimension into learning contexts.

We found that as realizing the personal contribution to the problems triggers emotional reactions, they in turn fuel social sensitivity and action, at the local or global level. We call this **proactive glocal sensitivity**, which is the developmental element of the **competency** or doing dimension within the content area of emotional intelligence.

Proactivity is an outcome of self-regulation (Goleman, 1998) in which the motivation to act ensues from knowledge and values. Self-regulation includes the capacity to respond flexibly to changing circumstances and to develop comfort with ambiguity and paradox. This competency facilitates working relationships, as equanimity and the suspension of judgment engender rapport-building and trust. Self-regulation also aids in resilience in the face of challenging circumstances and repeated setbacks, both of which are common occurrences in facing large and small systemic problems.

Glocal indicates a capacity to interact, understand and negotiate at local and global levels. Sustainability is not only a matter of personal choices but also choices for the greater good. Individual decision making towards more sustainable practices only goes so far. More substantive action on initiatives and policies takes place within communities, organizations and government, and this is where social skills are vital to build the necessary trust to make progress on change.

Sensitivity refers to the acknowledgement of organizational, local, regional, national or even sectoral cultural norms, as well as the ability to adjust to the emotional states of individuals. A well-documented and effective way to develop this competency is through service project work (see Vazquez Maguirre & Garcia de la Torre, Chapter 12; and Shutel, Becker and Audino, Chapter 11 c in this book).

Content area: spiritual intelligence

The spiritual intelligence content area refers to connecting with internal and external resources through regular introspective or meditative practices, in the pursuit of alignment of purpose, values and behaviors (Cashman, 2008; Doppelt, 2012; Scharmer & Kaufer, 2013).

The findings of the exploratory study connecting the leaders' sense of purpose or personal mission as a motivation to act for the greater good (Rimanoczy, 2010) were validated in other studies (Hurst, 2014; Kroth & Boverie, 2000; Visser & Crane, 2010). While traumatic events or midlife crisis tend to trigger questions about life's purpose, that inquiry could also be introduced intentionally earlier in life, to influence leaders' worldview.

For this reason, we incorporated the element of *purpose and mission* into the **knowledge** dimension of Spiritual Intelligence. Reflecting on one's *purpose and mission* and its connection to social sensitivity or the larger good had been observed by Frankl (1965), who emphasized that making a social contribution provided meaning to our life. This was also suggested by Wong's (1998) Personal Meaning Profile, where statements such as "I believe I can make a difference in the world; I strive to make the world a better place; it is important that I dedicate my life to a cause; I make a significant contribution to society; and I attempt to leave behind a good and lasting legacy" (p. 138) became indicators of self-transcendence.

Wheeler, Colbert, and Freeman (2003) note the connection between ethical aspects and life purpose, through social sensitivity and the aspiration for justice, integrity, reverence, respect and mutual prosperity that infuse people's decisions.

TABLE 1.10 Purpose, mission

	DIMENSIONS		
CONTENT AREAS	Knowledge (knowing, thinking)	Values (being)	Competencies (doing)
Ecological Worldview	Ecoliteracy	Biospheric	Protective/restorative action
Systemic Perspective	Systems theory	Sense of interconnectedness	Stakeholder engagement
Emotional Intelligence	Self/other-awareness Compassion	Compassion	Proactive glocal sensitivity
Spiritual Intelligence	Purpose, mission	Oneness with all that is	Contemplative Practices

Neal (2008) considered that when we are fully present we notice our 'deeper self', and profound questions can arise: Who am I? Who do I want to be? Why am I doing what I do? Considering one's priorities and values prompts an inquiry into purpose, such as what is the purpose of our talents and what difference can we make in the world? Such questions can be integrated as part of an assignment, in relation to the content of a course. These questions are important when shifting from a paucity of awareness or unexamined adherence to cultural norms toward sustainability-conscious behaviors and habits.

Scharmer and Kaufer (2013) integrate a spiritual dimension by "connecting to intention and awareness" in a management context (p. 141). Although not specifically positing their approach as a sustainability mindset, Scharmer and Kaufer (2013) speak explicitly to transforming thought (see Chapter 3) and propose a transition "from ego to eco" (in Chapter 6) in which diverse cross-sector innovation leads to a co-creation that benefits all stakeholders.

Leaders and students who reflect on their larger purpose develop more profound levels of engagement towards sustainable actions than those motivated by the desire to create a competitive advantage (Rimanoczy, 2014). Goleman (1998) pointed at the motivation present in "the passion to work for reasons that go beyond money or status" (p. 88).

There seems to be a connection between leaders championing sustainability initiatives and the deep-felt sense of *oneness with all that is* (Bonnett, 2002; Rimanoczy, 2010; Scharmer & Kaufer, 2013; Wiek et al., 2011). We include this developmental element within the **values** dimension of Spiritual Intelligence, referring to the conscious experience of being connected to the web of life (Capra, 1997). Management theory and practice traditionally position nature as offering resources: food, water, raw materials, minerals and air. This utilitarian point of view is based on a belief of human superiority that entitles humans to appropriate and

TABLE 1.11 Oneness with all that is

	DIMENSIONS		
CONTENT AREAS	Knowledge (knowing, thinking)	Values (being)	Competencies (doing)
Ecological Worldview	Ecoliteracy	Biospheric	Protective/restorative action
Systemic Perspective	Systems theory	Sense of interconnectedness	Stakeholder engagement
Emotional Intelligence	Self/other-awareness Compassion	Compassion	Proactive glocal sensitivity
Spiritual Intelligence	Purpose, mission	Oneness with all that is	Contemplative Practices

manipulate the natural world to fit our needs and desires, with little regard for environmental (or social) impacts.

In contrast, operating from the value of **oneness with all that is** means that we see ourselves as *part of* nature, thoroughly embedded in it, nurtured by it and nurturing it, not above or beyond it. The economy does not exist without secure, adequate, ongoing provisioning of natural resources, an enveloping global system that is in many ways being threatened and impacted by our actions and behaviors. This sense reflects a shift from a utilitarian "take-make-waste" approach to a more sustainable "borrow-use-return" approach to materials, reusing and restoring whenever possible. Individuals with this sense also develop a caring attitude for other manifestations of life, with a sense of responsibility, stewardship, protection and restoration. An interesting activity that the authors implemented with students was inviting them to spend one hour in nature, alone, without a phone, book, or any electronic device, just observing. This was a very powerful exercise that generated profound insights.

The **competency** dimension of Spiritual Intelligence introduces an unusual focus in management education: the developmental elements of **mindfulness and reflective practices**. While the concept of **mindfulness** originates in the Buddhist tradition, described as the faculty of attentively noticing the present moment, meaning the surrounding environment and one's reactions to it, there are indications of a connection between mindfulness practices and environmental or social sensitivity (Ericson, Kjønstad, & Barstad, 2014: Jacob, Jovic, & Brinkerhoff, 2009; Rimanoczy, 2010). Some executive leaders and educators are realizing the benefits, enough to get the attention of *The Wall Street Journal* (Gardiner, 2012). **Mindfulness** has the effect of calming the mind and creating focus, as well as a sense of peace, and it has been taught as a meditative practice in the West (Kabat-Zinn, 1994). It is a useful way to shift from an 'automated' execution mode to a state of conscious

TABLE 1.12 Contemplative practices

CONTENT AREAS	DIMENSIONS		
	Knowledge (knowing, thinking)	*Values (being)*	*Competencies (doing)*
Ecological Worldview	Ecoliteracy	Biospheric	Protective/restorative action
Systemic Perspective	Systems theory	Sense of interconnectedness	Stakeholder engagement
Emotional Intelligence	Self/other-awareness Compassion	Compassion	Proactive glocal sensitivity
Spiritual Intelligence	Purpose, mission	Oneness with all that is	Contemplative Practices

observation. The authors and many colleagues are implementing a few minutes of silent or guided meditation at the start of their regular classes, which has proven to be a welcome activity.

The concept of 'conscious capitalism' (Mackey & Sisodia, 2014), exemplified in companies like Whole Foods, described how conscious leaders played a major role in their companies to help them outperform the market. Other authors have signaled the importance of shifting business schools to "spaces where consciousness is awakened," and they connect it with students moving into social action as opposed to training future "servants of power" (Kurucz, Colbert, & Marcus, 2014, p. 439).

While *mindfulness* helps us to pay attention to the present moment, *reflection* is the intentional pause aimed at pondering patterns, relationships, and connections among events, questions or possibilities. Management culture's increasingly fast pace rewards and even expects rapid response, which is not conducive to pausing and reflecting. Identifying the impact of actions or decisions before they are made requires a *reflective practice*, a critical skill for a sustainable organization and planet.

This section described the model to develop the sustainability mindset with students, presenting the four content areas of ecological worldview, systems perspective, emotional intelligence and spiritual intelligence, and the aspects to be developed in the dimensions of knowledge (thinking), values (being) and competencies (doing).

The development of the sustainability mindset is enhanced by projects or initiatives that invite students to make a difference in the community or their organization, an experiential component that both accelerates the development of the four content areas, while it develops their self-confidence, as they realize they can proactively shape a better world.

In the next section we will describe how the sustainability mindset can be of value in organizational contexts.

Sustainability mindset in use

The area of social, environmental and economic sustainability attracts scholars from diverse disciplines. As a research frontier, sustainability appeals to a cross-disciplinary body of researchers that has yet to produce an overarching integrative theory. The sustainability mindset opens a nascent perspective that transcends boundaries and that can be integrated into management learning and education.

Forged by the work of Dweck on the origins of mindsets, their role in motivation and impact on achievement, and interpersonal processes (2006), to cultivating a global mindset defined as one that combines an openness to and awareness of diversity across cultures (Gupta and Govindarajan, 2002), we come to value the influence of mindset in management studies. From a broader perspective, the sustainability mindset is a lens that encompasses social and environmental aspects, self-awareness, connection with purpose, and social sensitivity, leading to an internal call to action.

We live and work in a world of natural systems where rising social and environmental pressures are redefining the way business creates value. In addition, the market forces of diminishing natural resources, extreme transparency and higher expectation levels are requiring a paradigm shift toward a new mindset, where our connection to the social and natural environment are the norm. In an Accenture 2013 survey with 1,000 CEOs of large companies in 27 industries across 103 countries, only 32% believed that the global economy was on track to meet the sustainability needs created by a growing population and rising environmental and resource constraints (www.accenture.com).

In the corporate world, innovative companies are developing new ways of growing and prospering while decreasing pollution and conserving ecosystem services or restoring natural resources. Esty and Winston (2006) used the term Eco-Advantage Mindset to describe a way of reframing and developing these new ways of approaching environmental issues by utilizing environmental thinking to strategize new opportunities. In their research they found this mindset critical to managing ecological risks, driving innovation and turning environmental pressures into competitive advantage by companies on a sustainability path.

Research conducted by Mitchell (2012) applied an Eco-Sustainability Conceptual Framework and Scorecard based on Esty and Winston's model in which the dimension of mindset played an instrumental role as a source of innovation within companies. Upon a closer review, elements of the sustainability mindset model were demonstrated with the Eco-Sustainability Scorecard: the findings revealed that decision making by the leadership team was based on core values reflected in the dimensions of *values and knowledge*, as featured in the sustainability mindset model (see Figure 1.2). In strategic thinking, leadership utilized systems thinking, considering both the short- and long-term horizons and attuned to intangible costs and benefits.

Sustainability mindset as part of organizational culture

The benefits of a sustainability mindset are realized when the knowledge, values and competencies become intrinsic to how organizations operate, becoming interwoven within and inextricable from the organizational culture: cost savings, managed risks, reputational enhancement, customer loyalty, employee engagement, new revenue streams and markets, for example. Contributions can be sourced from every department and division in a firm to improve organizational strength and agility.

How a sustainability mindset becomes embedded within an organization is a reflection of the top leadership, and it is unlikely to be adequately integrated without that support. There is, fortunately, a mission-driven movement of leaders from NGOs, government, non-profits, social enterprises and small to large companies which represent an enlightened, new breed of inspiring entrepreneurs (Russo, 2010; Sisodia, Wolfe & Sheth, 2015). As the business case for sustainability becomes the norm, while the new generations will be faced with challenges of a never-anticipated magnitude, we have the opportunity to connect the head and the heart with action, to inspire employees and business partners in embracing sustainable business practices along with personal mindfulness practices that foster an evolution of consciousness.

As managers adopt a sustainability mindset throughout all levels, they instill new ways of problem solving, embedding systems thinking, managing risks, spurring innovation and transforming environmental and social pressures into competitive advantage. In this process, the sustainability mindset starts to be translated into action, with stakeholders as part of the organizational culture. Ravasi and Schultz (2006) posit that the organizational culture is a set of shared mental assumptions that guide interpretation and action in organizations by defining appropriate behavior for various situations, including sustainability issues. This is where the sustainability mindset can be communicated in the way companies describe their culture in their employee handbook, statement of company values, code of conduct, in request for proposals, in job descriptions, annual sustainability reports, storytelling on their website and other communication outlets.

Limitations

The sustainability mindset conceptual model and framework has been developed on the foundation of the findings of an exploratory qualitative study with a narrow focus on corporate executive officers, social entrepreneurs and senior leaders. Some of the research examples cited in this paper were highlighted from a select group of leaders engaged in sustainability innovations. Although the mindset model has been used since 2010 with undergraduate and graduate students, future research could extend the sustainability mindset model use with an assessment tool to measure the validity of the model.

The findings of that study were contrasted with literature positing three dimensions impacting sustainability motivations: knowledge (thinking), values (being) and competency (doing). Furthermore, it focused on the content areas and elements identified in the study, which were later encountered in other studies and literature. The authors by no means assume that the knowledge, values and competencies described in this chapter are the only ones that may play a role in a sustainability mindset.

The model is presented as a scaffolding to organize contents and facilitate the development of such learning goals. Sustainability is in itself a systemic concept, which implies a certain transdisciplinarity and "messiness". Within the values dimension, for example, are inclinations such as a sense of *interconnectedness, oneness with all that is* and *biospheric orientation*, which may seem to overlap, as might *systems theory* and *ecoliteracy*. These terms are used within specific definitions, and as such they posit opportunities for future research. Additional research could explore the dimensions of values and knowledge; how innovative action occurs along the pathways between the quadrants; the potentially transformative impact of a program to develop the sustainability mindset using this model, and the lasting impact in a longitudinal study of students. A PRME Working Group on the Sustainability

Mindset, with members from more than 26 countries, is currently engaged in further research.

As economic, environmental and social equity issues become more complex, leaders will inevitability face challenges requiring a paradigm shift, such as the one proposed in the sustainability mindset model, extending its use further in management training and education. In order for managers to address multiple competing demands, they need to execute organizational strategy and balance the inconsistent tensions between social or environmental missions and profits, or global demands and local needs (Greenwood, Kodeih, Micelotta, & Lounsbury, 2011; Kraatz & Block, 2008). Additional research could further investigate the use of the sustainability mindset conceptual model in decision making and how the model is applied across different cultures.

In many ways, additional research would add to a body of literature that aligns with management and management education studies. The sustainability mindset model crosses multiple dimensions as well as disciplines and holds both potential and promise for a new generation of globally responsible leadership.

Conclusion

Evidence supporting the sustainability mindset model is showing up in scholarly journals in a widening variety of disciplines, including the travel and tourism industry (Ulrike, Davis, Bowser, Jiang, & Brown, 2014), engineering education (Polastri & Alberts, 2014) and management education (Fang et al., 2004; Kurucz et al., 2014, Rimanoczy, 2014).

The recognition that leaders are facing more situations that require them to access their self-awareness, spirituality and emotional intelligence in order to be successful has become imperative as a more enlightened form of business acumen (Laszlo & Brown, 2014). In this new role, management educators and leaders will benefit from using the sustainability mindset in creating learning hubs and work environments where people can experience a deeper sense of connection to and caring for others and their planet. The model was developed for the purpose of helping faculty and coaches create programs for management students and business leaders to cultivate the mindset, and is being explored and assessed by LEAP!, the PRME Working Group on the Sustainability Mindset, in which the authors are involved. Perhaps these explorations will provide indications of the potential applications of the sustainability mindset model for management studies, facilitating dialogue among multiple stakeholders, and use by management decision makers, spurring innovation, storytelling, executive coaching and leadership development as a tool to develop globally responsible leaders for the world.

> Taking this class in my final semester made me realize why I decided to get an MBA in the first place. It gave me the opportunity to stop and reflect on the choices I've made and understand why they're important to me. . . .This journey has certainly impacted my life in a positive way. I'm now more interested

in making a difference than making money. I'm more conscious of my role in life. I still need to figure that out, but I'm definitely on the right path.

(Student, MBA Fordham University)

References

Adkins, C. P., Gentile, M. C., Ingols, C., & Trefalt, S. (2011). Teaching "How" – Not "Whether" – to manage with integrity: Undergraduate and MBA application of the "Giving Voice to Values" curriculum. *Management Education for Integrity*, 107–133.
Allen-Gil, S., Walker, L., Thomas, G., & Shevory, T. (2005). Forming a community partnership to enhance education in sustainability. *International Journal of Sustainability in Higher Education*, 6(4), 392–402.
Argyris, C. (1987). Reasoning, action strategies, and defensive routines: The case of OD practitioners. In R. A. Woodman & A. A. Pasmore (Eds.), *Research in organizational change and development* (Vol. 1, pp. 89–128). Greenwich: JAI Press.
Baron, C., & Cayer, M. (2011). Fostering post-conventional consciousness in leaders: Why and how? *Journal of Management Development*, 30(4), 344–365.
Beringer, A., Wright, T., & Malone, L. (2008). Sustainability in higher education in Atlantic Canada. *International Journal of Sustainability in Higher Education*, 9(1), 48–67.
Bonnett, M. (2002). Education for sustainability as a frame of mind. *Environmental Education Research*, 8(1), 9–20.
Boulding, K. E. (1956). General systems theory – the skeleton of science. *Management Science*, 2(3), 197–208. https://doi.org/10.1287/mnsc.2.3.197
Capra, F. (1997). *The web of life: A new scientific understanding of living systems* (1st Anchor Books trade paperback ed.). New York, NY: Anchor Books.
Capra, F., & Mattei, U. (2015). *The ecology of law: Toward a legal system in tune with nature and community*. Oakland, CA: Berrett-Koehler Publishers.
Cashman, K. (2008). *Leadership from the inside out: Becoming a leader for life*. Retrieved from ReadHowYouWant.com
Cseh, M., Davis, E. B., & Khilji, S. E. (2013). Developing a global mindset: Learning of global leaders. *European Journal of Training and Development*, 37(5), 489–499. doi:10.1108/03090591311327303
Delbecq, A. L. (2008). Spirituality and leadership effectiveness: Inner growth matters. In J. Gallos (Ed.), *Business leadership: A Jossey-Bass reader* (2nd ed., pp. 485–503). New York, NY: John Wiley and Sons.
Divecha, S., & Brown, B. C. (2013). Integral sustainability: Correlating action logics with sustainability to provide insight into the dynamics of change. *Journal of Integral Theory and Practice*, 8(3/4), 197.
Doppelt, B. (2012). *The power of sustainable thinking: "How to Create a Positive Future for the Climate, the Planet, Your Organization and Your Life"*. London: Routledge.
Drucker, P. F. (1994). *Post-capitalist society*. London: Routledge.
Dweck, C. (2006). *Mindset: The new psychology of success*. New York, NY: Random House Publishing.
Eisenstein, C. (2013). *The more beautiful world our hearts know is possible (Sacred activism)*. Berkeley, CA: North Atlantic Books.
Elkington, J. (1998). *Cannibals with forks: The triple bottom line of 21st century business*. Gabriola Island, BC; Stony Creek, CT: New Society Publishers.
Ericson, T., Kjønstad, B. G., & Barstad, A. (2014). Mindfulness and sustainability. *Ecological Economics*, 104, 73–79.

Esty, D. C., & Winston, A. S. (2006). *Green to gold*. New Haven, CT: Yale University Press.

Fang, F., Kang, S.-P., & Liu, S. (2004). *Measuring mindset change in the systemic transformation of education*. Paper presented at the The National Convention of the Association for Educational Communications and Technology, Chicago, IL.

Forray, J., Leigh, J., & Kenworthy, A. L. (2015). Special section cluster on responsible management education: Nurturing an emerging PRME ethos. *Academy of Management Learning & Education, 14*(2), 293–296. doi:10.5465/amle.2015.0072

Francis, C. (2011). Critical pedagogy, ecoliteracy & planetary crisis: The ecopedagogy movement. *Environmental Education Research, 17*(6), 851–851. doi:10.1080/13504622.2011.626972

Frankl, V. E. (1965). The philosophical foundations of logotherapie. *Universitas, 8*(1), 171.

Freeman, R. E., Wicks, A. C., & Parmar, B. (2004). Stakeholder theory and "the corporate objective revisited". *Organization Science, 15*(3), 364–369.

Gardiner, B. (April 3, 2012. Business skills and Buddhist mindfulness. *The Wall Street Journal*. Retrieved from www.wsj.com/articles/SB10001424052702303816504577305820565167202

Gintis, H., & Khurana, R. (2007). Corporate honesty and business education: A behavior model: Free enterprise: Values in action conference series, 2005–2006. In P. J. Zak (Ed.), *Moral markets: The critical role of values in the economy*. Princeton, NJ: Princeton University Press. SSRN: https://ssrn.com/abstract=929173

Gladwin, T. N., Kennelly, J. J., & Krause, T.-S. (1995). Shifting paradigms for sustainable development: Implications. *The Academy of Management Review, 20*(4), 874.

Goleman, D. (1995). *Emotional intelligence*. New York: Bantam Books.

Goleman, D. (1998). What makes a leader? *Harvard Business Review, 76*(6), 92–+.

Goleman, D. (2009). *Ecological intelligence: How knowing the hidden impacts of what we buy can change everything*. New York: Crown Business.

Goleman, D., Boyatzis, R. E., & McKee, A. (2002). The *new leaders: Transforming the art of leadership into the science of results*. London: Little, Brown.

Greenwood, R. M., Kodeih, F., Micelotta, E. R., & Lounsbury, M. 2011. Institutional complexity and organizational responses. *Academy of Management Annals, 5*, 317–371.

Gupta, A. K., & Govindarajan, V. (2002). Cultivating a global mindset. *The Academy of Management Executive, 16*(1): 116–126. doi:10.5465/ame.2002.6640211. Retrieved from www.accenture.com/Microsites/ungc-ceo-study/Pages/home.aspx

Hawken, P. (1993). *The ecology of commerce: A declaration of sustainability*. New York: Harper-Collins.

Hawken, P., Lovins, A. B., & Lovins, L. H. (2013). *Natural capitalism: The next industrial revolution*. London: Routledge.

Hörisch, J., Freeman, R. E., & Schaltegger, S. (2014). Applying stakeholder theory in sustainability management links, similarities, dissimilarities, and a conceptual framework. *Organization & Environment, 27*(4), 328–346.

Hühn, M. P. (2013). You reap what you sow: How MBA programs undermine ethics. *Journal of Business Ethics, 121*(4), 527–541. https://doi.org/10.1007/s10551-013-1733-z

Hurst, A. 2014. *The purpose economy: how your desire for impact, personal growth and community is changing the world*. Boise, ID: Elevate.

Hutchison, E. D. (2016). *Essentials of human behavior: Integrating person, environment, and the life course*. Thousand Oaks, CA: Sage Publications.

Jacob, J., Jovic, E., & Brinkerhoff, M. B. (2009). Personal and planetary well-being: Mindfulness meditation, pro-environmental behavior and personal quality of life in a survey from the social justice and ecological sustainability movement. *Social Indicators Research, 93*(2), 275–294.

Kabat-Zinn, J. (1994). *Wherever you go, there you are: Mindfulness meditation in everyday life*. New York: Hyperion.

Kassel, K. (2014). *The thinking executive's guide to sustainability*. New York: Business Expert Press.

Kearney, R. (1984). *Dialogues with contemporary continental thinkers: The phenomenological heritage: Paul Ricoeur, Emmanuel Levinas, Herbert Marcuse, Stanislas Breton, Jacques Derrida*. Manchester: Manchester University Press.

Kegan, R. (1982). *The evolving self*. Cambridge: Harvard University Press.

Ketola, T. (2008). A holistic corporate responsibility model: Integrating values, discourses and actions. *Journal of Business Ethics, 80*(3), 419–435.

Kohlberg, L. (1984). *Essays on moral development. Vol. II: The psychology of moral development*. San Francisco: Harper & Row.

Kolb, D.A. (1984). *Experiential learning: Experience as the source of learning and development*. Englewood Cliffs, NJ: Prentice-Hall.

Kraatz, M. S., & Block, E. 2008. Organizational implications of institutional pluralism. In R. Greenwood, C. Oliver, K. Sahlin, & R. Suddaby (Eds.), *The Sage handbook of organizational institutionalism* (pp. 243–275). Thousand Oaks, CA: Sage Publications.

Kreb, C. J. (2008). *The ecological world view*. Oakland, CA: University of California Press.

Krishnan, V. R. (2008). Does management education make students better actors? A longitudinal study of change in values and self monitoring. *Great Lakes Herald, 2*, 35–48.

Kroth, M., & Boverie, P. (2000). Life mission and adult learning. *Adult Education Quarterly, 50*, 134–149.

Kuhn, T. S., & Hacking, I. (2012). *The structure of scientific revolutions* (4th ed.). Chicago and London: The University of Chicago Press.

Kurucz, E. C., Colbert, B. A., & Marcus, J. (2014). Sustainability as a provocation to rethink management education: Building a progressive educative practice. *Management Learning, 45*(4), 437–457. doi:10.1177/1350507613486421

Laszlo, C. (2008). *Sustainable value: How the world's leading companies are doing well by doing good*. Stanford, CA: Stanford Business Books.

Laszlo, C., & Brown, J. (2014). *Flourishing enterprise: The new spirit of business*. Stanford, CA: Stanford University Press.

Laszlo, C., & Zhexembayeva, N. (2011). *Embedded sustainability: The next big competitive advantage*. Stanford, CA: Stanford University Press.

Lewis, M. W. (2000). Exploring paradox: Toward a more comprehensive guide. *Academy of Management Review, 25*(4), 760–776.

Linnenluecke, M. K., & Griffiths, A. (2013). Firms and sustainability: Mapping the intellectual origins and structure of the corporate sustainability field. *Global Environmental Change, 23*(1), 382–391. doi:http://dx.doi.org/10.1016/j.gloenvcha.2012.07.007

Lissack, M. R. (1999). Complexity: The science, its vocabulary, and its relation to organizations. *Emergence, 1*(1), 110–126. doi:10.1207/s15327000em0101_7

Mackey, J., & Sisodia, R. (2014). *Conscious capitalism: Liberating the heroic spirit of business*. Cambridge, MA: Harvard Business School Publishing Corporation.

Magretta, J. (2008). Growth through global sustainability: An interview with Monsant's CEO, Robert B. Shapiro. In H. B. Review (Ed.), *Harvard business review on profiting from green business* (pp. 59–84). Boston, MA: Harvard Business School Publishing Corporation

Meadows, D. H. (2008). Thinking in systems: A primer. White River Junction, VT: Chelsea Green Pub.

Meadows, D. H., Meadows, D. H., Randers, J., & Behrens III, W. W. (1972). *The limits to growth: A report to the club of Rome (1972)*. New York, NY: Universe Books.

Mezher, T. (2011). Building future sustainable cities: The need for a new mindset. *Construction Innovation, 11*(2), 136–141.

Mezirow, J. (1994). Understanding transformation theory. *Adult Education Quarterly, 44*(4), 222–232. doi:10.1177/074171369404400403

Mitchell, S. F. (2012) *An empirical investigation: How small to mid-sized enterprises use innovation on the path toward ecological sustainability.* Doctoral dissertation. University of New Hampshire.

Moosmayer, D. C. (2013). *Questioning self-interest: Addressing the hidden moral impact of management theory and education.* Retrieved September 28, 2016, from http://pd.aom.org/2013/submission.asp?mode=ShowSession&SessionID=257

Muraca, B. (2012). Towards a fair degrowth-society: Justice and the right to a "good life" beyond growth. *Futures, 44*(6), 535–545.

Natrass, B., & Altomare, M. (1999). *The natural step for business.* Gabriela Island, Canada: Turtle Island.

Neal, J. A. (2008). *Leadership and spirituality in the workplace.* Retrieved July 15, 2009, www.judineal.com/pages/pubs/leadership.htm

Perry, W. (1968). *Forms of intellectual and ethical development in the college years.* New York, NY: Holt, Winehart & Winston.

Polastri, P., & Alberts, T. E. (2014). Developing a globalized and sustainable mindset in 21st century engineering students. *IDEAS, 18*, 83–92.

Porter, M. E., & Kramer, M. R. (2011). Creating shared value. *Harvard Business Review, 89*(1/2), 62–77.

Post, J. E., & Altman, B. W. (1994). Managing the environmental change process: Barriers and opportunities. *Journal of Organizational Change Management, 7*(4), 64.

Ravasi, D., & Schultz, M. (2006). Responding to organizational identity threats: Exploring the role of organizational culture. *Academy of Management Journal, 49*(3), 433–458.

Reinhardt, F. L. (2008). Bringing the environment down to earth. In H. B. Review (Ed.), *Harvard business review on profiting from green business* (pp. 35–58). Boston, MA: Harvard Business School Publishing Corporation.

Rimanoczy, I. (2014). A matter of being: Developing sustainability-minded leaders. *Journal of Management for Global Sustainability, 2*(1), 95–122.

Rimanoczy, I. (2016). *Stop teaching: Principles and practices for responsible management education.* New York, NY: Business Expert Press.

Rimanoczy, I. B. (2010). *Business leaders committing to and fostering sustainability initiatives.* Doctoral dissertation. Teachers College, Columbia University.

Russo, M. V. (2010). *Companies on a mission.* Stanford, CA: Stanford Business Books.

Salovey, P., Mayer, J., & Caruso, D. (2004). Emotional intelligence: Theory, findings, and implications. *Psychological Inquiry*, 197–215.

Salzmann, O., Ionescu-somers, A., & Steger, U. (2005). The business case for corporate sustainability: Literature review and research options. *European Management Journal, 23*(1), 27–36.

Sayer, R. A. (2000). *Realism and social science.* London; Thousand Oaks, CA: Sage.

Scharmer, O., & Hub, G. (2010). Seven acupuncture points for shifting capitalism to create a regenerative ecosystem economy. *Oxford Leadership Journal, 1*(3), 1–21.

Scharmer, O., & Kaufer, K. (2013). Leading from the emerging future from ego-system to eco-system economies. Oakland, CA: Berrett-Koehler.

Schein, S. (2015). *A new psychology for sustainability leadership the hidden power of ecological worldviews.* Sheffield, UK: Greenleaf Publishing.

Schneider, F., Kallis, G., & Martinez-Alier, J. (2010). Crisis or opportunity? Economic degrowth for social equity and ecological sustainability. Introduction to this special issue. *Journal of cleaner production, 18*(6), 511–518.

Senge, P. M. (2006). *The fifth discipline.* London: Random House Business.

Senge, P. M. (2008). *The necessary revolution: How individuals and organizations are working together to create a sustainable world.* New York, NY: Doubleday.

Sharp, Z., & Zaidma, N. (2010). Strategization of CSR. *Journal of Business Ethics, 93*(1), 51–71.

Sisodia, R., Wolfe, D., & Sheth, J. N. (2015). *Firms of endearment: How world-class companies profit from passion and purpose.* Upper Saddle River, NJ: Pearson Education.

Sison, A. J. G. (2009). From CSR to corporate citizenship: Anglo-American and continental European perspectives *Journal of Business Ethics, 89*(Supplement 3), 235–246.

Spitzeck, H. (2011). An integrated model of humanistic management. *Journal of Business Ethics, 99*(1), 51–62.

Sterling, S. (2011). Transformative learning and sustainability: Sketching the conceptual ground. *Learning and Teaching in Higher Education, 5,* 17–33.

Story, J. S. P., Barbuto, J. E., Luthans, F., & Bovaird, J. A. (2014). Meeting the challenges of effective international HRM: Analysis of the antecedents of global mindset. *Human Resource Management, 53*(1), 131–155. doi:10.1002/hrm.21568

Tudway, R., & Pascal, A.-M. (2006). Corporate governance, shareholder value and societal expectations. *Corporate Governance, 6*(3), 305.

Ulrike, G., Davis, E., Bowser, G., Jiang, J., & Brown, M. (2014). Creating global leaders with sustainability mindsets. *Journal of Teaching in Travel & Tourism, 14*(2), 164–183.

Van Lopik, W. (2013). Learning sustainability in a tribal college context. In P. F. Barlett & G. W. Chase (Eds.), *Sustainability in higher education: Stories and strategies for transformation* (pp. 107–114). Cambridge, MA: MIT Press.

Visser, W., & Courtice, P. (2011, October 21). *Sustainability leadership: Linking theory and practice.* Retrieved from SSRN: https://ssrn.com/abstract=1947221 or http://dx.doi.org/10.2139/ssrn.1947221

Visser, W., & Crane, A. (2010, February 25). Corporate sustainability and the individual: Understanding what drives sustainability professionals as change agents. Retrieved from SSRN: https://ssrn.com/abstract=1559087 or http://dx.doi.org/10.2139/ssrn.1559087

Wheeler, D., Colbert, B., & Freeman, R. E. (2003). Focusing on value: Corporate social responsibility, sustainability and a stakeholder approach in a network world. *Journal of General Management, 28*(3), 1–28.

Wiek, A., Withycombe, L., & Redman, C. L. (2011). Key competencies in sustainability: a reference framework for academic program development. *Sustainability Science, 6*(2), 203–218.

Wilber, K. (2001). *Sex, ecology, spirituality: The spirit of evolution.* Boulder, CO: Shambhala Publications.

Willard, B. (2002). *The sustainability advantage: Seven business case benefits of a triple bottom line.* Gabriola Island, BC: New Society Publishers.

Willard, B. (2005). *The next sustainability wave: building boardroom buy-in.* Gabriola Island, BC: New Society Publishers.

Willard, B. (2009). *The sustainability champion's guidebook: How to transform your company.* Gabriola Island, BC: New Society Publishers.

Williams, D., & Brown, J. (2013). *Learning gardens and sustainability education: Bringing life to schools and schools to life.* London: Routledge.

Wong, P. T. P. (1998). Implicit theories of meaningful life and the development of the Personal Meaning Profile. In P. T. P. Wong & P. S. Fry (Eds.), *The human quest for meaning: A handbook of psychological research and clinical applications.* London: Lawrence Erlbaum Associates.

Wong, P. T. P. (2012, July). The meaning mindset: Measurement and implications. *International Journal of Existential Psychology and Psychotherapy, 4*(1).

World Commission on Environment and Development. (1987). *Our common future*. Oxford: Oxford University Press.

Wu, Y., Huang, S., Kuo, L., & Wu, W. (2010). Management education for sustainability: A web-based content analysis. *Academy of Management Learning & Education, 9*(3), 520–531. Retrieved from www.jstor.org/stable/25782035

Yeager, D. S., & Dweck, C. S. (2012). Mindsets that promote resilience: When students believe that personal characteristics can be developed. *Educational Psychologist, 47*(4), 302–314. doi: 10.1080/00461520.2012.722805

Young, S., & Nagpal, S. (2013). Meeting the growing demand for sustainability-focused management education: A case study of a PRME academic institution. *Higher Education Research & Development, 32*(3), 493–506. doi:10.1080/07294360.2012.695339

Zohar, D. (2012). *Spiritual intelligence: The ultimate intelligence*. London: Bloomsbury Publishing.

2

SUSTAINABILITY AND THE BEING DIMENSION

The heart of the matter

Isabel Rimanoczy and Karthyeni Sridaran

Examples of corporate innovations, best practice efforts in industries and corporations that are successfully embedding sustainability into their organizational systems and highlighting the admirable will of imaginative entrepreneurs become good cases to discuss and learn from. Despite great examples of innovation, many initiatives still fall mostly into the category of "eco-efficiency", aiming at reducing the harm and less on creating better living conditions for all in the ecosystem. And the question rises again and again: with more information and technological solutions available, why is change so slow?

This chapter suggests that the missing link may lay in a dimension mostly unattended in management education: the Being Dimension. The authors reach into data from two qualitative research studies: the first study explored spiritually aware business leaders from Western and Eastern backgrounds to see how their spiritual values or beliefs influenced their behaviors, activities and relations in the workplace. The second study approached the phenomenon from another angle, studying exemplary business leaders championing sustainability initiatives to see if there were any spiritual values or beliefs motivating them behind their uncommon but exceptional business behavior.

As a result of this exploration from these two complementary studies, the spiritual domain is recognized as a fundamental tacit dimension on which an inner mind-shift can accelerate external transformations to address the ultimate need for human well-being in the world. After presenting their two independent studies, the authors then mapped for commonalities between the two research findings. They propose suitable activities in management education with the aim to inspire a new generation of graduates from the classroom to the boardroom with not just knowledge and skills but more importantly the values, will, and vision to transform into responsible corporate citizens of the future.

Introduction

In the year 2006, an international task force started a conversation about what role management education played in shaping the next generation of responsible leaders that the world was calling for. The task force had diverse members: academics, deans, university presidents, representatives of the United Nations Global Compact, the Association to Advance Collegiate Schools of Business (AACSB), the Aspen Institute, the student organization NetImpact, the European Foundation for Management Development (EFMD), and the Globally Responsible Leadership Initiative (GRLI). The task force finally identified six guiding principles, which became the Principles for Responsible Management Education (PRME), addressing purpose, values, pedagogical approaches, research, partnerships, and dialogue in management education (Waddock, Rasche, Werhane, & Unruh, 2010).

Although the principles didn't indicate contents to be taught, they pointed at the importance of revisiting the purpose of management and the values underlying managerial decisions, suggesting values of global social responsibility (Adams & Petrella, 2010). In particular, these two principles – purpose and values – hinted at the fact that while individuals may have a rational understanding of problems and a technical mastery of tools to address them, there was a whole other layer of factors influencing what could be global socially and environmentally responsible behavior. The knowledge and skills were definitely important, and many scholars focused on identifying the content and sustainability competencies that had to be developed (Wiek, Withycombe, & Redman, 2011), but the motivation and engagement to act in a responsible way were equally important and posed an educational challenge: how can this be developed?

Petersen-Boring (2010) indicates that sustainability education "is not as much about delivering content as it is about cultivating the skills, dispositions, and values that equip students to move towards sustainability" (p. xv). This perspective certainly brings a new approach to sustainability education, which, particularly in business schools, is these days mostly centered on successful case studies, on providing rationales for doing good in order to do well, on highlighting competitive advantages, on the eco-opportunities of corporate social responsibility (CSR), or on the catastrophic scenarios of inaction. For instance, *The Journal of Business Ethics* responded to this growing trend by introducing a new case section which provides a forum for publishing and assessing a range of teaching material (Falkenberg & Woiceshyn, 2008).

The right question as we design courses seems to be not how to teach *about* sustainability, but rather how to encourage students to move *towards* sustainability, how to nurture them to be leaders in a sustainability revolution (Jensen, 2013, p. 25). This is not something that results from a left-brain speculation: passion lies at the foundation and involves a paradigm change, a journey requiring the "transformation of virtues, of hearts and minds" (Cladis, 2013, p. 40). If we want to find solutions, we need to step out of our current interpretations and paradigms, and find answers that are not just technological and data-driven: "to sustain what is worth sustaining we must re-examine values, draw on cultural wisdom, and re-energize spiritual and philosophical traditions" (Petersen-Boring, p. xiv).

Gurleen Grewal (2013, p. 163) cites Aldo Leopold, who in stating his teaching objectives in 1947 held modern science and culture responsible for the "fallacy in present-day conservation," privileging only the economic in "the human relation to land" (1968, p. 337). Educators need to transform "the mindset of [the] students, so they can become more receptive and compassionate," and that "ought to be an important goal of teaching [for] sustainability" (Grewal, p. 163).

Some pioneering institutions, like the UK-based Schumacher College, have been developing responsible leaders for over two decades using holistic pedagogical approaches to address moral and spiritual qualities, with the tagline 'Transformative Learning for Sustainable Living' (Sterling, 2011). Ethics is increasingly integrated into the classroom dialogue (Arce & Gentile, 2015), but the mainstream of management education has not been that receptive to the missing epistemic (Sterling, 2011) and spiritual dimension in the curricula. Nevertheless, there is a growing focus on the relevance of self-transcendent values as antecedents of socially and environmentally responsible management attitudes (Sundermann, Brieger, Seidel & Strathoff, 2016), and that "the way to achieve sustainable, harmonious living in all spheres is through lived morality and spirituality at the personal level. The journey for world transformation starts indeed at the individual level" (Dhiman, Heaton, Marques, & Mitroff, 2016).

But this brings us back to the question: how to develop this deeper moral and spiritual engagement? Can and should it be developed in the context of management education?

The authors consider that the best way to answer these questions is to explore the connections between moral and spiritual engagement and sustainability-minded leaders. In presenting their studies, they consider what could be done in educational institutes to support the growth of a new generation of conscious leaders. In the next section, two studies will be briefly presented that explore the connection between sustainable actions for the greater good and spiritual values/practices. The first study explores spiritually aware business leaders to see how their spiritual values or beliefs influenced their behaviors, and the second study approaches the phenomenon from the opposite end, studying exemplary business leaders who championed sustainability initiatives to see what role their spiritual values played in their unusual business behavior.

STUDY 1 (Sridaran, 2014) Spiritually inspired leaders: their influence on the workplace research motivations

The first study presents how the inner spiritual dimensions of business leaders impacted their outer world of work based on a longitudinal research that explored this, among other issues in a cross-cultural investigation. As an educator at several Australian business schools, I was motivated to align my personal and professional life with meaningful questions that I felt needed to be addressed. Noticing high levels of work-related stress amongst business professionals in my social circle, I was equally dismayed at the general lack of genuine vision beyond the ambitions to drive bottom-line concerns. I wondered whether spiritual or religious values might reduce workplace stress and assist business practitioners to function more ethically and sustainably and cause less harm to people and the planet. I was inspired in the 1990s by Peter Senge, who was blazing the scene at that time with concepts that challenged the "business as usual" ethos, calling to examine mental models of decision makers in business – essentially promoting inner existential work. I was intrigued and made the leap from there to seek a wisdom-based spiritual model of business where individuals functioned from a higher moral code. I decided to study business leaders who had a conscious intent to be good and do good – leaders with a desire to leave a genuinely positive impact at work beyond the common lip service many leaders provide to ethics and sustainability in business. It led me to seek and study such individuals in the business world to see how they were wired and what legacies they left at work.

In the era of globalization, business leadership involves the ability to influence across national and cultural boundaries (Mobley and Dorfman, 2003) characterized by diversity and cultural systems significantly different from their own inner belief systems. Decision makers in business corporations large or small require a more inclusive mindset to function fairly and ethically in the world, and several scholars had suggested that spirituality is a critical component (Barley & Kunda, 1992; Cunha, Rego & D'Oliveira, 2006; Sengupta, 2010) Therefore, I was motivated to investigate if spiritually inspired business leaders fared better at navigating and negotiating the challenges. I was curious to find out if business leaders were to invest time and effort in developing their core values anchored on an inner spiritual inquiry, are they more likely to improve in their external conduct through an expanded awareness and consciousness?

Workplace culture has a huge impact upon worker morale and well-being, and it is becoming common in the post-modern era to expect business organizations to be conscious (Vasconcelos, 2011) and to be instruments of social responsibility (Gioia, 2003). Jackson (1999) argues that when dealing in foreign cultures, adopting spiritual principles and values based on world religions provides a deeper foundation for principles of international business ethics. He suggests that rather than using external compliance and control approaches, spiritual and religious values provide greater guidance through inner moral judgments. Could a new brand of organizational leadership with leaders espousing high levels of inner consciousness make a difference? These were reasons to explore if universal spiritual principles present a potentially potent dimension to guide executives navigating unpredictable and unfamiliar business terrains. Gauging by escalating corporate scandals and transgressions, business ethics education driven by compliance or code of conduct appears to be barely making a dent on the psyche of practitioners in the business world. The study explored if spiritually inspired leaders were more ethical and espoused a more inclusive compassionate care at work. I also ventured to study the impact of spiritually inspired leadership in nurturing the holistic well-being of associates at work.

Adopting a cross-cultural perspective, the study addressed the "Eastern versus Western" perspective on spirituality to test for differences and similarities and aimed to demystify the concept of spirituality. Seen as a universal principle, it follows on the premise that it ought to be relevant in all disciplines, across all cultural circumstances. In this respect, I gave careful consideration to the distinction between spirituality and religiosity and investigated the intricacies on how they applied in Western work environments, which are typically secular, versus Eastern work environments, which are traditionally robust in their celebration of religious and cultural values.

Methodology and data analysis

Questions explored in this research centred around three main themes:

1. The link between the tacit dimension of spirituality and its relevance to the workplace
2. The attributes of a spiritually inspired leader
3. The impact of spiritually inspired business leaders on the workplace environment, workplace relationships and outcomes

This was an empirical and qualitative research conducted using a heuristics methodology comprised of six distinct stages as depicted in Figure 2.1.

The scope of the research was limited to twelve organizations (six organizations in Malaysia representing the East and six more from Australia representing the West) in Phase one. In Phase two, three organizations participated in the in-depth case-study analysis (two organizations in the East and one in the West), with a total of fifty-seven participants from a variety of religious and spiritual backgrounds.

The research was unique in its methodological use of Heuristics inquiry, rarely used in business management research. A derivative of the phenomenological approach (Janesick, 2000; Patton, 2002) more commonly used in the humanistic psychology disciplines, the heuristics methodology showed its merits as it allowed the researcher to systematically investigate tacit human experience and be fully present as a participant observer throughout the research process using reflexive strategies. This included the researcher's own experience in engaging with the concept of spirituality, both intellectually, experientially, professionally and personally. Etherington (2004) makes a case for reflexive research, which in contrast to traditional impersonal approaches acknowledges the impact of the researcher's own history, beliefs and culture on the processes and outcomes of inquiry allowing for a level of close rigor that is required of good qualitative research. The value of this was achieved, through the incubation phase of the heuristics research design (see Figure 2.1) when I undertook an eight-month intense spiritual study in an ashram in India, to reconcile with my own spiritual uncertainties. My self-disclosure on my personal spiritual adventures often helped me gain an unspoken mutual respect with my respondents, as I soon found out, each one of them had amazing stories of their own spiritual explorations to share. For this reason, my ashram sojourn proved invaluable during fieldwork, as it helped to quickly establish a level of trust and agency with little or no time wasted in establishing rapport

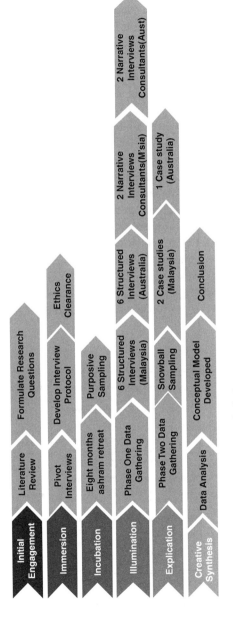

FIGURE 2.1 Heuristics methodology and research design

with my research subjects. Thus, despite the subject of spirituality being an inquiry that was subtle, sensitive and inherently difficult to be captured or measured, heuristics provided a good tool for entrance into this tacit dimension (Sela-Smith, 2002) with relative ease. The heuristics methodology demands that the research question must hold a significant value and passion for the researcher (Moustakas, 1990). Indeed, my personal spiritual journey very much shaped my professional interest in the workplace spirituality research field, leading to formulation of the research questions based on the following research problems and objectives, as presented in Figure 2.2.

The research sample that was sought were business leaders with a heightened sense of spiritual awareness and who were engaged in an internal spiritual process within themselves through a variety of religious and spiritual beliefs and practices. Many times, the research called for subjects to engage in inward introspection on the spot to explain the inner source of their actions. For most subjects, this integral part of who they are in their core personalities was not easy to reveal, or to articulate. Indeed, the spiritual dimension is an area of life which is often taken for granted and assumed to exist without any need for questioning or explication. The heuristics inquiry required them to do exactly that. This would not be possible if there had not been mutual trust, which was often seamlessly achieved with self-disclosure on one another's spiritual journeys, immensely aiding the inquiry.

By virtue, the heuristic process includes an empirical observable phenomenon, but perhaps more essentially it allows for the capture of various tacit contemplative and intuitive knowledge. In the process, whilst the study focused on their work

Research Problem	Research Questions	Research Objectives
■ Business environments of the present day are dynamic and constantly changing with emerging emphasis on meaning and purpose at work. Spiritually aware business leaders and managers from uniquely divergent Eastern and Western backgrounds are studied to see how their spiritual values or beliefs influence behaviour, activity and relations at the workplace.	1. How aware are key managers or leaders of their own spiritual beliefs and values? 2. What are some of the workplace value systems observed among organisational members? 3. What are some of the spiritual dimensions observed/ practiced in the workplace? 4. To what degree have spiritual dimensions influenced or enhanced workplace behaviour and activity?	■ To establish if there was awareness and use of tacit spiritual values that promotes greater meaning, purpose, and motivation and worker satisfaction at the workplace. ■ To propose an effective model for transformation of work environment based on a socio-spiritual paradigm.

FIGURE 2.2 Research problems, questions and objectives

engagements, inevitably it also exposed other areas of the key subject's lives, including their social and family roles.

This method resulted in a fish-bowl triangulation of data through informal conversations and formal sources of data collected at multiple levels to create a composite picture of the primary subject. This meant analyzing a single subject from multiple lenses; for example, apart from noting their own accounts about themselves, I triangulated the data on these primary subjects based on data gathered from as many other sources as possible. This included their current/former bosses and colleagues, peers at the same level, direct reports at subordinate levels, independent consultants, and close friends and family members, all of whom knew the primary subjects closely. They were each observed in their workplace as well as in their homes and other social environments. Data was gathered primarily through structured interviews, narrative interviews, participant observation, on-site visits, as well as an examination of printed material. The Nvivo software package was used to organize and analyze data for thematic structures in both phases of the research design.

Findings

Demystifying spirituality

One of the key aims of this research was to demarcate the differences and links between spirituality and religiosity, with the intention to lay to rest the tensions and discomfort felt across many scholarly discussions on this subject. I validated the significance of both concepts in varying cultural contexts of the East and West, and was able to highlight the universality and significance of spiritual precepts relevant to human life. Indeed, without a spiritual dimension, there is no life, as it is the elusive life-giving principle cloaked in human consciousness (Cowan, 1993). Its relevance in human endeavours, such as within the business world, is becoming difficult to ignore.

Much of the criticisms around the study of workplace spirituality and spiritual leadership are due to the lack of clear definitions on what constitutes spirituality (Benefiel, 2005). This research contends that the value of understanding spirituality is not in its definition but more in its relevance and manifestations within human systems, which had been amply demonstrated in the findings of this research.

It was interesting to note that the Western cohort pragmatically tended to de-link spirituality from religiosity to maintain a secular work environment. On the other hand, the Eastern subjects predominantly adopted a more symbiotic viewpoint, perceiving spirituality to co-exist within religious structures, or conversely saw religion existing to support spiritual frameworks. Regardless, spirituality appeared to be an existential question for all of the research subjects, and they expressed it differently from one subject to the next. Some had a keen awareness of their "inner-world", pursued consciously through regular practice of tacit reflection via religious or other forms of spiritual constructions. The important point is that spirituality was seen to be a universal concept relevant to all regardless of religious creed.

Triggers that led to spiritual seeking

Data indicated that participants had different triggers that led to a deeper inner inquiry. In some cases, these triggers tended to be traumatic or difficult circumstances that chipped away at their sense of self, forcing them to perceive things differently. The experiences of these participants seem to indicate that a spiritual search begins for individuals in one of three ways:

1   Through trauma (physical or emotional pain or suffering)
2   Influence of significant others
3   Natural progression of search for deeper meaning or contentment in life

Figure 2.3 depicts the many different ways in which an individual, conscious of the value of a deep spiritual mooring, regularly engages in spiritual practices such as meditation, devotional activities or reflective inner processes, which strengthen the spiritual conscience and core of the individual. Barnett, Krell, and Sendry (2000) provide a useful scale on which to categorize the variety of pathways through which an individual may choose to experience spirituality. It provides a useful categorization of the spiritual practices or habits of the participants in this research. Their spiritual values were often personal and private, cloaked in practices that are culturally embedded, whether religious or spiritual, with many pathways for practice and expression.

The being (intrinsic) – doing (extrinsic) dimensions

The in-depth case study of leaders in three organizational settings showed that regular spiritual practice brought higher levels of equanimity in their behaviors.

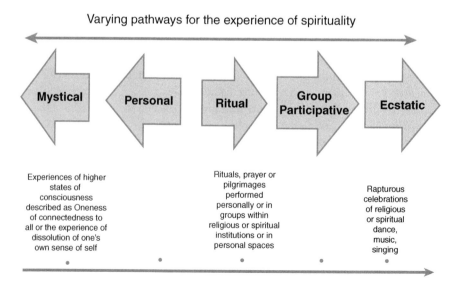

Varying pathways for the experience of spirituality

Mystical — Personal — Ritual — Group Participative — Ecstatic

Experiences of higher states of consciousness described as Oneness of connectedness to all or the experience of dissolution of one's own sense of self

Rituals, prayer or pilgrimages performed personally or in groups within religious or spiritual institutions or in personal spaces

Rapturous celebrations of religious or spiritual dance, music, singing

FIGURE 2.3   Categorization of spiritual paths

Source: Adapted from Barnett, Krell, and Sendry (2000).

Figure 2.4 depicts the relationship between the being and doing dimensions. I was fortunate enough to witness and capture first-hand events during fieldwork, including tense moments of crisis at work. On several occasions, it was also possible to witness how the leaders reacted calmly but with sharp precision to daily difficulties ranging from corrupt business environments to toxic work cultures. These spiritually inspired business subjects cited that their spiritual convictions carried them through moments when their personal moral codes were challenged. This interface between how their inner tacit dimension informs and directs their external world of work is depicted in Figure 2.4. It seeks to portray how their inner being, which was intrinsically inspired by their own spiritual practice, appears to be an anchoring factor that helps guide their decision making in the extrinsic environment, with resulting actions and presence that in turn was felt to be inspiring for others.

On such occasions, these leaders displayed strength of character by making unpopular decisions or taking decisions that called for personal sacrifice while maintaining an inner resilience and keeping an optimistic attitude for the future without breaking in the face of unfair adversity. Such integrity and grit during tough times in turn becomes a source of admiration and loyalty with their work colleagues. The research captured evidence of how people, whether they are co-workers, family members or casual associates, tend to look up to spiritual leaders as "wise elders" for guidance and hope. It testifies to the view of Bryttting and Trollestad (2000) that leading by values or value-based management is not a matter of creating ethical codes or common values. Instead, as they argue, it is the art of inspiring groups and individuals to reflect and become aware of some moral assumptions and that it is the glue that binds organizations together, creating a sense of community and belonging.

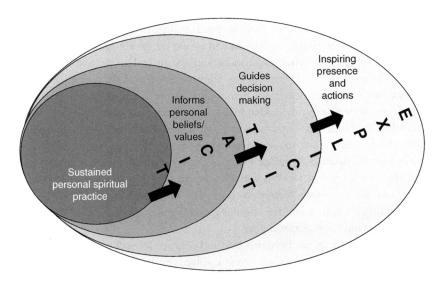

FIGURE 2.4   Tacit inner and explicit outer interface

Profile of spiritually inspired leaders

Figure 2.5 presents a collection of values and traits from all key respondents categorized to represent the social, psychological, physical and spiritual dimensions. It therefore is a composite model of the sum total of values and traits from research respondents to illustrate the full dimension of a spiritually inspired leader. Each research respondent showed some of these traits to varying degrees. In other words, the more values from the diagram displayed by an individual, to that degree he or she may be assumed to be spiritually inspired. The figure is an attempt to display the full spectrum of how such leaders' tacit inner realms have an observable outer extrinsic impact upon others in their relationships, with a special focus on their impact on co-workers. It captures and depicts the in-depth full profile of the human dimensions anchored on core spiritual values and encapsulates the full findings of this study, highlighting how the inner spiritual dimensions of a business leader have a strong influence upon their physical, psychological and social dimensions. These findings are useful to provide an understanding of why spiritually inspired leaders make for better leaders in the current and future era.

The sixteen business professionals both from the Eastern and Western sample of this research openly claimed to be spiritually inspired. Findings indicate that these leaders' workplace values were consistent with their personal values, which in turn they insisted are influenced by their deeply held spiritual beliefs. It was evident that decisions of the business leaders studied in this research arose from a strong spiritual intelligence. Zohar (2005) explains that spiritual intelligence is the ability to access higher meanings, values, abiding purposes and unconscious aspects of the self and to embed these meanings, values and purposes in living a richer and more creative life. It is important to note that these individuals were conscious of the fact that their spiritual dimension needed to be honed. Therefore, they made unique culture-specific attempts to maintain a spiritual practice that continuously evolved them onto higher or deeper spiritual moorings. This included regulating their physical, psychological and social dimensions to support their deepening spiritual core states. It displays how the spirituality of a person is interdependent on experiences within all their human dimensions (physical, psychological, social and spiritual). The socio-spiritual paradigm model presented in Figure 2.6 is a culmination of all findings from this study. Spiritual and/or religious values are driven through the organization either through symbolisms and subtle means, hidden in language, ideals, principles, moral and ethical standards and at other times through explicit organizational policies or procedures which clearly reflect a link to an underlying spiritual value of the respective leader.

The research findings show that the main impact spiritually inspired leaders have upon their colleagues at work is that they are trusted, and in turn, they create a climate of trust. Employees seem to be motivated to support their inspiring leader's causes, which lends to a culture of willingness to exert efforts beyond the call of duty in achieving organizational goals.

The leaders too expressed genuine care and concern for staff members and stood in their defense even when failures were involved, rarely blaming and even taking responsibility for failed intended outcomes. This high level of trust is built over a

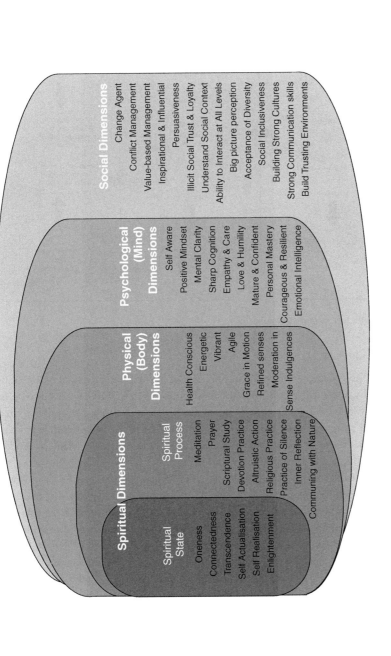

FIGURE 2.5 In-depth profile of spiritually inspired leaders

Spiritual Dimensions

Spiritual State
- Oneness
- Connectedness
- Transcendence
- Self Actualisation
- Self Realisation
- Enlightenment

Spiritual Process
- Meditation
- Prayer
- Scriptural Study
- Devotion Practice
- Altruistic Action
- Religious Practice
- Practice of Silence
- Inner Reflection
- Communing with Nature

Physical (Body) Dimensions
- Health Conscious
- Energetic
- Vibrant
- Agile
- Grace in Motion
- Refined senses
- Moderation in Sense Indulgences

Psychological (Mind) Dimensions
- Self Aware
- Positive Mindset
- Mental Clarity
- Sharp Cognition
- Empathy & Care
- Love & Humility
- Mature & Confident
- Personal Mastery
- Courageous & Resilient
- Emotional Intelligence

Social Dimensions
- Change Agent
- Conflict Management
- Value-based Management
- Inspirational & Influential
- Persuasiveness
- Illicit Social Trust & Loyalty
- Understand Social Context
- Ability to Interact at All Levels
- Big picture perception
- Acceptance of Diversity
- Social Inclusiveness
- Building Strong Cultures
- Strong Communication skills
- Build Trusting Environments

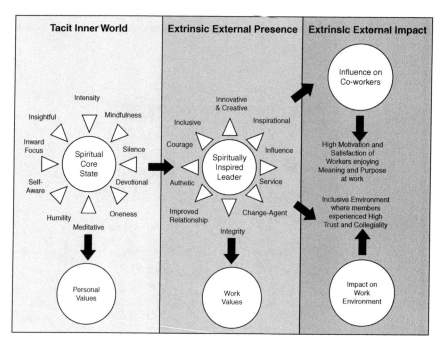

FIGURE 2.6   Socio-spiritual paradigm

period of time, and the spiritually inspired leader is often perceived to be decent and trustworthy, hence their decisions and contributions at work are perceived to be fair and wise. While the leader's spiritual inclinations were not readily perceptible to most colleagues, many reported that they "knew" the leader had a spiritual foundation, which underlies his or her actions and motivations in the workplace. Many co-workers looked to the leader for inspiration, and in both the Malaysian and Australian case studies, the leader was likened to a "wise elder" whose opinions and decisions were highly regarded. Earning the loyalty and commitment of co-workers led to a sense of enjoyment and feeling of satisfaction at work for the leader, and for the followers, there was a good sense of meaning and purpose for the tasks performed at work. Such leaders were also seen to be open to receiving good ideas from others, and hence there is voluntary involvement and sharing of knowledge and information with the leader. The subtle impact of spiritually inspired leadership is a certain organizational climate which is based on trust and mutual respect, resulting in inspired work, both for the leader and his or her co-workers in a genuine spirit of esprit de corps.

Connecting these findings to the focus on sustainability-related initiatives, it was observed that these leaders' influence also extended beyond the work organization, often engaging in social activism or charitable causes and championing community initiatives, bringing positive change through their influence and integrity within their professional as well as their personal lives. However, a clear limitation of this research project was that it included only participants who self-perceived to be spiritually aware without including any business leaders who did not consider themselves spiritually aware. Thus, any relevant comparisons between those who are spiritually inspired and those who were not spiritually inspired were not drawn. Also, as an exploratory qualitative study, the research does not have a sufficient sample size to draw any generalized conclusion, although it is an early exploration towards an in-depth understanding of the inner tacit world of spiritually inspired leadership. This study was also limited to two countries, with data collected from Australia and Malaysia to draw some narrow cross-cultural comparisons.

STUDY 2 (Rimanoczy, 2010) Motivations of business leaders championing sustainability initiatives

Research motivation

The foregoing section of this chapter discussed research into the disposition of spiritually inspired leaders to act for the greater good in the context of their organization. This section explores a study that looks at the connection of spirituality and sustainability from the opposite direction.

In 2005 some academics began to reflect on their (unintended) contribution to developing profit-focused leaders that had no comprehension of the environmental or social long-term impact of their actions. If what we were teaching was at fault, what should we be teaching instead? I was starting my doctoral studies and decided to explore the knowledge and motivations of business leaders who acted in a socially and environmentally positive way, championing initiatives that transformed their organization. I thought that if we could understand what they knew, what inspired or prompted them to act in an unusual way, we might be able to find aspects to intentionally develop in our classrooms.

Method and data analysis

I designed a qualitative, descriptive exploratory study (Denzin and Lincoln, 1998, p. 89), using a multiple case method (Creswell, 1998, p. 55). A group of exemplary individuals was selected, who had personally championed in their organizations the type of changes that qualified for 'sustainability' (reduced the negative impact or made a positive impact in community and/or the environment), without being asked to do so (Rimanoczy, 2010). The study focused on sixteen business leaders in the United States, age 37–75, from a variety of industries: food, technology, apparel, restaurant, retail, household products and pharmaceutical. The research explored the following questions:

1   What do business leaders need in order to begin or champion initiatives that contribute to the common good of communities or the environment?
2   How and what do business leaders learn about implementing these initiatives?
3   How could educators or coaches support the process?

A questionnaire was prepared to explore the questions from different angles. From the three research questions, the first one focused on what influenced or created the 'readiness to act'. This was a very important question given the interest in finding ways to intentionally develop leaders acting in this way, as well as the third one that invited them to give spontaneous advice for educators. The second question related to supporting leaders in the implementation of sustainability initiatives. The data from the interviews was then organized into "families" or categories. Figure 2.7 presents the categories of findings related to the first question.

I specifically explored the readiness connected with intentionality, meaning when the leaders acted in a very conscious and intentional way. Statements collected in the interviews indicated that the intentionality was rooted in a sense of "personal mission" (the need to contribute, with spirituality playing a definite role) and in social sensitivity. The social sensitivity was found to be developed early in life through upbringing experiences and role models, or resulting from an awakening as adults,

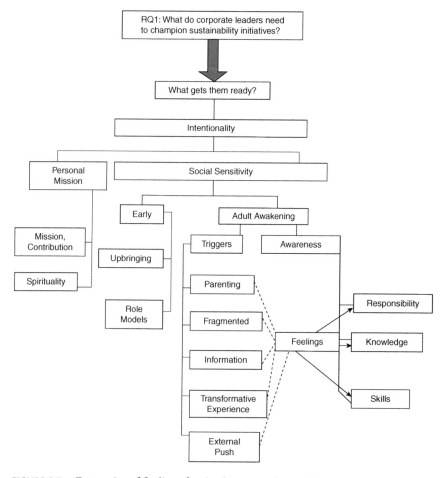

FIGURE 2.7 Categories of findings for the first research question

through triggers such as the experience of parenting, access to information about the state of the planet, transformative experiences, a sense of living a fragmented life or through an external push, like a mentor or someone prompting them to act.

Several aspects creating the readiness corresponded to "non-replicable" triggers, meaning triggers that are uniquely different to each respondent and cannot be intentionally replicated by anyone else, such as childhood experiences, meaningful encounters, traumatic events such as the loss of a loved one, accidents and health challenges, and the experience of becoming a parent. Particular attention, however, was given by the researcher to the aspects that could provide guidance for adult educators, for example:

- The role of inspiring mentors
- Access to information about the state of the planet and reflecting how they contributed to the problems
- Connecting fragmented information about world challenges and acquiring a 'big picture'
- People pushing or challenging them to reflect and act
- Introspective practices leading to self-exploration
- Revision of their espoused values and values in action
- Pondering existential questions such as Who am I? Why am I here? What is my purpose?

These questions and experiences created a number of feelings, such as anxiety, sadness, guilt, despair, anger, and an urge to act, which in turn reinforced their sense of responsibility, the desire to share their newly acquired knowledge with others, and the need to use their gifts and skills to find solutions (Rimanoczy, 2014).

Several individuals indicated the important role that introspective practices such as meditation, mindfulness exercise, yoga and contact with nature played in developing their motivation and engagement to act in a socially or environmentally responsible way.

Findings

The findings of this study highlighted three interconnected factors contributing to the leaders' engagement:

1   *What they learned*: Information about the state of the planet played a critical role (the "knowing").
2   *How they related to that information*: Reflective and introspective practices led the subjects to connect data and facts with their personal contribution to the problems, to assess their personal values, and to explore deeper questions of identity, responsibility, purpose, mission, legacy (the "being").
3   *How they felt as a result*: The feelings associated with how they related created a sense of urgency in taking action.

The findings of the study provided data about the aspects that contributed to creating a paradigm shift, such as eco-literacy, or social and economic impacts of industrial practices, and showed the development of new thinking processes (systems thinking, innovative and creative thinking). Useful insights were also obtained about the competencies and skills that the leaders exhibited to carry out their sustainability initiatives. In this chapter I will exclusively focus on the findings related to the role that spirituality played in their motivations and engagement in a sustainability worldview and actions.

The spiritual aspects are seen in this study as related to the "being" dimension – a construct that Adams (2008, p. 63) uses to name aspects on a continuum related to self-realization, valuing intangibles, the greater good, searching for qualitative growth and having enough. On the other end of the continuum, Adams refers to materialism, consumption, greed, cost-effectiveness, quantitative growth and financial performance. In my study, I used Adams' "being" dimension, adapting it to include self-exploration and introspective practices; scrutiny of values, and expressions related to the search for purpose, desire to make a difference, sense of interconnectedness, compassion and empathy. These aspects can be developed and are seen as key for responsible leaders who can make decisions with the greater good in mind, going beyond the more traditional profit and self-interest motivation (Lopez, Martinez, & Specht, 2013).

The leaders interviewed in the study were asked if spirituality played a role in engaging in their initiatives, a question that brought up a variety of reactions, from acknowledgement to rejection. "I don't believe that there is a higher being dictating what I have to do", one person responded, "I just act based on my values, and I know what is right". Religion-neutral terms were better accepted, like making a difference, having a sense of purpose, strong values or having a life dream. Some referred to a sense of mission, the need to find meaning in their life, a deeply felt social mission, awareness of their mortality and a desire to make a difference. Taking spirituality in the broader sense described in the previous sentence, thirteen out of sixteen individuals responded affirming that spirituality had some kind of influence on their initiatives, a response that was larger than anticipated. The influence of religion or spirituality balancing profit motivations has been seen in studies of leaders with declared strong religious beliefs (Kutcher, Bragger, Rodriguez-Srednicki, & Masco, 2010; Reave, 2005; Vives, 2006), social entrepreneurs (Dodd, & Gotsis, 2007) and with American Indian entrepreneurs (Hunt-Oxendine & Dent, 2010), but was not expected for this particular group of leaders.

Two individuals had the sense that there was something they "had to do" but they did not know what it was, and they thought of their sustainability initiatives as a way of addressing that sentiment, albeit they were unsure if there was more to it. Interestingly, for all the others the personal mission (a code originated in the literature review and the conceptual framework) was not a factor that they experienced before in their life and was the motivation to act, but rather it was in retrospect that they came to see their initiatives as a life dream or a mission. During the course of the interview, they provided responses indicating that the "being" aspects were not what prepared them to act in a business-unusual way, but the aspects emerged and developed as they reflected on the state of the planet and their personal contribution or responsibility. The fact that purpose can become a motivation reinforced in action matches the observations of Kroth and Boverie (2000), who found that individuals maintained a stronger motivation when they thought of how their actions connected to their life purpose.

Given the characteristics of the leaders of this study, which were selected for their role in championing sustainability initiatives within a mostly traditional business context, it is not surprising that they were not from the start socially or environmentally oriented business people motivated by purpose, but rather formed in the traditional tenets of accountability to the shareholders. One interviewee expressed the wish that someone would have asked him about his purpose when he was in his thirties because "I would have started twenty years earlier".

The data from these interviews presented interesting data about the role information plays (what we learn about what is happening), but particularly when the information is connected to the personal values of the individual.

"What does this mean for me?" "How am I contributing to the problems?" "How does this match my values?" The introspective questions became the real trigger for a transformation in the studied leaders' worldviews. The questions were profound, existential and related to identity, beliefs, values, sense of purpose, thoughts of a personal mission, desire to live a meaningful live and making a difference. Pondering these questions was not a one-time event, but a process that extended over long periods of time. The cognitive dissonance between the leaders' espoused values and their values in action was accompanied by feelings of guilt, sadness, desperation, anger and uncertainty, which ultimately fueled their action.

The findings of this study provided interesting input about the role of the "being dimension" as transformational learning that motivates leaders toward socially and environmentally sensitive behavior. The findings also suggested the opportunity to intentionally develop those "being" aspects, something that is rarely addressed in management education programs. Spirituality, in this broader sense of the "being dimension" that includes self-scrutiny, has an emancipatory role (Lerner, 2000, p. 165; Pope Francis, 2015), which manifests in intentionally working to transform the world for the better.

The study has limitations due to working with an elite sample. The candidates were selected from within an available pool, and it was not possible to create a gender or ethnically balanced sample. The materials were based on self-report of candidates that met the criteria and volunteered to participate in the research, and the data was not crossed with peers or other people knowing them.

Convergences

The two studies presented here addressed the relationship of spirituality and leadership actions for the greater good, approaching it from two opposing ends. Do spiritually oriented leaders tend to act for the greater good? On the other

FIGURE 2.8 Spiritual practice and leadership behaviors, explored from two angles

hand, do leaders acting for the greater good have a spiritual motivation? (see Figure 2.8).

The authors conducted their research not knowing about each other's work until they met at a conference of the Academy of Management, where both were presenting their studies. It is interesting thus to observe the convergence of findings, which we will address in this section with a particularly pragmatic focus: what can management educators do with this information? For this purpose, let's start with the trigger factors of spirituality.

Triggers of spirituality

In Study 1, Sridaran (2014) observes that the experiences of these participants seem to indicate that a spiritual search typically begins for individuals in one of three ways:

1 Through trauma (physical or emotional pain or suffering)
2 Influence of significant others
3 Natural progression of search for deeper meaning or contentment in life

The first point on trauma was also noted by Neal (2008), who suggested that traumatic or difficult events trigger deeper questions, which she calls "the key spiritual questions": Who am I and what are my deepest values? What do I really care about? What is my purpose in life? Why am I here and what am I meant to be doing? If I am true to myself, what should I be doing next? These questions become a fuel to action, as observed in individuals working for the greater good (Daloz, Keen, Keen, & Parks, 1996).

In Rimanoczy's 2010 study, the map of findings (see Figure 2.7) shows how intentional acts for the greater good originate in a sense of personal mission, combined with an awakened social sensitivity. The factors that developed social sensitivity in adult life are of particular interest for management educators, because we cannot replicate childhood conditions. Several individuals in the study mentioned traumatic experiences, and while we wouldn't replicate those either, the feelings that the individuals expressed when confronted with information about the state of the planet were equally traumatic. This finding connects with Mezirow's theory of transformative learning (1991), who described the power of "disorienting dilemmas" to uncover our assumptions, beliefs and elicit a profound change in our perspectives. This was also later observed in subsequent classes with higher education students.

> *I am excited yet scared, hopeful yet doubtful, opportunistic yet limited, together and at the same time alone, powerful with the ability to create and construct, yet at the same time powerless, clear-headed yet confused.*
>
> *(Craig, USA)*

> *The personal conflict I felt between ascribing to the current, flawed value system, participating in the economy as yet another disenchanted twenty-something working hard to consume meaningless goods . . . versus rejecting mainstream notions for a more holistic and feminine view, conserving and giving back to the earth rather than exploiting it . . . is something I struggled coming to terms with during this course. I felt like I was constantly reminded of the hypocrisies of my "noble" environmental work.*
>
> *(Anne M., USA)*

The influence of respected others in Sridaran's study was also found in Rimanoczy's study, where several individuals indicated the role informal mentors and teachers had played for them, as well as individuals they encountered who had made very different life choices, therefore offering a mirror to self-scrutinize personal choices and lifestyle.

The third trigger, "natural progression of search for deeper meaning" indicated by Sridaran might be accelerated via challenging questions and prompts. One leader in Rimanoczy's study reflected that he wished someone had asked him the "deeper questions" about meaning and purpose when he was in college, because he might have started earlier to make a difference (2010). This convergence of findings about triggers raises some interesting questions for educators:

- What can we do to engage the feelings of the students, not just their rational minds?
- How can we maximize the role we can play in challenging, inspiring and in allowing power to emerge in our students?
- What type of interventions can we offer to prompt the progression of a search for deeper meaning?

Sridaran's study observes that individuals "conscious of the value of a deep spiritual mooring regularly engage in reflective practices such as meditation, devotional activities or reflective inner processes which strengthen the spiritual conscience and core." In one of the courses she taught at Monash University, entitled Organisational Wellness, "Spiritual Health" is one out of twelve topics presented to final-year undergraduate students within the Management department. The subject covered various topics, presenting ways to prevent toxicity and promote wellness in work organizations. On Spiritual Health, students were taught the difference between spirituality and religiosity and the close interrelationship between the two concepts, clearing misconceptions and removing the taboo of the topic. In their final assessment, students had to make a choice of four topics to journal about from twelve different topics covered during the entire semester. Consistently in all semesters, a high percentage of students (80–90%) chose the topic on Spiritual Health to journal about in their final assessment, confirming that there is a thirst for exploring this dimension amongst young adults seeking to explore spiritual wellness in their professional and personal lives. In another post-graduate program on Management Competencies, students were challenged to explore their "self-awareness" and explore their deep values, which often brought robust exploration of their tacit dimensions, frequently bringing into question existential questions of "Who am I?" in the context of why they pursue the goals they do.

This was also a finding in the second study, where several leaders expressed having regular introspective or meditative practices. While this is something done in private, it has to be noted that an increasing number of corporations are offering meditation or reflective practices to their employees (Dane & Brummel, 2014). In fact, both the authors of this chapter regularly include a meditative practice in their classroom, mostly at the beginning, using silence, guided visualization, musical meditation or other tools. Convinced by findings from her research, Sridaran now introduces a two-minute silent meditation in all subjects she teaches in Australia, and student feedback about this initiative in her classrooms has been largely encouraging and positive. The meditation sessions are conducted at any point during the class, particularly when there is a wane in student energy or distractions with their technological gadgetry. The two-minute meditative initiative helps students to centre themselves in the present moment, and these sessions appear to help students re-focus internally into what's happening within their body and mind to help break the drift of their attention away from the present moment and away from the class lesson. These experimental initiatives in the classroom have led to many students showing a keenness to learn about meditation and spirituality and engaging in further conversations about these topics, some finding it the "most valuable learning from the whole semester":

I have never in my life meditated before taking this course, and today, especially in tense situations or before I walk into what I know will be a stressful day, I look inside myself and do a form of "self coaching." I let my inner voice calm myself down, and it truly brings calmness to my life. I apply this to situations big and small, where I am presented with an opportunity to live sustainably or not as well as to work this way or not.
(Keith, USA)

I have been using the meditation app (Headspace) that you recommended to us in class, and it has made a world of difference in my life. I now notice I'm much calmer, and most of all I feel greater focus and clarity and much less agitated.
(Maggie, international student from Philippines in Melbourne, Australia)

Can we please make sure we practice meditation this week? I truly missed it last week when we ran out of time.

(David, international student from Mexico in Melbourne, Australia)

Figure 2.5 depicts in a clear graphic how a sustained personal spiritual practice informs the personal values and beliefs, mostly in a tacit form. This becomes the foundation of a mindset that will tacitly guide and influence the decision making. At that point, the decisions become visible actions, which have the explicit power of inspiring others into action, too.

Two students put it into these words:

I enjoyed the stop-and-reflect and meditation exercise as it taught me to slow down from my busy lifestyle and take time to think and remember the things in life important to me. And, I must admit that working on my team's Passion Project was clearly the biggest and will be the most memorable highlight to me in the long run. It was just an amazing experience to put so much time and effort into something that truly mattered to me.

(Mel, USA)

I feel different from the beginning of the class. I have never been concerned or aware of sustainability on the planet. This class has opened my eyes and motivated me to take on actions. I see myself paying more attention to environment. Sustainability is a trendy topic that I have been discussing with my boyfriend. At least, I influence him to make a change too. I'm so proud to say that my Facebook [page] Sustainability and Environment has many members more than I expected. The more people have awareness, I think they will think about it, and hopefully they will be take action little by little. This has a lot of value in my life.

(Eve J., Thailand)

Resilience and hope

Sridaran observed that the spiritually oriented leaders in her study were often faced with situations which "called for personal sacrifice while maintaining an inner resilience and keeping an optimistic attitude for the future without breaking in the face of unfair adversity." When individuals are prompted to "reflect and become aware of some moral assumptions [. . .] that it is the glue that binds organizations together, creating a sense of community and belonging". Rimanoczy found this same aspect in the observations of several students of the sustainability mindset course taught at Fordham's MBA program in the US:

I am now different than when I started this journey because I now understand that I personally CAN make a difference in this world. When discussing the risks of climate change, so often the question comes up if individuals can truly make a difference. And, after this journey I can now answer that question confidently with an emphatic YES! Look at the power that one person joining us made . . . . she was able to gain support of others on her project of no impact week. I have learned from this experience, that if only one person shares their message it has a chain reaction effect by one person telling one person and telling another person, and now we have a group of people to get things done.

(Nelson, USA)

Students inspired each other with their ideas on specific projects to make a difference they developed a shared interest, and were profoundly motivated to invest time and energy. They developed a sense of resiliency in the face of the planetary challenges, with a positive and hopeful attitude.

Figure 2.5 presented the different dimensions Sridaran developed based on Study 1, which is adapted in Figure 2.9 to highlight the overlaps in multidimensional values originating in Rimanoczy's study. These became learning outcomes in the sustainability mindset course.

Finally, the model developed by Sridaran displayed in Figure 2.6 shows the connection between the tacit inner world of a spiritually inspired individual, their extrinsic external presence and the extrinsic impact on their work environments. Figure 2.10 highlights the intersection of the values on the Socio-Spiritual Paradigm with the values incorporated in the sustainability mindset course. These highlighted overlaps indicate that although the two studies were geographically dispersed and unrelated to one another, the significant similarities in findings do suggest that spiritual seeking remains a deeply personal quest of responsible leaders regardless of their cultural backgrounds from different corners of the globe. These are spirited individuals who are energized by a deeper sense of meaning and purpose beyond paychecks and performance. It was unforeseen that both studies would come to complement one another. By chance, while one (Study 1) sought to see the expression of the inner spiritual world on the external world of work, the other (Study 2) discovered that leaders who were good corporate citizens had private spiritual attributes. Some of the findings in Study 1 were uniquely different from those of Study 2, due in part to the central focus of the research on spirituality and religiosity. For example, Study 1 found the study of scriptures and devotional practice as a factor, while it was not a relevant factor in Study 2, where in turn the CSR initiatives were more important. Therefore, both studies together offer a convincing testimony that this inner psychological spiritual construct has a significant influence upon the behavior of responsible leaders. Hence, it stands to reason that the spiritually anchored being is correlated to positive outcomes for the organizational culture (Study 1) as well as to communities beyond (Study 2). Other authors have argued that the spiritual construct is linked to positive organizational outcomes (Marschke, Preziosi & Harrington, 2011), citing that both psychological and social theories have established a link between higher spiritual motives and positive economic outcomes. Thus, both Sridaran's and Rimanoczy's studies jointly argue for ways and means to more progressively introduce this significant but elusive dimension into business curricula.

Although Study 2 did not focus on the impact of leaders' behavior on the organizational culture and working environment, and the Socio-Spiritual Paradigm does not include the impact on the environment or the larger community, Sridaran notes that "the leaders' influence also extended beyond the work organization,

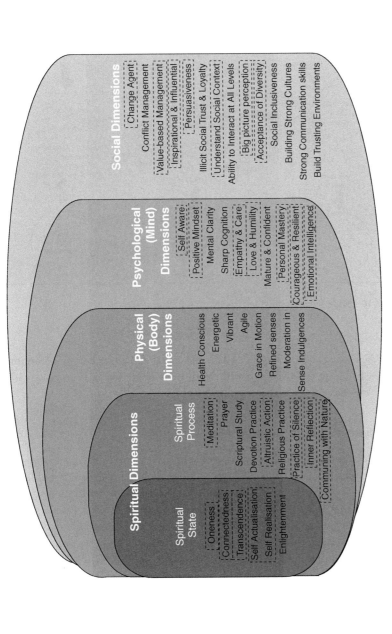

Spiritual Dimensions

Spiritual State

Oneness
Connectedness
Transcendence
Self Actualisation
Self Realisation
Enlightenment

Spiritual Process

Meditation
Prayer
Scriptural Study
Devotion Practice
Altruistic Action
Religious Practice
Practice of Silence
Inner Reflection
Communing with Nature

Physical (Body) Dimensions

Health Conscious
Energetic
Vibrant
Agile
Grace in Motion
Refined senses
Moderation in Sense Indulgences

Psychological (Mind) Dimensions

Self Aware
Positive Mindset
Mental Clarity
Sharp Cognition
Empathy & Care
Love & Humility
Mature & Confident
Personal Mastery
Courageous & Resilient
Emotional Intelligence

Social Dimensions

Change Agent
Conflict Management
Value-based Management
Inspirational & Influential
Persuasiveness
Illicit Social Trust & Loyalty
Understand Social Context
Ability to Interact at All Levels
Big picture perception
Acceptance of Diversity
Social Inclusiveness
Building Strong Cultures
Strong Communication skills
Build Trusting Environments

FIGURE 2.9 Overlaps between Study 1 and Study 2

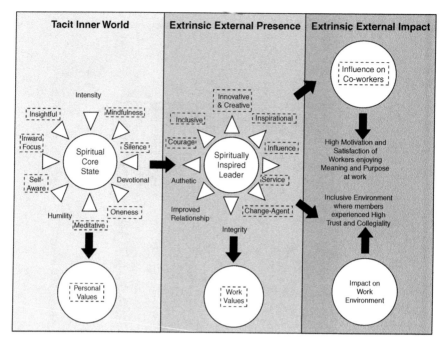

FIGURE 2.10 Intersections between Study 1 and Study 2

often engaging in social activism or charitable causes and championing community initiatives, bringing positive change through their influence and integrity within their professional as well as their personal lives."

Developing the being dimension

The previous section presented how two scholars explored in far-away geographies (Australia, Asia and USA) the connections between spirituality and leaders acting with the greater good in mind. The motivations were similar: there is a lack of alignment between personal and professional lives, which causes stress. Leaders are acting with a myopic short-term vision, which is causing harm to people and planet. This common concern led us, however, to ask related questions: are leaders with spiritual practices acting more ethically or sustainability? Why do some leaders act in sustainable ways? Could a spiritual or religious practice close the gap in values, reduce stress and have leaders act more ethically and sustainably?

As we were analyzing the findings of the respective studies, we both were motivated with a new purpose: is there something in these findings that we could include in our courses? Are there some aspects that could be fostered, prompted or developed in the next generation? Given the fact that we were both engaged in higher education institutions, including the "being" dimension was not usual content. To this date, universities and colleges around the world are mostly focused on developing cognitive skills and competencies, staying secular and carefully avoiding the "tricky" areas of personal values, beliefs, purpose and spirituality, especially since it can be confused with religiosity (Khurana, 2007).

At the same time, we had a growing sense that we were missing an important dimension, validated by other scholars gathering in networks such as the Management, Spirituality and Religion (MSR) division of the Academy of Management, or the Humanistic Network. Several scholars indicated that in order to prepare students with the skills and competencies required by the current (and future) planetary challenges, it was not sufficient to develop their intellectual understanding of sustainability. It is necessary to develop a new worldview or mindset (Doppelt, 2012; Fairfield, 2017). By focusing on intellectual knowledge and primarily engaging with rational, linear cognitive faculties, students are ill prepared for the increasing complexity of the world.

This oversight inevitably means that a whole other dimension of our human self has no place in the educational context. The cost? As is becoming obvious, the rapid maladies of modern times from stress to addictions, including socially acceptable techno-games and connectivity, are threatening to unravel human progress into paradoxical decline in overall quality of human life (see Sharma, Chapter 5 and Naim, Chapter xx in this book). The tacit, intuitive, heuristics dimension has proven to be equally, if not more, valuable in the present age of globalization to promote creative innovative solutions (Huang, Davison & Gu, 2011). Reflecting on the quality of life and leadership decisions of the leaders we studied, we each on our own continent gained conviction that the unattended "being" dimension was perhaps the critical missing link causing such ecological and social strife.

As a result, we both began to translate some aspects into developmental goals, and sought exercises, readings, videos or activities aiming at those goals. We selected activities that, while unconventional, would not be extremely disruptive or create distress in students. In this section we are sharing some of these developmental goals and examples of pedagogical approaches.[1]

Setting the stage

An important consideration when incorporating unconventional exercises or activities into the classroom is to clearly set the stage, so that students know what to expect. An explanation of what we will do, why it is important, how we will do it and what they may get out of it is a powerful introduction, which not only addresses the different learning preferences in the room but also provides structure and lowers anxiety levels. Even a clarification that this "may be new for you" acts as a welcome warning. Indications and examples of how corporate executive education is increasingly incorporating these types of developmental goals helps to ease the uncertainty and create a more accepting atmosphere (Rimanoczy, 2016).

Developmental goal: oneness with nature

Description: To develop in the students the sense that they are a part of a larger eco-system, providing a systems perspective in analyzing problems and develop solutions from within the framework of oneness with nature.

Activities to experience nature

There are many possibilities to immerse students in nature. Whatever the activity chosen, it is important to accompany with reflection. Offer prompt questions, such as what did I learn about myself in nature? What did I learn about nature that relates to my life? This can be in form of a written posting, a creative production of a video, a dialogue in class, a debrief in pairs followed by a larger group dialogue.

- Walk in nature, alone, with no gadgets. Concentrate just on observing and noticing. When back in your room, write down your thoughts.
- Meet for class outside – in a garden, park, Japanese garden.
- Visit a zoo.
- Distribute seeds and invite students to plant and grow them.
- Identify and explore nature's services that we take for granted.

Exploration of nature through questions

- How is nature present in this classroom?
- How are we a part of nature?
- What is our relationship with nature: control, domination, stewardship, users, protectors, agents of restoration?
- Discuss how nature is integrated into their decisions, in their workplace or in their profession, in the different subjects they are taking at school.

Developmental goal: increased self-awareness

Description: To develop introspective habits, to understand self, practicing revision of the personal motives, values, as well as anchors of their own identity.

Activities

These exercises can be done using silent reflection, journaling, questions posted on Blackboard, sharing in duos, debrief, and face-to-face dialogues.

- Invite students to use markers and a flipchart to draw "Who am I" using only images, no words.
- Complete a personality assessment (i.e., DISC, MBTI – Learning styles inventory, etc.).

- Values of our culture: Explore growth, wealth, independence, achievement, speed, comfort, control, knowledge, and competition as anchors of the un-sustainability.
- Exercise 'In your shoes': Identify their personally most unacceptable person, and enact a skit 'walking in his/her shoes.' Work in duos, debrief.
- Explore My Contribution: Identify an unacceptable circumstance (planet, society, news) and explore what is our personal, individual contribution to the problem. Alternative: Work in duos, identifying an unacceptable circumstance at work or home, and identify the personal (unintentional) contribution to the problem.
- Debrief and explore how this connects with the challenges we face individually and in our society, and what we individually can do.

Developmental goal: mindfulness

Description: Learn to slow down, incorporate practices to quiet the mind, achieve moments of inner peace, connect with the higher self, experience higher alertness and consciousness.

Activities

Use individual reflection, sharing impressions in duos or trios, dialogues in the larger group. Debrief and make connections with how they felt and how this is different from their everyday experience. What are the consequences of speeding up and slowing down? What would they like to try out/change within themselves? Use prompt questions to post reflections and journaling. As the facilitator, control your own pace and rhythm, explain to the students that it will be slower sometimes than they are used to, and explain the purpose. Introduce segments with different pace. You are the example of what you are trying to convey, and you will demonstrate in your own pace what slowing down means.

- Start the classes with a 3- to 4-minute meditation.
- Walk or sit in nature.
- Use music in the room.
- Invite them to notice their body posture, the internal bodily sensations inside, their breathing.
- Invite them to go to a coffee shop with no phone or device, stay 45 minutes just being there, as an assignment. Then they write down about the experience. Debrief.

Developmental goal: reflective practice

Description: To develop habits of reflection to pause and ponder situations without jumping to quick answers.

Activities

Explain the power of silent reflection, and discuss how pausing is different from the way we behave in our everyday life. Facilitate dialogue and debriefs, exploring what their experience is when pausing to reflect, when sitting in silence in the room, when hand-writing thoughts, and how could this make our life different, easier, more gratifying. Explore personal challenges, limiting thoughts, constraints and objections.

* Use a few silent minutes for individual reflection before starting a dialogue or sharing thoughts in a group.
* Debrief how it felt to sit in silence, writing down thoughts before talking.
* Encourage writing and handwriting thoughts.

Developmental goal: purpose

Description: To include the dimension of the personal larger purpose into their decisions, life plans and choices. To weigh options with the criteria in mind of what brings meaning to their life, what difference they want to make.

Activities

The activities can include inspirational readings, videos, poetry, interviews with the homeless or the elderly, or individuals who are doing greater-good work in the area. Use questions to post reflections, journaling, work with learning partners, and dialogues.

* Write an acceptance speech for an award for an amazing achievement you did, that you will receive in seven years. Describe what you did, what obstacles you had and who helped you.
* Drawing: Me and what is missing to be fully me. Share, debrief, and extract meaning.
* Questions to ponder: What are my values and how are they manifested in what I do? If I could do anything, what would I do? On my deathbed, what is my advice to my younger self?

Conclusions

What started as a serendipitous encounter of two scholars exploring a similar connection – between spiritual practices and leadership behaviors – became an interesting overlap and discovery of convergence in the findings. As a result of the authors' research, both put special attention on designing courses or learning interventions that could address the missing "being" dimension with their students. In one case, it took the shape of an elective course to develop the sustainability mindset, which made it easier to engage the students in a variety of activities and experiences.

In the other case, it was the creative imagination of the teacher that allowed for the inclusion of atypical exercises in the context of more traditional courses. She invited students to explore the difference between spirituality and religiosity using simple metaphors in the classroom to lift the fog on these concepts, which are often cause for confusion, and introduced silent meditations in all subjects in both undergraduate and post-graduate courses. These activities had positive responses from students.

It should be noted that a number of colleagues from the PRME[2] Working Group on the Sustainability Mindset have over the past few years included multiple activities and processes to develop the "being" dimension.

Whether as periodical activities, as a regular habit (like starting the class with a minute of silence or a guided meditation), or as singular exercises (visit to a museum, walk in nature), what has been observed is the transformational learning impact of this type of activities is promising. It is not because of the activity per se, but because space is created for addressing aspects that are essential to our human nature that are artificially kept out of our educational institutions. While an increasing number of corporations realize the importance of developing wholeness and making space for meditative practices in the workplace, educators are missing an opportunity to contribute to a more integral development of their students by not including those deeper questions in their classroom dialogues. It may take some training to play a facilitator role, stepping periodically out of the well-known expert role, but the benefits may be profound as students and instructors develop a greater self-awareness, a clearer consciousness of their values and purpose, and are able to intentionally act in shaping a better world.

> *I'm also realizing that sustainability is about learning about yourself, and who you are as a person as a means of taking the next step and living the most sustainable lifestyle for yourself. One thing I'm learning through this class is that I think sustainability is partly a personal experience where we need to first discover ourselves and what is important to us, our values, how we think as a person, then we can effectively move forward and work on what is important to us.*
>
> *(Charles, a student)*

> *Having trained to facilitate students learning of Developing a Sustainability Mindset has been one of the most rewarding learning experiences for me. Experiencing students' realization that we all must do something to contribute to the common good and becoming aware of how we are driven to consume, has been a very powerful experience.*
> *(Dr. Aixa A. Ritz, Associate Professor, International School of Hospitality and Tourism Management, Fairleigh Dickinson University)*

Notes

1 Adapted from Rimanoczy, I. (2016). A holistic learning approach for responsible management education. In R. Sunley & J. Leigh (Eds.), *Educating for responsible management: Putting theory into practice*. Sheffield, UK: Greenleaf Publishing.
2 www.unprme.org/working/groups/

References

Adams, C., & Petrella, L. (2010). Collaboration, connections and change: The UN global compact, the global reporting initiative, principles for responsible management education and the globally responsible leadership initiative. *Sustainability Accounting, Management and Policy Journal, 1*(2), 292–296.

Adams, J. D. (2008). Six dimensions of mental models. In J. Wirtenberg, W. G. Russell, & D. Lipsky (Eds.), *The sustainable enterprise fieldbook: When it all comes together* (pp. 60–70). Sheffield, UK: Greenfield Publishing.

Arce, D. G., & Gentile, M. C. (2015). Giving voice to values as a leverage point in business ethics education. *Journal of Business Ethics, 131*(3), 535–542.

Barley, S. R., & Kunda, G. (1992). Design and devotion: Surges of rational and normative ideologies of control in managerial discourse. *Administrative Science Quarterly, 37*, 363–399.

Barnett, C. K., Krell, T. C., & Sendry, J. (2000). Learning to learn about spirituality: A categorical approach to introducing the topic into management courses. *Journal of Management Education, 24*(5), 562–579.

Benefiel, M. (2005). The second half of the journey: Spiritual leadership for organizational transformation. *The Leadership Quarterly, 16*(5), 723–747.

Brytting, T., & Trollestad, C. (2000). Managerial thinking on value-based management. *International Journal of Value-Based Management, 13*, 55–77.

Cladis, M. S. (2013). The culture of sustainability. In W. P. Boring & W. Forbes (Eds.), *Teaching sustainability: Perspectives from the humanities and social sciences* (pp. 38–48). Nacogdoches, TX: Stephen F. Austin State University Press.

Cowan, J. (1993). *The common table: Reflections and meditations on community and spirituality in the workplace.* New York, NY: Harper Business.

Creswell, J. W. (1998). *Qualitative inquiry and research design: Choosing among five traditions.* Thousand Oaks, CA: Sage.

Cunha, M. P., Rego, A., & D'Oliveira, T. (2006). Organizational spiritualties: An ideology-based typology. *Business & Society, 45*(2), 211–234.

Daloz, L. A., Keen, C. H., Keen, J. P., & Parks, S. D. (1996). *Common fire: Leading lives of commitment in a complex world.* Boston: Beacon Press.

Dane, E., & Brummel, B. J. (2014). Examining workplace mindfulness and its relations to job performance and turnover intention. *Human Relations, 67*(1), 105–128.

Denzin, N. K., & Lincoln, Y. S. (1998). *Strategies of qualitative inquiry.* Thousand Oaks, CA: Sage.

Dhiman, S. K, Heaton, D. P., Marques, J., & Mitroff, I. (2016(1),p1-1. Making sustainability meaningful: A holistic approach. *Academy of Management Proceedings*

Dodd, S. D., & Gotsis, G. (2007). The interrelationships between entrepreneurship and religion. *The International Journal of Entrepreneurship and Innovation, 8*(2), 93–104.

Doppelt, B. (2012). *From me to we: The five transformational commitments required to rescue the planet, your organization, & your life.* Sheffield, UK: Greenleaf Publishing.

Etherington, K. (2004). *Becoming a reflexive researcher-using ourselves in research.* London: Jessica Kingsley Publishers.

Fairfield, K. (2017, March 24). Educating for change in mindset and worldview on sustainability: One teacher's story. *International Conference on Business Management and Technology.*

Falkenberg, L., & Woiceshyn, J. (2008). Enhancing business ethics: Using cases to teach moral reasoning. *Journal of Business Ethics, 79*(3), 213–217.

Francis, P. (2015). Laudato si: On care for our common home. *Our Sunday Visitor.*

Gioia, D. A. (2003). Business organization as instrument of societal responsibility. *Organization, 10*(3), 435–438.

Grewal, G. (2013). Contemplative poetics and pedagogy for sustainability. In Wendy Petersen Boring & William Forbes (Eds.), *Teaching sustainability: Perspectives from the humanities and social sciences* (pp. 162–172). Nacogdoches, TX: Stephen F. Austin State University Press.

Huang, Q., Davison, R. M., & Gu, J. (2011), The impact of trust, guanxi orientation and face on the intention of Chinese employees and managers to engage in peer-to-peer tacit and explicit knowledge sharing. *Information Systems Journal, 21*, 557–577. doi:10.1111/j.1365-2575.2010.00361.x

Hunt-Oxendine, C., & Dent, E. (2010). Sustainability strategies of American Indian entrepreneurs. Management, Spirituality & Religion Conference Paper Abstracts. *Academy of Management Annual Meeting Proceedings*, August, 1–17. doi:10.5465/AMBPP.2010.54503765

Jackson, K. T. (1999). 'Spirituality as a Foundation for Freedom and Creative Imagination in International Business Ethics', *Journal of Business Ethics* 19, 61–70.

Janesick, V. J. (2000). The choreography of qualitative research design. In N. K. Denzin & Y. S. Lincoln (Eds.), *Handbook of qualitative research* (pp. 379–399). Thousand Oaks, CA: Sage Publications.

Jensen, J. (2013). Learning outcomes for sustainability in the humanities. In W. P. Boring & W. Forbes (Eds.), *Teaching sustainability: Perspectives from the humanities and social sciences* (pp. 23–37). Nacogdoches, TX: Stephen F. Austin State University Press.

Khurana, R. (2007). *From higher aims to hired hands: The social transformation of American business schools and the unfulfilled promise of management as a profession.* Princeton, NJ: Princeton University Press.

Kroth, M., & Boverie, P. (2000). Life mission and adult learning. *Adult Education Quarterly, 50*, 134–149.

Kutcher, E. J., Bragger, J. D., Rodriguez-Srednicki, O., & Masco, J. L. (2010). The role of religiosity in stress, job attitudes, and organizational citizenship behavior. *Journal of Business Ethics, 95*(2), 319–337.

Leopold, A. (1968). *A Sand County Almanac and sketches here and there* (pp. 336–337). New York: Oxford University Press.

Lerner, M. (2000). *Spirit matters.* Charlottesville, VA: Hampton Roads.

Lopez, K. J., Martínez, Z. L., & Specht, L. B. (2013). The economy of communion model. A spirituality-based view of global sustainability and its application to management education. *Journal of Management for Global Sustainability, 1*, 71–90.

Marschke, E., Preziosi, R., & Harrington, W. J. (2011). How sales personnel view the relationship between job satisfaction and spirituality in the workplace. *Journal of Organizational Culture, Communication and Conflict, 15*(2), 71.

Mezirow J. (1991). *Transformative dimensions of adult learning.* San Francisco: Jossey-Bass.

Mobley, W. H., & Dorfman, P. W. (Eds.). (2003). *Advances in global leadership* (Vol. 3, p. 3). Oxford, UK: Elsevier Science Ltd.

Moustakas, C. (Ed.). (1990). *Heuristic research: Design, methodology, and applications.* Thousand Oaks, CA: Sage Publications.

Neal, J. A. (2008). *Leadership and spirituality in the workplace.* Retrieved March 10, 2017. Retrieved from http://judineal.com/pages/pubs/leadership.htm

Patton, M. Q. (2002). *Qualitative research and evaluation methods* (3rd ed.). Thousand Oaks, CA: Sage Publications.

Peterson-Boring, W. (2010). "Sustainability and the Western Civilization Curriculum: Reflections on Cross-pollinating the Humanities and Environmental History". *Environmental History, 15*(2): 288-304

Reave, L. (2005). Spiritual values and practices related to leadership effectiveness. *The Leadership Quarterly, 16*(5), 655–687.

Rimanoczy, I. (2014). A matter of being: Developing sustainability-minded leaders. *Journal of Management for Global Sustainability*, *2*(1), 95–122.

Rimanoczy, I. (2016). *Stop teaching: Principles and practices for responsible management education.* New York, NY: Business Expert Press.

Rimanoczy, I. B. (2010). *Business leaders committing to and fostering sustainability initiatives. Doctoral dissertation.* Teachers College, Columbia University, New York.

Sela-Smith, S. (2002). Heuristic research: A review and critique of Moustakas's method. *Journal of Humanistic Psychology*, *42*(3), 53–88.

Sengupta, S. S. (2010). Correlates of spiritual orientation & managerial effectiveness. *Indian Journal of Industrial Relations*, 45–60.

Sridaran, K. (2014). *Workplace spirituality: Profile and influence of spiritually inspired business leaders – a cross cultural perspective.* Doctoral dissertation. Monash University, Melbourne.

Sterling, S. (2011). Transformative learning and sustainability: Sketching the conceptual ground. *Learning and Teaching in Higher Education*, *5*(11), 17–33.

Sundermann, A., Brieger, S. A., Seidel, J., & Strathoff, P. (2016). Leadership for sustainability: The role of values, sustainability understanding, and education. *Academy of Management Proceedings.* doi: 10.5465/AMBPP.2016.16066

Vasconcelos, A. F. (2011). Societal marketing concept and spirituality in the workplace theory: finding the common ground. *Cadernos EBAPE. BR*, *9*(1), 96–115.

Vives, A. (2006). Social and environmental responsibility in small and medium enterprises in Latin America. *The Journal of Corporate Citizenship*, *21*, 39.

Waddock, S., Rasche, A., Werhane, P., & Unruh, G. (2010). The principles for responsible management education – where do we go from here? In D. Fisher and D. Swanson (Eds.), *Assessing business ethics education* (pp. 13–28). Charlotte, NC: Information Age Publishing.

Wiek, A., Withycombe, L., & Redman, C. L. (2011). Key competencies in sustainability: a reference framework for academic program development. *Sustainability Science*, *6*(2), 203–218.

Zohar, D. (2005). Spiritually intelligent leadership. *Leader to Leader*, *38*, 45–51.

3

VALUES, SUSTAINABILITY, AND IMPLICATIONS FOR MANAGEMENT EDUCATION

Marta Fabiano Sambiase, Silvia M. Russi De Domenico, and Janette Brunstein

Introduction

The sustainability mindset model proposed by Rimanoczy, Kassel, and Mitchel (2016) is composed of three dimensions: Knowledge/Thinking, Values/Being, and Action/Doing. This chapter aims to contribute to the comprehension of the Values dimension while guiding principles for sustainability attitudes and behaviors through management education in the formation of future management leaders.

'Values' and 'sustainability' are two terms, in different areas, commonly used both by scientists and the general population, with different meanings and levels of usage. The word 'sustainability' is not new. It comes from 'sustain'; 'unsustainable', from the 18th century; 'to sustain' (verb), from the 19th century, and it means 'to hold down, to prevent falls', 'to keep', and 'to nurture physically or morally'. It was only in the 20th century that the idea of preserving and renovating resources transformed into the well-known term 'sustainability', representing, mainly, longevity (Cunha, 1982, p. 746; Dictionary.com, 2016). The notion of 'longevity' has inspired the term 'sustainable development', which was adopted by the United Nations for the upkeep of resources and survival of societies both today and in the future (WCED, 1987).

The term 'value' has two meanings, which started being used from 1303 and 1330, respectively. The first one indicates the quantity of any goods or medium of exchange considered equal to something; the latter expresses a set of individual qualities (Rohan, 2000; Simpson & Weiner, 1998). Around 1380, the word appeared in the plural form, indicating principles or patterns that guide an individual's or a society's life, or the individual judgment coming from a society over what is valued as important in life (Simpson & Weiner, 1998).

Approximately six centuries later, in the first half of the 19th century in Germany, the philosophical study of value appeared, labeled 'axiology'. Max Scheler, one of the most famous axiologists, although not having presented a formal definition of 'value', emphasized the need to express with accuracy what we mean when using the term 'value' – a task that has been the object of several knowledge fields, such as anthropology, sociology, and, mainly, psychology, or more specifically, social psychology in its two lines, psychological and social. The studies, especially contributions by Rokeach (1973) and Schwartz (1992), are studied within a psychological perspective. These scholars theorize that the value locus lies in the individual and is related, above all, to cognition.

However, from the sociological social psychology point of view (Thomas & Znaniecki, 2006), values are determined by what is valued, whether it is concrete or abstract, considering the meaning that a certain group, in a certain time and space, has attributed to it.

Since the first Industrial Revolution, society has become increasingly materialistic. Only during the last three decades, when information about the negative effects of this materialism started to spread throughout the world due to new technologies, did this way of consuming start to be questioned. The concept of sustainability began to make sense to scholars, policymakers, and the public. In this sense, the academic environment is fundamental for promoting knowledge, reflections, and stimuli that may come to reorient beliefs, through transformative learning.

Gouvêa (2008, p. 22) argues that:

> The intention of value researches in general must be coated with an ethical and social-political ideal of building a better world, offering companies a new existence perspective in which they awaken to their social calling, realize the need to effectively contribute towards this ideal, aiming, for instance, the survival itself of the human race and a sustainable social-economical development.

Such an assertion prompts us to compare the two perspectives from social psychology. The psychological line, which comprehends personal values as representations of the common needs to all individuals in any culture, with which human beings must deal in order for the species to survive, within an evolutionist perspective (Schwartz, 1992). The sociological line defines values as social constructions, inter-subjectively defined (Thomas & Znaniecki, 2006). In the latter approach, within a certain period or periods of time, and for a certain group or groups, sustainability starts becoming a social value. Torregrosa (2004) already claimed that the line between one social psychology branch and another does not contribute towards the understanding of the phenomena, making it necessary to look at both approaches in order to comprehend the world and try to preserve both it and the societies living in it.

Values for sustainable development and sustainability

The meaning of sustainability has shifted somewhat over time, as has its significance. The United Nations Declaration (UN, 1942) posed the universal values of peace, freedom, social progress, equal rights, and human dignity as urgently necessary. These values, included in the Charter of the United Nations and in the Universal Declaration of Human Rights, are no less valid today than when, over half a century ago, representatives of many different nations and cultures drafted these documents. However, they are much more broadly accepted today than they were a few decades ago. Annan (2003, para.1) claims that "the Universal Declaration, in particular, has been accepted in legal systems across the world, and has become a point of reference for people who long for human rights in every country." These documents express an optimistic view and not a description of the existing reality.

In the mid-1970s, however, forecast models of the future of the world economy classified resources as finite and warned that their misuse would lead to a global collapse as soon as the 21st century arrived. Taking this into consideration, in 1972 the UN held a meeting with the Member States in Stockholm, and 'sustainable development' appeared as a response to the balance of economic, social, and ecological approaches (Corazza, 2005; Freeman, 1996).

Since then, the idea of sustainable development (SD) has been used by many groups in various ways. The definition that is most taken into consideration is from the *Brundtland Report* of the World Commission for Economic Development (WCED, 1987). In this document, SD is regarded as a process of change in which the exploitation of resources, the direction of investments, the orientation of technological development, and the institutional changes are carried out in a manner consistent with the current and future needs of societies (Banerjee, 2002; Claro, Claro & Amancio, 2005; Romeiro, 2001).

With the advancement of globalization, such intentions were reaffirmed by the United Nations Millennium Declaration, in the year 2000, which defined fundamental values as essential for international relations in the 21st century, and also to achieve sustainable development in the form of freedom, equality, solidarity, tolerance, respect for nature, and shared responsibility (UN, 2000). The UN recognizes that, in addition to the responsibilities of its members towards individual societies, they also have a collective responsibility to uphold the principles of human dignity, equality, and equity at a global level.

In order to translate these espoused values into actions, the UN has identified key goals to which they have assigned special significance. Thus, the 8th, and later the 17th, Millennium Goals for sustainable development were created, seeking to guide decisions in various areas of expertise (UN_SD, 2016). These goals present an opportunity to bring the countries and citizens of the world together, embarking on a new path to improve society.

In addition to the international institutions, corporations are important agents in society today due to employing a considerable amount of people; they are either the main or at least a major player in generating wealth for countries, and they are also responsible for using natural resources on a large scale. Considering such information, the United Nations Global Compact (UN_GC, 2016, no page) encourages companies to:

> Do business responsibly by aligning their strategies and operations with ten principles on human rights, labor, environment, and anti-corruption; and take strategic actions to advance broader societal goals, such as the UN Sustainable Development Goals, with an emphasis on collaboration and innovation.

The UN Global Compact is a voluntary initiative that relies on public accountability, transparency, and disclosure to complement regulation and to provide space for innovation and collective action (UN_GC, 2016, no page):

> We need business to give practical meaning and reach to the values and principles that connect cultures and people everywhere.
> *Ban Ki-moon, Secretary-General of the United Nations.*

The Ten Principles of the UN Global Compact are derived from the Universal Declaration of Human Rights, the International Labor Organization's Declaration on Fundamental Principles and Rights at Work, the Rio Declaration of Environment and Development, and the United Nations Convention Against Corruption (UN_GC, 2016).

Launched in July 2000, the UN Global Compact is a leadership platform for the development, implementation, and disclosure of responsible and sustainable corporate policies and practices. By doing this, businesses, as the primary driver of globalization, can help ensure that markets, commerce, technology, and finance advance in ways that benefit economies and societies everywhere, and contribute to a more sustainable and inclusive global economy.

The principles for corporations are:

Human Rights

Principle 1: Businesses should support and respect the protection of internationally proclaimed human rights; and
   Principle 2: Make sure that they are not complicit in human rights abuses.

Labor

Principle 3: Businesses should uphold the freedom of association and the effective recognition of the right to collective bargaining;
   Principle 4: The elimination of all forms of forced and compulsory labor;
   Principle 5: The effective abolition of child labor; and

Principle 6: The elimination of discrimination in respect of employment and occupation.

Environment

Principle 7: Businesses should support a precautionary approach to environmental challenges;

Principle 8: Undertake initiatives to promote greater environmental responsibility; and

Principle 9: Encourage the development and diffusion of environmentally friendly technologies.

Anti-Corruption

Principle 10: Businesses should work against corruption in all its forms, including extortion and bribery.

More specifically, in business administration and management of organizations, the Principles for Responsible Management Education emerge as an initiative supported by the Global Compact (PRME, 2016). These guidelines aim to engage universities in the development of managers who may take into consideration the issue of sustainability in their actions within organizations and in society. They consist of six principles:

Principle 1 | Purpose: We will develop the capabilities of students to be future generators of sustainable value for business and society at large and to work for an inclusive and sustainable global economy.

Principle 2 | Values: We will incorporate into our academic activities and curricula the values of global social responsibility as portrayed in international initiatives such as the United Nations Global Compact.

Principle 3 | Method: We will create educational frameworks, materials, processes, and environments that enable learning experiences for responsible leadership.

Principle 4 | Research: We will engage in conceptual and empirical research that advances our understanding about the role, dynamics, and impact of corporations in the creation of sustainable social, environmental, and economic value.

Principle 5 | Partnership: We will interact with managers of business corporations to extend our knowledge of their challenges in meeting social and environmental responsibilities and to explore jointly effective approaches to meeting these challenges.

Principle 6 | Dialog: We will facilitate and support dialog and debate among educators, students, business, government, consumers, media, civil society organizations, and other interested groups and stake-holders on critical issues related to global social responsibility and sustainability.

It is clear from these policymaking institutions and their efforts that, since the 1970s, a global trend has been building in assigning a value to sustainability, and that education, specifically that of future managers, may be a path towards other groups recognizing it as something that must be valued.

Within the PRME management education guidelines, the second principle suggests incorporating the values of global social responsibility into academic activities and curricula, as portrayed in international initiatives such as the United Nations Global Compact. A movement in favor of widening the discussion on the definition and enactment of sustainability is apparent. However, in the sense of understanding individual attitudes and in relation to sustainability as a social value, more research and discussion is necessary in regard to personal values from the perspective of social psychology.

Basic values theory

Despite differences among the several value experts, especially until the first half of the 20th century, there was agreement about some characteristics of such a concept: values are concepts or beliefs about final desirable states or behaviors, which transcend specific situations. They are classified in terms of relative importance, forming a value system, which guides the selection or evaluation of behaviors and events (Rokeach, 1973).

Personal values represent human needs (Rokeach, 1973; Schwartz, 1992, Schwartz et al., 2012) and, unlike attitudes, which refer to various concrete and abstract objects, personal values are few and are the foundation for our attitudes, according to Rokeach (1973). From certain gaps left in this author's studies, Schwartz (1992) has developed the Basic Values Theory, which has been established as one of the most recognized and applied theories in empirical studies (Almeida & Sobral, 2009).

Considering that values are the expression of three needs with which all individuals, of any society, must deal (biological needs, coordinating social interaction needs, and survival and well-being of group needs), Schwartz (1992) defined values as being hierarchizing goals with motivational content, which serve as principles in individuals' and groups' lives, in different life contexts.

According to this theory, all human beings supposedly possess the same value categories, named motivational types,[1] regardless of the culture of the society in which they are raised. Schwartz started with ten types of values in 1992, and, in 2012, he refined his theory by subdividing some motivational types and adding two new ones (face and humility), to more completely cover the spectrum of human motivations (Table 3.1).

TABLE 3.1 Motivational types and their conceptual definition in terms of motivational content

Value	Subtype	Conceptual definition
Self-direction	Thought	Freedom to cultivate one's own ideas and abilities
	Action	Freedom to determine one's own actions
Stimulation	–	Excitement, novelty, and change
Hedonism	–	Pleasure and sensuous gratification
Achievement	–	Success according to social standards
Power	Dominance	Power through exercising control over people
	Resources	Power through control of material and social resources
Face	–	Security and power through maintaining one's public image and avoiding humiliation
Security	Personal	Safety in one's immediate environment
	Societal	Safety and stability in wider society
Tradition	–	Maintaining and preserving cultural, family, or religious traditions
Conformity	Rules	Compliance with rules, laws, and formal obligations
	Interpersonal	Avoidance of upsetting or harming other people
Humility	–	Recognizing one's insignificance in the larger scheme of things
Benevolence	Dependability	Being a reliable and trustworthy member of the in-group
	Caring	Devotion to the welfare of in-group members
Universalism	Concern	Commitment to equality, justice, and protection for all people
	Nature	Preservation of the natural environment
	Tolerance	Acceptance and understanding of those who are different from oneself

Source: Based on Schwartz et al. (2012)

The motivational types, on the other hand, regarding the motivational goals they express, are in similarity or conflict relationships amongst themselves, setting a circular and continuous relationship structure (Figure 3.1).

Compatibility amongst value types happens via the sharing of motivational guidance with adjacent values of the continuum. Providing more details, Schwartz (2013) explains this when taking the ten motivational types into consideration:

- Power and achievement emphasize social superiority and esteem
- Achievement and hedonism both express self-centeredness
- Hedonism and stimulation entail a desire for effectively pleasant arousal

- Stimulation and self-direction involve an intrinsic motivation for mastery and openness to change
- Self-direction and universalism express reliance upon one's own judgment and comfort with the diversity of existence
- Universalism and benevolence both entail concern for the enhancement of others and transcendence of selfish interests
- Benevolence and tradition/conformity all promote devotion to one's in-group
- Tradition/conformity and security all emphasize conservation of order and harmony in relationships
- Security and power both stress avoiding or overcoming the threat of uncertainties by controlling relationships and resources

The Basic Values structure presented by Schwartz (1992; Schwartz et al., 2012), therefore, is founded on compatibility relations between certain values and conflict relations between those that oppose each other. Thus, relations between the different, first-order motivational types, as the 19 motivational types can be considered, define four second-order types of values, related in pairs, into two bipolar dimensions, which are: Self-Transcendence—Self Enhancement and Openness to Change—Conservation (Figure 3.1). The first dimension gathers Self-Transcendence values (benevolence and universalism), which are found to be opposed to Self-Enhancement values (power and achievement), while the second dimension opposes Openness to Change values (self-direction and stimulation) to Conservation values (tradition, conformity, and security). Some motivational types (hedonism, face, and humility) may be placed, depending on the sample, in some other set of second-order types of values.

On the other hand, the motivational types may be gathered with regards to the social or personal focus they express, in terms of their goals. Therefore, values such as universalism, benevolence, humility, conformity, tradition, and security-societal express social focus, whereas the other values express individual focus. This leads us to think that people who prioritize social focus values may be more open to searching for sustainability.

Values, attitudes, and behaviors towards sustainability

Schwartz (2013) clarifies that the main goal of values research is related to individual differences that occur given the priority that each individual attributes to the motivational types, leading to differences in behavior.

As previously presented, the Basic Values Theory specifies dynamic relations amongst value types. One of its first implications is that adjacent motivational types must keep similar associations with other variables. The second consequence of the circular structure is that associations of motivational types with many other variables form a predictable pattern. If an attitude or behavior variable presents a stronger, positive correlation with a certain motivational type, and a negative correlation with another, then the expected association pattern with all other motivational types must follow the same circular value structure.

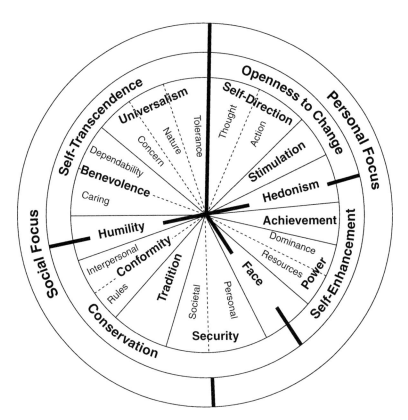

FIGURE 3.1 Circular motivational continuum of 19 values

Source: Adapted from Schwartz et al. (2012).

Verlanken and Holland (2002) point out how values can influence behavior:

1   First, values must be activated; a value's accessibility and importance in relation to other values are crucial to its activation, which does not necessarily occur in a conscious way.
2   Values motivate actions, and actions that promote valued goals are appealing.
3   People define situations based on values they consider important; different values suggest different actions.
4   The higher the priority given to a certain value, the more will an individual set an action plan in order to direct its expression in behavior. Priority values may be more easily accessed because they are more available; that explains why the value hierarchy relates to behavior.

Next, a few studies that show such considerations are presented.

Values and cooperation

An empirical example presented by Schwartz (2013), supported by Natan and Bornstein, studied interpersonal cooperation, a desirable behavior for the promotion of the sustainability mindset. A hypothesis was set based on the consequences of each choice made by the respondents expressing a motivational goal amongst the ten motivational types from Schwartz's theory (Schwartz, 2012) before it was changed to 19 values. Taking into consideration: (1) that when allocating resources for oneself and for others, the relevant superior value is self-enhancement (which includes power and achievement as value types), and (2) there are consequences of cooperative and non-cooperative behavior for each of the ten motivational goals. The following hypothesis was elaborated:

1   Motivational types that do not promote cooperation are power, achievement, and hedonism.

The power motivational type emphasizes competition, and also legitimizes the maximization of self-gain, even if there may be cost to others as a result. On the other hand, the achievement motivational type also predicts non-cooperative behavior because it promotes self-interest, being weaker than 'power' because it will provide a less-solid social status, which is the main goal of the achievement value. The hedonism motivational type predicts non-cooperative behavior, because cooperation implies making sacrifices.

2   Motivational types that do promote cooperation are benevolence, universalism, and conformity.

Experimental settings probably turn cooperation into more of a conventional common decency and expression of consideration than a basic commitment towards social justice; thus, making it more related to benevolence goals than to universalism. Conformity is also a predictor of cooperation due to its normative nature, and, therefore, a conventional behavior in society.

3   Values of self-direction, stimulation, security, and tradition are less relevant as cooperation predictors and, therefore, should have an almost null correlation.

All three hypotheses have been confirmed. Benevolence was the value type with the highest correlation with cooperation, and power had the lowest correlation. Most importantly, the order of correlations has followed the theoretic structure. Self-direction, stimulation, security, and tradition had near-zero correlations. Thus, Schwartz (2013, p. 128) concludes that "a commitment to values that promote cooperation (benevolence), in the absence of conflict with a commitment to values opposed to cooperation (power), was necessary to elicit a high level of cooperation". The specific behavior analysis is facilitated by the circular values theory structure (Figure 3.1); while some types explain correlations well, other types help understand the opposite, lower, correlations better.

Sagiv, Sverdlik, and Schwarz (2011) also investigated the impact of values on perceptional and behavioral choices in cooperation versus competition dilemmas. The authors simulated interpersonal (Study 1) and intergroup (Study 2) studies by using two games designed to provide unambiguous situations in terms of values that could be attained by competing or cooperating, as the authors explain.

"The Paired Charity Game (Study 1) framed the conflict situation in terms of cooperation – by donating the money given to them, participants could contribute to others" (Sagiv, Sverdlik & Schwarz, 2011, p. 75). Results show that contribution had a positive correlation with universalism and benevolence values, highlighting caring towards others; it also had a negative correlation with power, achievement, and hedonism values, due to promoting self-interest.

"The Group Charity Game (Study 2) was designed to frame the situation in terms of competition. It highlighted participants' chances to lose their money (if they contributed) or to win out over others (if they did not contribute)" (Sagiv, Sverdlik & Schwarz, 2011, p. 75). In Study 2, a situation that was relevant to the power value was created, reflecting a favorable situation to control, win, and overcome others, opposed to the benevolence value (which reflects concern and caring towards group members). As a result, contribution had an emphasis on the positive correlation of benevolence over power.

Using these two examples of cooperative behavior and values, educators could highlight situations where the advantages of cooperation are shown. Presentations of company cases, for instance, may show the mutual gains due to cooperation, such as defended by the Theory and Cooperation Games (Brandenburger & Nalebuff, 2011), inspiring the future manager to search for other kinds of reasonability rather than the classical, pure competition type (Brunstein, Sambiase & Novaes, 2016).

Torres, Schwartz, and Nascimento (2016) have encountered the same predictive validity evidence of the theory with the instrument for 19 motivational types (Schwartz et al., 2012). As expected, most reported behaviors were positively predicted by their motivating value and were negatively predicted by the opposed motivational type.

Attitudes and predisposition to behavior

To illustrate the processes which connect values to attitudes and behavior, an illustrative example is presented by Schwartz (2005): John, who, when getting a challenging proposition from his boss, which would require moving to a different city, reacts with enthusiasm. He finds the proposition appealing because it best serves the self-direction, stimulation, and achievement values, which, due to being more important to him, end up getting activated in a way that causes him to express agreement and enthusiasm behavior. If John had as a high priority those values related to security, he probably would not find the proposition appealing, since its actions become less pleasing and valued as they obstruct goals from those values that have priority. Through a continuous comprehension of circumstances being processed in terms of positive or negative, appropriate or inappropriate, and convenient or inconvenient, people take on a 'position' regarding the world surrounding them; such a position is called an 'attitude' (Torres & Neiva, 2011).

Values with a high priority are consistent goals that guide people to pursue and pay attention to situational aspects that are relevant to the prioritized value. Values also influence the planning of actions. Therefore, the higher the priority one gives to a value, the more one will elaborate action plans that can value it in the expression of one's behavior. Possibly, John may have acted at work in a way that pursued values which expressed self-direction, stimulation, and achievement.

On the other hand, a later examination of conscience may change a decision's attractiveness when considering its consequences, such as happened to John when he told the news to his family. A series of obstacles to moving to another city arose: for his wife, the effects on the family's quality of life and, for their daughter, the impact on her relationships with her friends. This awakened in John behaviors related to the benevolence value type. The values system influences attention, perception, and interpretation of situations. The individual's value hierarchy may influence their attitudes and their behavior, guiding them or not towards sustainability.

Pro-sustainability values and attitudes

Research points to the importance of values and attitudes towards promoting pro-sustainability behavior (Bechtel, Verdugo & Pinheiro, 1999; Dunlap & Van Liere, 1978; Dunlap, Van Liere, Mertig & Jones, 2000; Schultz & Zelezny, 1999; Stern, Dietz & Guagnano, 1998; Stern & Dietz, 1994; Stern, Dietz & Kalof, 1993; Thompson & Barton, 1994; Vaske & Donnelly, 1999; Weigel & Weigel, 1978).

There are many terms used in the literature to name pro-sustainability behavior (i.e., a behavior in favor of the 'sustainability' social value). One of the terms used is a pro-environmental behavior, with emphasis on protection of resources (Corral-Verdugo, 2005). Another term used is ecocentric behavior, where the ecosystem is placed in the center of human decisions; in this sense, Coelho, Gouveia, and Milfont (2006) have identified that the 'universalism' motivational type was consistently the one that best explained 'ecocentrism', corroborating what has been found in previous studies (Karp, 1996; Schultz & Zelezny, 1999).

Karp (1996) verified, for instance, that out of the four superior categories of secondary values suggested by Schwartz (1992), self-transcendence and openness to change were strong predictors of pro-environmental behavior. People who scored higher in the self-transcendence dimension presented a higher degree of ecocentric attitudes and commitment to participating in environment-friendly activities. More specifically, people with higher scores in the universalism motivational type presented a higher predisposition to acting in a way that favors sustainability.

According to Nordlund and Garvil (2002), environment-friendly behavior involves conflict between the individual's immediate self-interests and the collective long-term interests. The authors conducted research where personal norms mediated value effects and the conscience problems in pro-environment behavior, found in individuals with a high priority of the self-transcendent value, showed higher care towards the environment than people with a higher priority of the self-enhancement value.

> These results are in accordance with findings in social dilemma research on social value orientation. Individuals with a cooperative value orientation have been found to give more weight to the collective consequences of their behavior and be more willing to make personal sacrifices for the common good than those with an individual value orientation.
>
> *(Nordlund & Garvill, 2002, p. 752)*

Almeida (2007), during a managing scope study, showed that the most favorable management attitude toward the balance among pro-environment behavior of companies is validated by a universalist desire for equality, and influenced by managers' personal value system being centered in others, as opposed to values centered in oneself. Selfish values have been found to be inhibitors of a socially responsible management attitude.

Depending on the value priority, individuals either present or do not present attitudes and behaviors which contribute to preserving the environment (De Boer, Hoogland & Boersema, 2007; Martin & Upham, 2016).

According to Schwartz (2005), life circumstances allow some values to be expressed more easily than others, but they can also impose barriers. For him, "people adapt their values to the circumstances" (p. 69), and he also asserts that "[the] importance attributed to a value depends on how easy obtaining that value is" (p. 69). Schwartz gives his statement an example by saying that individuals with jobs that bear freedom of choice increase the importance of self-achievement values as opposed to conformity values.

In the same sense, it can be thought that if students, during their Management education, are exposed to a pro-sustainability environment, where discussion on the theme takes place in different circumstances, such as classes and university events, values that express related goals will become more important to them, for example, the self-transcendence value – mainly universalism value type favors pro-sustainability behavior.

Jacobi (2003, p. 189) has already warned about the need to question "values and premises which guide predominant social practices, implying a change in the way of thinking and transformation in the knowledge and educational practices". In the next section, the way that this change can be made in the educational environment will be discussed.

Education, values, and sustainability

The debate on education has been associated with the action of adhering to socially agreed-upon, shared values, which are achieved through a set of individual and collective projects, and which historically change (Machado, 1999). It is in this sense that the sustainability idea presents as a collective value and a societal project with which teaching institutions must start engaging. There are three important instances to be considered when it comes to discussing education, values, and sustainability: institutional, organizational, and didactical-pedagogical. To achieve the goals of this chapter, the first two will be addressed briefly, and the latter will be discussed in more detail.

At the macro-institutional level, as previously stated, the world has watched the promulgation of conferences, letters, and declarations since the 1970s, about principles that were pre-established by a set of educational values with the purpose of consolidating a sustainable society project (PRME, 2016; UNESCO, 2012; ULSF, 2010). Such movement drives universities around the world forward, prompting them to become signatories who promise to pursue these goals and values (Wright, 2004). It also unleashes, at an organizational level, a series of initiatives from the higher education institutions to incorporate these values into their mission and vision, which will translate into their political, pedagogical projects, in changing their curricula, and in initiatives that affect the management of the campus itself (Alabaster & Blair, 1996; Calder & Clugston, 2003; Lotz-Sisitka, 2004; Shriberg, 2003; Wals & Blewitt, 2010). As a consequence, from a didactical-pedagogical perspective, classroom experiments start soaring and being studied throughout the whole world (Annandale & Morrison-Sounders, 2007; Brunnquell, Brunstein & Jaime, 2015; Collins & Kearins, 2007; Kearins & Springett, 2003; Springett, 2005; Svoboda & Whalen, 2004).

However, there is an intrinsic difficulty when it comes to thinking about steering management education towards sustainability, because it presupposes favoring a new justification in teaching management, and its values are based on a logic that, until very recently, was not part of the Management teaching agenda. And when they are present in the curricula, they are often isolated within the context of only one subject, or the personal initiative from one committed professor, surrounded by a group of others who either put these same values into debate only very little or not at all, or even worse, they contradict them. These are crippling and difficult matters, given that the sustainability logic presupposes, at times, asking the manager to give up part of their profit, or to produce less, which is contrary to an entire set of rules that for years has been the foundation of the organizational logic and dynamics. Another issue is faculty who are unprepared to talk about these matters in the classroom (Brunstein, Godoy & da Silva, 2014).

In addition, when starting their professional activities, such as internships, students typically find little space in which to reinforce the sustainability value. Our experience is that it is frequently the opposite; actions toward sustainable practices are threatened by the rampant market competition, by the individual interest's predominance over the collective, by the disbelief in the possibility of change, and even by the lack of consensus that surrounds the concept of sustainable development (poverty, equity, environmental preservation, etc.), whether it is from the organizational level or not.

Thus, our focus is to find ways to promote sustainability-oriented values in management education classroom courses. In this chapter, four pedagogical approaches that may contribute towards thinking on sustainability and values targeting education in management schools will be highlighted, inspired by the work of Kearins and Springett (2003), and in the studies on Mezirow's (2009) critical reflection: a) *the engagement approach* – engaging the students in the debate about values and sustainability in organizations; b) *the sense approach* – encouraging the identification, in the classroom, with sustainability values, projects, and ideals in organizations, providing them with sense; c) *the reflection approach* – favoring the exercise of reflexivity and of critical reflection on values and sustainability in organizations; and d) *the action approach* – involving the students in activities and projects which promote action. These four approaches are circular and, sometimes, concurring, as Figure 3.2 exemplifies:

1 **Engaging in the debate on values and sustainability in organizations:** *promoting dialogues in the classroom and involving students in discussion*

This approach is about creating an atmosphere that favors dialogue and encouraging the students to discuss values and sustainability within the organizations' universe, which is not a simple task. Sustainability presupposes a paradigmatic review (Wals, 2010) that introduces a new agenda into the business world which professors

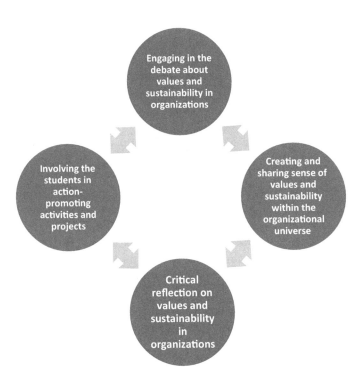

FIGURE 3.2 Mobilizing approaches to values and sustainability-oriented teaching

Source: Authors, inspired by Kearins and Springett (2003).

and students are not completely familiar with or convinced by. It requires an epistemic change that is not reduced to doing better things, or making things better, but to seeing things from a different perspective (Sterling, 2011). Finally, it demands a change in mental habits and daily routine, implying leaving one's comfort zone, which may be quite painful (Hibbert & Cunliffe, 2015). In this sense, creating a trustworthy, free, and safe point of view, which is open to different opinions, and which values atmosphere, is fundamental. The quality of such dialogue and the students' engagement represents a thermometer for pedagogical action in this field.

2 Creating and sharing sense on values and sustainability in the organizational universe: *identifying with pro-sustainability projects and ideals*

For Schaefer, Corner, and Kearins (2015), sustainability necessarily requires feeling and a connectivity process with others and with nature. Here, it is about favoring opportunities so that these connections are made, causing the students to identify with pro-sustainability values and to connect with its projects, turning it into an identificatory ideal. Such a process presupposes strengthening the discussion on sustainability in the management field, and also looking at the causes of unsustainability as well as its consequences (Schaefer, Corner & Kearins, 2015). To do so, it is important to go beyond the more pragmatic, technical, or legal matters that sustainability involves – while a competitive advantage object only – stimulating a reflection process on the values contained in the economic growth and the consumer society logic which have led us to the unsustainable situation in which we find ourselves. The construction of this shared sense in the classroom, and its link with students' professional and life projects, stimulates acknowledgment and adherence to certain value groups that are considered relevant in a sustainable society.

3 Favoring the exercise of critical reflection on values and organizational sustainability: *reflexivity and critical reflection*

In this approach, the professor stimulates the students to exercise their reflective practice, which involves making them recognize and question the values that guide their answers towards a certain situation and context, and from there, observing how they judge their own conduct and that of companies. Regarding critical reflection, the task is to provoke disorienting dilemmas in the classroom that, as Mezirow (2009) observes, are capable of making the students think not only about the *problem's content* (the way they see it, feel about it, act towards it), or about the *process* (reviewing strategies and processes to resolve a problem), but, above all, thinking about the *problem's premises and conjectures* (they are prompted to revisit their previously acquired knowledge, questioning the problem in itself: 'why am I thinking about it?', 'is this important?', and 'should I worry about this?'). In the case of sustainability-oriented values, promoting this deeper level of reflection demands a continuous exercise of questioning and searching for answers in the classroom, for instance: 'what values guide the relationships between company and society?'; 'what values direct strategic decisions anchored in consumption and production goals?'; 'what values influence their actions as future managers?'; and others.

4   **The students' involvement in activities and projects that promote action:** *transformative learning and new competencies development*

In order to have a transformative learning process that leads to the review of beliefs and values (Cranton & Taylor, 2012), there must be an opening and permeability to new ideas. Such a transformation can occur due to some positive or negative fact or event, which causes the individual to assess one's beliefs and values (Brookfield, 1987).

It is important to clarify that it is not possible to transform others, their values, and beliefs, but it is possible to create an environment that stimulates such change. However, to create such availability in the classroom, pedagogical experiences must be focused on the students' action. This means that the students should participate in workshops, campus intervention projects, the community, research, and all sorts of experiences that lead them to experiment and to think about problem resolution, innovation, and any way in which to re-read phenomena and the organizational space from the sustainability perspective. This is what will contribute, at a discursive level, towards building the students' reasoning capacity in favor of sustainability, and, regarding the concrete, objective actions level, to the development of new methods and competencies.

Table 3.2, synthesized from Brunnquell, Brunstein, and Jaime's study (2015), illustrates teaching goals and strategies used by Management professors who incorporate discussions regarding sustainability into their classes. The authors show how professors sought to engage students in thinking about, for example, the coherence of companies' practices and their motivations, as well as the coherence and impacts of their own actions as individuals. Beyond this, these professors have also brought their students' attention to the role of the manager and the executive responsibility for building a more sustainable society. Finally, they have summoned their students to reflect on the conjectures that guide their actions, organizational conduct, and management professionals' actions. To this end, they employ a set of didactical strategies in which the students take over as protagonists: they write blogs on sustainability; produce documentaries about sustainable management practices; participate in company games; and engage in consulting activities, elaborate upon business plans and strategically plan with a focus on sustainability.

The relevance of stimulating the students to get in contact with social reality is highlighted above all:

> when students hold workshops, visit a social project, a fair, etc. On these occasions, they are exposed to tensions that mark the construction of sustainability, because they can witness disputes and cooperation between different stakeholders involved in solving certain problems. All this corresponds to what authors like Annandale and Morrison-Sounders (2007), Collins and

TABLE 3.2 Teaching objectives and methodological strategies

Teaching Objectives	Teaching Strategies
• Indicated the intention to surpass traditional views of the subject, replacing them with others • Rendered administrators responsible for their decisions and led them to consider indicators that surpass economic and financial analysis • Added discussions on ethics, transparency, communication with stakeholders, and social justice to the traditional objectives of their subjects • Sought to develop communication skills and commitment attitude towards sustainability among their students • Placed the evolution of Administration Science within a historical perspective, based on the good and the bad of what it has provided for society, discussing its implications for contemporary management • Demonstrated a concern towards reviewing the role of administrators and the practice of management itself • Placed students in a position to confront a management model that seemed to indicate signs of exhaustion, and invited them to think about the need for a new model that would take into consideration elements which, until recently, had not been part of the functions of administrators • Led the students to think about consistency in company actions, and the professors' and students' behavior	**Audiovisual Resources** − *Videos and films*: To make the students think about certain situations or problems, as well as to evaluate management practices, taking sustainability into account − *Documentary production*: The students visited an organization and made a documentary about how sustainability was incorporated into management practices and the organization process. − *Blog*: Space for reflection and production of texts related to sustainability **Games** − *Board game*: The traditional board game *War* was intended to make students reflect on the process of decision-making and the values that were behind these actions − *Business games*: Business games immerse the participant in complex situations that require them to make difficult decisions and, as the protagonist, responsibly assess the consequences of their actions on sustainability issues **Simulation of Management Practices** − *Plans Development*: Communication Plans, Business Plans, and Strategic Plans − *Problem Solving*: Design, thinking, methodology − *Consulting*: Practical consulting exercise **Visits and Tours** − *Technical visit*: Sustainable management model in organizations − *Visiting a fair*: Entrepreneur fair excursion in order to understand Brazilian companies and their actions in accordance with sustainability − *Visiting a social project*: Bring the students closer to social projects − *Ecological trail*: Contact with the environment around their city − *Fieldwork*: Monitoring the production cycle of an extractive activity **Event Organization** − *Workshop*: The students organized the Entrepreneurship Workshop regarding sustainability

Source: Elaborated from Brunnquell, Brunstein, and Jaime (2015)

Kearins (2007), and Kearins and Springett (2003) highlight when they refer to the need for students to establish contact with the communities; the need to engage in solving real problems in their surroundings, suggesting solutions; to participate in activities that simulate conflicts of interests between different actors; to exercise the negotiations of these dissents in an attempt to build possible consensus and to experience situations that reproduce the actual conditions of the business world, with their time limits, budget constraints, market conditions and social pressures.

(Brunnquell, Brunstein & Jaime, 2015, p. 335)

In summary, sustainability-oriented teaching offers an opportunity to make a difference to an entire generation of business administration and management students if there is the living quality of a continuous circle that involves engaging, sensing, reflection, and action stimulated by numerous, active pedagogical paths (Springett, 2005).

Final considerations

For many years, the planet's resources were considered sufficient to handle all of humankind's demands. However, consumer society, strongly developed in the 20th century, has revealed itself to be more avid than the Earth's regenerating capacity, leading to several environmental, social, and economic imbalances.

As such awareness was brought about by different agents, such as the media, governments, and civil society organizations, (the absence of) sustainability started becoming part of the day-to-day lives of individuals and societies.

Thus, sustainability has been constituting itself as a social value (from Thomas and Znaniecki's perspective, 2006), now that it has acquired meaning to people in a determined time and space. According to these authors, once a social value is constituted, individuals start presenting different attitudes toward such a value. Here, it is understood that these attitudes may vary due to the personal values hierarchy present in each individual, as is explained by the Theory of Basic Values (Schwartz, 1992; Schwartz et al., 2012).

Self-transcendent-oriented personal values (i.e., values which represent motivations related to society's and the environment's well-being, mainly through the universalism value type), have been related to pro-sustainability attitudes and behaviors, as the many studies previously commented on have shown. Personal values of openness to change, with stimulation and self-direction value types, are also considered, since they involve internal motivation and make it easier to change.

On the other hand, according to Schwartz (2005), it is possible that the individual gives more importance to a certain value if it is more present in a certain environment. In this sense, schools, and particularly management education courses, have an essential role in ensuring that their students start prioritizing values that lead to pro-sustainability attitudes and behaviors (e.g., green consumption, recycling habits, recycling and waste reduction, sustainability innovation).

In order to do so, in-classroom discussions regarding the consequences of sustainability, from the theories presented by the professors as applied to the different subjects that form the curricula, will make critical reflection possible for the students on how we have come where we are now and possible ways out. Using didactical-pedagogical resources, such as disorienting dilemmas and dramatization, may be useful, since this allows the students to experience such situations. Several studies on Critical Reflection and Transformative Learning have exemplified teaching-learning strategies adopted in the educational environment at a higher-education level (Brunnquell, Brunstein & Jaime, 2015) that make it possible for the students to reflect on the meaning of sustainability and its consequences for organizations, societies, and the planet.

On the other hand, a university environment that promotes self-transcendence and openness to change values, due to allowing interaction between people from different nationalities on-campus, as well as offering programs, internships, and exchange programs which provide undergraduate students with the means to get in contact with different social, economic, and environmental realities which demand solving, are also recommended.

Regarding business management undergraduate students, whose collective thought is mainly oriented towards economic results, the challenge faced is to create conditions in business schools so that future managers are able to identify with the 'sustainability' social value, and to become aware of their own value system through assessing and reflecting on it.

Note

1 In this text, motivational types are also called types of values.

References

Alabaster, T., & Blair, D. (1996). Greening the university. In J. Huckle & S. Sterling (Eds.), *Education for sustainability* (pp. 86–104). London: Earthscan Publications.

Almeida, F. J. R. (2007). Ética e desempenho social das organizações: Um modelo teórico de análise dos fatores culturais e contextuais. *Revista de Administração Contemporânea, 11*(3), 105–125.

Almeida, F. J. R., & Sobral, F. J. B. A. (2009). O sistema de valores humanos de administradores brasileiros: Adaptação da escala PVQ para o estudo de valores no Brasil. *Revista de Administração Mackenzie, 10*(3), 101–126.

Annan, K. (2003). *Universal values – peace, freedom, social progress, equal rights, human dignity.* Acutely needed, secretary-general says at Tubingen University, Germany. Retrieved from www.un.org/press/en/2003/sgsm9076.doc.htm

Annandale, D., & Morrison-Sounders, A. (2007). Teaching process sustainability: A role-playing case focused on finding new solutions to a waste-water management problem. In C. Galea (Ed.), *Teaching business sustainability Vol. 2. Cases, simulations and experiential approaches* (pp. 180–198). Sheffield: Greenleaf.

Banerjee, S. B. (2002). Organisational strategies for sustainable development: Developing a research agenda for the new Millennium. *Australian Journal of Management, 27*, Special Issue.

Bechtel, R. B., Verdugo, V. C., & de Pinheiro, J. Q. (1999). Environmental belief systems: United States, Brazil, and Mexico. *Journal of Cross-Cultural Psychology, 30*(1), 122–128.

Brandenburger, A. M., & Nalebuff, B. J. (2011). *Co-opetition.* New York: Bantam Doubleday Dell Publishing Group.

Brookfield, S. (1987). *Developing critical thinkers.* Milton Keynes: Open University Press.

Brunnquell, C., Brunstein, J., & Jaime, P. (2015). Education for sustainability, critical reflection and transformative learning: Professors' experiences in Brazilian administration courses. *International Journal of Innovation and Sustainable Development, 9*(3–4), 321–342. doi: http://doi.org/10.1504/IJISD.2015.071858

Brunstein, J., Godoy, A. S., & da Silva, H. C. C. (Eds.). (2014). *Educação para sustentabilidade nas escolas de Administração.* São Carlos: Rima.

Brunstein, J., Sambiase, M. F., & Novaes, M. B. C. (2016). Critical reflection and transformative learning: The development of shared value rationality in the teaching of strategy for sustainability. In *Handbook of sustainability in management education* (1st ed.). Edward Elgar Publishing.

Calder, W., & Clugston, R. (2003) Progress toward sustainability in higher education. *Environmental Law Review, 33*(1), 10003–20023.

Claro, P. B. O., Claro, D. P., & Amancio, R. (2005). Entendemos sustentabilidade em sua plenitude? Análise de fatores que influenciam a interpretação do conceito. *Proceedings from EnANPAD 2005*: XXIX Encontro da ANPAD.

Coelho, J. A. P. M., Gouveia, V. V., & Milfont, T. L. (2006). Valores humanos como explicadores de atitudes ambientais e intenção de comportamento pró-ambiental. *Psicol. Estud, 11*(1), 199–207.

Collins, E., & Kearins, K. (2007). Exposing students to the potential and risks of stakeholder engagement when teaching sustainability: A classroom exercise. *Journal of Management Education, 31*(4), 521–540.

Corazza, R. I. (2005). Tecnologia e meio ambiente no debate sobre os limites do crescimento: notas à luz de contribuições selecionadas de Georgescu-Roegen. *Revista Economia, 6*(2), 435–461.

Corral-Verdugo, V. (2005). Psicologia ambiental: objeto, "realidades" sócio físicas e visões culturais de interações ambiente-comportamento. *Psicologia USP, 16*(1–2), 71–87.

Cranton, P., & Taylor, E. W. (2012). *The handbook of transformative learning: Theory, research, and practice.* New York, NY: John Wiley & Sons.

Cunha, A. G. (1982). *Dicionário Etimológico da Língua Portuguesa.* Editora Nova Fronteira, 2ª edição.

Davis, K. (1960). Can business afford to ignore social responsibilities? *California Management Review, 2*(3), 70–76.

Dawson, L. M. (1969). The human concept: New philosophy for business: Marketing concept outmoded today. *Business Horizons, 12*(6), 29–38.

De Boer, J., Hoogland, C. T., & Boersema, J. J. (2007). Towards more sustainable food choices: Value priorities and motivational orientations. *Food Quality and Preference, 18*(7), 985–996.

Dictionary.com (2016). Unabridged. Retrieved December 5, 2016, from *Dictionary.com* website www.dictionary.com/browse/sustainability.

Dunlap, R. E., & Van Liere, K. D. (1978). The new environmental paradigm. *The Journal of Environmental Education, 9*(4), 10–19.

Dunlap, R. E., Van Liere, K. D., Mertig, A. G., & Jones, R. E. (2000). New trends in measuring environmental attitudes: Measuring endorsement of the new ecological paradigm: A revised NEP scale. *Journal of Social Issues, 56*(3), 425–442.

Elbing, A. O. (1970). The value issue of business: The responsibility of the businessman. *Academy of Management Journal, 13*(1), 79–89.

Freeman, C. (1996). The greening of technology and models of innovation. *Technological Forecasting and Social Change, 53*(1), 27–39.

Gouvêa, R. Q. (2008). Da filosofia dos Valores a uma ciência dos valores. In M. L. M. Teixeira (Ed.), *Valores humanos & Gestão* (pp. 17–52). São Paulo: Editora Senac.

Hibbert, P., & Cunliffe, A. (2015). Responsible management: Engaging moral reflexive practice through threshold concepts. *Journal of Business Ethics, 127*(1), 177–188.

Jacobi, P. (2003). Educação ambiental, cidadania e sustentabilidade. *Cadernos de Pesquisa, 118*(3), 189–205.

Karp, D. G. (1996). Values and their effect on pro-environmental behavior. In R. B. Bechtel (Ed.), *Environment and behavior: An introduction.* Thousand Oaks, Oaks: Sage.

Kearins, K., & Springett, D. (2003). Educating for sustainability: Developing critical skills. *Journal of Management Education, 27*(2), 188–204.

Lotz-Sisitka, H. (2004). Stories of transformation: Guest editorial. *International Journal of Sustainability in Higher Education, 5*(1), 8–10.

Machado, N. J. (1999). *Educação projetos e valores* (Vol. 5). Escrituras Editora e Distribuidora de Livros Ltda.

Martin, C. J., & Upham, P. (2016). Grassroots social innovation and the mobilisation of values in collaborative consumption: A conceptual model. *Journal of Cleaner Production, 134*, 204–213.

Mezirow, J. (1994). Understanding transformation theory. *Adult Education Quarterly, 44*(4), 222–244.

Mezirow, J. (2009). Transformative learning. In J. Mezirow, E. W. Taylor, & Associates (Org.) *Transformative learning in practice: Insights from community, workplace, and higher education* (pp. 18–31). San Francisco: Jossey-Bass.

Nordlund, A. M., & Garvill, J. (2002). Value structures behind pro-environmental behavior. *Environment and Behavior, 34*(6), 740–756.

PRME. (2016). *Principles for responsible management education* – United Nations. Retrieved October 22, 2016, www.unprme.org/index.php

Rimanoczy, I., Kassel, K., & Mitchell, S. (2016). The sustainable mindset: Connecting being, thinking, and doing in management education. *Academy of Management Meeting*, California, USA.

Rohan, M. A. (2000). A rose by any name? The values construct. *Personality and Social Psychology Review, 4*(3), 255–277.

Rokeach, M. (1973). *The nature of human values.* New York: Free Press.

Romeiro, A. R. (2001). Economia ou economia política da sustentabilidade? *Texto para Discussão.* IE/UNICAMP, Campinas, n. 102, set.

Sagiv, L., Sverdlik, N., & Schwarz, N. (2011). To compete or to cooperate? Values' impact on perception and action in social dilemma games. *European Journal of Social Psychology, 41*(1), 64–77.

Schaefer, K., Corner, P. D., & Kearins, K. (2015). Social, environmental and sustainable entrepreneurship research: What is needed for sustainability-as-flourishing? *Organization & Environment, 28*(4), 394–413.

Schultz, P. W., & Zelezny, L. (1999). Values as predictors of environmental attitudes: Evidence for consistency across 14 countries. *Journal of Environmental Psychology, 19*(3), 255–265.

Schwartz, S. H. (1992). Universals in the content and structure of values: Theoretical advances and empirical tests in 20 countries. In M. Zanna (Ed.), *Advances in experimental social psychology.* San Diego: Academic Press.

Schwartz, S. H. (2005). Robustness and fruitfulness of a theory of universals in individual human values. In A. Tamayo & J. Porto (Eds.), *Valores e trabalho [Values and work].* Brasilia: Editora Universidade de Brasília.

Schwartz, S. H. (2013). Value priorities and behavior: Applying a theory of integrated value systems (1–24). In C. Seligman, J. M. Olson, & M. P. Zanna (Eds.), *The psychology of values: The Ontario symposium* Vol. 8 (pp. 1–343), University of Western Ontario. Psychology Press.

Schwartz, S. H., & Bilsky, W. (1990). Toward a theory of the universal content and structure of values: Extensions and cross-cultural replications. *Journal of Personality and Social Psychology*, *58*(5), 878.

Schwartz, S. H., Cieciuch, J., Vecchione, M., Davidov, E., Fischer, R., Beierlein, C., & Dirilen-Gumus, O. (2012). Refining the theory of basic individual values. *Journal of Personality and Social Psychology*, *103*(4), 663.

Shriberg, M. P. (2003). Sustainability in US higher education: Organizational factors influencing campus environmental performance and leadership. *International Journal of Sustainability in Higher Education*, *4*(1), 192.

Simpson, J. A., & Weiner, E. S. C. (1998). *The Oxford English dictionary* (Vol. XIX). Oxford: Oxford University Press.

Springett, D. (2005). Education for sustainability in the business studies curriculum: A call for a critical agenda. *Business Strategy and the Environment*, *14*(3), 146–159.

Sterling, S. (2011). Transformative learning and sustainability: Sketching the conceptual ground. *Learning and Teaching in Higher Education*, *5*(11), 17–33.

Stern, P. C., & Dietz, T. (1994). The value basis of environmental concern. *Journal of Social Issues*, *50*(3), 65–84.

Stern, P. C., Dietz, T., & Guagnano, G. (1998). The new environmental paradigm in social psychological perspective. *Environment & Behavior*, *27*, 723–745.

Stern, P. C., Dietz, T., & Kalof, L. (1993). Value orientations, gender, and environmental concern. *Environment and Behavior*, *25*(5), 322–348.

Svoboda, S., & Whalen, J. (2004). Using experiential simulation to teach sustainability. *Greener Management International*, *48*, 57.

Taylor, E. W., & Cranton, P. (2012). *The handbook of transformative learning: Theory, research, and practice*. John Wiley & Sons.

Thomas, W. I., & Znaniecki, F. (2006). *The polish peasant in Europe and America*. Madrid: Centro de Investigaciones Sociológicas.

Thompson, S. C., & Barton, M. (1994). Ecocentric and anthropocentric attitudes toward the environment. *Journal of Environmental Psychology*, *14*, 149–157.

Torregrosa, R. J. (2004). Social psychology: Social or sociological? In A. H. Eagly, R. M. Boron, & V. L. Hamilton (Eds.), *The social psychology of group identity and social conflict*. Washington: American Psychological Association.

Torres, C., & Neiva, E. R. (2011). *Psicologia Social*. Artmed Editora.

Torres, C. V., Schwartz, S. H., & Nascimento, T. G. (2016). A teoria de valores refinada: Associações com comportamento e evidências de validade discriminante e preditiva. *Psicologia USP*, *27*(2), 341–356.

ULSF. (2010). *Talloires declaration signatories list*. University Leaders for a Sustainable Future. Retrieved September 15, 2016, from www.ulsf.org

UN. (1942). *United Nations declaration*. Retrieved October 25, 2016, from www.un.org/en/sections/history-united-nations-charter/1942-declaration-united-nations/

UN. (2000). *United Nations millennium declaration*. Retrieved October 22, 2016, from www.un.org/millennium/declaration/ares552e.htm

UN_GC. (2016). *United Nations global compact*. Retrieved October 25, 2016, from www.unglobalcompact.org/docs/news_events/8.1/GC_brochure_FINAL.pdf

UN_SD. (2016). *United Nations – sustainable development goals*. Retrieved October 22, 2016, from www.un.org/sustainabledevelopment/

UNESCO. (2012). *United Nations: Rio +20 – the future we want.* Proceedings from Rio+20 United Nations Conference on Sustainable Development, 1–53.

Vaske, J. J., & Donnelly, M. P. (1999). A value-attitude-behavior model predicting wildland preservation voting intentions. *Society & Natural Resources, 12*(6), 523–537.

Verlanken, B., & Holland, R. W. (2002). Motivated decision making: Effects of activation and self-centrality of values on choices and behavior. *Journal of Personality and Social Psychology, 82*(3), 434–447.

Wals, A. E. (2010). Mirroring, gestaltswitching and transformative social learning: Stepping stones for developing sustainability competence. *International Journal of Sustainability in Higher Education, 11*(4), 380–390.

Wals, A. E., & Blewitt, J. (2010). Third wave sustainability in higher education: Some (inter)national trends and developments. In P. Jones, D. Selby, & S. Sterling (Eds.), *Sustainability education: Perspectives and practice across higher education* (pp. 55–74). London: Earthscan.

WCED – World Commission for Economic Development. (1987). *Our common future.* Oxford: Oxford University Press.

Weigel, R., & Weigel, J. (1978). Environmental concern – the development of a measure. *Environment and Behavior, 10*, 3–15.

Wright, T. S. A. (2004). The evolution of sustainability declarations in higher education. In P. B. Corcoran, & A. E. J. Wals (Eds.), *Higher education and the challenge of sustainability: Problematic, promise and practice* (pp. 7–19). Dordrecht: Kluwer Academic Publishers.

4

MOTIVATION FOR THE SUSTAINABILITY MINDSET

Angus W.H. Yip

Part 1: the theories

Background

According to the triple bottom line in corporate sustainability proposed by John Elkington (2004), the traditional bottom line (i.e., profit) is an important element alongside the environmental and social bottom lines. This clearly spells out that achieving corporate sustainability should benefit companies, environment and society. As making profit out of business is one of the three pillars in corporate sustainability (the other two are environment and society), for many business executives making profit (or benefits to companies) has been a strong motivation and legitimate mission to create and maximize shareholder value. Unfortunately, there is always a struggle between the short-term and the long-term because current sacrifices may be needed in exchange for benefits in the longer run: business sustainability is about time (Bansal and DesJardine, 2014). Therefore, motivation is actually a complex issue for practicing sustainability that is worthy of in-depth analysis.

Motivation is of utmost importance in the sustainability mindset model (Kassel, Rimanoczy & Mitchell, 2016) because it leads to business leaders' actions and then to their organization's actions. In the four different dimensions of the sustainability mindset model, namely Ecological World View, Systems Perspective, Emotional Intelligence and Spiritual Intelligence, each of them has its respective dimensional contexts of knowledge (thinking), values (being) and competency (doing). The real impact rests on the actual behavior, i.e., doing. In other words, even when business leaders and their subordinates are well versed in these dimensional contexts, it does not necessarily produce desired actions. The missing link is the motivation, in which there are many internal and external factors that could drive or deter actions. As practicality is at the top of the agenda in management education, most students are eager to learn not only the theories but also their application. Therefore, exploring motivation so as to bridge the gap between mindset and behavior would seem to be crucial in management education for applying concepts to practice.

Scope and limitations

There are numerous frameworks and models of motivation, and this chapter will not describe each of them in detail. Instead, a holistic view is adopted encompassing different drivers (motivators) in motivation. For instance, although "motivation" is a subcomponent of the emotional intelligence content area in values dimension (Kassel, Rimanoczy & Mitchell, 2016), it is more about the intrinsic motivation in the sustainability mindset model. It refers to "the passion to work for reasons that go beyond money or status or a propensity to pursue goals with energy and persistence", but the extrinsic motivation like rewards and punishments also play an important role. In addition, motivation can be at the individual level and at the organizational level, so there are different sets of drivers to be considered before taking action. The selected theories and models cover the motivational issues at both individual and organizational levels and provide insights from different perspectives.

ESG reporting as a case study

A case study approach is appropriate for students to grasp an abstract concept like motivation. Using Environmental, Social and Governance (ESG) reporting, cases can demonstrate the complexity of motivational issues, which allows students to experience the tough journey from a mindset to an action. ESG reporting is also known as sustainability reporting or corporate social responsibility (CSR) reporting, and in many countries it is already a semi-mandatory ("comply or explain") or mandatory requirement for listed companies to issue every year (e.g., U.S., U.K., Australia, China, South Africa, Singapore, Hong Kong, etc.; Hong Kong Exchange, 2015). ESG reporting is used as a case study to explore the motivational problem, especially with small and medium-sized enterprises (SMEs), because most of them may not have sufficient motivation to do ESG reporting due to lack of knowledge and vision (Bansal and DesJardine, 2014). The case study approach makes it easier for students to understand how the theories and concepts are applied in the real world.

A brief history of ESG reporting

ESG reporting addresses the economic, environmental and governance issues. It is used to internalize and improve an organization's commitment to sustainable development in a way that can be shown to various stakeholders (Ioannou & Serafeim, 2014). Social reporting first appeared in The Netherlands and France in the 1970s, and this paved the way for environmental reporting in Austria, Switzerland and Germany (Buhr, 2007). In the 1980s, the negative screening approach based on social ethical performance (i.e., excluding companies based on certain criteria) was adopted by the UK and the US ethical investment funds (Harte, Lewis, & Owen, 1991). The US-based Coalition for Environmentally Responsible Economies (CERES) developed the CERES/Valdez Principles for a set of environmental reporting guidelines after the Exxon *Valdez* disaster in 1989 (Le Lievre, 2009). From the 1990s, riding on the trend of the development of other non-financial measures of firm value (e.g., Kaplan and Norton, 1992), the disclosure became more comprehensive. A well-known retailer, Body Shop International, published its first-ever Values Report in 1995, exemplifying the trend (Sillanpää, 1998). The United Nations Environment Program (UNEP) and CERES launched the Global Reporting Initiative (GRI) in 1997 to develop the triple bottom line reporting guidelines, aiming to make sustainability reporting as rigorous as financial reporting. A growing number of companies began to voluntarily report on sustainability issues starting in the 1990s (Burritt & Schaltegger, 2010). During the 2000s, the growing concern about social inequality and climate change put pressure on companies to disclosure their ESG issues (Kolk, 2003). The financial tsunami in 2008 elicited a general feeling of distrust regarding companies' ability to self-regulate (Roth, 2009), and different stakeholders demanded governments to require more stringent sustainability reporting.

The United Nations Principles for Responsible Investment (UNPRI) launched the sustainable stock exchange initiative, and UNPRI's investors asked the top 30 stock exchanges worldwide to encourage firms to adopt integrated reporting (PRI, 2006). In 2009, South Africa regulators decided to adopt mandatory integrated reporting, with the issuance of the King III Report on Corporate Governance. As of 1 March 2010, the Johannesburg Stock Exchange required companies to submit integrated ESG reports, the first of its kind (Eccles & Saltzman, 2011). Following the Gulf of Mexico oil spill in April 2010, the US government raised expectations for regulation on mandatory sustainability disclosure (White, 2012).

The impact of mandatory ESG reporting

As per the research conducted by Ioannou and Serafeim (2014), who analyzed country and firm-level data from 58 countries, the results show that after the adoption of the mandatory sustainability reporting laws and regulations, the social responsibility of business leaders increases, and both sustainable development and employee training become a higher priority for companies. In addition, corporate governance and ethical practices are enhanced that reduce bribery and corruption and increase managerial credibility (Sullivan, 2009).

Doane (2002) believes that reporting should be regulated by the state in order to protect the citizens and to ensure that the appropriate information is provided. This belief was exhibited later, when Dawkins and Ngunjiri (2008) did a descriptive and comparative analysis of corporate social responsibility reporting in South Africa. In general, the frequency and level of ESG reporting in South African companies was significantly higher than that of the Fortune Global 100, which indicates a greater willingness to convey social responsibility in their disclosure practices. The success can be largely attributed to legal and regulatory measures that compel legitimate business practice (Dawkins and Ngunjiri, 2008).

Despite the successful implementation of mandatory ESG reporting in South Africa, businesses in South Africa have complained that the reporting requirements are too onerous and costly (Rensburg & Botha, 2014). In addition, some companies are disingenuous about sustainability reporting and provide superficial and/or misleading information, as demonstrated by high-profile scandals in recent years, for instance, Parmalat and Enron cases (Dawkins and Ngunjiri, 2008). The disingenuous act to report ESG information may be more serious for SMEs because most of them lack awareness and knowledge of sustainability (Bansal and DesJardine, 2014).

Global sustainability challenge

There is substantial growth in the number of companies reporting their ESG activities. Corporate Register observed that the number of companies that produced CSR-sustainability (or ESG) reports had been growing from less than 2,000 in 2002 to more than 10,000 in 2015 (CorporateRegister.com). The increasing number of companies reporting ESG issues clearly shows the general acceptance of the triple bottom line (Elkington, 1997) as a mainstream practice, though there are a few opposing political views like libertarian and nationalism. The concept of the triple bottom line (economic, social and environmental accounting) requires that a company's responsibility expand to other stakeholders rather than just the shareholders. ESG reporting is a form of commitment made by commercial enterprises towards corporate social responsibility, taking care of social and environmental aspects in addition to economic profit. However, many CFOs and other senior executives are lax about reporting ESG issues. In fact, sustainability reporting has not yet penetrated the corporate world widely or deeply (Hoffelder, 2012).

Hong Kong is a major financial centre in the world and was ranked the first in the global initial public offering (IPO) rankings (*The Wall Street Journal*, 1 December 2015). Taking a closer look, the ESG reporting situation of Hong Kong is similar to that of the West. According to the Hong Kong Exchange (2011), many Hong Kong listed companies were not yet ready to report ESG issues. Hong Kong Exchange (2012) commented that among the 106 responses from the listed companies to the *Consultation Paper on ESG Reporting Guide* (published in December 2011), only 20 respondents (19%) were from issuers. This represents approximately only 1.3% of Hong Kong issuers.

Many companies initiate reporting in order to avoid being perceived as laggards in their sector. Others undertake reporting as a public-relations exercise or because their corporate customers have begun peppering them with questions about ESG performance – these are all defensive approaches (MacLean and Rebernak, 2007). Defensive approaches are a problem because the need to report is not linked to core business strategy and may lead to "green washing".

Though more and more companies report their ESG issues, the impact is superficial, not enough to create the real change of business discourse and paradigm (Ramus and Montiel, 2005). From the consultancy experience of the author, many senior executives of SMEs recognize and agree to the importance of ESG issues, but do not feel the urgency. The author considers that the reason is related to the mindset.

The mindsets are obstacles, a deep and structural challenge. The mindsets are heavily framed by the conventional education system that is overweighting economic benefits (i.e., shareholder orientation and short-termism; Amaeshi and Grayson, 2009). ESG reporting is generally viewed as a longer-term issue, and its urgency is not as immediate as getting a deal done yielding a huge profit.

Specific challenge to SMEs

ESG reporting became mainstream in the last two decades, but it has not trickled down to many smaller companies (Hoffelder, 2012). The situation is worse in SMEs as ESG activities in the companies have still received relatively little attention, and there is a lack of know-how and experience to support the systematic integration of ESG practices in the management process (Dukauskaite, Jonkute, & Staniskis, 2011). ESG issues are complex and uncertain in terms of their boundary (i.e., what is in and what is out), which can make them very difficult to articulate (Amaeshi and Grayson, 2009). In addition, especially some SMEs do not think ESG issues relate to their core business and are reluctant to report due to the added costs and administrative burden, as per the *Consultation Conclusions on ESG Guide* (August 2012) issued by Hong Kong Exchange.

Theories and models for analysis

In order to explore the motivational problem, some relevant theories and models are selected for investigating the different, both internal (intrinsic) and external (extrinsic), drivers. The intrinsic motivators act as a "pulling force" while the extrinsic motivators act as a "pushing force". It is important that these forces are complementary to drive action. The following models offer a more comprehensive view on the nature of motivation, both on the individual and corporate levels. The models on the individual level can be used to deeply understand decision makers' concerns, which in turn will affect organizational behavior. Therefore, the motivators at individual and corporate levels influence one another when making decisions.

Fogg's Behavior Model

Fogg's Behavior Model (Fogg, 2009) focuses at the individual level (Figure 4.1). It shows that three elements – Motivation, Ability and Trigger – must converge at the same moment for a behavior to occur. Motivation and ability can be traded off (i.e.,

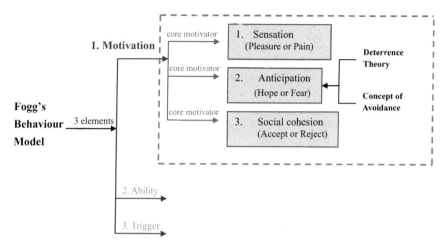

FIGURE 4.1   Combination of Fogg's Behavior Model, deterrence theory and concept of avoidance

if motivation is very high, ability can be low(. The focus of the sustainability challenge in this analysis is motivation, so the element of motivation in Fogg's Behavior Model will be examined in detail.

Fogg's Behavior Model highlights three core motivators: (1) Sensation, (2) Anticipation, and (3) Social Cohesion. Each of these motivators has two sides: Pleasure/Pain for Sensation, Hope/Fear for Anticipation, and Acceptance/Rejection for Social Cohesion.

According to Fogg (2009), the core motivator #1, Sensation (Pleasure/Pain), is an intrinsic factor, it is a primitive response and it functions adaptively in the activities related to self-preservation and propagation of genes. The core motivator #2, Anticipation (Hope/Fear), is characterized by anticipation of an outcome (incident). It is an extrinsic factor because it is the result of an incident. Hope is the anticipation of something good happening, whereas Fear is the anticipation of something bad (e.g., loss). The core motivator #3, Social Cohesion (Acceptance/Rejection), controls much of social behavior and is an extrinsic factor. People are motivated to do things that win them social acceptance or avoid them being socially rejected. Both sides of each core motivator can either facilitate or prevent certain behaviors.

Deterrence theory and the concept of avoidance

Deterrence theory and the concept of avoidance are used for further analyzing the core motivator #2, Anticipation (Hope/Fear). Classical deterrence theory was first formulated by Beccaria (1809) and Bentham (1843) and holds that crime is deterred by threat of punishment. Becker (1968) used economic theory and fiscal psychology to expand the deterrence theory. Becker's neo-classical deterrence theory contends that those considering an illegal act utilize probability of detection and financial value of the penalty to undertake a cost-benefit analysis of the crime.

The concept of avoidance is associated with the general theory of deterrence and is where offenders expend resources on activities to decrease both the chance of detection and any anticipated punishment by reducing the probability of that punishment, or by limiting the penalty if detected (Nussim and Tabbach, 2009). The extrinsic nature of core motivator #2, Anticipation, in Fogg's Behavior Model is connected with Deterrence Theory and Concept of Avoidance as they refer to external incidents; therefore they can be viewed together as a whole (Figure 4.1).

Stakeholder theory

The interconnectivity in the modern economy makes the stakeholder view crucial for understanding different parties' thoughts and taking care of their concerns before making important decisions. In business, stakeholders may be divided into internal and external stakeholders. Internally, they are employees at different levels. Externally, they are shareholders, bankers, customers, suppliers, regulators, trade union, government, NGOs, etc. There are also some less visible but important stakeholders like nature and future generations.

Stakeholder theory presents and explains relationships that are observable in the real world (Donaldson & Preston, 1995). Information is viewed as a major element that can be used by an organisation to manage stakeholders to gain their support or distract their opposition (Gray, Owen, & Adams, 1996). Stakeholder theory tries to systematically articulate which stakeholder(s) deserve or require management attention. There is a right to obtain or an obligation to provide information if responsibility and accountability exist among an organisation and its stakeholders.

Stakeholder analysis starts with the identification of organisational stakeholders that have the right to information and prioritisation of their interest (Gray, 2001). Conflict may exist when it comes to deciding the recipients and the amount of information to be disclosed. There are also conflicting demands from stakeholders with different interests. According to Ullmann (1985), the more critical the stakeholders are to the success and viability of the organisation, the more likely that the organisation will satisfy their demands. In a broader perspective, when nature is understood as a critical stakeholder, as we depend on adequate ongoing natural resources and stable climate conditions to conduct business, it becomes another stakeholder to be satisfied.

Analysis of the motivational problem

According to the Hong Kong Trade and Development Council, SMEs are an important driving force in Hong Kong's economic development. As of December 2015, there were about 317,000 SMEs in Hong Kong. They constituted more than 98% of the territory's business units and accounted for about 46% of private sector employment. The current dilemma is that most SMEs do ESG reporting mainly as a compliance obligation (Arend, 2014). If the reporting is done on voluntary basis, it is not surprising that only a few will do it.

The deeper problem is the real effort and resources put into the reporting even when they do it. As mentioned previously, while many countries' stock exchanges already have the requirement to disclose ESG issues, most SMEs may only fulfil the minimum, and sustainable business practices are not effectively embedded into the operations and business models. The previously discussed conceptual frameworks can be applied to analyse the root causes of the problem and shed light on possible solutions.

From the perspectives of Fogg's Behavior Model, deterrence theory and the concept of avoidance

As to Sensation (Pleasure/Pain), the first core motivator in Fogg's Behavior Model, "Pleasure" is perceived as fulfilling needs, and vice versa. ESG reporting is a more accepted practice for large companies as they may use it to enhance their image and branding. For customers, this creates a sense of loyalty, and for employees a sense of belonging to something they feel proud of. Of course, all of these contribute to the financial benefits to companies. In the case of SMEs, the way they feel the pleasure is to benefit from a good image of corporate citizenship, especially when they want to grow or sell products to larger companies, where stricter supply chain management is in place.

As for the second core motivator, Anticipation (Hope/Fear), key executives are responsible for the penalty if organizations do not comply with the ESG reporting requirement promulgated by stock exchanges. This could act as a "Fear" factor and explains why regulations are so important to drive the reporting action. However, the "Fear" factor may be diluted by the semi-mandatory requirement (i.e., "comply or explain") as some stock exchanges are adopting this, for example, Hong Kong. Under semi-mandatory requirement, no penalty of substance will be imposed for non-compliance. Of course, if companies do not report, they are required to explain the reasons in their annual reports, and they may become target companies for regulators to follow on.

A deeper insight can be obtained by using the Deterrence Theory and the concept of Avoidance: those non-compliant companies will try to deter the negative impacts of non-compliance, and the concept of avoidance suggests that issuing ESG reports could just be viewed as a cost to avoid being targeted by regulators. This may result in issuing a sloppy ESG report because the effort paid by the companies is limited by minimizing the expense on preparing ESG reports in order to achieve the maximum benefit (i.e., not being caught by regulators). This logic applies to SMEs, as they are listed, they need to comply and may be prone to do the same.

A substantiated conclusion can be drawn: that more and more companies, especially the large ones, report their ESG issues in order to build up their reputation (Gomer and Jones, 2010). From the perspective of the third core motivator, Social Cohesion (Acceptance/Rejection), this could create social pressure on key executives to follow. MacLean and Rebernak (2007) pointed out that in the short run many companies' real motive is driven by the defensive attitude (i.e., they do not want to be a laggard in their peer groups). To go further, a possible consequence could be "green washing", which eventually creates even more waste because "form" is now held up over "substance", and the resources might be spent on some ineffective or useless activities.

From the perspective of stakeholder theory

In ESG reporting, stakeholder engagement is an important step for identifying the types of information required by different stakeholders. ESG reports are read not only by shareholders but also by other stakeholders because companies are accountable to different stakeholders in the society. Stakeholder theory explains the motivation from another angle. It is an extrinsic factor that focuses on the interaction among stakeholders, which motivates business leaders to take action in response to their stakeholders' preferences. The more influential the stakeholders are, the more power to influence the management they have.

In the case of ESG reporting, stakeholder theory can be further used to understand the detailed requirements of the stakeholders. Hence the managerial motivation to best respond to the ESG reporting comes from the most influential stakeholder(s). The importance of different stakeholders, their insights and preferences can be established by engaging the stakeholders. This echoes the competency (doing) dimension subcomponent of the Systems Perspective in the sustainability mindset model, as this dimension includes engagement with all relevant stakeholders. The following steps summarise the methodology of engaging stakeholders for ESG reporting:

1   *The key stakeholders and the company's perception of their power over the company may impact the decisions on what and who to disclose in the ESG report.* The company stakeholders can be identified by interviewing the management of the business after explaining the stakeholder definition to them. This process could be done by internal staff or external consultants; it depends on whether the company has the expertise. Then, management's views on the stakeholders' influence and the stakeholders' dependence on the company are collected and prioritized by using the "Stakeholder influence – dependency matrix" (Figure 4.2). As stakeholder engagement is a significant component in ESG reporting, students need to practise this process for application purpose.

2   Conduct in-depth face-to-face/telephone semi-structured interviews by using the sample ESG report content (Table 4.1) with the identified stakeholders to find out what they want to see most from the ESG report.

3   *Data obtained from the interviews is critically analysed; common trends and critical points are highlighted for further discussion.* For example, if "Customers" is the most important key stakeholder of the company, then "Product Responsibility" may be an area of higher concern in the ESG report, so the company is likely to put more effort in disclosing the performance in this area. If "Employees" are the most important stakeholder and their main concern is "Workplace Quality", then more disclosure

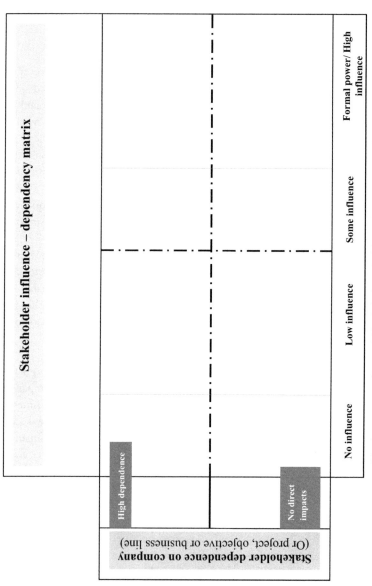

Stakeholder influence – dependency matrix

Stakeholder influence on company
(or objective, project or business line)

No influence | Low influence | Some influence | Formal power/ High influence

Stakeholder dependence on company
(Or project, objective or business line)

High dependence

No direct impacts

FIGURE 4.2 Stakeholder influence – dependency matrix

TABLE 4.1 A sample of areas and aspects in ESG report content

Areas	Aspects
Workplace quality	Working conditions
	Health and safety
	Development and training
	Labor standards
Environmental protection	Emissions
	Use of resources
	The environment and natural resources
Operating practices	Supply chain management
	Product responsibility
	Anti-corruption
Community involvement	Community investment

should be on this area. As there are four aspects under this area, namely working conditions, health and safety, development and training and labor standards, further precise preference on the aspects can be identified through interviews.

The gist of stakeholder theory is to engage your stakeholders because motivation is believed to come from pleasing the stakeholders. This theory can be applied to different tasks, for example, strategy formulation, policy making and implementation. Through the stakeholder engagement process, the key stakeholders are identified and their requirements are clarified, which make the actions taken more focused and effective.

Issues and implications

As for the three core motivators in Fogg's Behavior Model, the main issue lies in the power to facilitate or prevent certain behaviour. For example, the first core motivator, "Sensation" alone, may not be strong enough to facilitate the desired behaviour; the other two core motivators, "Anticipation" and/or "Social Cohesion", need to be used to reinforce the facilitation. Sometimes no single motivator works well alone. Although three motivators together may not always guarantee a success, the overall motivation is more enhanced than when no motivator is adopted.

According to the Model, the other two elements, Ability and Trigger, also play an important role because three elements, Motivation, Ability and Trigger, have to be in place for a behavior to occur. These three elements are mutually reinforcing over a period of time to reach incremental readiness to act (Schein, 2015). The implication for management is that a behavioral change does not originate in one single cause, but it is actually a combination of different elements. This also has an implication in management education: students are required to appreciate the interaction of multiple factors in motivation, and a systems-thinking point of view is needed.

Another management implication is that Motivation and Ability can be traded off (i.e., if motivation is very high, ability can be low). For example, if a person or an organization is motivated enough, they can quickly develop sustainability knowledge and skills. However, according to the author's experience, some complex issues may occur. For instance, if all the stakeholders' opinions support the importance of ESG reporting as a long-term benefit to the subject company, to a certain extent, this should have motivated the management to put more effort and resources in the reporting. But the management of SMEs may think that it could be delayed for a while (i.e., important but not urgent) because they generally cannot see the linkage between ESG reporting and its immediate benefits. It may be that they do not see the immediate threat of not reporting.

Reporting ESG issues as the "Pleasure" motivator seems not strong enough, and this leads us to the importance of the Fear motivator. If the ESG reporting is a semi-mandatory or mandatory one, it should motivate the management to change behaviors. The lack of motivation is characterized by complexity and is sometimes due to the failure to connect the short-term cost and the long-term benefit.

Freedman and Stagliano (1992) pointed out that there may be no single motivation for making a social disclosure; it is probably a consequence of each manager's particular perception of the world she faces. Therefore, understanding the key decision maker's perception of the factor that is of highest concern can lead us to figure out the most crucial motivator.

Stakeholder theory offers a good insight for motivating an organisation, and this theory can enable the students in management education to view the world from different perspectives. Van der Laan (2009) commented that there are two fundamental conceptions or factors forming the basis for organisational responses to solicited disclosure. The first is the amount of power the requesting stakeholder holds in the organisational environment, and the second is the extent to which the organisation perceives the duty to account to the requesting stakeholder. These two factors should be stressed and elaborated in management education. By beginning a stakeholder engagement process to identify key stakeholders and understand their preferred disclosures, organisational motivation can be enhanced.

Understanding management's perspective and motivations are truly helpful. For SMEs, it is common that the management is also the company's owner (e.g., a family-owned business). The decision making is highly centralised, and manager/owner preferences may be dominant and overriding. For example, if the management of a small listed company wants to further raise capital, then "attracting investors" will be viewed as the short-term top priority of the company. This could be a golden opportunity to bridge the long-term and short-term gap by showing that a good ESG report may help to attract institutional investors. Referring to the literature, Emelianova, Ferns, and Sethi (2008) commented that there was a recognition that public perception and trust in corporate messages will have significant long-term impacts. The impacts are on:

- a company's financial viability;
- its access to investment capital, especially from large institutional investors;

- its ability to attract and retain intellectual talent; and
- its ability to gain and sustain strategic competitive advantage in the marketplace.

Institutional investors are more and more interested in using ESG information for their portfolio decisions (Konigs and Schiereck, 2008). When asked if voluntary reporting is investor driven or initiated by the stock exchanges, about 90% were initiated by investors and around 10% were based on exchange effort (Thompson Jr, 2012). Good ESG performance can help companies save costs, enhance staff morale, build up corporate image, reduce risks, and all these are favourable to potential investors.

In a nutshell, linking up management's preference and ESG performance is highly effective to gain management's commitment. Of course, the key is to persuade the management of the linkage. This applies to companies of any size, but it is more prominent for SMEs because of their highly centralised structure. Most SMEs' decision making mainly rests on one key executive, who may be the founder or a major family member.

Last, but not least, practicality also serves as a major motivator, and it belongs to the second core motivator, Anticipation (Hope), in Fogg's Behavior Model. Extrapolating from this second core motivator, being detailed, concrete and quantifiable helps to create hope and make the hope more believable. Taking the example of the small listed company wanting to attract investors by using the ESG report, some practical issues should be outlined and communicated to the management team:

1   *A clear strategy of using the ESG report for attracting potential investors should be discussed with the top management by the internal or external sustainability consultant(s).* This can be achieved by a better communication of the ESG issues to potential investors. A proactive approach should be used when meeting with potential investors, especially institutional investors, by clearly linking the ESG issues to the company's competitive edge, risk management, retention of talents and corporate image, etc.

2   *Using the growth opportunity, always the investors' concern though not a definite result, to motivate the top management to integrate sustainability into their business strategy.* For instance, more resources are put into R&D to advance their production process to further cut down greenhouse gas emissions. This could lead them to outperform other competitors, meeting the future more stringent environmental regulations and create a stronger opportunity to export their products to other developed markets.

3   *Creating a clear mapping of ESG activities that save costs, manage risk and help in talent retention.* A very concrete picture is needed to show how the benefits of ESG activities link up with the company's core competence and competitive edge. This should be presented in a quantified manner showing the ESG report's economic value. The consequence of an ineffective ESG report should also be visualized and quantified.

Conclusion

In order to motivate an organisation, we need to motivate the management and the individuals. This chapter discussed selected theories in relation to the sustainability mindset model, capturing both intrinsic and extrinsic motivators, at individual and corporate levels. Here is the summary of the main learning points:

1   It is usual that no single motivator alone can work well; it has to be a mix of all.
2   Understanding management's want is the first step toward articulating the logic of being sustainable and motivating them to allocate more resources in sustainability.
3   The common barrier of motivating people or organisations to practice sustainability is trading short-term costs for long-term benefits, especially for SME.
4   A linkage between the short-term costs and the benefits of sustainable practice must be shown to gain support from business leaders. This cost-benefit analysis has to be clearly spelt out. For instance, the upfront costs could be offset by short-term cost savings and long-term enhancement of corporate image and branding.
5   Systemic view is important in sustainability policies making and implementation. Stakeholder theory can be used to motivate decision makers and stakeholder engagement is a crucial process for success.
6   Being practical, detailed, concrete and quantifiable can create hope as well as increase the perception of the realisation of hope.

With respect to management education, motivating people is a critical issue for putting mindset to action. Students are encouraged to walk through the methodology through case studies to understand its application.

Part 2: the teaching

Motivation for sustainability mindset – teaching at higher education

This chapter focuses on the Knowing (Head) dimension of the sustainability mindset model. Theories, models and conceptual frameworks of motivation are presented with a case study of ESG reporting. The purpose is to make the abstract concepts more tangible for learning and applying. With the same thought, teaching conceptual texts has to be made interesting for motivating students to stay focused on, retain and apply the concepts learnt from the classroom. A case study approach can achieve the objectives of keeping focus and retaining the concepts.

The theory of motivation is taught in group discussions in class about motivational problems in case studies, for example, "how to motivate commercial firms to stop or prevent them from green washing?", "How to motivate SMEs to practice sustainability?" By applying the theory of Learning by Doing (Anzai and Simon, 1979), each student is required to do an individual project based on a real organization to investigate the existing/potential motivational problem(s) in practicing sustainability. This lets students learn the practicality aspect of enacting the sustainability mindset, which incorporates different dimensions by using different motivators.

The format of teaching this topic is twofold: (1) group discussion to share one another's viewpoints in class and (2) individual projects to let students explore the concepts in the context of the real world. The following sections detail the activities to be conducted in the learning process.

Group discussion

A case is given to each student one week in advance of the lecture; the case is the brief of subject company's general background and the current status of their sustainability performance. After teaching all the theories and models in the first half of the class, a question will be posted, for example, "What might motivate the management to stop green washing?" It must be emphasized to the students that they use the theories and models in their analysis and in the structuring of their answers. The procedure for group discussion is as follows:

- Students are grouped in teams of four to six people each.
- Ten minutes are given for individual reflection.
- Then 30 minutes are allowed for group discussion and preparing the analysis and suggestions by writing on a flip chart.
- Each group sends a representative to present their work to the class in 10 minutes.
- After all groups have finished, it is "Challenge" time for each group – each group needs to spend not more than 5 minutes to answer two questions from the floor.
- The lecturer uses approximately 15 minutes for debriefing.
- Finally, each student has 5 minutes of quiet and personal time to write down the three most important things learnt today as a self-reflection.

Learning outcomes include the deeper understanding of the theories and models taught in class, more thinking and feedback exchanged during the group discussion.

Individual project

The case study approach is again used in this learning-by-doing exercise. Each student needs to base the project on his/her own organisation or must pick an organisation to explore the motivational problem in sustainability. Each student critically analyses the sustainability issue(s) and challenge(s) within the organisation.

For instance, it could be "Lack of green office practices", "Lack of attention in regard to reducing dumping waste in landfills" or "Discrimination in certain areas", etc. The students need to collect relevant information and data from the organisation, interview relevant personnel and, if possible, make a site visit. The motivational problem has to be discussed in detail by using the theories and models taught in class.

The students are assessed on the degree of practicality and effectiveness for the motivational strategies they design for the organisation. The assessment methods include a 20-minute solo presentation with question-and-answer time, and if possible, the organisation is welcomed to join the presentation. Finally, a written report with no more than 3,000 words is required.

Learning outcomes include applying the theories and models by analysing real organisations, collecting primary information and data, encouraging interaction between the student and the organisation.

Note

* SMEs herein this chapter refer to the small/medium capitalized listed companies. They are not constituent stocks of Hang Seng Index, and the top management is generally designated by the largest shareholder.

References

Amaeshi, K., & Grayson, D. (2009). *The challenges of mainstreaming environmental, social and governance (ESG) issues in investment decisions.* Corporate Responsibility, market valuation and measuring the financial and non-financial performance of the firm. Retrieved from http://citeseerx.ist.psu.edu/viewdoc/download?doi=10.1.1.466.1773&rep=rep1&type=pdf

Anzai, Y., & Simon, H. A. (1979). The theory of learning by doing. *Psychological Review, 86*(2), 124.

Arend, R. J. (2014). Social and environmental performance at SMEs: Considering motivations, capabilities, and instrumentalism. *Journal of Business Ethics, 125*(4), 541–561.

Bansal, P., & DesJardine, M. R. (2014). Business sustainability: It is about time. *Strategic Organization, 12*(1), 70–78.

Beccaria, C. (1809), *Essays on crimes and punishment.* Indianapolis: Bobbs-Merrill.

Becker, G. S. (1968). Crime and punishment: An economic approach. *Journal of Political Economy, 76*(2), 169–217.

Bentham, J. (1843). *Principles of penal law.* Edinburgh: Tait.

Buhr, N. (2007). Histories of and rationales for sustainability reporting. *Sustainability Accounting and Accountability,* 57–69.

Burritt, R. L., & Schaltegger, S. (2010). Sustainability accounting and reporting: Fad or trend? *Accounting, Auditing & Accountability Journal, 23*(7), 829–846.

Condon, L. (2004). Sustainability and small to medium sized enterprises: How to engage them. *Australian Journal of Environmental Education, 20*(01), 57–67.

Corporate Register. Retrieved from www.corporateregister.com

Dawkins, C., & Ngunjiri, F. W. (2008). Corporate social responsibility reporting in South Africa: A descriptive and comparative analysis. *Journal of Business Communication, 45*(3), 286–307.

Doane, M. A. (2002). *The emergence of cinematic time: Modernity, contingency, the archive.* Boston, MA: Harvard University Press.

Donaldson, T., & Preston, L. E. (1995). The stakeholder theory of the corporation: Concepts, evidence and implications. *Academy of Management Review,* 20(1), 65–91.

Dukauskaite, D., Jonkute, G., & Staniskis, J. K. (2011). Social responsibility as a tool to achieve sustainable development in SMEs. *Environmental Research, Engineering and Management,* 3(57), 67–81.

Eccles, R. G., & Saltzman, D. (2011, Summer). Achieving sustainability through integrated reporting. *Stanford Social Innovation Review, 59.*

The Edelman Trust (2009). *2009 The Edelman trust barometer.* Retrieved from www.edelman.com/assets/uploads/2014/01/2009-Trust-Barometer-Global-Deck.pdf

Elkington, J. (1997). *Cannibals with forks: the triple bottom line of 21st century business.* BC Canada: New Society Publishers.

Elkington, J. (2004/2013). Enter the triple bottom line. In A. Henriques & J. Richardson (Eds.), *The triple bottom line: Does it all add up* (pp. 1–16). London: Routledge.

Emelianova, O., Ferns, B., and Sethi, S. (2008). In his own words: The effectiveness of CEO as spokesperson on CSR-Sustainability issues – analysis of data from the Sethi CSR monitor. *Corporate Reputation Review, 11*(2), 116–129.

Fogg, B. J. (2009), Persuasive '09 Proceedings of the 4th International Conference on Persuasive Technology, ACM, New York.

Freedman, M., & Stagliano, M. J. (1992). European unification, accounting harmonisation, and social disclosure. *The International Journal of Accounting,* 27(2), 112–122.

Gomer, S., and Jones, A. (2010). Survey: "How companies manage sustainability: McKinsey Global Survey result". McKinsey & Company. Retrieved from www.mckinsey.com/business-functions/sustainability-and-resource-productivity/our-insights/how-companies-manage-sustainability-mckinsey-global-survey-results

Gray, R. (2001). Thirty years of social accounting, reporting and auditing: What (if anything) have we learnt? *Business Ethics: A European Review,* 10(1), 9–15.

Gray, R., Owen, D., & Adams, C. (1996). *Accounting and accountability.* Upper Saddle River, NJ: Prentice Hall.

Harte, G., Lewis, L., & Owen, D. (1991). Ethical investment and the corporate reporting function. *Critical Perspectives on Accounting,* 2(3), 227–253.

Hoffelder, K. (2012, November). The value of sustainability. *Accounting &Tax,* 17–18.

Hong Kong Exchange. (2011, December). *Consultation paper on ESG reporting guide.* Hong Kong Exchange. Retrieved from www.hkex.com.hk/eng/newsconsul/mktconsul/Documents/cp201112.pdf

Hong Kong Exchange. (2012, August). *Consultation conclusions on ESG guide.* Hong Kong Exchange. Retrieved from www.hkex.com.hk/eng/newsconsul/mktconsul/Documents/cp201112cc.pdf

Hong Kong Exchange. (2015, 2015). *Consultation paper on ESG reporting guide.* Hong Kong Exchange. Retrieved from www.hkex.com.hk/eng/newsconsul/mktconsul/Documents/cp201507.pdf

Ioannou, I., & Serafeim, G. (2014). The consequences of mandatory corporate sustainability reporting. *Harvard Business School Research Working Paper No. 11–100.*

Kaplan, R. S., & Norton, D. P. (1992, January/February). The balanced scorecard – measures that drive performance. *Harvard Business Review,* 71–79.

Kassel, K., Rimanoczy, I., & Mitchell, S. (2016). *The sustainable mindset: Connecting being, thinking, and doing in management education.* Paper accepted for presentation at the Academy of Management Annual Meeting 2016, Anaheim, CA.

Kolk, A. (2003). Trends in sustainability reporting by the Fortune Global 250. *Business Strategy and the Environment, 12*(5), 279–291.

Konigs, A., & Schiereck, D. (2008), Intangibles reporting – the financial communication challenge in response to corporate responsibility requirements. *Zeitschrift für Wirtschafts- und Unternehmensethik, 9*(2), 193–195.

Le Lievre, R. (2009). Friedman was right about the corporation, but can the free market solve global warming? In *2009 committee for the Australasian Postgraduate Philosophy Conference Sydney, Canberra* (p. 30).

MacLean, R., & Rebernak, K. (2007). Closing the credibility gap: The challenges of corporate responsibility reporting. *Environmental Quality Management, 16*(4), 1–6.

Nussim, J., & Tabbach, A. (2009). Deterrence or avoidance. *International Review of Law and Economics, 29*, 314–323.

PRI. (2006). *Principles for responsible investment.* Retrieved from www.unpri.org/about

Ramus, C. A., & Montiel, I. (2005). When are corporate environmental policies a form of greenwashing? *Business & Society, 44*(4), 377–414.

Rensburg, R., & Botha, E. (2014). Is integrated reporting the silver bullet of financial communication? A stakeholder perspective from South Africa. *Public Relations Review, 40*(2), 144–152.

Roth, F. (2009). The effect of the financial crisis on systemic trust. Intereconomics, 44(4), 203-208.

Schein, S. (2015). *A new psychology for sustainability leadership: the hidden power of ecological worldviews.* Sheffield: Greenleaf Publishing.

Sillanpää, M. (1998). The body shop values report – towards integrated stakeholder auditing. *Journal of Business Ethics, 17*(13), 1443–1456.

Sullivan, J. D. (2009). The moral compass of companies: Business ethics and corporate governance as anti-corruption tools. *Global Corporate Governance Forum.*

Ullmann, A. A. (1985). Data in search of a theory: A critical examination of the relationships among performance, social disclosure, and economic performance of U.S. firms. *Academy of Management Review, 10*(3), 540–547.

Van der Laan, S. (2009). The role of theory in explaining motivation for corporate social disclosures: Voluntary disclosures vs 'solicited' disclosures. *Australasian Accounting Business & Finance Journal, 3*(4), 15A.

The Wall Street Journal (2015, December 1). Hong Kong is no. 1 again for IPOs globally. Retrieved from www.wsj.com/articles/hong-kong-is-no-1-again-for-ipos-globally-1449120929

White, S. E. (2012). The rising global interest in sustainability and corporate social responsibility reporting. *Thomson Reuter.* Retrieved from http://sustainability.thomsonreuters.com/2012/10/05/the-rising-global-interest-in-sustainability-and-corporate-social-responsibility-reporting/

5

A VALUE-CENTRIC APPROACH TO EUDAIMONIA (HUMAN FLOURISHING) AND SUSTAINABILITY

Radha R. Sharma

Introduction: values and value system for sustainability

The term *values* was derived from the Latin word *valere* in 1300, implying "be strong, be well, be of value". Values have been defined as "the social principles, goals or standards held or accepted by an individual, class, society etc." (www.business dictionary.com). Another perspective defines values as "stable, evaluative beliefs that guide our preference or outcomes or courses of action in a variety of situations" (McShane, Glinow & Sharma, 2011, p. 98). Values are developed by an individual and reinforced in the process of socialization with those the person came in contact with, such as family, friends, teachers, religious institutions, etc., in addition to personal experiences. People generally arrange values in an order of preference referred to as a 'value system'. Thus, people have personal values as well as some shared values in the form of organizational values, team values and cultural values. When personal values match with the dominant organizational values, value-congruence occurs, which leads to employee commitment, job satisfaction and organizational citizenship. However, when there is incongruence between individual and organizational values, the person feels stressed, dissatisfied, burnt out or intends to quit the organization (McShane, Glinow & Sharma, 2011, pp. 100–101). Values and ethics provide the foundation to sustainability in all human endeavors, encompassing economic, social or technological fields. The value-centric approach provides guidance on how to integrate our traditional values with emerging knowledge and modern management. It uses multiple concepts from Greek, Latin and Indian texts and suggests ways to incorporate these into education and business.

According to management scholars Courtice and Van Der Kamp (2013) and Stibbe (2009), subject-specific knowledge is not adequate for managers to deal with sustainability challenges; they need values, dispositions, skills and attitudes to slow down or contain the declining situation. The National Business Ethics Survey

(2014) of the US revealed that effective ethics and compliance programs reduced employee misconduct and improved every key measure of workplace behavior. They found that at large companies with effective ethical programs, 87% of the employees reported violations when they observed them to higher-ups for action, compared to just 32% who report wrongdoing when ethical programs are lacking. Their study also found that perception of ethical leadership is based on the leaders' personal conduct; therefore, they recommended that when hiring a leader, personal character and integrity should be one of the job expectations. This will contribute to the creation of a socially and economically responsible organization, which will protect the dignity of people and promote well-being.

The chapter draws on traditional Western and Indian wisdom throwing light on values and virtues and provides a paradigm for sustainable organizations and society, and ends with a case for use with management students as a curricular exercise aimed at an in-depth exploration of the concepts covered.

The context

Management education's aim all along has been to "prepare the students for managerial roles, to help them gain a better understanding of the industrial and business world and its needs, enrich their skills and provide them with competencies relevant to their careers" (Baruch and Lemming, 1996, p. 27). To impart these skills and to maximize shareholder value, the management institutions focused on providing hard knowledge in functional areas – namely, finance, marketing, operations and others, and some soft skills (Kozminski, 2011). Thus, management education began focusing on providing cutting-edge knowledge, sharpened tools and versatile technology for maximizing economic returns rather than developing a holistic person and a value-centric professional. This focus also got impetus from Milton Friedman (1970, pp. 32–33), who argued that "the social responsibility of business is to increase its profits". In his view a company's responsibility is to its owners (shareholders) and not to society at large; he posited that "only people can have responsibilities" (pp. 122-24).

Globalization, advancing technology, increasing workforce diversity and changing work conditions have accelerated complexity and intensified competition. This has sometimes led to unhealthy competition and unethical practices for business growth which, together with self-serving policies, led to economic crisis, having cascading effects across geographies. This also led to bankruptcies, loss of wealth and jobs, personal miseries and health problems (Sharma & Madan, 2017, pp. 237–258). Ethical violations, financial irregularities, abusive supervision and dysfunctional behavior in organizations have become common features of the contemporary business landscape. While there have been business scandals in the past century too, the recent debacles have drawn attention to values and ethics in education, as educational institutions are supposed to lay the ethical foundation of the future workforce (Ferrell & Ferrell, 2014). There have been scathing attacks on curriculum, pedagogy, unhealthy competition among various internal stakeholders, institutional culture and even leadership in higher education in general and management education in particular. Critics have accused business schools of teaching ways to bend the rules to make the numbers, while others have maintained that business schools gloss over ethical conduct in examining business transactions and might go so far as to encourage students to bypass policies, procedures and even the law, to ensure favorable financial results (Bontis & Mould-Mograbi, 2006). One observes that the emphasis of management education, so far, has been on the 'knowing component' and less on the 'doing' and 'being components' (Datar, Garvin & Cullen, 2010). The 'knowing dimension' in the context of sustainability was later highlighted by Rimanoczy, (2014). Based on Datar et al.'s study of 31 European and 17 American leading business schools, they have recommended a right balance of the 'doing component' and the 'being component'. While the doing component is based on practice involving skills and capabilities, the being component deals with self-awareness and reflection on values and beliefs that come from developing the 'being'. The focus on the being component for personal development and motivation will enable the students to connect with the full range of people in the organization they will work with, or in the case of executives it will improve their relations with their colleagues.

How values impact the 'being dimension'

Values find manifestation in behavior and have been described as espoused values and enacted values (Argyris and Schon, 1996; Kabanoff & Daly, 2002). Espoused values are manifestations of an organization's core morals, which may be developed into a code of conduct. Espoused values are what we say that we would do at an individual or organizational level, but sometimes people in the corporate world do not practice what they preach, and their enacted values do not abide by espoused corporate values. In some cases, leaders abide by the espoused organizational values but the lower-level employees do not show commitment to these espoused corporate values, which affects the organization's image.

Enacted values are the manifestation of the values which guide our decisions and behavior. The congruence between espoused and enacted values is essential for people in leadership roles, as a gap between the two undermines their perceived personal integrity, leadership effectiveness and organizational sustainability. It is observed that organizations adopt sustainability practices not only for economic returns but also for concern for society and the environment. Thus, organizations need to incorporate a triple bottom line (people, profit and planet) approach in their espoused values and ensure that these are enacted by all the employees.

Values have been classified in different ways. Social psychologist Rokeach (1973) categorized the list of values into two: (1) instrumental values which signify the means and (2) terminal values which signify the ends. According to Rokeach, based on their value orientation, people adopt means (instrumental values) to reach their goal. These means may be ethical or unethical. Building on Rokeach's classification, Schwartz (1992) and his colleagues have identified 57 values and have classified these into 10 categories and two bipolar dimensions (Table 5.1).

TABLE 5.1 Schwartz's classification of values

Openness to change cluster	←——→ *Conservation cluster*
Self direction (creativity, independent thought)	Conformity-tradition (adherence to social norms)
Stimulation (excitement and challenge)	Security (safety and stability)
Hedonism (self-indulgence/gratification)	

Self transcendence	←——→ *Self enhancement*
Universalism (concern for welfare of all people and nature)	Achievement (pursuit of personal success)
Benevolence (concern for others in one's life)	Power (dominance over others)
	Hedonism (self-indulgence/gratification)

Source: Adapted from Schwartz, 1992 and Schwartz, & Sagie, 2000.

As described in Table 5.1, individuals would have a dominant orientation for one or the other type of values and will behave accordingly in most situations. Thus, values direct an individual's behavior. However, three conditions have been identified (Maio, Olson, Lindsay & Bernar, 2001) that can strengthen the association between personal values and behavior. These are (1) reminding or re-stressing the values (e.g., respect for others, generosity); (2) a logical reason for applying a specific value in a specific situation (e.g., switching off lights when leaving one's office room to save energy); and (3) a situation that facilitates applying our values (e.g., openness to culture by promoting cultural diversity in teams). Thus, the values that are recognized by leaders or other influential individuals in an organization are likely to be adopted by most of the employees. Similarly, the values of quality, customer centricity and gender equality displayed and frequently communicated in the organization get strengthened among employees (Debruyne & Dullweber, 2015).

A study by Chandrakumara (2011) in the Australian context revealed dynamic relationships between values and management practices, and behavioral and performance outcomes. The study used values as an independent, dependent and a moderator variable. The findings yielded that managers and leaders need to understand the changing patterns of values pertaining to different generations of employees and adapt themselves and their organizations accordingly.

Values are related to the norms of a culture, but they are more global and abstract than the norms. Norms are rules for behavior in specific situations, whereas values identify what should be judged as good or evil. Cultures vary in values and people reflect different values. Due to this, people may take part in a ceremony even if their personal values do not match. If a group member expresses a value that is in serious conflict with the group's norms, the group's authority may carry out various ways of encouraging conformity or stigmatizing the non-conforming behavior of its members. Therefore, if organizational leadership advocates and promotes values for green management, respect for diversity and gender equality, then the culture of the organization will develop accordingly, and people in the organization will develop sustainability mindset.

Development of ethics and values

Derived from the Greek word 'ethos', *ethics* means custom, habit, character or disposition. It refers to guidelines or rules that are developed for a society, an organization or an individual (BBC www.bbc.co.uk/ethics/introduction/intro_1.shtml). Ethics is defined as "the science of the ideal human character" or "the science of moral duty" (Rushworth, 2003, p. 63), a moral principle or code. Thus, business ethics becomes the application of these moral codes in all business transactions, not only by the corporation but also by its employees, in a manner that establishes transparency and trust in the organization.

Values are described as the guiding principles in one's life (Ross, Schwartz & Surkiss, 1999). Values, as defined in earlier paragraphs, are broad preferences concerning appropriate courses of action or outcomes. As such, values reflect a person's sense of right and wrong or what "ought" to be (e.g., "Equal rights for all", "Excellence deserves admiration", and "People should be treated with respect and dignity" are representative of values). Values tend to influence attitudes and behavior.

Personal values

These values are acquired from various sources during the process of development. The foundation for values is laid within an individual's family, which inculcates the value of distinguishing what is right and wrong long before other influences come in life. A child generally reflects the values of the parents (Siegel & Kohn, 1959). Once the child goes to school, his/her interaction with teachers and peers begins to shape his/her values. If the family follows a religion, the teachings of the religion affect what is valued as right and wrong behavior. According to Massey (1979), a child is not born with values but acquires these in three distinct periods: (a) imprint period from birth to 7 years, (b) modeling period from 8–13 years, where the child generally imitates others, and (c) socialization period from 13–21 years, where peers play a significant role in the formation of values.

Thus, the personal values acquired during these periods become reference points regarding goodness, appropriateness, importance, usefulness or desirability of a behavior. Values are the guiding principles in one's life. In other words, 'value' acts as a bridge for an individual's decision between good or bad, right or wrong, and the most important or least important issue. As such, an individual's value system guides and helps him/her solve common human problems by comparative rankings of values. In this way, how a person would behave in a given situation would fit into this pattern if we know his/her value system.

Consequently, personal values in group functioning take the form of cultural values, which may be in agreement with or divergent from prevailing norms. The cultural values evolve over a period of time and provide cultural reference to assess an individual's values, as these are largely shared by their members. Some of the personal values which are important for lasting relationships and sustainability mindset are described as follows

Empathy

The most important value in our life revolves around empathy to build lasting relationships. Empathy is the capacity to understand what another person is experiencing from within the other person's frame of reference (Bellet & Michael, 1991). We need to be able to accept others for who they are, rather than what they can do for us. We focus on how we can grow together rather than how to grow at the cost of others. In cross-cultural settings, empathy assumes a greater significance for humanistic behavior. Trevisani (2005) has provided four dimensions for using an empathic component in the intercultural context:

> *Behavioral empathy*: Ability to understand the nature and cause of a single or a chain of behaviors of a different culture.
> *Emotional empathy*: Ability to feel the emotions of others from a different culture. Also appreciate the intensity of emotions when these are expressed in public and private. It also involves understanding how emotions are linked with people or situations.
> *Relational empathy*: Ability to understand the relationship patterns in different cultural contexts. Whether relationship is voluntary or mandatory, who are the decision makers and decision influencers and how they can affect professional decisions.
> *Cognitive empathy*: Understanding the mental frameworks of people from another culture which reflects their cultural values, beliefs, ideologies and behavior.

Mutual Respect

One problem which comes in the way of sustainability of an organization or society is human conflict resulting from disagreement, misunderstanding and lack of respect for diversity (Mortensen, 2005, pp. 62–63). Mutual respect is described as proper regard for the dignity of a person or position, which forms the basis for trust, meaningful communication and interpersonal relationships. Mutual trust and respect are pre-requisites for open communication and honest dialogue about values, goals and expectations. It can be observed when two people do not agree on everything but don't get ruffled by small disagreements and are willing to work things out because they care for each other. Mutual respect also manifests in gender equality and respect and appreciation of cultural diversity in social and organizational settings.

Love

"If there is one substance by which everything is held together and you want to give it a name, you can call it love. It is the basis of all existence "His Holiness Sri

Sri Ravi Shankar (2005, p. 5). Love has a variety of connotations, including feelings, emotions, attitude, attraction, interpersonal affection or attachment. The value system that builds strong relationships is based on sacrificial love for others. Instead of focusing on only one's own desires, one also needs to consider the needs of the other person. Sacrificial love demands one's willingness to give up something in order to fulfil the other person's desire. This reduces conflicts and develops lasting relationship. Psychologically, love is considered to be the basis for human bonding. Love is not only interpersonal but could also be impersonal (e.g., love for goals or principles which people greatly value and are deeply committed to, such as passion for green management, equitable society and gender equality) (His Holiness Sri Sri Ravi Shankar, (2005, pp. 6–10).

Honesty

Honesty is one of the most personal values (Sharma, 2010; Sharma & Taneja, 2011). It is a moral characteristic which manifests in words and actions such as truthfulness, integrity, straightforwardness and is valued (Wikipedia). Honest people are trustworthy and are preferred as employees, colleagues and friends. Honest people admit their flaws and work towards improving themselves. They enjoy a good reputation and build organizational reputation, too. Honesty helps in procurement of appropriate quality of material, ethical marketing and building organizational brand. In recent years, one has observed that many companies have lost not only their reputation but also their business because they did not pursue honesty in their functioning. Thus honesty, as a value, is essential for reputation and survival of an employee, and for brand equity and the sustainability of an organization.

The Indian perspective on values

Purushartha: a holistic view

Purushartha, a concept derived from Indian scriptures (*Vedanta, Mahabharata*), implies desired and desirable "object of human pursuit" or valid goals of life, which are pursued or 'ought to be' pursued by people (Hiriyanna, 2000, pp. 1–10). We find a number of examples of this in ancient Indian scriptures *viz.*, *Ramayana* and *Mahabharata*. *Ramayana* is an epic which narrates the journey of *virtue* to annihilate vice. The *Mahabharata* contains philosophical material, such as a discussion of the four "goals of life" or *purusharthas*.

These are also referred to as four classifications of human values, pursuance of which makes one's life meaningful. The four *purusharthas* are:

1   *Dharma* (principles, the norms, righteousness and moral values)
2   *Artha* (acquisition of wealth, power, fame, prosperity and economic values)
3   *Kama* (pleasure, love, fulfillment of desires for sensuous pleasures, psychological values)
4   *Moksa* or *Moksha* (liberation, spiritual values)

In the context of the *purushartha* concept, *dharma* is not religious beliefs and practices, but a system of ethical and human values for holistic pursuit of life or deriving meaning in life. *Artha*– money is not only a means for some security, but it is also a means for getting the pleasures and comforts of life. The best way to acquire money is to specialize in a particular field which is compatible to one's nature and capacities in an ethical way, which also is a means to serve the society. Though *artha* and *kama* are desirable human pursuits for pleasure in life, these need to be regulated by *dharma*. Accordingly, all human pursuits, whether personal or collective, ought to be in conformity with the norms of *dharma*, implying that ethics and morality need to be adopted in earning money and also while indulging in pleasures of life.

The *purushartha of dharma* has a wide scope, and it emphasizes personal as well as social values involving virtues, duties, rights, laws, right conduct, obligation to others, a sense of responsibility for 'doing good' to others and not harming them. Thus, the inner urge to do the right thing is far stronger than external controls, regulations and law imposed for responsible behavior.

Artha and *kama purusharthas* have an inherent tension, thus the scholars proposed "action with renunciation" or "craving-free, *dharma-driven action*", called *Nishkam Karma* to resolve the tension (Dharma, 2013). A mind free from all the worries, a sense of wanting, insecurity and fear, hankerings and egoistic problems can have blissful experience – *moksha*, which literally means *liberation*. Such a state of existence alone is real freedom; liberation is not to be confused with a state to be attained after death. The acceptance of *moksha* as a life goal and life value involves faith in the existence of a transcendental reality. Mother Teresa is an excellent example of pursuing *moksha*. Not all human beings can aspire for *moksha*, but if they pursue their life goals of *artha* and *kama* with *dharma*, it will result in positive socio-economic change and will promote human dignity and well-being (Hiriyanna, 1932, 2000). This can be explained with the help of stories from Ramayan (Indian scripture) or fables from different cultures.

At the societal level, *dharma* regulates the conduct of those who are in public/corporate governance. In the Indian scriptures such as *Ramayana* and *Mahabharata*, the ethical guidance for exercise of state powers was termed as *rajdharma* (*raj* = *state* + *dharma* = *duty*). The guiding value of *rajdharma* is *nyaya* (i.e., justice). The duty of a king/ruler was to establish a just social order and to work for the security and well-being of his people. It is noteworthy that *dharma* in the Indian wisdom tradition was not linked to any religion; rather, it was a secular idea, and decisions were taken after considerable moral deliberation, keeping in view the '*kala*' meaning time and '*desh*' implying demand of the situation.

The question arises how to integrate these concepts in the modern curriculum. The most effective way would be to integrate the holistic worldview and human values in the curriculum, which currently focuses on imparting of general and specialized knowledge and skills. Evidence of integrating this with the curriculum can be found in the ancient Indian gurukula system of education, and in the ancient Indian universities of *Takshashila*, *Vallabhi*, *Nalanda*, and *Vikramshila*, which flourished from the 7th century BC to the 11th century AD (http://indiansaga.com/history/golden_education.html, accessed on July 10, 2016).

This experiment was tried in modern times by two luminary Indians *viz.*, Madan Mohan Malaviya and Rabindranath Tagore (both born in 1861), who incorporated holistic and universalistic Indian ideas and values systems in their philosophy of education. Malaviya (Bharat Ratna, a recipient of the highest civilian honor in India), inspired by the ancient Indian '*gurukula*' system of education and the tradition of great Indian universities, established a residential university, Banaras Hindu University (BHU), in 1916. The university offers the latest knowledge of science and technology along with traditional Indian knowledge in *Sanskrit Vidya* (Sanskrit literature), *Dharma Vigyan* (science of religion), *Sankaya* (one of the six leading systems of Hindu philosophy involving yoga, meditation, etc.), and *Ayurveda* (traditional science of Ayurvedic medicine). The unique feature of the university has been the teaching of *dharma* to all the university students for building their moral character, arousing patriotic feelings for serving the society and connecting them with their cultural heritage.

But after Indian independence and adoption of secular principles, the teaching of *dharma* was discontinued, as it was considered to be linked with religion. *Artha*, creating wealth beyond need, is always very tempting to individuals; therefore, *artha* needs to be governed by *dharma*.

The other luminary, Tagore, laid emphasis on the emotional and aesthetic aspects of personality to develop, among students, universal human sensitivities and sensibilities. "Sensibility" is likely to be emotional or moral in nature and has internal orientation, whereas sensitivity has to do with senses and is mostly externally oriented. His vision resulted in the founding of a unique institution of higher learning, the university of Visva Bharati in 1921.

> Visva-Bharati represents India where she has her wealth of mind which is for all. Visva-Bharati acknowledges India's obligation to offer to others the hospitality of her best culture and India's right to accept from others their best.
> *(Tagore, www.visvabharati.ac.in/, retrieved on May 20, 2017)*

The objective of the foregoing discussion on the *purushartha* scheme of life for socio-economic well-being and linking it with education was to highlight that *purushartha*-based values provide a conceptual base for developing a holistic viewpoint to live, relate and grow in the present world. The global economic crisis, despite all the scientific and technological knowledge, and conflicts in various parts of the world, manifest the deficit of a *common dharma*. A global philosophy of human, social and ecological well-being can be developed by creatively integrating the Western and the Eastern concepts and ideals. Equally important is attitude change through value education.

Virtue, practical wisdom and eudaimonia

A virtue has been described as a character trait or an enduring tendency (e.g., generosity or honesty), a disposition which has many facets. Virtue has been an area of research in psychology, and by the mid-20th century, research on personality had overlapping interest in character. Allport (1921; Allport & Vernon, 1930) stressed the need for separating personality and character to make the study of personality traits scientific and relegating virtue and character as subject matter within ethics. However, the Five Factor Model of personality included the two traditional virtues 'Agreeableness' (A) and 'Conscientiousness' (C) (Digman, 1990). There has been increasing interest in virtues and good life (explained later) in psychology (Fowler, 2005; 2010). MacIntyre (1984) posited that "the concept of the good life is prior to the concept of a virtue", highlighting that Aristotle began *Nicomachean Ethics* (NE) with eudaimonia (human flourishing). The rationale behind this was that virtues are character excellences or signature strengths that enable one to pursue a good life in the form of acquiring knowledge or having a social network or helping one to flourish as a human being (Fowers, 2010a).

Psychologists who do research on virtues focus on a single or a list of virtues. Virtues are associated with emotions and emotional reactions, values, desires, choices, perceptions, interests, attitudes, expectations and sensibilities (Stanford Encyclopedia, 2003). Mere possession of the trait and being honest due to 'fear of being caught' or to make one look good in a situation is not enough to identify a person as honest. Rather, one needs an honesty mindset where there is a range of considerations to be honest, and a conviction and whole-hearted acceptance that to behave otherwise would be dishonest. Additionally, virtue would manifest in supporting a right cause, emotional reaction to honest situations, choice of honest friends, dislike and disapproval of dishonest behavior, deploring dishonesty and the like. Therefore, in view of the multi-faceted nature of the virtue, it may not be appropriate to base one's judgement about one's virtue on a single incident or behavior without knowing the intention behind the action (Sreenivasan, 2002). Similarly, it may be difficult to find a person with a perfect virtue (e.g., generosity, as the person may not be generous in every single situation) (Athanassoulis, 2000). Thus, people have varying degrees of a virtue; someone with a higher degree of a virtue could be called fairly virtuous. There are a few ancient concepts such as phronesis (practical wisdom), eudaemonia (human good/flourishing), and modern developments in psychology such as positivity (Robinson, 1999) and signature strengths described in the following paragraphs which need to be intertwined with ethics and values for developing a sustainable mindset in the personal, social and organizational life.

Phronesis is Greek word that refers to a type of wisdom or intelligence translated as 'practical wisdom' or prudence. According to Aristotle, "phronesis is both necessary and sufficient for being virtuous; because phronesis is practical" (http://en.wikipedia.org/wiki/Phronesis, accessed on February 4, 15); it is concerned with how to behave in specific situations. While an individual can learn the principles of behavior and action, due to unfamiliarity with a situation, one may behave in a way which may offend or hurt others; therefore, one requires experience of that context. For smooth relationship with stakeholders inside and outside the organization, practical wisdom is important.

Practical wisdom, then, is the knowledge or understanding that enables its possessor to appropriately and intelligently act in any given situation. The lack of wisdom may manifest itself in insensitive remarks or impulsive or short-sighted behavior, which may have repercussions for the people involved or may lead to a conflict. It has been observed that infrastructure development projects often involve cutting of trees and taking possession of green areas which irritate local people. Even though approved by the competent authority, it may lead to agitation or violence, if not handled tactfully. It would be prudent to discuss the matter with the stakeholders involved and offer alternatives before destroying the green field. Ignoring stakeholders, then, will not be an appropriate mindset for sustainability. Practical wisdom to behave appropriately in a situation, therefore, is equally important in maintaining positive and long-term relationships.

Eudaemonia or *eudemonia* is a Greek word made up of two words *eu* ("good") and *daimon* ("spirit"). It has been described in several ways. A perusal of Aristotle's works reveals that in the Greek tradition *eudaimonia* was used to imply the highest human good. In Aristotle's view, virtue and its exercise are the most important constituents in *eudaimonia*. Thus, to direct a person's desires and actions to *eudaimonia*, the rational part of the mind must appeal to emotions and spirits. For example, a person engaging in rape for self-pleasure may not realize the horrible consequences of it on the victim, but when he is shown the consequences of such an incident on a video, he can develop feelings of guilt and remorse to such an extent that he may totally transform. In order to develop a sustainability mindset, people need to be exposed to the consequences of their lack of concern for society and environment.

In moral philosophy, *eudaimonia* has been used to describe the right actions as those that result in the *well-being* of others, emphasizing *well-being* (Robinson, 1999). In Positive Psychology, it refers to a contented state of being healthy, happy and prosperous. It has also been used to imply happiness or welfare; another translation suggested by Robinson (1999) is "human flourishing". Thus, *eudaimonia* can be considered a theory that places the personal happiness of a person and one's complete life at the core of *ethical concern* (Eudaimonia, 2015).

Hence, to bring about a change in people's attitude, a change agent needs both positive and negative approaches for guiding them to the right path. An example of this could be that people need to be made aware of the consequences of global warming, ethnic conflict or child abuse, etc. Adopting Plato's approach of showing horrendous pictures or reports of the consequence can make people feel guilty and change their mindset or course of action. Alternatively, showing the positive effects of human flourishing will promote happiness and well-being. Thus, faculty in business schools can incorporate YouTube videos and documentaries featuring examples of businesses as agents of world benefit, or engage the students in initiatives such as AIM2 Flourish.com, where students identify profitable entrepreneurs that work for the greater good. Incorporating these tools in their teaching methodology, professors can sensitize students to the Sustainable Development Goals (SDGs) and facilitate development of a sustainability mindset among them (Rimanoczy, 2017). These tools can also be used during management development programs for managers and industry professionals for promoting a sustainability mindset. Even social entrepreneurship can be developed around it.

Leveraging positive psychology and signature strengths for sustainability

For the greater part of the 20th century, Psychology, as a subject, dealt with the study of the weaknesses and pathologies of the human mind. These led to the development of effective diagnosis and treatment for many mental disorders, but in this pursuit a significant part of psychology was overlooked. The part that deals with the inherent strengths of the human mind and the further improvement thereof is called positive psychology. Positive psychologists are concerned with:

* positive experiences
* enduring psychological traits
* positive relationships
* positive institutions

The movement started when University of Pennsylvania psychologist Martin Seligman (1999), during his presidency of the American Psychological Association, set Positive Psychology as the theme for his term. Subsequently, the first Positive Psychology Summit took place in 1999 and later the First International Conference on Positive Psychology in 2002. Positive Psychology evolved from humanistic psychology derived from the work of psychologists like Abraham Carl Rogers (1980), Erich Fromm (1997), and Maslow (1999). Its link can also be seen with various religions, philosophies and cultures in the foregoing paragraphs, which discuss happiness and satisfaction but differ in the values for their attainment.

Seligman and Csikszentmihalyi (2000) posited that the focus of psychological theories needed to change from deficits to virtues. They observed that psychology, as a science, began contributing to healing, resilience and strength since World War II. Seligman (1998, 1999) advocated that three areas needed to be explored in Positive Psychology, with focus on positive personal and interpersonal traits, positive experiences, and positive institutions and communities, which he referred to as a 'strengths' approach. If one wanted to enhance positive personal experiences, one needed to focus on positive personal and interpersonal traits. Seligman (2002) posits that 'authentic happiness' includes positive emotions and, more importantly, meaning and engagement. Thus, authentic happiness can be achieved indirectly by living an engaged and meaningful life using one's strengths.

Signature strengths are "(s)trengths of character that a person consciously owns, celebrates and exercises every day in work, love, play and parenting" (Seligman, 2002, p. 89). In other words, it is the ability of an individual to give consistent and high/excellent performance in a given activity. Signature strengths are innate and are demonstrated by ownership, authenticity, yearning and expression of zest and enthusiasm while using these, resulting in a rapid learning curve and creation of projects around these strengths. Other strengths can be increased by an individual by focused efforts and dedication. These strengths can help an individual's development if one (a) identifies one's strength/s; (b) integrates it/them by self-reflection and finds ways to put these to use; and (c) changes one's behavior accordingly. Even organizations can use the strengths of their employees to enhance the employee engagement (Black, 2001), customer loyalty and employee retention and enhanced performance (Harter and Schmidt, 2002). When a strength is put to use, not only does the performance improve, but the individual derives positive personal experience, as well.

Dahlsgaard, Peterson, and Seligman (2002) have evolved a list of 24 strengths and categorized these under six virtues.

A perusal of Table 5.2, with content adapted from Dahlsgaard et al., reveals that 24 strengths have been classified under six virtues of human goodness, which are referred to in philosophical/religious discussions as well. The strengths under Wisdom & Knowledge are cognitive in nature; the strengths under Courage are emotional strengths; those under Humanity & Love are interpersonal in nature; and those under Justice are civic strengths. The strengths under Temperance protect a person from engaging in excesses and involve forgiveness, humility, prudence and self-regulation.

TABLE 5.2 Values in Action (VIA) classification of character strengths

Wisdom & Knowledge (cognitive)	Courage (emotional)	Humanity & Love (interpersonal)	Justice (civic)	Temperance (protecting excess)	Transcendence (connecting to larger universe & providing meaning)
Creativity, originality	Bravery/ valour	Intimacy/ reciprocal attachment	Citizenship/ duty loyalty/ teamwork	Forgiveness/ mercy	Appreciation of beauty/ excellence
Curiosity/ interest	Industry/ perspective/ diligence	Kindness/ generosity/ nurturance/ altruism	Fairness/ equity	Modesty/ humility	Gratitude
Judgement/ active open-mindedness	Integrity/ honesty/ authenticity	Social intelligence	leadership	Prudence/ caution	Hope/ optimism
Love & learning	Vitality/zest/ enthusiasm			Self regulation/ self control	Playfulness/ humour
Perceptive					Spirituality/ religiousness/ sense of purpose

Source: Adapted from Dahlsgaard, K; Peterson, C. and Seligman, MEP (2002, 2005).

Similarly, the virtue of Transcendence enables one to connect to the larger world and provides meaning in life. This is facilitated by strengths of appreciation, gratitude, optimism, humor, spirituality and sense of purpose. Schwartz and Sharpe (2006) have commented that strengths and virtues should be understood as integrated and not independent. Also, a very high virtue is not necessarily better because it may produce deformations of character (e.g., a person may be modest but too much of modesty may be mistaken as a weak personality), and therefore people should strive for an average level of virtues. They stressed that practical wisdom is a master virtue, which can orchestrate other virtues to deal with problems of specificity (specific case), relevance (specific context) and conflicts and make life happy and effective. Practical wisdom, as discussed earlier, needs to be integrated with one's signature strengths to be happy and effective in dealing with situations.

Awareness programs are being run by students for recycling papers, sorting garbage according to being biodegradable/non-degradable, and fair trade practices in various countries, as a part of PRME and CSR initiatives of academic institutions. In India, students have been engaged in generating awareness about the harmful effects of fireworks by promoting 'saying no to crackers', which last for weeks during festive seasons, as a means to promote clean air for good health and to protect from environmental pollution. This has brought down sales of firecrackers and fireworks substantially (Sahay, 2012). School children collect newspapers for recycling, use car pools, avoid use of plastic bottles, carry water bottles, and use paper bags instead of plastic bags, all of which are yielding good results. Integrating traditional and modern values from across cultures, not only in curricula, and sharing these through mass and social media will facilitate change in the mindset in this interconnected world and lead to a sustainable society. The case at the end of the chapter, 'A part-time job with full-time challenge', will develop a better understanding of the phenomenon.

Just as there are individual virtues, there are also organizational virtues, such as moral goals or a values-based culture. It is not just pursuance of economic goals which will lead to organizational sustainability, but also organizational virtues and organizational culture which provide fulfillment to its members and ensure the well-being of people in the organization. It is possible for an organization to be profitable without virtue (cf., Cameron & Kazaa, 2002), but this will not lead to organizational sustainability in terms of continued effective existence. Business and leadership need to focus beyond "wealth creation for shareholders" to "wealth creation for the optimal benefit of all the stakeholders" including shareholders, employees, customers, community, nature, society and future generations. This can be possible by adopting a value-centric approach right from the early stages of life, which will provide a foundation to personal values and pursuance of *purushartha* in personal and professional life. Virtues, signature strengths and practical wisdom will improve interpersonal relations and develop positivity at the workplace, which will promote employee well-being and human flourishing. At the organizational level, these qualities will facilitate alignment between espoused and enacted values and will promote a value-based organizational culture, where organizational functions will be discharged with integrity and responsibility, which in turn will lead to brand equity and organizational sustainability.

Summary

Organizations have been undergoing metamorphosis over the years due to liberalization of the economies, increasing global business and trade combined with misuse of technology and social media, exposure to a variety of unethical practices and cyber-crimes, which has led to a decline in values in the society. Also, traditional values are eroding, institutions of family and marriage are giving way to divorces and new forms of relationships, causing emotional and social insecurity and workplace problems. Consequently, anxiety, depression, aggression and delinquency are on the rise, and violence is taking place at institutions, organizations and in the society (Sharma & Cooper, 2017: 4–5).

As spiritual teachings and religious values have taken a back seat in a multicultural world, values need to be imparted through the curriculum in educational institutions from early stages to higher education levels. This is imperative for management education, which prepares students for business and industry. In this context, the values of honesty, mutual respect, compassion, gender equality, cultural diversity and practical wisdom have assumed great significance. It is natural for the youth of today to look for happiness, but authentic happiness will come from their engagement with meaningful work, purpose or activities using their signature strength. Concern for others and a sense of responsibility towards various stakeholders, including the environment, are important in a globally connected world. Social awareness can be created about values and ethics and the consequences of not adhering to these, using social media and other technologies as effective tools. The traditional Western and Indian wisdom throw light on values and virtues and provide a paradigm for sustainable organizations and society.

Class exercise

Please go through the case, form small groups and discuss the questions given at its end. Having discussed in small groups, share the analysis with the whole class and gain insight about:

1   How do values affect an individual's behavior?
2   How do values/ethics of employees can impact sustainability of an organization?
3   What measures should an organization adopt to promote values and ethics in an organization?

The part-time job with a full-time challenge[1,2]

George went to college and worked part-time at a car parts store. He had been hired at the store because his good friend John was one of the night managers and had put in a good word for him. The job was ideal for George's school situation since the store was located directly across the street from his college, and the hours did not interfere with his school schedule. Not only were the location and hours convenient, but the work was fun and entertaining because George got to work with John, one of his good friends and the manager.

George usually worked at night when he and John were the only two employees in the store. He really enjoyed the job and intended to stay there until he finished college. About one month into the job, George began to notice strange things going on: John would disappear for 30 minutes at a time. At first George did not think much of it and, for the most part, just did what he was told to do. Another month passed and he started noticing that John was constantly in the back room checking the inventory. The only reason this seemed odd was because George had worked with other managers, and they had not done this.

When John would return from the back of the store, he would have a list filled with different part numbers. He would then sit at one of the computers and begin to print multiple invoices. To add to the peculiarity of this situation, George also observed John opening his cash drawer and removing money on numerous occasions. When George questioned John about what he was doing, John said that he was dealing with returns from earlier that day and that it was a routine procedure regularly done at night.

Another week or two passed, and John continued to do the same thing. George questioned him again, but this time George was a little more insistent on a truthful answer. John said that he would tell George the secret if he would not let anyone else in on it. Eager to know what was going on, George agreed.

John got on a computer and began to type in the identification numbers of different parts in order to see how many of each were currently in the inventory system. He then walked to the back of the store and checked to see if the inventory in the computer was correct. If yes, it was no big deal and he did nothing. However, if John did discover an extra part that was not identified in the inventory database, he made minor adjustments, searched the sales history of that particular part, and retrieved various invoice numbers and dates that he used to perform a cash refund. He would keep the cash for himself and sign off on the return with his own management approval.

It was blatantly obvious to George that this was wrong. He knew that it was dishonest and illegal. Still, he was confused about what to do about the whole situation. Which side was he supposed to take? He had been friends with John for over five years, and they had been through a lot together. On the other hand, John's actions were wrong and could have serious legal repercussions. George never thought of himself as a "rat", and he did not want to be involved in this situation. However, he now *was* involved and faced a difficult challenge. Where was he supposed to start? How should he approach the situation? George knew he wanted to talk to his friend, but he did not want to come off as a "goodie-two-shoes."

What should George say to John, and when, and where?

Notes

1 This material is part of the *Giving Voice to Values* (GVV) curriculum. The Yale School of Management was the founding partner, along with the Aspen Institute, which also served as the incubator for GVV. From 2009 to 2015, GVV was hosted and supported by Babson College. Darden Business Publishing is pleased to present this material in its original form. Names and other situational details have been disguised. It was written as a basis for class discussion rather than to illustrate effective or ineffective handling of an administrative situation. Copyright © 2010 by Mary Gentile. All rights reserved. *To order free copies, send an e-mail to sales@dardenbusinesspublishing.com. No part of this publication may be altered without permission.*

2 This case was prepared by Caleb Ashby with guidance from Professor Minette Drumwright, University of Texas at Austin. This case was inspired by interviews and observations of actual experiences, but names and other situational details have been changed for confidentiality and teaching purposes.

Questions on the case:

1 Discuss John's values in the case.
2 Had you been in George's position, what would you have done?
3 What impact would John's behavior have on organizational sustainability?

References

Allport, G.W. (1921). Personality and character. *Psychological Bulletin, 18,* 441–455. doi:10.1037/h0066265

Allport, G.W., & Vernon, P.E. (1930). The field of personality. *Psychological Bulletin, 27,* 677–730. doi:10.1037/h0072589

Argyris, C., & Schon, D.A. (1996), *Organizational Learning II.* Reading, MA: Addison Wesley.

Athanassoulis, N. (2000). A response to Harman: Virtue ethics and character traits. *Proceedings of the Aristotelian Society* (New Series), *100,* 215–221.

Baruch, Y., & Lemming, A. (1996). Programming the MBA- the quest for curriculum. *Journal of Management Development, 15*(7), 27–36.· doi:10.1108/02621719610122785

BBC. Retrieved February 22, 2017, from www.bbc.co.uk/ethics/introduction/intro_1. shtml

Bellet, P.S., & Maloney, M.J. (1991). The importance of empathy as an interviewing skill in medicine. *JAMA*, *226*(13), 1831–1832.

Black, B. (2001). The road to recovery. *Gappup Management Journal*, *1*, 10–12.

Bontis, N., & Mould-Mograbi, A. (2006). Ethical values and leadership: A study of business schools in Canada. *International Journal of Governance and Ethics*, *2*(3/4), 217–236.

Cameron, K.S., & Caza, A. (2002). Organizational and leadership virtues and the role of forgiveness. *Journal of Leadership and Organizational Studies*, *9*, 33–48.

Chandrakumara, A. (2011). Value of values for practicing managers and leaders. *Problems and Perspectives in Management*, *9*(2), 80–88.

Courtice, P., and Van Der Kamp, M. (2013). Developing Leaders for the Future, Working Paper of the Cambridge Program for Sustainability Leadership, commissioned by the Academy of Business in Society.

Dahlsgaard, K., Peterson, C., & Seligman, M. E. P. (2002). *Virtues cover across culture and history.* Unpublished Manuscript, University of Pennsylvania.

Dahlsgaard, K., Peterson, C., & Seligman, M. E. P. (2005). Shared virtue: The convergence of valued human strengths across culture and history. *Review of General Psychology*, *9*(3), 203–213.

Datar, S.M., Garvin, D.A., & Cullen, P.G. (2010). *Rethinking the MBA: Business education at a crossroads.* Boston, MA: Harvard Business Press.

Debruyne, F., & Dullweber, A. (2015). The five disciplines of customer experience leaders. Retrieved from www.bain.com/publications/articles/the-five-disciplines-of-customer-experience-leaders.aspx

Dharma, the Columbia Encyclopedia(6th ed.). (2013). Columbia University Press, Gale.

Digman, J. M. (1990). Personality structure: Emergence of the five-factor model. *Annual Review of Psychology*, *41*, 417–440.

Eudaimonia. (2015). Retrieved April 2, 2015, from http://positivepsychologyprogram.com/eudaimonia/

Ferrell, O. C., & Ferrell, J. F. (2014, January 1). *Business ethics: Ethical decision making &cases.* Mason: OH: Cengage Learning, Business & Economics.

Fowler, B.J. (2005). *Virtue and psychology: Pursuing excellence in ordinary practices.* Washington, DC: APA Press. doi:10.1037/11219–000.

Fowler, B.J. (2010). *Aristotle on eudaimonia: On the virtue of returning to the source.* Unpublished manuscript.

Freidman, M. (1970, September 13). The social responsibility of business is to increase its profits. *New York Times Magazine*, 32–33, 122–124.

Fromm, E. (1997). *On being human.* New York: Continuum.

Harter, J.K., & Schmidt, F.L. (2002). *Employee engagement, satisfaction and business – unit-level outcomes: Meta-analysis.* Gallup Technical Report.

Hiriyanna, M. (1932). *Outlines of Indian philosophy* (p. 73). London: George Allen and Unwin.

Hiriyanna, M. (2000). Philosophy of values. In R. Perrett (Ed.), *Indian philosophy: Theory of value* (pp. 1–10). London: Routledge.

His Holiness Sri Sri Ravi Shankar. (2005). *Celebrating Love (The Art of Living)* (Kindle ed.).

Kabanoff, B., & Daly, J. (2002). Espoused values in organizations. *Australian Journal of Management*, *27*, special issue, 89–104.

Kozminski, A. K. (2008). In W. Gasparski (Ed.), *Responsible management education* (pp. 19–20). Warsaw: Wydawnictwa Akademickie i Profesjonalne.

Kozminski, A.K. (2011).*PRME progress report 2011.* Retrieved from www.unprme.org/reports/KozminskiUniversityPRME.pdf

MacIntyre, A. (1984). *After virtue: A study in moral theory* (2nd ed.). Notre Dame, IN: University of Notre Dame Press.

Madan Mohan Malviya Founder of Banaras Hindu University: Mahamana Pandit Madan Mohan Malviya.(2006). Banaras Hindu University, p. 19. Retrieved June 10, 2012

Maio, G. R., Olson, J. M., Lindsay, A.,& Bernar, M. M. (2001). Addressing discrepancies between values and behavior: The motivating effect of reasons. *Journal of Experimental Social Psychology*, *37*(2), 104–117.

Maslow, A.H. (1999). *Towards a psychology of being* (3rd ed.). New York, NY: John Wiley & Sons.

Massey, M. E. (1979). *The people puzzle: Understanding yourself and others.* Reston, VA: Reston Publication co. ISBN 0835954773 9780835954778.

McShane, S., Glinow, M. A. V.,& Sharma, R. R. (2011). *Organizational behavior: Emerging knowledge &practice for the real world.* New Delhi: McGraw-Hill Companies, 665p.

Mortensen, D.C. (2005).*Human conflict: Disagreement, misunderstanding, and problematic talk.* Wisconsin: Rowman & Littlefield Publishers.

The National Business Ethics Survey. (2014). Issue 46, March, 2015.

National Ethics Survey. (2014, March 29).*The state of ethics in large companies.* Retrieved from www.ethics.org/nbes/

Purushartha: Sanskrit-English Dictionary. Germany: Koeln University.

Rimanoczy, I. (2014).A matter of being: Developing sustainability-minded leaders. *Journal of Management for Global Sustainability*, *2*(1), 95–122.

Robinson, D. N. (1999). *Aristotle's psychology.* New York: Joe Christensen Inc. ISBN 0-9672066-0-X ISBN 978-0967206608.

Rogers, C. (1980). *A way of being.* Boston: Houghton Mifflin.

Rokeach, M. (1973). *The nature of human values.* New York: The Free Press.

Ross, M., Schwartz, S.H.,& Surkiss, S. (1999). Basic individual values, work values &meaning of work. *Journal of Applied Psychology*, *48*(1), 49–71.

Rushworth, K. (2003). *How good people make tough choices: Resolving the dilemmas of ethical living* (p. 63). New York: Harper Collins.

Sahay, V. (2012). Should we say no to Diwali firecrackers? Why or why not? *Live Life Quora Size.* Retrieved February 22, 2017, from www.quora.com/Should-we-say-no-to-Diwali-firecrackers-Why-or-why-not#!n=90

Schwartz, B.,& Sharpe, K.E. (2006). Practical wisdom: Aristotle meets positive psychology. *Journal of Happiness Studies*, 7, 377–395.

Schwartz, S.H. (1992). Universals in the content and structure of values: Theoretical advances and empirical tests in 20 countries. *Advances in Experimental Social Psychology*, *25*, 1–65.

Schwartz, S.H.,& Sagie, G. 2000.Value consensus &importance: A cross national study. *Journal of Cross cultural Psychology*, *31*, 465–497.

Seligman, M.E.P. (1998). Positive social sciences. *APA Monitor*, *29*(4), 2–5.

Seligman, M.E.P. (1999). *Positive psychology.* Presidential address delivered at the 107th annual convention of the American Psychological Association, Boston.

Seligman, M.E.P. (2002) *Authentic Happiness.* New York: Free Press.

Seligman, M.E.P.,& Csikszentmihalyi, M. (2000). Positive psychology: An introduction. *American Psychologist*, *55*(1), 5–14.

Sharma, R. R. (2010). Preventing corruption through spiritual leadership in organisations. *Organisation & Management*, *1*(139), 135–152.

Sharma, R.R.,& Cooper, C. (2017).*Executive burnout: Eastern & Western concepts, models and approaches for mitigation* (pp. 4–5). Bingley, UK: Emerald Group Publishing.

Sharma, R.R.,& Madan, A.O. (2017). Exploring the Nexus between organizational crimes and the dark side of behavior: Strategies for prevention &mitigation. In A. Stachowicz-Stanusch, G. Mangia, & A. Caldarelli (Eds.), *Organizational social irresponsibility* (pp. 237–258). Charlotte, NC: Information Age Publishing Inc.

Sharma, R. R.,& Taneja, S. (2011). Research &practice of business ethics. *Organisation & Management*, *1*(13), 37–58.

Siegel, A. E., &Kohn, L. G. (1959). Permissiveness, permission, and aggression: The effects of adult presence or absence on aggression in children's play. *Child Development*, *36*, 131–141.

Sreenivasan, G. (2002). Errors about errors: Virtue theory and trait attribution. *Mind*, 111 (January), 47–68.

Stanford Encyclopedia.(2003, July 18). Retrieved April 1, 2015, from http://plato.stanford.edu/entries/ethics-virtue/ substantive revision Thu March 8, 2012

Stibbe, A. (Ed.). (2009). *Handbook of sustainability literacy: Skills for a changing world.* Totnes, UK: Green Books.

Sutherland, E. H. (1961). *White collar crime.* New York, NY: Holt, Rinehart and Winston.

Tagore, R. Retrieved May 20, 2017, from www.visvabharati.ac.in/

Trevisani, D. (2005). *Negoziazione Interculturale. Comunicazione oltre le barriere culturali.* Milan: Franco Angeli (Title translation: *Intercultural Negotiation: Communication Beyond Cultural Barriers*).

Wikipedia. Retrieved March 31, 2017, from https://en.wikipedia.org/wiki/Virtue

6

COSMODERN EDUCATION

Emotional, spiritual, and ecological literacy to develop a sustainability mindset

Javier Collado-Ruano[1]

Introduction: sustainable development goals for people and planet

Sustainable development has gained momentum since the Member States of the United Nations committed to the Sustainable Development Goals (SDGs) for the year 2030. The final declaration signed by world leaders is known as *Transforming our World: The 2030 Agenda for Sustainable Development* (United Nations, 2015), and it includes climate change, conservation of terrestrial ecosystems, seas and oceans, as well as other systemic and global goals on health, gender, poverty, and education. In sum, the 17 SDGs and 169 targets recognize the socio-ecological problems that characterize the current global civilization beyond their national borders. The continued exploitation of materials and energy resources of the Earth by the models of production and consumption has caused a great ecological and social footprint that has been disclosed as unsustainable (Wackernagel & Ress, 1996).

A society that walks towards sustainable development must learn to reduce its ecological destruction, reusing and recycling materials. Sustainable development is a dynamic process that requires a new transdisciplinary organization of knowledge to *feel-think-act* in harmony with the co-evolutionary processes of nature (Collado, 2016c). Sustainability is a complex and transdimensional process that is inside and outside of human beings at the same time. For this reason, sustainable development cannot be reduced to just three dimensions (social, economic, and environmental), as happens in almost all statements of the UN system. This reductionist view does not allow us to internalize the complex phenomena that are inter-retro-acting constantly in the *continuum* of life during its co-evolution with the environment. Our emotions, spirituality, and interiority are also a fundamental dimension for the achievement of the SDGs through a comprehensive and sustainable human development (Collado, 2016d) (Krishna, 2013) (Maturana, 2007).

In this line of thought, I have developed a conceptual model claiming to promote triple literacy in all educational levels: (1) *emotional literacy* to develop the ability to recognize students' emotions and empathize with others, (2) *spiritual literacy* to create an inner dialogue and critically analyze our "glocal" problems, and (3) *ecological literacy* (ecoliteracy) to understand the principles of organization of ecological communities and to use those principles for creating more resilient and sustainable human communities. In short, emotional, spiritual, and ecological literacy help students/citizens to *feel-think-act* in harmony with nature and contribute to the emergence of a consciousness of resilience. This triple literacy process represents a qualitative leap in human training to create more just, equitable, democratic, sustainable and resilient societies. Many tools, resources, exercises, projects, curricular content, and activities to achieve the triple literacy can be applied in higher education.

Transdisciplinary pedagogical approach

Our students require a non-reductionist epistemological approach to understand the complex and globalized society (of the current globalization), with its positive and negative aspects. Consequently, this chapter addresses the socio-ecological problems from the transdisciplinary methodology proposed by nuclear physicist Basarab Nicolescu (2008) and the "Complexity Theory" formulated by sociologist Edgar Morin (1999). This epistemological combination is characterized by creating an "ecology of knowledge" that is in, between, and beyond scientific and academic disciplines. It also implies openness to the inner spiritual self-awareness, worldviews of indigenous peoples, and other perceptive, affective, emotional, rhetorical, poetic, epistemic, creative, artistic, cognitive, and philosophical dimensions of our human condition.

As it can be appreciated in Figure 6.1, the theoretical-methodological combination adopted in this research seeks to develop an epistemological tool to train students from primary school to university. The transdisciplinary methodology of Nicolescu (2008) is based on quantum physics and comprises three axioms: multiple levels of reality (ontology), the logic of the Included Middle, and knowledge as complex and emergent (epistemology). Those axioms support our vision of the human condition as provisional and open-ended in the profound mysteries of the Universe. In turn, the Complexity Theory of Morin (1999) formulates seven interrelated and complementary principles based on natural phenomena: (1) systemic or organizational principle, (2) holographic principle, (3) retroactive circle principle, (4) recursive circle principle, (5) self-eco-organization principle: autonomy and dependence, (6) dialogical principle, and (7) principle of reintroduction of knowledge in all knowledge. In sum, the main intention of those principles is to identify fundamental problems that are overlooked or neglected in education, and should be taught in the future. This methodological and theoretical combination helps students to recognize different ontological and perception levels of their reality. It represents an important epistemological tool to develop a sustainability mindset

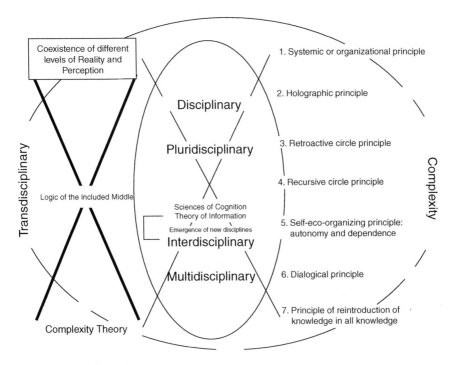

FIGURE 6.1 Epistemological combination

Source: Self-elaboration. Epistemological combination of transdisciplinary methodology (Nicolescu, 2008) with Complexity Theory (Morin, 1999).

in higher education, where students can learn with activities focused on *feeling-thinking-acting* in harmony with other people, the planet, and the *sacred*.

In other words, these epistemological combinations allow higher education students to generate holistic knowledge and resilient attitudes. Although different physical laws govern in each ontological level of nature (macro, meso, and micro), our human perception also has different levels to understand our reality (Nicolescu, 2008). While every elementary particle or quantic entity has wave-particle duality – integrating both classical concepts of "particle" and "wave" at the same time – the Logic of the Included Middle (Lupasco, 1994) acts as a *quanta* integrating different elements and phenomena with a poly-logic approach. This means different logics act together in the same space and time, despite their self-contradictions. Then, students learn to practice the seven principles proposed by Morin (1999) to understand their personal reality in a complex world. They learn that different levels of reality compose our own identity: cosmic, planetary, regional, national, and local. That is why the achievement of the SDGs requires that all educators promote a transdisciplinary mindset with projects, exercises, and activities focused on practical applications in the personal and contextual reality of their students. Learning to understand all dimensions of sustainable development requires this complex and transdisciplinary approach in education to solve problems and develop a sustainability mindset.

For this reason, this work approaches affectivity, emotions, intuitions, spirituality, reason, and imagination in order to organize transdisciplinary knowledge to learn how to *feel-think-act* in harmony with the interdependent processes of nature, as well as with each other, individually, organizationally, and culturally. According to neuroscience, our actions are preceded by emotional feelings and thoughts that arise from our interiority or inner being. Neurologist Antonio Damasio (2010, p. 110) claims: "while emotions are actions accompanied by ideas and certain modes of thinking, emotional feelings are mostly perceptions of what our bodies do during the emoting, along with perceptions of our state of mind during that same period of time." As a result, it can be concluded that we externalize what is *inside* of us, and vice versa, because we also internalize what happens *outside* of us. Sustainability needs to be addressed with a human training model that is more focused on the complexity of the relationships of our inner-outer dimensions (Krishnamurti, 1966). That is why emotional, spiritual, and ecological literacy are essential in all levels of higher education. The threefold literacy practice combines teaching of practical skills and theoretical expertise, which helps management educators in integrating critical and transdisciplinary contents into their courses and programs.

How to develop a sustainable human being in harmony with nature? How to guide global citizens to preserve life on planet Earth, avoiding the epistemic illusion of social and material progress based on unlimited economic growth? What is the role of emotions and spirituality to understand our individual responsibilities with respect to planetary unsustainability? What is the role of emotional, spiritual, and ecological literacy to achieve resilient and sustainable development? What are the best practices in higher education to develop a sustainable mindset with students? This research argues that these questions can be addressed in our classrooms if we create an inter-epistemological dialogue. Since the scholarly microcosm embodies the macrocosm of social structures, the common future of humanity on Earth requires a sustainable mindset to learn how to *feel-think-act* in harmony with our environment.

Thus, educational curricula must consider the complexity in all levels of identity through which the human race is shaped, without falling into reductionist, one-dimensional or homogenized logics. Higher education students must learn that our identity is composed by multiple dependencies with our social and natural environment. "[The] eco-bio-anthropo-social conceptual loop is a loop in which the thought of natural complexity should allow developing the thought of social and political complexity," says Morin (1983, p. 120). From this vision, our identity is a unique result of multiple relationships. Every culture is more or less hybrid, mixed, made of intersections, feedback loops. There are no finished or perfect cultures because each culture carries sufficiency, insufficiencies, functionalities, and dysfunctionalities.

Therefore, it is necessary to promote a mindset transformation that facilitates the development of a "complex thought" capable of building a new kind of identity for the emerging global citizenship. "Teaching the human condition means teaching the cosmic, physical, and earthly condition of the individual-society-species," asserts Morin (1999, pp. 21–23). Our planetary identity is based on the idea that humans are part of nature (governed by natural laws), whose historical approach addresses together the past of people, life, Earth, and the universe (Collado, 2016b). This integral view of cosmic, planetary, and human history is known as "Big History" by the scientific community (Christian, 2010), and allows us to understand better the complexity of social relations with nature, where humankind is considered an important element of co-evolutionary processes. So the next questions are: How to raise sustainability awareness within a cosmic education? How to promote a sustainability mindset in schools and universities? How to implement practical applications to achieve the SDGs?

Cosmic education in primary and secondary schools

From this co-evolutionary vision that integrates the human being in his earthly and cosmic context, the concept of sustainable development gains a new sidereal dimension to see how all living forms that co-inhabit in Gaia represent an exceptional miracle in the universe. This type of "Cosmic Education" was formulated in 1935 by the biologist, medical doctor, psychiatrist, anthropologist, philosopher, educator, and pedagogue Maria Montessori. As shown in Figure 6.2, the Montessori method is a set of knowledge, practices, and recommendations characterized by emphasis on the interdependence of all natural elements. This method seeks to create conditions for children age 6 to 12 years – future global citizens – that strengthen their feelings of cooperation, respect, and love in relation with their own nature and the cosmos. "Life is a cosmic agent. How shall this truth be presented to the children so as to strike their imagination?" Montessori reflected (2004, p. 32). Aligned with Big History, Cosmic Education is based on giving children the freedom to explore, study, and learn about the early universe, the origin of life, human evolution, language development, and the history of mathematics. They learn to appreciate how diverse cosmic forces operate and interact according to the complex laws and co-evolutionary strategies of nature: "another – and stronger – factor in evolutionary processes is concerned with the cosmic function of each living being, and even of inanimate natural objects, working in collaboration for the fulfillment of the Purpose of Life" (Montessori, 2004, p. 42, own translation). This cosmic vision in pedagogy is an essential seed to achieving the blossoming of a conscious global citizenship ready to comply with the SDGs (Collado, 2016a).

In sum, Montessori's education promotes sustainable human development where students feel creative, deeply, and self-aware about how the whole and the parts are interrelated. The epistemological core of this pedagogical approach is aligned with the thought of Indian educator Jiddu Krishnamurti (1977, p. 26): "to learn the mind must remain highly sensitive, and learning implies we see every problem, not as an

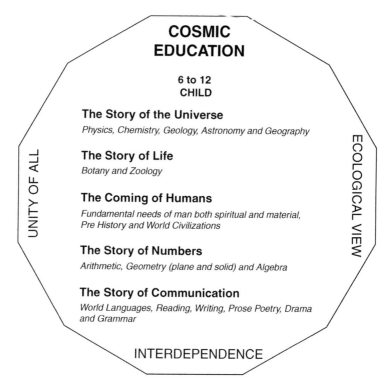

FIGURE 6.2 Cosmic education

Source: Self-elaboration. Adapted from Montessori's Cosmic Education method.

isolated event, but as a fact related to others." Hence Krishnamurti (1977, p. 185) says, "We need, internally, a great revolution. And to have the possibility to make this great psychological and mental revolution we must go beyond the limits of our own mind." For this reason, self-awareness and management of our emotional intelligence are essential elements that all models of education must include in their pedagogical praxis to develop individuals towards a paradigm of Cosmodernity (Collado, 2016e). This means learning to co-evolve in harmony with all ecosystems of Mother Earth.

The paradigm of Cosmodernity: an emerging perspective in higher education to develop a sustainability mindset

At the dawn of the third millennium, training the human condition in higher education requires adequate and pertinent contextualization. The atomic particles that compose life on our planet, and that compose us, were born in the first seconds of the cosmos. Our carbon atoms were created in a sun before our current one, and our molecules were formed on Earth (Morin, 2011). The human species is a cosmo-bio-genetic entity coming from the same co-evolution of the universe. Thus, reflection about the meaning of higher education in the globalized era of the 21st century demands both a holistic and an analytic approach to understand the complexity of our current world.

In this sense, Collado, Galeffi, and Ponczek (2014) define the "Paradigm of Cosmodernity" as the civilizational metamorphosis where humans reinvent their relationship with nature – the *sacred* dimension in indigenous worldviews. This means to stop exploiting nature, to learn from it, and to create new biomimetic models that allow us to develop a sustainability mindset. Unlike the Industrial Revolution, the Biomimetic Revolution involves the appearance of a new epistemological horizon that focuses on what we can learn from nature, rather than focusing on what we can exploit to obtain raw materials for industry.

From this cosmodern perspective, Nicolescu (2014) claims that scientific knowledge of an external physical universe converges with the spiritual knowledge of an inner emotional universe. This transdisciplinary approach is the pure essence that defines the Cosmodern Education. While Cosmic Education is focused on external knowledge, Cosmodern Education combines the outside and inside dimensions. As I will explain later, Nature is the best model to follow if we want to achieve the SDGs. Nature is the best transdisciplinary example because its levels of reality combine outside and inside dimensions at the same time. Then, many practical applications can be introduced in higher education to develop a sustainability mindset by teaching that we are, and are inseparable from, nature. Humans are interconnected with all of the ontological levels of reality, and this fact opens the possibility to rethink our pedagogical practices in higher education. However, the first thing we must take into account in management education is learning to unlearn.

Learning to unlearn means questioning all educational frameworks – tools, resources, exercises, practices, projects, activities, and curricular contents. Humanity cannot achieve the SDGs by repeating the mistakes from the past. Solving the current socio-ecological problems demands a multidimensional rebirth of our sociosphere and technosphere, in order to be in harmony with the biosphere. In this context, education is at the same time the problem and the solution, because it develops our collective imagination and our personality. While primary and secondary education promotes a general understanding of many disciplines (such as mathematics, literature, natural sciences, history, arts, philosophy, etc.), traditional higher education is very specific and reductionist in siloed disciplines. Although we may need those professionals with specific skills and competencies to solve many problems, the achievement of the SDGs demands another kind of human training focused on practical applications.

According to anthropologist Cristina Núñez (2012, p. 109), "our transdisciplinary education experience for sustainability includes the spiritual dimension as a core for creating relevant knowledge within our societies, at local and global levels." This means that educational success cannot be reduced to a simple quantification carried out by standardized tests of reading, science, or mathematics, as happens with PISA[2] tests developed by the OECD. The real educational success lies in understanding that students have spiritual, emotional, and psychosomatic experiences with the intention to develop deep connections with other people, with life, with nature, and with the cosmos. Theory and practice belong together in the paradigm of Cosmodernity, as ideas and sensorial experimentation converge to develop a meaningful learning in all educational levels.

In this sense, combining the thoughts of Montessori and Krishnamurti is a good way to understand that sustainability is a complex and transdimensional process, which is at the same time inside and outside of human beings. This cosmodern approach constitutes an epistemological openness that seeks to integrate and combine multiple cosmic, physical, ethical, emotional, affective, cultural, and artistic dimensions of a human being who constantly co-evolves in systemic and interdependent processes of energy, matter, and information (Maturana & Varela, 1980). Herein lies the need to reintroduce all of these dimensions in the teaching and learning processes of higher education, because they are human dimensions directly linked to the imbalances of our current world. "The psychological transformation is more important than outer change. The outer fundamental changes are not possible unless there is a radical transformation, a true revolution in the psyche," explains Krishnamurti (1977, p. 192), and "outer changes and reforms are necessary, but they are always destroyed by our inner state of confusion, disorder, and violence." Thus, emotional feelings, spirituality, and interiority are important facets to achieve the mental, social, and environmental balance needed to improve human welfare in a resilient and sustainable manner with all ecosystems on Earth. What is the role of emotions to manage sustainability? How can emotions help us to achieve the SDGs? What does emotional literacy mean? How could we promote practical applications to develop a sustainability mindset toward our inner universe? These questions will be explored next.

Emotional literacy: learning to explore our inner universe

Emotional literacy is a psychopedagogical innovation focused on the endogenous development of people to shape their interiority inside a universe of emotions (Bisquerra, 2015). The scientific foundations provided by social psychology, neuroscience, and psychoneuroimmunology support emotional education to meet social needs that are not met by traditional academic subjects. From a historical point of view, human emotions have been little studied by modern scientific psychology, but in recent decades more attention went to this fundamental human dimension. According to the specialized literature, Michael Beldoch first used the term "emotional intelligence" in his book *The Communication of Emotional Meaning* in 1964. In the early 1990s, social psychologists Peter Salovey and John Mayer (1990, p. 189) proposed the Theory of Emotional Intelligence, defining emotional intelligence "as the subset of social intelligence that involves the ability to monitor one's own and others' feelings and emotions, to discriminate among them and to use this information to guide one's thinking and actions."

However, the term was popularized in 1995 with publication of the book *Emotional Intelligence*, written by psychologist and science journalist Daniel Goleman (1995, pp. 55–56), who reports five basic domains: (1) knowing one's emotions (self-awareness); (2) managing emotions (resilience/ mood management); (3) motivating oneself (self motivation); (4) recognizing emotions in others (empathy); and 5) handling relationships (social competence). Since then, there have been different theoretical models, but they have never been exempt from criticism alleging a lack of indicators or gauges of this type of intelligence. But, how could we measure emotions and feelings? How to measure our passions and affects? According to scientific agreement, it is clear that emotional intelligence cannot be measurable today, at least with intelligence tests that have been applied since the 1910s to predict the school performance of children. Educator Ken Robinson (2011) states that most aspects measured in intelligence quotient (IQ) tests only reflect a measure of linguistic, logical (mathematical), and spatial skills, but they do not consider other intellectual dimensions such as creativity. Hence the controversy between the scientific communities to assess what types of intelligence exist.

In 1983, the Theory of Multiple Intelligences, created by neuropsychologist Howard Gardner, became a pioneering model that opened the debate to redefine intelligence. Since then, numerous authors have been proposing and criticizing models focused on the study of intelligence. While the traditional definition of intelligence was rather reductionist and focused on cognitive aspects, Gardner's theory (1983) focused more on the multiples ways in which we think and learn. Despite the great academic controversy, many schools of thought are using this model to understand the multidimensional nature of human intelligence (Zohar & Marshall, 2000). For Gardner and his team, there are eight types of intelligence, and each person develops some more than others depending on their personal skills and social influence. They are: (1) verbal-linguistic intelligence, (2) logical-mathematical intelligence, (3) visual-spatial intelligence, (4) musical-rhythmic and harmonic intelligence, (5) bodily-kinesthetic intelligence, (6) intrapersonal intelligence, (7) interpersonal intelligence, and (8) naturalist intelligence. Extending these ideas about intelligence, Gardner and Hatch (1989) suggest that interpersonal intelligence recognizes and responds to the moods, temperaments, motivations, and desires of others, whereas intrapersonal intelligence focuses on self-knowledge and access to one's feelings.

Currently, Gardner and Hatch are also investigating the existence of a ninth intelligence: the "existential intelligence." This intelligence refers to the sensitivity and capacity to tackle deep questions about human existence, such as the meaning of life, why we die, and how we get here. Therefore, a theoretical and conceptual model of multiple forms of intelligence is very close to the Theory of Emotional Intelligences (Salovey & Mayer, 1990). This suggests that emotional intelligence plays an important role in *internalizing* the resilient and sustainable behavior necessary for the compliance of the SDGs because this biological phenomena goes beyond our cultural constructions.

From a phylogenetic evolutionary standpoint, the human species has developed the ability to combine reason with an inner universe of emotions and feelings that have accompanied it for thousands of years during its evolution. Emotions have been passed down from generation to generation and are a feature and indispensable part of our human nature. Without them, we would be psychopaths with antisocial personality disorders. "As we all know from experience when it comes to shaping our decisions and our actions, feelings count every bit as much – and often more – than thought," argues Goleman (1995, p. 18), adding that "each emotion offers a distinctive readiness to act; each points us in a direction that has worked well to handle the recurring challenges of human life." According to some socio-biologists, these automatic reactions of *emotion-action* were recorded in some form in our nervous system and were crucial to surviving during the long period of human prehistory.

As mentioned before, the specification introduced by the neurologist Antonio Damasio (2010, p. 110) is important here: "while emotions are actions accompanied by ideas and certain modes of thinking, emotional feelings are mostly perceptions of what our bodies do during the emoting, along with perceptions of our state of mind during that same period of time." Thus, neuroscience affirms that emotional feelings "color" our life from beginning to end, regardless of our nationality, ethnicity, culture, race, or religion. In this sense, it is curious that most international events I have attended always talk about "universal values" and not about "universal emotional feelings." In my opinion, this is a transcendental epistemic mistake we must correct if we want to achieve the SDGs. When we try to identify the universal values that are present in all cultures of the world, we run the serious risk of homogenizing the rich and complex cultural diversity of peoples (Collado, 2016c).

According to the estimation made by philosopher Kenneth Shouler (2010), there are currently around 4,200 religions worldwide. In turn, the research project *Ethnologue* reckoned there were around 7,102 living languages for a population of 7.1 billion people in 2015. After colonization and imperialism, it is clear that epistemic approaches that "universalize" values almost always have a strong Western imprint, as it happened with the Universal Declaration of Human Rights. On the contrary, by focusing the discourse of sustainability using a transcultural biological phenomenon, such as human emotional feelings, education gains a new epistemological perspective of *feeling-thinking-acting* to build "other possible worlds."

Therefore, it is clear that governments are failing in their educational reforms because they are trying to face the complex problems of our current globalized world by making the same mistakes of the past. In this process, they are alienating millions of young adults in higher education who do not see any use in university attendance, especially in the West. In order to face the dangers of the future, with the collective aim to meet the SDGs by 2030, we will need a holistic, systemic, and transversal reflection on the appearance of human beings in the Big History, without forgetting the epistemic worldviews and cultural traditions of each particular context. Emotional literacy is within the latest movements of pedagogical renewal and regeneration. This educational perspective redefines the Theory of Multiple Intelligences and provides meaningful learning to train new citizens.

In this line of thought, psychotherapist Claude Steiner postulated the term "emotional literacy" in 1997 to describe the ability to know the emotions, the ability to empathize with the emotions of others, and the art of learning to manage our emotions to solve emotional problems resulting from interaction with others. According to this view, emotional literacy helps us understand our inner emotional universe to facilitate relations of social coexistence. We carry the responsibility for our actions by emphasizing the emotional training of individuals and seeking to improve interpersonal relationships. "An open heart is the foundation of emotional literacy and a prerequisite for the next two stages of emotional literacy training: Surveying the Emotional Landscape and Taking Responsibility," argues Steiner (2003, p. 57), and "that is why the training starts here, by learning how to give and take affection – or in plain English, by learning to love." Educating for emotional literacy is a dual process of personal development and collective activity (i.e., self-development and community building), where the sense of welfare grows along with others in a common and shared environment. For this reason, parents, families, neighborhoods, communities, religious organizations, media, and also formal education institutions must develop emotional literacy to achieve a sustainability mindset (Steiner, 1997).

This human training for emotional literacy is defended by neurologist Antonio Damasio (*in* Bisquerra, 2015, p. 34), who considers that:

> it is necessary that political and educational leaders come to understand how important is the knowledge about emotion and feeling because many of the reactions we consider pathological have to do with emotions, mainly with social emotions, and with the ease that social conflicts are triggered.

This kind of *emotional education* seems to be a fertile and prosperous path that leads us to the heart of an education that prepares us to achieve sustainable development. According to integral educators Kerul Kassel, Isabel Rimanoczy, and Shelley Mitchell (2016, p. 8),

> Sustainability Mindset is a way of thinking and being that results from a broad understanding of the ecosystem's manifestations as well as an introspective focus on one's personal values and higher self, and finds its expression in actions for the greater good of the whole.

The authors incorporate the dimensions of values (being) and knowledge (thinking), expressed in actions or competencies (doing). This vision broadens epistemic horizons to achieve the SDGs, since it seeks to transform entire global citizenship from the root: making them affectively responsible for current ecological and civilizational crisis.

From a similar pedagogical worldview, educational psychologist Rafael Bisquerra (2015) is inspired in the ontological structure of the outer universe to organize the universe of emotions of our interiority. In his book *Universe of Emotions*, there is strong *cosmomimetic* creativity with rich theoretical contributions to emotional education. While the universe is formed by galaxies, the universe of emotions is composed by families of emotions, which Bisquerra (2015) metaphorically referred to as galaxies of emotions. They are massive clusters of affective phenomena and the largest structures in which emotions are agglutinated. "It is estimated there are around 100,000 million galaxies in the universe. Emotions are processed in the brain, where there are estimated about 100,000 million neurons," explains Bisquerra (2015, p. 21), while arguing "this curious numerical coincidence is another excuse to propose a parallel between the cosmic universe and the universe of emotions processed in the brain." Analogous to the "wheel of basic emotions" designed by medical doctor Robert Plutchik (2003) in his Theory of Psychoevolution or the Circumplex Model of Affects proposed by psychologist James Russell (1980), the "universe of emotions" also represents a didactic, psychopedagogical, and psychotherapeutic resource. The universe of emotions is based on knowledge and scientific theories, but Bisquerra recognizes that its configuration is opened to different interpretations due to the intangibility of emotions. In its original sense, astronomy is the science that studies the celestial bodies of the universe (galaxies, stars, planets, satellites, etc.), and it is divided into four main branches of knowledge: positional astronomy, celestial mechanics, astrophysics, and cosmology. In his emotional model, Bisquerra argues that:

> *Positional Astronomy* aims to locate the stars in the celestial sphere. It describes the movement of the stars, planets, satellites, and phenomena such as eclipses. The application into the universe of emotions is in determining the position of various emotions in space. *Celestial mechanics* aims to interpret the movements of positional astronomy. It studies the movement of the Moon, the planets around the Sun, their satellites, and calculates the orbits of comets and asteroids. Its application into the universe of emotions is to analyze the movement from one emotion to another. *Astrophysics* studies the stars as physical bodies, analyzing their composition, structure and evolution. Its application into emotions is to analyze the intrinsic traits of each one of them. *Cosmology* studies the origins, structure and evolution of the universe as a whole. . . . Its application to the emotions is to study their origin and primitive functions, and their evolution.
>
> *(Bisquerra, 2015, pp. 19–20, own translation)*

With this *cosmomimetic* vision, Bisquerra (2015) defines the epistemological model to create his vision of the emotional universe. "We must make it clear that all emotions are good. The problem is what we do with them. The way we manage them determines the effects they will have on our welfare and on the others," says Bisquerra (2015, p. 47), adding: "while all emotions have value, some make us feel good and other make us feel bad. Hence some are called positive and other negative depending on whether or not they provide wellbeing."While the constellations of positive emotions (joy, love, and happiness) are represented at the top, the constellations of negative emotions (fear, anger, and sadness) are at the bottom. The existence of these two constellations represents our emotional polarity: joy-sadness, love-hate, etc. Values and attitudes are located in the emotional intergalactic space because of their role in the affective states present in our actions.

Here lies the importance of understanding how "universal values" emerge from the emotional feelings of our inner universe. If human beings did not have the ability to feel emotions, we would be a psychopathic species incapable of understanding the planetary emergency of current unsustainability. In fact, this is what happens with some large corporations at the transnational level (Hathaway & Boff, 2014; Ketola, 2008). They are entities without conscience or emotional feelings that are guiding the course of humanity towards climate catastrophe in their insatiable desire for economic profit. For this reason, "before a child learns the alphabet and some notions about the world, he should learn what is the soul, truth and love, and what forces sleep in the soul," explains pacifist activist Mahatma Gandhi (2001, p. 100), arguing that "an even more essential part of education should be teaching a child to win the battle of life to conquer hatred with love, falsehood with truth, and violence with his own suffering." In the educational philosophy of *Gandhiji* (as he is popularly known in India), love is a feeling that fights against violence to be a law of truth and life. In this sense, love is the most powerful energy to transform our world society. The promotion of love emerges as a practical exercise to develop a sustainability mindset. Our students must conceive sustainability as a *feel-thought-act* of love within a complex and interdependent process that spans multiple cosmic, ecological, political, economic, epistemic, emotional, and spiritual dimensions.

Spiritual literacy and the religious dimension of the human being

Different philosophical and pedagogical movements seek to develop social and emotional learning in a school environment, to form integral human beings. A good example is the Waldorf education postulated by philosopher Rudolf Steiner in the early 20th century, which promotes the physical, spiritual, emotional, intellectual, and artistic development of students with the aim of developing free, socially competent, and morally responsible individuals. Steiner's theosophical training led him to connect anthroposophy to education, applying the process of rebirth in pedagogy to expand the material world into the spiritual world. From his epistemological perspective, Steiner (1992, pp. 5–6) explains that

> anthroposophy is therefore the knowledge of the spiritual man, and that knowledge is not confined to man but is a knowledge of everything which the spiritual man can perceive in the spiritual world, just as the physical man observes physical things in the world. . . . The knowledge which he acquires may likewise be called "spiritual science."

Thus, the material world merges with the spiritual world in addressing the integrity of the human being.

This endogenous development is also present in the perspective of spiritual evolution and material reincarnation of Indian philosopher Sri Aurobindo:

> If evolution is a truth and is not only a physical evolution of species, but an evolution of consciousness, it must be a spiritual and not only a physical fact. . . . If there is evolution of a conscious individual, then there must be rebirth. Rebirth is a logical necessity and a spiritual fact of which we can have the experience.
>
> *(Aurobindo, 2003, p. 343)*

According to Aurobindo (2003, p. 34–35), "it is often through intensity of emotion that the psychic being awakens and there is an opening of the inner doors to the Divine," which means that the soul grows during its experience in the evolution of life by experimenting emotions with the purpose of developing its own nature.

Based on these ideas, physicists and philosophers Danah Zohar and Ian Marshall (2000, p. 9) created the concept of Spiritual Intelligence (SQ) to refer to the *soul of intelligence*:

> SQ is the intelligence that rests in that deep part of the self that is connected to wisdom from beyond the ego, or conscious mind; it is the intelligence with which we not only recognize existing values, but with which we creatively discover new values.

For Zohar and Marshall, SQ is not culture-dependent or value-dependent – it creates the very possibility of having values in our cultures. Influenced by the Vedanta philosophy of Swami Vivekananda and Mahatma Gandhi, Zohar and Marshall (2000, p. 263) put forward seven practical steps to promote spiritual literacy: (1) become aware of where I am now; (2) feel strongly what I want to change; (3) reflect on what my own center is and on my deepest motivations; (4) discover and dissolve obstacles; (5) explore many possibilities to go forward; (6) commit myself to a path; and (7) remain aware that there are many paths. Taken together, these steps are aimed at connecting the "spiritual being" to the whole, having a feeling of integrity. For this reason, these practical steps must be brought into higher education to promote a spiritual worldview and a sustainability mindset.

There are many good exercises and activities of practical application in higher education to apply those theories on emotional and spiritual literacy. The relationship between emotional feelings and socio-ecological well-being is based on contemporary scientific studies, but also on the millenary wisdom of traditional medicine and ancient philosophy of indigenous peoples who still survive. Nowadays, biomedical science investigates therapies such as acupuncture, yoga, meditation, Tai Chi, Qigong, Reiki, relaxation therapy, music therapy, and laughter therapy. In this sense, the specialist psychologist in interiority, spirituality, and emotional education, Luis López (2015, p. 47), considers that "interiority is the human *capacity that allows developing the consciousness of one's self and the environment, giving sense and meaning to our existence.*" For this reason, many authors seem to agree that emotional education is a parallel and complementary path to spiritual education and the education of our interiority in the complex processes of human development.

In this line of thought, López and his team conducted a rigorous study of 44 methods of relaxation and meditation to understand their practical application in education. The study suggests there are nine basic psychotherapeutic skills that can be employed in higher education to develop our interiority: (1) attention, (2) breathing, (3) visualization, (4) voice, (5) relaxation, (6) sensory awareness, (7) posture, (8) body energy, and (9) movement (López, 2015, pp. 77–78). Interiority awareness is a key component of developing a sustainability mindset. In fact, López is coordinating the program TREVA (Spanish initials for "Experiential Relaxation Techniques Applied in Classroom") to improve emotional intelligence and interiority at the University of Barcelona and also in secondary schools. As a result of this long process of research and experience, the TREVA project has developed many pedagogical innovations, including resources, practices, and tools with practical applications. "Learning to feel is to develop emotional awareness (self-knowledge, understanding of own and others' emotions), and other psychotherapeutic and perceptual skills," argues López (2015, p. 122). A sustainability mindset emerges when students learn to *feel-think-act* spiritually with the parts and the whole.

The book *The Tao of Liberation: Exploring the Ecology of Transformation*, by ecologist Mark Hathaway and theologian Leonardo Boff (2014, p. 376), also advocates for the spiritual dimension: "The spirituality of each person is in some sense unique, and our own spirituality may draw on a variety of religious or philosophical traditions, as well as our own personal experience." However, they also warn that "most of humanity draws on religious traditions as a key source of spiritual insight. It is nearly impossible to consider spirituality without also considering the influence – both potentially positive and negative – of religion" (Hathaway & Boff, 2014, p. 376). Therefore, it is necessary to differentiate spirituality from the historical interests that have prevailed and continue to occur within religions. To this end, the work *Why Religion Matters*, written by Huston Smith (2003), is a good study that helps us establish an interreligious dialogue of most practiced and influential beliefs today: Christianity (33% of the world population), Islam (21%), Hinduism (14%), Buddhism (6%), traditional Chinese religion (6%), and Judaism (0.25%) (Shouler, 2010).

As shown in Figure 6.3, the diagram has a form of the mandala with the flower of life in the center representing the common wisdom of native indigenous peoples. The mandala addresses the interpretations that the main religious beliefs have about the relationship between reality and selfhood. At the top, the levels of reality are reflected in the levels of selfhood of the bottom through four circles of different intensity. This figure depicts the many similarities between the six most influential religions practiced today by approximately 80.25% of the world population. If we

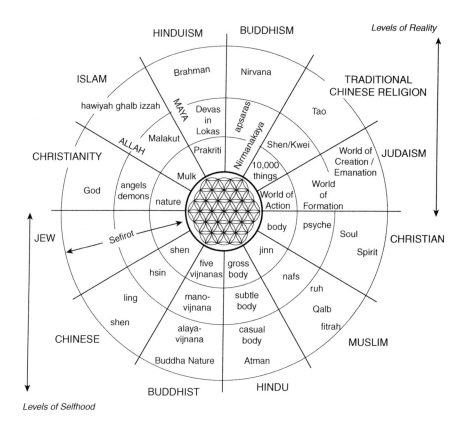

FIGURE 6.3 Levels of reality and levels of selfhood in the most influential religious beliefs, with flower of life

Source: Self-elaboration. Inspired by Smith (2003, p. 224).

also note that 16% of world citizenship is secular, not religious, agnostic, and atheist, it means that only 4% of the world population, about 275 million people, practice the other 4,195 religious worldviews identified by Shouler (2010). Thus, the mandala helps us to develop an interreligious dialogue between the most influential religions of today (see Table 6.1).

Throughout human history, religion has been a risk factor for all the wars that took place, especially in the Middle East. This is an area of great instability due to a complex network of ethnic, racial, political, and economic factors that arise by the coexistence of three monotheistic religions: Judaism, Christianity, and Islam. Currently, interreligious conflicts are suffered in countries such as Nigeria (Christians and Muslims), Israel (Jewish and Muslim), Thailand (Buddhists and Muslims), Sudan (Muslims and non-Muslims), Afghanistan (fundamentalist Muslims and non-Muslim radicals), and in Bosnia and Kosovo (Catholics, Muslims, and Orthodox). At the

TABLE 6.1 Interfaith comparison of philosophical and religious doctrines most practiced today (in 2010 there were around 6,875 million citizens)

Religion	Christianity	Islam	Hinduism	Buddhism	Traditional Chinese Religion	Judaism
Symbol						
Founder	Jesus	Muhammad (Muslims)	It has no founder	Siddhartha Gautama (Buddha)	It has no founder	Abraham
Conception	Monotheist	Monotheist	Monotheist and polytheistic	Not theistic	Polytheistic	Monotheist
Place of worship	Church	Mosque	Temple or house	Temple	Temple	Synagogue
Holy Scriptures	Bible (Old and New Testaments)	Koran (114 Psalm)	4 Vedas, Upanishad, Mahabharata, Bhagavad-Gita, Ramayana	Vinaya, Sutra, Abhidharma	Oral tradition	Torah (Mishna and Talmud)
Mainstream	Catholicism, Protestantism, Orthodox, evangelical, Pentecostal	Sunnism, Shiism, Sufism, Jainism	Vaishnavism, krishnaism, Shaivism, Shaktism	Theravada, Mahayana, Vajrayana	Confucianism, Taoism,	Orthodox, Reform, Conservative, Reconstructionist, Karaite, Hasidic
Followers (Millions)	2,100–2,300	1,500–2,040	900	375–500	394–800	14
% World population	33%	21%	14%	6%	6%	0.25%

Source: Self-elaboration.

same time, intra-religious conflicts are getting more visibility within Islam, between Shi'ites and Sunnis, in countries such as Syria, Lebanon, or Iraq. In these countries, the so-called Islamic State is emerging and threatening the world through terrorism practiced by its followers in a "holy war" against the West.

All of these confrontations seem to indicate that we have developed a wrong way to seek our spirituality. Instead of cultivating and researching the mind and our relationship with the sacred, we have preferred to maintain dogmatic beliefs, mistaking them with religion and spiritual growth. For this reason, all liberating education must transgress these epistemic paradigms and promote an investigative mind that questions and finds out for itself, rather than reproduces and imitates contents of a certain "holy book" written thousands of years ago. In line with this, the Indian theosophist Padmanabhan Krishna (2013, p. 27) remarks that

> Jesus did not become Christ through a church or a belief, but through his own understanding and his own research. Buddha attained enlightenment and understanding through his own meditation, his own research. We must understand this and correct the situation in our educational system.

The pedagogy of freedom (Freire, 1971, 1997) must guide each individual of global citizenship in their own intellectual, emotional, and spiritual research, questioning the epistemic paradigms where they live in. What is my identity? Why is this my nationality? Why should I follow this particular religion? What are my responsibilities with nature given my human condition and ability for reflection? Only by researching and having our own *insights* will we learn to give these answers. Repeating the answers of Jesus, Buddha, Mohammed, or other spiritual leaders we will not be cultivating our own conscience to safeguard life on Earth. Each response is unique and non-transferable.

Critical thinking is one of the most important skills that students must learn in higher education to become spiritually literate. For this reason, it is important to reinvent the sacred dimension from their individual hermeneutic, which involves learning to dialogue in an intra-religious form. According to the philosopher, theophysicist, and expert in religious comparisons, Raimon Panikkar (1999, p. 74): "If interreligious dialogue is to be a real dialogue, an intrareligious dialogue must accompany it, i.e., it must begin with my questioning myself and the relativity of my beliefs." Panikkar offers a meeting point between East and West, and his work is an ongoing intercultural and interreligious dialogue that leads to cross-fertilization between cultures and civilizations: where everyone learns from everyone. "Each language is a world of its own . . . each culture is a galaxy with its own criteria of goodness, beauty, and truth" (Panikkar, 1998a, p. 29). The truth is pluralistic, and this means no one has all the elements to judge other cultures. Pluralism makes us aware of our contingency and our limits to judge, showing how to coexist with a cultural diversity that implies galaxies of worldviews with their own criteria of reality.

According to Panikkar (1998b), every culture and civilization has three ontonomic orders (myth, logos, and mystery) and an interrelated cosmotheandric dimension. This means that Human History, Cosmic Existence, and Divine Destiny are inseparable. Thus, Panikkar (1998b) unifies and reconciles the physical and the religious cosmology, giving a new philosophical and spiritual sense to the *ontonomy of science*. This is the pure essence of the Cosmodernity paradigm (Collado, Galeffi & Ponczek, 2014), as has been explained previously. In sum, the pluralistic consciousness reminds us that every culture or religion is intrinsically open to being fertilized by others since the understanding of our human identity/condition in the universe requires comprehensive solidarity among all beings to bring us to the knowledge of the ontological structure of reality. Therefore, we must develop a comprehensive look at the teaching and learning processes that take place in our educational institutions. A sustainable mindset seems to be emerging from this cosmodern philosophy of nature.

Educating for a sustainable world requires that we rethink how we teach our students about their place in nature and the universe. The model of Cosmodern Education presented in this chapter takes the cultivation of emotional, spiritual, and ecological literacy as its foundation and expands this foundation to integrate ecological intelligence. *Feeling-thinking-acting* in harmony with the co-evolution processes of nature is the main goal of Cosmodern Education. This model recognizes emotional, spiritual, and ecological intelligence as essential dimensions to develop a sustainability mindset, where science, culture, and spirituality are interlinked in the cosmos for a resilient and sustainable human development on Earth. Next, we will explore how to connect our emotions and spirituality with nature and how to include ecoliteracy's practical applications in higher education.

Ecological literacy to co-evolve harmonically with nature

After 3.8 billions years, nature is the only "business" that has never failed. To achieve a sustainable development, it is necessary to better understand the principles and strategies of nature. In this sense, ecological literacy is required to learn resilience lessons from nature and build a more just and democratic society, better integrated with the biosphere. The notion of "ecoliteracy" or "ecological literacy" was developed by physicist Fritjof Capra (1998) to describe the organizational principles of ecosystems with the main goal of building sustainable human communities. *Ecoliteracy* includes a systems thinking approach in terms of relationships, connectedness, and context. The growing realization of the earth as a common home forms a compelling reason for creating a sustainable world for future generations as our collective and urgent task (Capra & Mattei, 2015). According to Capra (1998), there are five basic principles in nature: (1) interdependence, (2) the cyclical nature of ecological processes; (3) a tendency to associate, establish links, and cooperate as essential characteristics of life, (4) flexibility, and (5) diversity.

Capra (1998, p. 20) argues that "understanding life must be seen as the scientific vanguard of the paradigm shift, from a mechanistic world conception to an ecological conception." He postulates that human systems should be governed by the following key criteria of a living system: (a) *organizational pattern* or configuration of relationships that are determined by the essential characteristics of the system; (b) *structure* or physical embodiment of the organizational pattern of the system; (c) *vital process* or involved activity in the continuous physical embodiment of the organizational pattern of the system (Capra, 1998, p. 175). In other words, Capra believes reconnecting with the web of life means rebuilding and maintaining sustainable communities in which we can satisfy our needs and aspirations without diminishing the chances of future generations. For this task we can learn a lot from ecosystems, true sustainable communities of plants, animals, and microorganisms. To understand them, we must become ecologically literate: "Being ecologically literate, being 'ecoliterate', means understanding the organizing principles of ecological communities (ecosystems) and using these principles to build sustainable human communities. We need to revitalize our communities including education, business, and policies" (Capra, 1998, p. 307).

Ecological literacy is inspired by nature to build more sustainable and resilient human communities on Earth. This bio-inspiration is the main foundation of biomimetics in science. The biomimetic approach is one of the most innovative responses in recent years to protect the environment and improve the quality of life through new sustainable habits of consumption and production. The term *biomimicry* comes from the ancient Greek *bios* (life) and *mīmēsis* (imitation). In the 1990s, the American science writer Janine M. Benyus popularized the term with her book *Biomimicry: Innovation Inspired by Nature*. Since then, biomimicry emerged as a new transdisciplinary science that considers and values nature as model, measure, and mentor. Biomimicry is looking for the inspiration and imitation of the natural processes to be applied in social systems, and thus find innovative solutions to complex problems – such as the SDGs demand. "Biomimicry uses an ecological standard to judge the correctness of our innovations. After 3.8 billion years of evolution, nature has discovered what works, what is appropriate, and what endures," notes Benyus (2012, p. 13), affirming that biomimicry "begins an era based not on what we can extract from the natural world, but what it can teach us." In this sense, the biomimetic vision represents a theoretical-pragmatic symbiosis between citizens from the North and the South, and also a fundamental tool to face climate change.

Benyus (2012, p. 22) recognized nine basic operational principles of biomimicry, based on the Laws of Nature, which can be used as an example of a beneficial model for human behavior: (1) Nature runs on natural sunlight; (2) Nature uses only energy and resources that it needs; (3) Nature fits form to function; (4) Nature recycles and finds uses for everything; (5) Nature rewards cooperation; (6) Nature depends on and develops diversity; (7) Nature requires expertise and resources; (8) Nature avoids internal excesses; and (9) Nature taps into the power of limits. These principles promote critical thinking with our students, inviting them to reflect and compare the inherent characteristics of ecosystems with the culture of human production. The natural world has designed co-evolutionary strategic processes that work and persist over billions of years, so it represents the best meta-model to imitate and create more resilience and sustainable civilizational models. Biomimicry can be used in management education to create practical activities and exercises to raise sustainability awareness.

At the same time, the natural world is the proper environment to develop ecological literacy with our students. Educating is a transcendental act in the lives of people that forces us to recognize problems outside of the classroom. It is necessary to challenge our own educational paradigm to encourage a culture of peace and sustainability that promotes social and democratic transformation. "This is not another reform, but a real structural transformation of the mindset, to raise, implement, and manage basic education," argues educator Moacir Gadotti (2000, p. 47), who claimed the need to create a "pedagogy of the Earth" or "eco-pedagogy" that goes beyond the traditional schooling logic to reach the entire society. For Gadotti (2000, p. 93), eco-pedagogy "is concerned with the 'promotion of life', relational content, experiences, attitudes, and values," so education should not be confused with the formal and institutionalized schooling processes. While the schooling logic is focused on speech, educational logic is focused on the process. "Founded on the principle of competitiveness, selection, and sorting, traditional pedagogies do not help in the development of citizens who need to be more cooperative and active" (Gadotti, 2000, p. 87). On the contrary, most educational organizations that do not behave like an isolated island in their social environment and that develop formal, non-formal, and informal networks are already fostering a sustainability mindset. A good example is the formal education system of Finland, where secondary schools train students in an interdisciplinary way through complex concepts such as sustainability, climate change, globalization, and so forth.

Final conclusions to develop a cosmodern education

Education is key to achieving a sustainable development for Gaia: being the seed that we must cultivate for our present and future flourishing. "Sustainability is not just a problem between us the humans," explains environmental educator Maria Novo (2009, p. 368), "it is also a serious problem of our relationship with the biosphere, the way we appropriate resources, exploit nature, manage the commons, and how we consider the limits of ecosystems." For this reason, it is urgent to transform the models of predatory behavior that human species exercise over Gaia, as well as the unequal distribution of wealth that only benefits a minority. In this regard, emotional, spiritual, and ecological literacy helps us to create new theoretical and practical horizons in management education. An emerging sustainability mindset emerges to live in Cosmodernity: where human beings co-evolve in sustainable and resilient harmony with all the ecosystems of our planet.

Educating to live in the paradigm of Cosmodernity means developing new processes of meaningful learning by exploring different types of human intelligence (rational, spiritual, social, emotional, ethical, etc.) that help us to *feel-think-act* in response to our current emergency situation. As it has been demonstrated in this chapter, evidence supporting emotional, spiritual, and ecological literacy is showing up in different cultural and academic contexts. This triple literacy helps students to develop a sustainability mindset. In fact, Cosmodern Education cannot be just about transmitting values and knowledge, but is a creative, constructive, and transformative act. Students must learn to develop a continuous self-conscious dialogue to *feel-think-act* with their emotional feelings, thoughts, and actions. For this reason, it is important to address the emotional, spiritual, and ecological literacy in management education. Emotional feelings, thoughts, and actions are part of the same phenomenon of inseparable interconnections that form the basis of our socio-ecological relations.

From this perspective of sustainability, it is important that higher education students know the cosmic universe as well as their inner emotional universe. While the knowledge of a cosmic universe allows students to assess the emergence of life in the Big History as an exceptional event that we must preserve and conserve at all costs, their emotional knowledge of their inner universe allows them to improve the quality of their relations with other people and with nature. Therefore, walking towards sustainability means setting the emotional course for our mental, social, and environmental well-being. We cannot let the markets of economic globalization continue managing the course, because it has a significant negative impact on our personal health and on the planet's health. The great transition to "other possible worlds" is a twofold process of internal and external transformation of the human condition that requires new transdisciplinary educational models aimed at creating strong links among emotions, spirituality, and the environment. This symbiosis represents the sustainability mindset that can be achieved by a Cosmodern Education, which allows us to improve our human ability to learn how to co-evolve in harmony with all ecosystems of nature.

A Cosmodern Education promotes a transdimensional understanding where the human being is seen as a unique species co-evolving in a shared ecosystem with more than ten million other species. We must learn to respect, preserve, and regenerate them. We cannot extinguish the infinite wisdom accumulated over billions of years of planetary biodiversity. It is urgent to transform humankind's domination approach to nature, launched during the Agricultural Revolution about 10,000 years ago, into an approach of stewardship (Benyus, 2012). Now it is time to learn how to co-evolve as a sub-system within the biophysical limits of Gaia: our Earth-Homeland (Morin & Kern, 2005). If we want to achieve the SDGs, it is essential to reflect on the human footprint on Earth, because it is causing extinction of species and a dramatic environmental degradation (Wackernagel & Ress, 1996). In this sense, emotional, spiritual, and ecological literacy appear as key areas to train our students how to respect our planet. This triple process seeks to reinvent our relationship with the *sacred*: moving from the exploitation of nature to create new resilient models, learning from nature in order to achieve a lasting sustainable development.

New higher education sustainability initiatives are being created around the world to transform run-up practical applications in management education and beyond. Higher education should reinforce its role of service to society, especially its activities aimed at achieving the SDGs, mainly through transdisciplinary tools, resources, exercises, practices, projects, curricular contents, and activities. Institutions of higher education should systematically take into account emotional, spiritual, and ecological literacy into their curricular contents to develop a sustainability mindset. Developing those skills should become a major focus of higher education, in order to facilitate the achievement of the SDGs. However, reflecting on the challenges concerning the SDGs carries many questions and approaches to implement practical applications in higher education. How can we all develop a sustainability mindset? According to integral educator Isabel Rimanoczy (2013, p. 2),

> each one of us can play a part in leading the change; actually we are already playing a part – we are just not necessarily aware if that is the part we would like to play, or aware that we choose the change we are contributing to unfold.

In conclusion, I invite all readers to explore their own inner feeling, thinking, and being dimensions for the fulfillment of the Sustainable Development Goals. Are you ready? I hope the transdisciplinary overview of Cosmodern Education can help you for a self and collective benefit.

Notes

1 Ph.D. Javier Collado-Ruano is titular professor in the National University of Education (UNAE) in Ecuador. He teaches Global Citizenship Education, Philosophy of Education, Big History, and International Relations. He has a Ph.D. in Creation of Knowledge by the Federal University of Bahia (Brazil), and a Ph.D. in Philosophy by the University of Salamanca (Spain). He is a Journalist and Director General at *Global Education* Magazine. E-mail: javier.collado@unae.edu.ec; website: www.javiercolladoruano.com
2 The Program for International Student Assessment (PISA) report is a worldwide study by the Organization for Economic Co-operation and Development (OECD) in member and non-member nations of 15-years-old school pupils' scholastic performance on mathematics, science, and reading.

References

Aurobindo, S. (2003). *The integral Yoga: Sri Aurobindo's teaching and method of practice.* Compiled by Sri Aurobindo Ashram. Pondicherry: Lotus Press.

Benyus, J. (2012). *Biomímesis. Cómo la ciencia innova inspirándose en la naturaleza.* Barcelona: Tusquets editores.

Bisquerra, R. (2015). *Universo de emociones.* Valencia: PalauGea.

Capra, F. (1998). *La trama de la vida. Una nueva perspectiva de los sistemas vivos.* Barcelona: ANAGRAMA.

Capra, F., & Mattei, U. (2015). *The ecology of law: Toward a legal system in tune with nature and community.* Oakland, CA: Berrett-Koehler Publishers.

Christian, D. (2010). *Mapas del tiempo: Introducción a la Gran Historia.* Barcelona: Ed. Crítica.

Collado-Ruano, J. (2016a). Una perspectiva transdisciplinar y biomimética a la educación para la ciudadanía mundial. *Educere,* nº 65, enero-abril, 113–129.

Collado-Ruano, J. (2016b). La bioética como ciencia transdisciplinar de la complejidad: una introducción coevolutiva desde la Gran Historia. *Revista Colombiana de Bioética, 11*(1), 54–67.

Collado-Ruano, J. (2016c). Epistemologia del Sur: una visión descolonial de los Objetivos de Desarrollo Sostenible. *Sankofa, 9*(17), 137–158.

Collado-Ruano, J. (2016d). *Educación emocional: retos para alcanzar un desarrollo sosteni-ble. CIEG*, n° 26, octubre – diciembre, pp. 27–46.

Collado-Ruano, J. (2016e). *Paradigmas epistemológicos en Filosofía, Ciencia y Educación. Ensayos Cosmodernos*. Saarbrücken: Editorial Académica Española.

Collado-Ruano, J., Galeffi, D., & Ponczek, R. (2014). O paradigma da cosmodernidad: uma abordagem transdisciplinar à Educação para a Cidadania Global proposta pela UNESCO. *Revista da FAEEBA: educação e contemporaneidade, 23*(42), 141–152.

Damasio, A. (2010). *Self comes to mind. Constructing the conscious brain*. New York: Pantheon.

Freire, P. (1971). *Pedagogía del oprimido*. Montevideo, Ed. San Santiago.

Freire, P. (1997). *La educación como práctica de la libertad*. México, DF: Siglo XXI Editores.

Gadotti, M. (2000). *Pedagogía da Terra*. São Paulo: Editora Peirópolis, 2000.

Gandhi, M. (2001). *Palabras para la paz*. Santander: Sal Terrae.

Gardner, H. (1983). *Frames of mind: The theory of multiple intelligence*. New York: Basic Books.

Gardner, H., & Hatch, T. (1989). Multiple intelligences go to school: The educational impli-cations of the theory of multiple intelligences. *Educational Researcher, 18*, 4–10.

Goleman, D. (1995). *Inteligência Emocional*. Rio de Janeiro: Objetiva.

Hathaway, M., & Boff, L. (2014). *El Tao de la liberación. Una ecología de la transformación*. Madrid: Trotta.

Kassel, K., Rimanoczy, I., & Mitchell, S. (2016). *The sustainable mindset: Connecting being, think-ing, and doing in management education*. Paper accepted for presentation at the Academy of Management Annual Meeting 2016, Anaheim, CA.

Ketola, T. (2008). *From psychopaths to responsible corporations: Waking up the inner sleeping beauty of companies*. New York: Nova Science Pub.

Krishna, P. (2013). *Educação, Ciência e Espiritualidade*. Brasilia, Editora Teosófica.

Krishnamurti, J. (1966). *A mutação interior*. São Paulo: Cultrix.

Krishnamurti, J. (1977). *A Suprema Realização*. São Paulo: Editora Cultrix.

López, L. (2015). *Educar la interioridad*. Barcelona: Plataforma Actual.

Lupasco, S. (1994). *O Homem e suas Três Éticas*. Lisboa: Instituto Piaget.

Maturana, H. (2007). *Emociones y lenguaje en educación y política*. Santiago: Centro de Estudios del Desarrollo.

Maturana, H., & Varela, F. (1980). *Autopoiesis and cognition. The realization of the living*. Dordrecht: Reidel Publishing Company.

Montessori, M. (2004). *Para educar o potencial humano*. São Paulo: Papirus Editora.

Morin, E. (1983). *El método II. La Vida de la Vida*. Madrid: Editorial Cátedra.

Morin, E. (1999). *Los siete saberes necesarios para la educación del futuro*. París: UNESCO.

Morin, E. (2011). *La Vía. Para el futuro de la humanidad*. Barcelona: Paidos.

Morin, E., & Kern, A. (2005). *Tierra-Patria*. Barcelona: Kairós.

Nicolescu, B. (2008). *O Manifesto da Transdisciplinaridade*. São Paulo: TRIOM.

Nicolescu, B. (2014). *From modernity to cosmodernity. Science, culture, and spirituality*. New York: SUNY.

Novo, M. (2009). *El desarrollo sostenible. Su dimensión ambiental y educativa*. Madrid: Ed. Universitas.

Núñez-Madrazo, M. C. (2012). Sustainability and spirituality: A transdisciplinary perspective. In *Transdisciplinarity and sustainability* (pp. 102–111). Texas: Atlas Publishing.

Panikkar, R. (1998a). *El Imperativo intercultural*. In *Unterwegs zur interkulturellen Philosophie*. Dokumentation des II. Internationalen Kongress für Interkulturelle Philosophie. IKO – Verlag für Interkulturelle Kommunikation.

Panikkar, R. (1998b). *The cosmotheandric experience. Emerging religious consciousness*. New Delhi: Motilal Banarsidass Publishers.

Panikkar, R. (1999). *The intra-religious dialogue.* New York: Paulist Press.

Plutchik, R. (2003). *Emotions and life: Perspectives from psychology, biology, and evolution.* Washington, DC: American Psychological Association.

Rimanoczy, I. (2013). *Big Bang being: Developing the sustainability mindset.* Sheffield: Greenleaf.

Robinson, K. (2011). *Out of our minds: Learning to be creative.* Mankato: Capstone.

Russell, J. (1980). A circumplex model of affect. *Journal of Personality and Social Psychology, 39*(6), 1161–1178.

Salovey, P., & Mayer, J. (1990). Emotional intelligence. *Imagination, Cognition and Personality, 9*(3), 185–211.

Shouler, K. (2010). *The everything world's religions book. Explore the beliefs, traditions, and cultures of ancient and modern religions.* Avon: Adams Media.

Smith, H. (2003). *Why religion matters. The fate of the human spirit in an age of disbelief.* San Francisco: HarperCollins.

Steiner, C. (1997). *Achieving emotional literacy.* New York: Avon Books.

Steiner, C. (2003). *Emotional literacy: Intelligence with a heart. Learn to achieve better personal and professional relationships.* Fawnskin: Personhood Press.

Steiner, R. (1992). *Approaches to anthroposophy. Human life from the perspective of spiritual science* (J. M. Thompson, Eds.). Sussex: Rudolf Steiner Press.

United Nations. (2015). *Transforming our world: The 2030 agenda for sustainable development.* Retrieved in September 25, 2016, https://sustainabledevelopment.un.org/content/doc uments/21252030%20Agenda%20for%20Sustainable%20Development%20web.pdf

Wackernagel, M., & Ress, W. (1996). *Our ecological footprint. Reducing human impact on the earth.* Gabriola Island: New Society Publishers.

Zohar, D., & Marshall, I. (2000). *SQ: Spiritual intelligence. The ultimate intelligence. Connecting with our spiritual intelligence.* London: Bloomsbury Publishing.

PART II

Curricular examples of embedding sustainability mindset within management education

7

EXPERIENTIAL LEARNING METHODS FOR TEACHING ENTREPRENEURSHIP WITH A SUSTAINABILITY MINDSET

Henrietta Onwuegbuzie and Ijeoma Ugwuanyi

Introduction

In the past, the emphasis of business has been uni-directional – focused mainly on profit-making (Elkington, 2004). Even when corporate social responsibility activities were carried out, they were often done only after the businesses reached a certain level of profitability and, in addition, was compelled to do so by regulation or restiveness on the part of the stakeholders affected by the business operations. The rising wave of terrorism spreading across the globe (Nagdy & Roser, 2016; Peters, 2015) has been fuelled by the growing disparity between the rich and the poor in most countries (Giddens, 2011). Sustainability-driven entrepreneurship, which triggers inclusive growth by seeking to improve the lives of others using profitable business models, offers a means to stem this tide.

This chapter explores experiential learning methods for effectively teaching entrepreneurship with a sustainability mindset. Sustainability mindset in this context relates to the concepts of being, thinking and doing that translates to the greater good of the entire ecosystem, including the abiotic and biotic components (Kassel, Rimanoczy,& Mitchell, 2016).

Theories and concepts that support experiential learning and teaching with a sustainability mindset are featured while practical projects carried out by students applying sustainable business principles are also presented. The central model adopted for teaching entrepreneurship is around using business as a tool for societal transformation. The students in the MBA and Executive MBA classes are therefore taught to design business models that are targeted at solving specific problems while making financial returns and being mindful of the environment. The paper also highlights the benefits that accrue from intentionally seeking to transform society positively through business. The chapter presents four approaches through which this can be achieved.

The first approach is the use of written and video case studies to provide examples of entrepreneurial journeys and challenges entrepreneurs face at different stages and circumstances of their business operations. The second approach involves practical hands-on projects that allow a first-hand learning experience. The third approach involves getting the students to *meet practice*. This entails inviting entrepreneurs to share their entrepreneurial journeys with students in class. The fourth approach allows learning through direct observation of business processes, and involves visits to existing businesses to observe how they operate, learn from what is being done right and recommend improvements regarding what is being done wrong or could be done better in the business.

All four approaches provide practical ways of learning and practicing entrepreneurship. Embedded in the strategies that have been outlined is the overall goal of creating entrepreneurs with a sustainability mindset that leads to greater social awareness. These approaches are discussed in detail in later sections.

Importance of teaching entrepreneurship with a sustainability mindset

The sustainability mindset is designed as, "*a way of thinking and being that results from a broad understanding of the ecosystem's manifestations as well as an introspective focus on one's personal values and higher self, and finds its expression in actions for the greater good of the whole*" (Kassel, Rimanoczy, & Mitchell, 2016, p. 2).

Sustainability is often associated with the triple bottom line of assessing business performance, which includes the social, financial and environmental impact (Elkington, 1994; McDonough & Braungart, 2002). This is contrasted with conventional business strategies targeted at achieving only financial goals. While this transition from the traditional focus on just financial goals to the triple bottom line is gradual (Elkington, 2004), business schools can accelerate this process by training existing and would-be managers/entrepreneurs to aim at achieving the triple bottom line, which ultimately leads to more sustainable (and possibly more profitable) operations.

Society is increasingly questioning the relevance of business schools and demanding that they make a stronger impact in response to the myriad of socio-economic challenges facing today's society. Most existing models of management training, through which managers are socialised, emphasise organisational profit, without regard to the consequences of their operations on the environment or society. This has led to what can be termed "predatory capitalism" (Acemoglu and Robinson, 2012), which creates a systematic neglect of environmental concerns and the socio-economic exclusion of the majority of populations (Akrivou and Huang, 2015). The emerging consequences are climate change and social exclusion of the majority, which has given rise to increasing societal ills such as terrorism and delinquency, which are now in the forefront of global concerns (United Nations Global Compact, 2007). It is becoming increasingly recognised that business as usual is leading to an unsustainable society and world economy, and that there is an urgent need to stem this tide by transiting from a profit focused orientation to a sustainability mindset. As business schools continue to be a major channel for the development of managers, it is pertinent to ensure that they are equipping managers to become leaders with a sustainability mindset. This chapter argues that business schools can shift the trend from a profit-only focus to one that intentionally includes social and environmental goals. This can be achieved through the kind of management training they provide (Akrivou and Huang, 2015).

Teaching entrepreneurship: a review

In the past few decades, there has been considerable concern over the rising rate of terrorism (Nagdy & Roser, 2016; Peters, 2015), unemployment (International Labour Organisation, 2014) and the high failure rates of startups (Brain, 2013). These problems pose a huge challenge to society. Educators, especially those in business schools, can play a major role in mitigating this challenge, as they can influence the development of individuals, managers and future world leaders with a more holistic, values-driven management perspective, such that management is understood to encompass societal and environmental well-being, besides financial gain. Furthermore, to solve the problem of growing unemployment, business schools should deliberately focus on producing graduates with a problem-solving and job-creation mindset, beyond improving job eligibility, which has been the traditional focus of most business schools. This can be achieved through a curriculum infused with a strong entrepreneurial orientation.

Over the years, there have been arguments as to whether entrepreneurs are born or made, or whether traits found in entrepreneurs can be taught; this argument is a result of the widespread myth that entrepreneurs are born with certain characteristics and traits that cannot be taught in the classrooms (Henry, Hill & Leitch, 2005; Blenker, Dreisler, Færgeman, & Kjeldsen, 2006; Read, Sarmiento & Street, 2006; Neck & Greene, 2011). Studies have, however, shown that entrepreneurs can be taught (Kuratko, 2005; Gibb, 2007), especially using experiential techniques (Sherman, Sebora, & Digman, 2008). This realisation should stir entrepreneurship educators to make the transition from traditional methods of passive lectures to alternative, experiential methods of transmitting entrepreneurial knowledge and skills (Kickul & Fayolle, 2007). Such methods could involve the use of live cases, company visits, interactions with entrepreneurs and simulations (Sherman, Sebora, & Digman, 2008).

Some authors argue that it is difficult to move entirely away from the traditional "lecturer-centred, passive" learning methods, especially when other traditional business courses like Information Systems, Marketing, Finance and Management also make up the development of entrepreneurship knowledge (Jones & English, 2004, p. 416). This chapter posits that passive lectures only are not effective in building functional competencies. This is buttressed by the current high failure rates of startups (Brain, 2013). Rather, including experiential learning methods ensures that students graduate with practical hands-on experience, which not only makes it easier for them to become entrepreneurs when they leave school but also increases their chances of success.

As previously noted, it is important that students graduate not only with knowledge about entrepreneurship but are also equipped with a sustainability mindset. This ultimately leads to sustainable development, because it accelerates the social inclusion of a significantly higher percentage of the population, while the business makes profits. The sustainability mindset can be achieved by exposing students to projects that allow them to experience how doing good is good for business. This can be done by getting the students to embark on business ventures aimed at solving specific problems, using profitable business models. Examples of this are shown in Table 7.1, where the students in the MBA programme at Lagos Business School embarked on problem-driven business initiatives. They were provided with minimal startup capital (the equivalent of $30) on purpose. This was aimed at helping them learn to be resourceful, by using what they have, to get what they want. The idea of starting a business that makes profit from solving problems is a departure from the traditional dichotomy between social entrepreneurship, which emphasises solving social and environmental problems, and commercially driven entrepreneurship, which tends to be solely profit-driven. Today's society, where insecurity and societal ills are increasingly fuelled by rising poverty levels and the absence of inclusive growth, requires business models that address these challenges in a way that leads to shared prosperity.

The social impact concept is still in the budding stages of development (Tracey & Phillips, 2007), and it is referred to in different ways by different authors. For some, it is referred to as the "social economy" (Mook, Quarter & Ryan, 2012). This term is used to describe organisations and individuals who are driven by financial and social bottom lines, including the need to satisfy all stakeholders of the entity. For them social economy business owners believe that the social and economic aspect of the society are reciprocal and must therefore be in equilibrium. Other authors refer to the individuals and organisations who exhibit the traits explained above as social entrepreneurs (Bornstein, 2007; Tracey & Phillips, 2007). While there are different perspectives on social entrepreneurship, the most common is the not-for-profit model. This model, however, tends to be unsustainable as it is financially dependent on donations, which are not constant in many instances.

Businesses can nevertheless address society's most pressing problems through profitable business models. Several examples are presented in Table 7.1. Similarly, an existing business can incorporate impact. For instance, an entrepreneur, who runs a dress-making factory, may decide to open a tailoring training school that accepts both fee-paying students as well as those who cannot afford to pay. The trainees who cannot afford the fees could work part-time for the sewing factory and, by so doing, work to earn their tuition. Ultimately, while ensuring skill acquisition for the trainees, the training centre also provides a steady source of skilled labour for the factory and provides the entrepreneur increased capacity at a lower cost than if he hired professionals for the job. The additional capacity also enables the entrepreneur

TABLE 7.1 Lagos Business School's MBA for-profit social impact projects started with an initial capital of $30

S/N	Name of Enterprise	Social problem (s)	Business Model	Sustainable Outcome (s)
1	GREENFIELDS ENTERPRISE	Poverty and lack of fair returns for farmers	"Our business, Greenfields Enterprise, aims to give farmers a fair return for their wages by creating access to markets and providing them with fair returns. Farmers of exotic vegetables and spices like Dill, Coriander, Celery, Parsley, Indian Palak, etc., are our target. We set out to achieve two objectives; first, to help the farmers reduce waste as a result of glut. Second, through increased sales and fair pricing, increase the returns farmers get from their produce and thus raise their standard of living. We have been able to achieve these objectives, in a mutually profitable manner, such that we both earn good margins, while our customers are happy to have a reliable source of fresh and exotic vegetables and fruits at affordable prices."	"Our customers are fruit and vegetable marts, supermarkets, hotels and restaurants. They represent an estimated demand size of over N100 million annually. A return on investment of over 30% is expected, even after paying our farmers a fair wage. Our immediate plans are centered on scaling up the business to enable us to exploit this opportunity even more and capture more value for the farmers and ourselves."
2	BHEALTHY BAKERY	Unhealthy pastries (high cholesterol content) and unemployment	"To solve the problem of consumption of unhealthy pastries, Bhealthy Bakery intends to nourish the community with quality and healthy pastries."	"Every year, we will train and mentor at least 24 unemployed youths on how to bake as well as how to start their business. The training, which costs N50,000 for a month, will be offered for free for those who cannot afford the fee; these trainees will work for us part-time in exchange of their tuition. After the training they will be left with the choice of being employed by us, or leave to start their own businesses."

(Continued)

TABLE 7.1 (Continued)

S/N	Name of Enterprise	Social problem (s)	Business Model	Sustainable Outcome (s)
3	TRESOR: Handmade treasures	Out-of-school children, unemployment	"About 10.5 million young children drop out of high school every year in Nigeria to cater for themselves and their families. Most of these drop-outs get involved in street hawking, prostitution, armed robbery and other social vices, just to make ends meet. Tresor intends to provide these children with skills in the art of bead making. Empowering these youths with skills allows them to become entrepreneurs in their own respect. They can then make and sell accessories for a profit."	"After training the students over a period of one month, during which they are taught different styles and designs to suit Tresor's customers, they are able to make items for sale. The students benefit from the market that Tresor provides through its network, while Tresor benefits from the pool of skilled labour that is always available to cater to the demands of its customers. The margins are also very high, providing a very profitable business for Tresor and its investors."
4	YOUTHS' REDEFINED CONSULTING	Youth unemployment	"Youths' Redefined Consulting (YRC) is an impact investing business that equips youths with both hard and soft skills as well as provides small and medium-scale businesses with recruitment and training services. Over 80% of youths are unemployable due to inadequate workplace skills. We intend to solve this problem by equipping young unemployed graduates with skills that will give them an edge in the labour market. We will train them specifically in the area of sales, marketing and customer service. The trainings will also include sessions on soft skills and values. An affordable fee of N3,000 per person is charged, and recruiters also pay us a fee for each staff recruited from our talent pool. With our lean startup, we can confidently train at least 100 youths annually. By providing SMEs with well trained staff, we also facilitate their growth and their ability to employ more people. The recruitment arm of our business also promises to generate significant revenue, as many companies face the challenge of finding well-trained staff."	"We plan to work with universities, which will recommend graduating students to us for training. We will also contact the human resource departments of major organisations, so that they are aware of the kind of services that we are poised to offer."

| 5 | Book City | Illiteracy, poor reading culture and insufficient educational resources in mainly public schools | Theme: Develop yourself; secure/empower your future. "Our business, Book City, seeks to establish book clubs where reading and writing skills are taught and developed, and also supply educational resources (books) to public school libraries. The business makes profit from book sales to higher income groups and book club subscriptions targeted at the middle income class through private schools." | "With a book market size of about N28.9million, the business should make a Return on Investment (ROI) of 40%. Our aim is to grow the business organically." |
| 6 | SPARKLE CLEANING SERVICES | Women's unemployment, good cleaning services | "Sparkle Cleaning Services aims at solving two problems: – To empower and create a sustainable source of income for jobless women, by engaging these women in providing cleaning services. We would start with a cluster of women we found in the region of Sango Tedo (town in Lagos State, Nigeria). – To provide good cleaning services for the average working-class family, corporate offices, event centers and estates." | "As the business grows we intend to start a training school, where young women and single mothers can be trained to carry out these services. During the training they would learn about integrity, loyalty and our company's standard operating procedures to ensure a uniform standard of cleaning. This training school would also be an avenue where individuals and corporate bodies can request for long-term cleaning contracts. From industry research estimates, the potential of the cleaning service market is over N3 billion. The growing population of working-class families, the thriving real estate sector and the number of events that take place on a daily basis account for this amount. We believe that we can capture a significant part of this market by building a strong and trustworthy brand while changing the lives of thousands of women." |

(Continued)

TABLE 7.1 (Continued)

S/N	Name of Enterprise	Social problem (s)	Business Model	Sustainable Outcome (s)
7	FUCHSIBELLA	Social needs: lack of finance to pursue further education, reduce crime rates, under-age pregnancies	"Most young persons in Nigeria find themselves financially incapable to continue their education. This has led to an increase in the number of school drop-outs, underage pregnancies and higher crime rates. Also, ladies within the ages of 18–40 who are fashion conscious have the need for trendy and bespoke accessories that can be worn to different events. Fuchsibella intends to meet these needs by bringing the two distinct groups together in a way that is mutually beneficial to both parties and thus create a win–win situation. The financially incapacitated makes accessories for the fashion-conscious ladies. The financially incapacitated gets paid and the money used to further their education."	"By training 100 students yearly, I will ensure that 500 lives are impacted directly with the average return of 50% on investments."
8	SUSU GROUND OATMEAL	Health challenges: diabetes, impaired glucose tolerance and unemployment	"Our product, SUSU GROUND OATMEAL is designed to give relief to persons that may be suffering from the health challenges mentioned. We have therefore put forward two strategic and sustainable solutions that can assist in solving the problems highlighted: (1) For every five oatmeal sold, one is given to an individual in the public hospitals who has diabetes, cholesterol or sugar problems. We are in partnership with the Lagos teaching hospital to make this possible. (2) We currently employ the services of young persons who do not have resources to continue their education. We have started with young persons in the Jakande area (in Lagos, Nigeria), where our factory is located. They receive a commission for every 10 packets of Susu oatmeal that they are able to sell."	"We have a projected profit of N1.05 million in 2015 with a projected 30% increase annually. This projection is in line with our expansion plans to other parts of Lagos and beyond."

9	COIR	Biodegradable products for export	"There is a shift towards biodegradable natural products in the western world, and we believe this has created a viable market for exportation of COIR products." "Coir Nigeria Limited plans to offer good-quality coir fibre and coco pith at internationally competitive prices and also based on the specifications of our customers."	"The financial model of our business is equity capital (70%) and bank finance (30%). We hope to break even by the third year. A sinking fund will be established from the fourth year with a dual purpose of debt servicing and working capital provision. Money from the sinking fund for the working capital purposes will be given at the existing interest rate."
10	ACCESS THRIFT TO CREDIT SCHEME	Lack of access to financial institutions	"Over 80% of Nigerians do not have access to financial institutions whilst only about 28.6 million adults in Nigeria have bank accounts. 80% of the unbanked population are women. We will provide financial services to women in the lowest cadre of the society."	"To surmount the challenge of apathy to savings, we will carry out direct marketing efforts and also organise sensitisation workshops. The operations of the business will be within appropriate regulatory framework to avoid regulatory challenges. To ensure transparency, thrift collectors will be properly screened and bound to the scheme contractually to prevent the risk of cross activities of thrift collectors."
11	ARETELINK ASSOCIATES	Lack of qualified teachers and lack of skills for gainful employment	"ARETELINK ASSOCIATES seeks to create a channel for unemployed graduates to develop a career in formal and vocational education by training and developing them into world-class tutors. By doing this, we will be contributing to raising the standard of education in Nigeria and providing an excellent learning experience for our students."	"We will support the economic and social progress of our host communities by maintaining excellent partnerships in various sectors. Our strategy will also involve the development of a volunteering programme while we give free English lessons to disadvantaged persons in the community. We will also protect the environment through efficient use of resources by uploading video tutorials of lessons on YouTube so as to reduce printing and energy use. A financial forecast over a two-year period pegs the revenue as N9.01M in year 1 and N18.02 in year 2. The gross profit is estimated at N6,49 million in year 1 and N14,240,000 in year 2."

(Continued)

TABLE 7.1 (Continued)

S/N	Name of Enterprise	Social problem (s)	Business Model	Sustainable Outcome (s)
12	ENVIROP LIMITED	Poor management of solid waste, unemployment	"Proper management of solid waste is critical to the health and well-being of urban residents. In Ibadan, several tons of solid waste is left uncollected on streets each day. This has caused clogged drains and has created breeding sites for pests that spread diseases. Envirop Limited aims to create a plastic products waste gathering, segregation and recycling hub in Ibadan, Nigeria. The unemployed will be engaged in the process of removing plastic wastes from neighbourhoods and thus contribute to a cleaner environment while generating income."	"Envirop is using a competitive compensation package (per kg and target-based monthly payment plans) to attract and keep solid waste collectors. We also hope to create a strong brand that will stand the test of any adverse macroeconomic conditions."
13	MOBALACHE SERVICING COMPANY	Lack of adequate skill in the hospitality industry in Port Harcourt and unemployment	"MOBALACHE servicing company is aimed at bridging the gap created by the problems listed through the provision of capacity-building programmes for possible employees of the hospitality industry. In the long run, this programme will help improve customers' experience in the hotels with well-trained staff; it will also lead to guaranteed continued patronage in these hotels."	"We will provide high-quality services consistently so as to ensure satisfaction of clients. We will also be in partnership with the youth associations and community leaders, from whom we could draw a pool of young unemployed persons for training. A 3-year financial forecast estimates revenue at N25million in the first year and N34 million by the third year. The gross profit is estimated at N6.5 million in the first year and N11million by the third year. The profit after tax is N2.79 million in the first year and N56 million by the third year. The retained earnings is pegged at N2.79 million in the 1st year and N4.13 million by the third year."

| 14 | PRIMUS RENEE ENGINEERING LTD | Lack of professional artisans, unemployment | "We discovered that businesses, estates, homes in Lekki/Ajah axis (in Lagos, Nigeria) are presently being underserved by handymen, who are known for being dishonest and dubious.

PRIMUS seeks to take all possible mechanical, electrical and plumbing (MEP) related burdens off their customers by providing round-the-clock electrical and mechanical services in a professional, reliable, convenient and secure manner to our target customers." | "To avoid the risk of uncertainties and insecurity associated with working with random skilled technicians, PRIMUS offers guaranteed quality service to its customers.

PRIMUS shall adopt the use of eco-friendly materials and offer the same standard in service to all its customers.

PRIMUS will address the social problem of unemployment/underemployment by having its labour pool drawn from a mix of versed professionals who will be supported by young trainees to be drawn from a pool of unemployed or underemployed youths."

"In year 1, the total sale was N1,34 million. Gross margin was at N1.34 million. In year 2, the total sale is estimated at N3.16 million. Gross margin is at N3,16 million. In year 3, total sale is estimated at N4.98 million. Gross margin is at N4. 98 million." |

(Continued)

TABLE 7.1 (Continued)

S/N	Name of Enterprise	Social problem (s)	Business Model	Sustainable Outcome (s)
15	KENVIC'S OIL (PALM OIL/PALM KERNAL OIL PRODUCTION & MARKETING COMPANY)	Shortage of vegetable oil	"Presently, Nigeria is experiencing shortages in supply of all grades of vegetable oil, especially red palm oil. Local market prices are currently double international. Kenvic proposes a business model that will increase the supply of crude palm oil and palm kernel for local consumption and eventually for exports."	"To combat fire in factory premises, there will be introduction of safety management practices and regular fire drills. Credit sales will be kept at a minimum to avoid bad debt. Production shall be monitored and controlled to ensure that it meets both NAFDAC and international specifications before packaging. The project will require the investment of 56 million Naira (including working capital requirement of 10.7 million). It is planned to raise the fund by a mix of lease financing (N19.7 million) and equity financing (N33.1 million). The project will breakeven within the first 12 months and all loans repaid within 30 months. Cash flows on the project indicate that the project will be self-sustaining after the first 12 months."
16	KUNSE NIGERIA LIMITED	Shortfall of about 30 million cubic meters in oxygen production in Nigeria	"This project intends to take advantage of the shortfall by producing oxygen in commercial quantities."	"Gross sales revenue in the first year will be N25.08 million. The corresponding production expenses will amount to N12.702 million, leaving earnings before interest and company tax of N12.378 million. The earnings before interest and company tax will increase to N20.475 million in the fifth year. With the impressive economic returns, a good technical team will be assembled by the promoters of this business. Equipment will be supplied by a reputable manufacturer; we would also see that technical support is available locally. This project is viable and is recommended for funding support from financing institution."

to take on larger orders, which bring in more revenue and profits. Furthermore, when fully trained, the trainees have three options available to them: (1) they could be employed to work full time for the company that trained them; (2) they could be employed by other entrepreneurs in the industry who need skilled workers; and (3) they could decide to become self-employed entrepreneurs as they have acquired the required training. The business model thus provides empowerment through skill acquisition; employment, by engaging them to work in the factory; or eligibility for employment by tailors in the industry. This model thus effectively addresses poverty alleviation, because the trainees acquire earning capacity/financial independence, and creates wealth for the entrepreneur, who can successfully execute large orders because of his pool of workers. Such business models accelerate inclusive growth, which leads to shared prosperity, more sustainable businesses and, ultimately, sustainable development. Such business models also provide an effective means of addressing the rising global insecurity, as those who may have turned to crime as a means of survival become gainfully engaged and are transformed into assets that contribute to society and economic growth. For-profit, social-purpose business models such as these reconcile the world of social entrepreneurship, which tends to be donor-dependent or non-profit and therefore financially vulnerable, with that of commercial entrepreneurship, which is usually profit focused alone. The absence of a financially viable business model tends to hinder the positive impact of social entrepreneurs. Thus, by designing for-profit business models with a social purpose, social problems can be tackled in a significant and more sustainable manner, creating a more sustainable solution. This ultimately results in a better operating environment and more sustainable businesses.

At the Lagos Business School (LBS), we began to expose our students to experiential exercises based on this "for-profit, social impact" business model since 2013. Approximately 25 students took part in the first set. They worked in groups of twos and threes, forming about 12 groups in total. They were asked to start a venture aimed at solving a problem using a profitable business model. They were also given minimal capital, the equivalent of $30. This was aimed at helping them learn the art of starting small, while thinking big. At first, the students found it difficult to reconcile social impact with profit, and they struggled with the idea that a business could be started with so little capital. Nevertheless, by the end of the 11-week project period, most of the students had started businesses that were impacting lives and making profit. They gained first-hand experience about solving problems using profitable business models, while being mindful of the environment. By socialising business school students with such projects, a category of business leaders who perceive success to include making a positive social and environmental impact beyond profit-making are developed.

This chapter therefore advocates that when potential entrepreneurs are taught with a sustainability mindset, they develop greater social consciousness that leads them to see business as a tool for transforming society (Stephan, Patterson & Kelly, 2013).

Theoretical framework

The underpinning theoretical framework of this chapter is the experiential learning theory (ELT). It is used to explain how experiential learning with a social impact dimension can produce entrepreneurs, with a sustainability mindset. Although the ELT does not directly have a social impact dimension, the principles anchored by the ELT supports the methods adopted in teaching entrepreneurship with a sustainability mindset. ELT explains that learning should be studied as a process, rather than considered in terms of outcomes (Corbett, 2005; Kolb, 1984). Focus should therefore be on the process of learning and factors that influence how individuals transform experience into knowledge. Entrepreneurial learning is perceived as a dynamic, continuous process (Cope, 2001, 2003, 2005; Deakins & Freel, 1998; McGill & Beaty, 2001; Minniti & Bygrave, 2001; Morris, Kuratko, Schindehutte & Spivack, 2011; Reuber & Fischer, 1999). In relation to entrepreneurship, this learning starts before the venture startup process and continues all through the existence of the business as a result of the interactions of the entrepreneur with the venture and the environment (Cope, 2005; Kolb, 1984; Rae, 2000). ELT thus explains how the experience acquired by individuals during the learning process influences subsequent entrepreneurial behaviours. Consequently, the belief is that when one has experienced how a business venture seeking to proffer solutions or impact society positively can be profitable, the person is likely to develop a tendency to set up businesses that seek to solve problems using profitable business models. The students who have gone through this sort of training would therefore have learned that problems represent potentially profitable business opportunities. The theory therefore explains how individuals acquire and transform their experiences into knowledge in the entrepreneurial process (Corbett, 2005).

Kolb (1984) argues that learning is a lifelong process and explains that individuals learn through experience, reflection, thought and experimentation. He identifies three learning modes – concrete experience, reflective observation and abstract conceptualisation. He uses these modes to explain how individuals acquire and transform information and experience into knowledge. Although individuals may experience the different learning modes, Kolb (1984) explains that different individuals tend towards some learning modes more than others. Also, different learning modes could be more appropriate at the different phases in the life-cycle of a venture. It is therefore important that different experiential learning methods are applied in seeking to transmit a sustainability mindset in entrepreneurship. The various learning methods allow the recipients an opportunity to learn according to their preferred mode, rather than compel them to follow any one method of learning.

Furthermore, the teaching methods proposed here cater to the learning modes presented by Kolb: concrete experience is provided by the hands-on projects the participants are expected to execute, which entails starting a venture with the aim of solving identified problems using profitable business models to ensure financial sustainability. Reflective observation is provided by the exercise of observing and analysing other existing businesses to learn from how well they are being run, determining what is not being done well and making recommendations for better outcomes, while aiming to achieve the triple bottom line. Abstract conceptualisation is achieved through discussions on case studies that present the journeys of entrepreneurs who are transforming society through their businesses, in a profitable way.

Because issues around sustainability are often complex and related to multiple areas of knowledge, imparting a sustainability mindset to students would usually involve a robust framework and process of learning, as explained by the experiential learning theory. Furthermore, Kassel, Rimanoczy, and Mitchell (2016) propose that sustainability mindset learning can be achieved through three dimensions:(1) thinking, which relates to upholding higher values; (2) acquiring knowledge of nature through relationships and self-knowledge (being) and (3) doing, which requires the capacity to apply knowledge and values to activities that lead to the greater good of all.

The three dimensions of thinking, acquiring knowledge and doing (Kassel, Rimanoczy & Mitchell, 2016) overlap favourably with the dimensions of Kolb's experiential learning theory and provide another lens to understand how a sustainability mindset model can be transmitted through the experiential process of teaching entrepreneurship as shown by the following comparisons:

Thinking – – – Reflective observation
Acquiring knowledge – – – Abstract conceptualisation
Doing – – – Concrete experience

This comparison suggests that the authors coincide in the way they conceptualise the learning process such that, while Kassel, Rimanoczy, and Mitchell (2016) look at the cause that leads to certain outcomes, Kolb (1984) considers the same process based on the outcomes. Consequently, thinking may be considered to lead to reflective observation; acquiring knowledge considered to give rise to abstract conceptualisation; and doing considered to lead to concrete experience.

The learning approaches are discussed further in the next section.

Ways of achieving experiential learning in entrepreneurship with a sustainability perspective

The first approach is the use of case studies to provide examples of entrepreneurs who intentionally make a positive impact on society through profitable business operations. These case studies showcase the advantages of the "for-profit, social purpose" or impact-driven model. They also portray challenges entrepreneurs face at different stages and circumstances of their business operations and how they overcome them. The case studies provide an opportunity to inspire the readers to act as well as learn from the examples of the entrepreneurs they read about, while avoiding their mistakes. For instance, one of the cases used in class is about an indigenous entrepreneur named Nike Davies-Okundaye, who trained indigent women and men with skills in art to lift them out of poverty, using a profitable business model. Being a successful artist, she set up a gallery where she exhibited her works and those of other well-known Nigerian artists. The gallery was also used to facilitate the sales of artworks by the people she trained in her workshops. She established her training workshops beside the gallery, to allow her trainees to exhibit their works alongside renowned artists, who attracted wealthy art collectors. By so doing, she raised thousands of men and women out of poverty. She practically pulled indigent people off the streets and encouraged them to learn different forms of art, with which they could earn a living.

She did not charge any fees and ensured that her trainees achieved financial independence through the sale of their works. She therefore had a financially sustainable way of empowering others. The entrepreneur, Okundaye, was also featured in the pioneer Aim-to-Flourish case collection,[1] which showcased entrepreneurs like her, who were doing for-profit businesses with a social impact – in other words, doing business for world benefit.

The second approach involves practical hands-on projects that allow a first-hand learning experience. Students are given seed capital to start a business venture that is impact-driven. They are charged with the task of solving any identified problem, using a profitable business model. Besides gaining practical experience, two other learning goals are sought: first, they experience how having an impact-driven business tends to attract customer patronage and, consequently, accelerate returns. Second, considering that they are intentionally provided with little capital ($30), they learn the importance of starting small, while thinking big. Table 7.1 provides several examples of the business ventures started by the students. One such example is the "Impact 500" business venture, which was eventually renamed Fuschibella. The business was aimed at improving 500 lives and targeted mainly at indigent girls who run the risk of not attending or dropping out of school because their parents cannot afford fees. The business aimed to train such girls to make ladies' accessories, like bangles, earrings and neck- pieces from indigenous fabrics known as "Ankara". The fabric gives them a unique African touch. As the initial capital was not sufficient to buy enough material to train all five girls, the student entrepreneur bought and sold conventional accessories till she multiplied her capital five times over. Having secured enough funds to buy the materials she needed, she proceeded to a low-income public school and approached the school principal, with her plan to train five of the most indigent female students, who could earn some money in their spare time and therefore ensure that their school fees are paid and support their families. The principal was delighted with the idea and very quickly selected the girls for the training. The training thus started with five indigent girls who were at risk of dropping out of school. The accessories are branded and marketed by the student entrepreneur, who paid the girls as they produced. Through this business, several girls are now assured of continuing their education, and they also contribute to their family purse. The business was started in 2015 and continues to enjoy good patronage to date. Besides enjoying a thriving local demand, some customers buy the products for export.

This business model aimed to empower through training in marketable skills, while providing access to markets through the network of the student entrepreneur to facilitate commercialisation. The success of the venture was therefore based on matching skills training, with access to markets.

The third approach involves getting the students to *meet practice*. This entails inviting entrepreneurs to share stories of their entrepreneurial journeys with students in class. In some instances, this approach is combined with case studies, such that the students would have read a case about the entrepreneur, who then comes to class to throw more light on the case and answer questions.

The fourth approach entails learning from observation. It involves an assignment requiring the students to visit existing businesses to observe how they operate, learn from what they are doing right and recommend improvements regarding what could be done better in the way the business is run.

These points are further explained in the following sections.

Case studies

The first aspect of experiential learning activity that is used in teaching entrepreneurship is the case study method. The cases are of various formats and lengths. They could be either short or long cases (Davis & Wilcock, 2003).

A case study provides different levels of learning. Reading the case allows for personal learning and abstract conceptualisation, as the participants reflect on the experience of the characters in the case and the business evolution. The case discussion in class presents different perspectives, which are shared and another level of learning is attained. Most cases present a challenge the class tries to resolve, and this process hones the participants' problem-solving skills and spurs innovative ideas. These various levels of learning, when based on a sustainability-driven case study, allows both conscious and subconscious development of a sustainability mindset. In addition, the levels of learning mentioned earlier are further related to the sustainability mindset values dimensions, such as interconnectedness, capacity to engage and collaborate with multiple stakeholders, as well as innovative thinking (Kassel, Rimanoczy & Mitchell, 2016).

The central idea is to engage the participants in ways that reflect the advantages of meeting the triple bottom line through entrepreneurship. During the case discussions, students are encouraged to critique the way entrepreneurs tackle the challenges and propose solutions that ensure positive social, economic and environmental impact. This will ensure that rather than reinvent the wheel, they enjoy the advantage of leveraging the experience of other entrepreneurs and become entrepreneurs who accelerate inclusive growth.

Practical hands-on projects

In this approach, participants are required to start a business venture aimed at solving identified problems or to seek to make a positive impact on society, using profitable business models. The goal is to help them realise that they can reconcile making a positive social and/or environmental impact with making profit. The assignment also helps them learn that every problem represents a potentially profitable business opportunity. The participants are scored based on how well their ventures provide effective solutions to the problems they choose to solve, as well as on the profitability of the business, to guarantee financial sustainability. So far, the experience has been that the students witness an accelerated business growth and profitability when their solutions are effective. For instance, the student who sought to empower underprivileged children by teaching them to make bead accessories for women found out that people were more willing to buy the beads when they were informed that the beads were made by underprivileged girls, who hope to earn enough from the sale of the beads to further their education. Experiencing the relationship between impact and profitability ultimately leads even the most capitalist-minded person to act with a sustainability mindset. If business leaders and entrepreneurs are trained with this orientation, it is likely to influence all of their activities, as well as the people who work with them. Consequently, over time, there will be no need for governments to harp on sustainability, as it would become the natural way for to people act.

This point is further illustrated in the business ventures listed in Table 7.1.

Another objective of this approach is for the students to learn that businesses can be started with little or no money. This goes against the common belief that a lot of money is required to start businesses. The capital students receive for their startup is therefore deliberately small ($30). This is aimed at reinforcing the fact that one does not need a lot of money to start a business and to help them learn that it is usually safer to start small, while thinking big. It is also intended to spur their creativity and compel them to develop better resource management skills. This is also another way of developing a sustainability mindset, as they are compelled to find ways to use available resources, especially at the initial stages of the business.

The experience so far from four years of carrying out such projects with students revealed an interesting trend. While some students genuinely aimed at solving problems and making an impact, others were more focused on making money and tried to appear to have some impact. They found it difficult to overcome monetary goals and genuinely seek to make an impact, although they had been told that the impact should be achieved through profitable business models. The outcome, however, showed that the students whose ventures genuinely aimed at solving social problems with profitable business models made more profit than others who were more focused on financial gain. For instance, the business in number 8 on Table 7.1 (Susu Ground Oatmeal) easily attracted customers because it was addressing the need of persons who suffered from diabetes, impaired glucose tolerance and also creating employment. Their business model entailed providing a healthy meal alternative to diabetic and cholesterol patients. In addition, they provided for those patients who could not afford the product through a system of giving out one free pack to such patients, for every five packs sold. This approach was communicated to customers as they marketed the product. Customers were therefore more willing to patronise them, with the goal of embracing an opportunity to give back to the less privileged, while meeting their needs. On the other hand, the business that was mainly profit-driven, and sought to provide freshly baked bread to students, was soon knocked out of business by a competitor who provided hot sandwiches and a drink. There was no commitment on the part of the customers to remain loyal to the fresh bread business, which was perceived as any other business. Even though the team argued that they had a social impact based on the staff they engaged to assist them with selling, the counter-argument was that every business engages staff, but impact-driven businesses tend to address problems that improve lives and engage staff in a way that empowers them to learn and grow as they work for the business.

Although the initial goal of the project was to help students understand that they could reconcile impact with profit, I was surprised to discover how this model consistently led to accelerated profits. Indeed, there was a positive relationship between the degree of impact by the business and the profitability of the business. The experience thus revealed that doing good is indeed good for business.

Giving students an opportunity to start their own businesses while in school provides them with immediate tactical skills and experience. It gives them an opportunity to learn quickly from their own successes and mistakes such that they graduate from the programme as experienced entrepreneurs with a sustainability mindset. Some sustainability mindset competencies developed in the course of starting impact-driven businesses include being able to seek *protective and restorative action* (Kassel, Rimanoczy & Mitchell, 2016), by proffering solutions to identified problems, using financially sustainable business models to ensure the solution is provided consistently. They also develop the competencies of *mindfulness and reflective practices* (Kassel, Rimanoczy & Mitchell, 2016) to further guide their business decisions, such that decisions are viewed with the lens of fairness to all stakeholders and ethical practices.

Inviting entrepreneurs to share real-life experiences: "meet practice"

This approach has a wonderful way of inspiring the participants. Listening to entrepreneurs share their journeys and the impact their businesses have made has a way of inspiring listeners to do the same. This approach is intermingled with company visits where the students listen to the entrepreneur relate his entrepreneurial journey in his operating environment, rather than in a classroom setting. They can therefore also learn from observation. The entrepreneurs and companies that are selected for these visits are those that exemplify a sustainability mindset in practice. This exercise develops the sustainability mindset knowledge dimensions of long-term thinking in making decisions (Kassel, Rimanoczy & Mitchell, 2016), as they aspire to resemble the role models they have seen and heard.

The opportunity to observe such companies and listen to the entrepreneurs helps the lessons learnt to resonate more strongly in the minds of the students/young entrepreneurs. They also have the opportunity to interact with the entrepreneurs and ask questions beyond the classroom or duration of the session. This also provides an avenue for the students to develop a mentor-mentee relationship with the entrepreneurs. As the students reflect on what they have heard and seen, they also get to develop the sustainability mindset competence of mindfulness and reflective practices (Kassel, Rimanoczy & Mitchell, 2016). By selecting entrepreneurs who already run impact-driven businesses, the mentees will more easily tend to become entrepreneurs with a sustainability mindset.

The stories of most successful entrepreneurs tend to reveal small beginnings and the steps that led to their gradual scaling. They therefore provide an effective means of dispelling the frequent belief that big businesses started big and, consequently, that a lot of money is required to start a business. The knowledge about starting small while thinking big will not only encourage more people to embark on entrepreneurship, but will also help them grow in a more sustainable way, as it is easier to manage a smaller business at the onset, while scaling gradually.

This approach of exposing students to the journey of experienced entrepreneurs therefore achieves the twin goal of inspiring entry into entrepreneurship and practising it with a sustainability mindset. Given the global magnitude of the unemployment problem, there is an urgent need to encourage entrepreneurship, which creates jobs. And if people are trained to practice entrepreneurship with a sustainability mindset, it accelerates the attainment of shared prosperity and sustainable development.

Analysing existing businesses to recommend improvements

This approach entails analysing existing businesses with the aim of understanding how they can be better run, as well as learning from the businesses being analysed. It could also be perceived as rendering consultancy services to the business owners. The participants are required to visit existing businesses to observe how they are run. They are expected to discern the strengths and weaknesses of the businesses and make recommendations to help the business run more efficiently and profitably, while infusing their operations with a significant social dimension.

A guideline is provided to help the students analyse the businesses they select to work on. The following questions are contained in the guideline: (1) What is the entrepreneur doing right? (2) What is he/she doing badly or not well enough? (3) What recommendations can be made for the business to run better and achieve the triple bottom line of a positive social, financial and environmental impact? and (4) What are some possible ways of evolving or scaling the business either through related offerings or innovative strategies? The participants are subsequently required to make presentations to the rest of the class using pictures or videos to explain their observations and recommendations. This session provides a great learning opportunity for each participant as they listen to each other's presentations. Consequently, the approach allows direct learning from the businesses that each student visits and peer learning opportunities as they listen to each other present their analyses in class.

This exercise allows for the development of the sustainability mindset dimensions of logical thinking and a sense of oneness (Kassel, Rimanoczy,& Mitchell, 2016).The logical way of thinking is flexible and inclusive, while the sense of oneness incorporates the interests of all stakeholders. In the spiritual intelligence sphere, the exercise strengthens the sense of *oneness* for all that exists, driven by the consciousness of *one's purpose and mission* to further achieve *mindfulness and reflective practices* in business.

All four approaches as proffered by this chapter, and based on the author's teaching experience, allow practical ways of imbibing and practicing entrepreneurship with a sustainability mindset.This will ultimately lead to fostering entrepreneurs who use business as a tool for transforming society from what it is to what it should be.

For-profit business models for social impact

This section presents different for-profit social-purpose business models.Table 7.1 shows 16 for-profit business models for creating social impact.They were designed by the MBA and E/MBA students at the Lagos Business School, Pan-Atlantic University. These business models are applied in the hands-on practical projects that the students execute during the Entrepreneurship course.A number of them have transformed these startups into full-time businesses after the MBA programme.

The business models are centred on solving social problems while making profit. For instance, in Table 7.1 (serial number 2), the BHEALTHY Bakery is aimed at solving the problem of consuming pastries made from unhealthy ingredients such as saturated fats and sugars.The market for this business exists mainly because there are health-conscious people who love pastries but would rather have them prepared with ingredients that are healthier.The business thus provides value in the form of healthier alternatives. In addition to this, the promoters of the business train indigent youths who work for them in return for their tuition for the training, as noted in the following statement by the student entrepreneurs:

> Every year, we will train and mentor at least 24 unemployed youths to bake as well as on how to start a business. The training, which costs N50,000 (US$299) for a month, will be offered free to those who cannot afford to pay. They will however work for us part-time, in exchange for their tuition.After the training they will have a choice of being employed by us, or leave to start their own businesses.
>
> This approach creates various levels of impact. On the first level, it empowers the trainees with skills they can use to earn a living or get jobs. It therefore reduces unemployment. On a second level, it generates capacity for the business to produce on a large scale at lower costs as labour is provided almost free by those who earn their tuition by working for the company and, consequently, more wealth is created. On a fourth level, it creates good will for the business as the community perceives it as an opportunity to train their youths and empower them with skills, enable them to obtain jobs or become entrepreneurs if they so choose.

The other solutions or impact-driven businesses started by the students had similar outcomes. The businesses were profitable not only because the product/ service offering was either meeting a need or solving a problem, but also because they were intentionally making a social impact, which made customers inclined to support them through increased patronage. For instance, the promoters of the SUSU GROUND OATMEAL business (serial number 8 on Table 7.1) noted the following:

> Our product, SUSU GROUND OATMEAL, is designed to give relief to persons suffering from diabetes and cholesterol. Our business provides two sustainable solutions that can assist in solving the problems:
>
> 1 For every five packs of oatmeal sold, one is given free to a patient in a public hospital who has diabetes or cholesterol problems, but cannot afford to buy this meal. We are working in partnership with the Lagos University Teaching Hospital (public hospital) to have the oatmeal delivered to poor patients in a consistent way.
>
> 2 We currently employ the services of young persons who do not have resources to continue their education, to help manufacture and sell the product. We have started with young persons who live where our factory is located. They get paid for helping in the production process, while those in sales receive a commission for every 10 packets of Susu oatmeal that they sell.

As mentioned earlier, the businesses the students execute are intended to serve as a tool for social transformation and inclusive economic growth, while returning profits to the promoters of the business.

Conclusion

This chapter presents different approaches through which future entrepreneurs can be trained to practice entrepreneurship with a sustainability mindset. Some dimensions of the sustainability mindset acquired as highlighted in the chapter include: *logic thinking, long-term thinking, interconnectedness, engagement with all relevant stakeholders*, a *developing sense of oneness, mindfulness* and *reflective practices*(Kassel, Rimanoczy,& Mitchell, 2016).

The four different approaches to teaching entrepreneurship with a sustainability mindset, as discussed in this chapter, are based on the lead author's teaching experience. The first entailed practical hands-on projects, which involves starting a problem or impact-driven business venture during the course, with the goal of solving problems using profitable business models to ensure sustainability. This allows learning by concrete experience. The second approach entailed the exercise of observing and analysing businesses, which allows learning from reflective observation. The third approach was the use of case studies on entrepreneurs who intentionally seek to impact society through their businesses, while the fourth entailed listening to such entrepreneurs share their journeys in person. Both the third and fourth approaches allow learning by abstract conceptualisation. These various approaches reinforce each other. Embedded in these approaches is the overall goal of connecting profitability to social impact with the aim of creating shared prosperity and a more sustainable operating environment, which leads to sustainable socioeconomic development.

It is therefore of utmost importance to develop current and future managers and/or entrepreneurs to inculcate a sustainability mindset in their business practices as opposed to being solely profit-driven. This chapter thus provides a guide on how managers and entrepreneurs can be taught to reconcile social impact with profitmaking, through a sustainability mindset. The approaches presented facilitate the development of socially sensitive entrepreneurs, who can bridge the gap between economic growth and social development and therefore accelerate the positive transformation of society in a sustainable way.

Note

1 Aim2Flourish is an initiative launched by Case Western Reserve University, where professors around the world invite their students to identify a local business that is profitable while working towards any of the Sustainable Development Goals identified by the United Nations Global Compact. The students interview the business leader, and if all criteria are met, they nominate the business for the Flourish Prizes. See www.aim2flourish.com.

References

Acemoglu, D., & Robinson, J. (2012). *Why nations fail: The origins of power, prosperity, and poverty*. New York: Crown Business.

Akrivou, K., & Bradbury-Huang, H. (2015). Educating integrated catalysts: Transforming business schools toward ethics and sustainability. *Academy of Management Learning & Education, 14*(2), 222–240.

Blenker, P., Dreisler, P., Færgeman, H. M., & Kjeldsen, J. (2006). Learning and teaching entrepreneurship: dilemmas, reflections and strategies. In *International entrepreneurship education* (p. 21). Gloucestershire, UK/Northamptom, MA: Edward Elgar Publishing.

Bornstein, D. (2007). *How to change the world: Social entrepreneurs and the power of new ideas.* Oxford: Oxford University Press

Brain, S. (2013). *Statistic brain: Statistic brain.* Retrieved August 30, 2016, from www.statisticbrain.com/

Cope, J. (2001). *The entrepreneurial experience: Towards a dynamic learning perspective of entrepreneurship.* Unpublished Thesis, Lancaster University Management School, Lancaster.

Cope, J. (2003). Entrepreneurial learning and critical reflection: Discontinuous events as triggers for higher-level learning. *Management Learning, 34*(4), 429–450.

Cope, J. (2005). Toward a dynamic learning perspective of entrepreneurship. *Entrepreneurship Theory and Practice, 29*(4), 373–397.

Corbett, A. C. (2005). Experiential learning within the process of opportunity identification and exploitation. *Entrepreneurship Theory and Practice, 29*(4), 473–491.

Davis, C., & Wilcock, E. (2003). *Teaching materials using case studies*(C. Baillie, Series Ed.). The UK Centre for Materials Education. Retrieved from www.materials.ac.uk/guides/1-casestudies.pdf

Deakins, D., & Freel, M. (1998). Entrepreneurial learning and growth processes in SMEs. *The Learning Organisation, 5*(3), 144–155.

Elkington, J. (1994). Towards the sustainable corporation: Win-win-win business strategies for sustainable development. *California Management Review, 36*(2), 90–100. http://dx.doi.org/10.2307/41165746

Elkington, J. (2004). Enter the triple bottom line. *The Triple Bottom Line: Does It All Add Up, 11*(12), 1–16.

Gibb, A. (2007). Creating the entrepreneurial university: Do we need a wholly different model of entrepreneurship. In *Handbook of research in entrepreneurship education*(Vol. 1, pp. 67–103). Gloucestershire, UK/Northamptom, MA: Edward Elgar Publishing.

Giddens, A. (2011). *Runaway world*. London: Profile Books.

Gupta, S., & Kumar, V. (2013). Sustainability as corporate culture of a brand for superior performance. *Journal of World Business, 48*(3), 311–320.

Henry, C., Hill, F., & Leitch, C. (2005). Entrepreneurship education and training: Can entrepreneurship be taught? Part I. *Education + Training, 47*(2), 98–111.

International Labour Organisation. (2014). *Global employment trends 2014*. Retrieved August 30, 2016, from www.ilo.org/global/about-the-ilo/multimedia/maps-and-charts/WCMS_233936/lang-en/index.htm

Jones, C., & English, J. (2004). A contemporary approach to entrepreneurship education. *Education + Training, 46*(8/9), 416–423.

Kassel, K., Rimanoczy, I., & Mitchell, S. F. (2016, January). The sustainable mindset: Connecting being, thinking, and doing in management education. In *Academy of management proceedings* (Vol. 2016, No. 1, p. 16659). Briarcliff Manor, NY: Academy of Management.

Kickul, J., & Fayolle, A. (2007). Cornerstones of change: Revisiting and challenging new perspectives on research in entrepreneurship education. In *Handbook of research in entrepreneurship education* (Vol. 1, pp. 1–17).

Kolb, D. A. (1984). *Experiential learning: Experience as the source of learning and development*. Englewood Cliffs, NJ: Prentice Hall.

Kuratko, D. F. (2005). The emergence of entrepreneurship education: Development, trends, and challenges. *Entrepreneurship Theory and Practice, 29*(5), 577–598.

McDonough, W., & Braungart, M. (2002). Design for the triple top line: new tools for sustainable commerce. *Corporate Environmental Strategy, 9*(3), 251–258.

McGill, I., & Beaty, L. (2001). *Action learning* (2nd ed.). London: Kogan Page.

Minniti, M., & Bygrave, W. (2001). A dynamic model of entrepreneurial learning. *Entrepreneurship Theory & Practice, 25*(3), 5–16.

Morris, M. H., Kuratko, D. F., Schindehutte, M., & Spivack, A. J. (2011). Framing the entrepreneurial experience. *Entrepreneurship Theory and Practice, 36*(1), 11–40.

Nagdy, M., & Roser, M. (2016). *Terrorism*. Published online at OurWorldInData.org. Retrieved from https://ourworldindata.org/terrorism/ [Online Resource].

Neck, H. M., & Greene, P. G. (2011). Entrepreneurship education: known worlds and new frontiers. *Journal of Small Business Management, 49*(1), 55–70.

Peters, M. A. (2015). *Education, globalization and the state in the age of terrorism*. London: Routledge.

Quarter, J., Mook, L., & Ryan, S. (2012). *Businesses with a difference: Balancing the social and the economic*. Toronto: University of Toronto Press.

Rae, D. (2000). Understanding entrepreneurial learning: A question of how? *International Journal of Entrepreneurial Behaviour & Research, 6*(3): 145–159.

Read, E., & Sarmiento, T. (2006). *The benefits of using "live" case studies in entrepreneurship education.* Coventry, UK: Coventry University.

Reuber, A. R., & Fischer. 1999. Understanding the consequences of founders' experience. *Journal of Small Business Management, 37*(2): 30–45.

Savitz, A. (2012). *The triple bottom line: How today's best-run companies are achieving economic, social and environmental success – and how you can too.* New York, NY: John Wiley & Sons.

Sherman, P. S., Sebora, T., & Digman, L. A. (2008). Experiential entrepreneurship in the classroom: Effects of teaching methods on entrepreneurial career choice intentions. *Journal of Entrepreneurship Education, 11*, 29–42.

Stephan, U., Patterson, M., & Kelly, C. (2013). Business-driven social change: A systematic review of the evidence. In *Network for Business Sustainability.* Retrieved from: nbs.net/knowledge

Tracey, P., & Phillips, N. (2007). The distinctive challenge of educating social entrepreneurs: A postscript and rejoinder to the special issue on entrepreneurship education. *Academy of Management Learning & Education, 6*(2), 264–271.

United Nations Global Compact. (2007). *The principles for responsible management education.* New York: United Nations Publications.

8

ENHANCING THE SUSTAINABILITY MINDSET THROUGH REAL-LIFE BUSINESS AS A FLOURISHING IMPACT PROJECT

amelia naim indrajaya

Introduction

The future attitudes and behaviors of business school graduates appear to be influenced by their value systems by the time they leave the business school, creating in many cases a fragmented understanding of reality (Rimanoczy, 2010). It is thus worthwhile to understand how management education changes the value systems of the business school graduate students. Krishnan (2008) shows that during a longitudinal study in a two-year MBA program, a group of students assessed in the beginning and at the end of the program showed that self-oriented values such as social power became more important, and others-oriented values such as being loyal became less important. While this was a one-time study, the traditional economist focus in management education may make people more selfish and less concerned about others, a change in value systems that does not seem to be along the lines that most organizations would prefer (Krishnan, 2008). Burns (1978) posited that transforming leadership is a process in which "leaders and followers help each other to advance to a higher level of morale and motivation". Hence, the objective of management education should be to transform students to a higher value system. The purpose is to prepare business school students to be transformational leaders who are able to help their followers to advance to a higher morale and motivation levels. Krishnan (2008) proposed the need for redesigning the value system of management education toward engaging not only the know-how but also the being dimension, specifically regarding spirituality and interconnectedness.

In order to foster business leaders with readiness to create business as an agent of world benefit (Lazslo et al., 2012; Cooperrider, Whitney & Stavos, 2008), it has been recommended to help them connect with their values through developing a sustainability mindset (Rimanoczy, 2014). The sustainability mindset incorporates the dimensions of values and knowledge in the form of competencies shown through action ("doing") (Kassel, Rimanoczy, & Mitchell, 2016). This integration between the being, knowing and doing creates a powerful impact, aligned with Sterling's (2011) approach of transformative learning for sustainability through epistemic learning, which integrates innovative and systemic characteristics with the spiritual component. The spiritual component has the potential to help students to see interconnectedness and the ability to see opportunities even in the middle of a crisis (Mitroff & Denton, 1999).

In the context of the rich Indonesian culture with a strong spiritual belief embedded in the way of life, this spiritual component becomes more significant. In Indonesia, spirituality has formed a hybrid with the strong religious belief (Muttaqin, 2012). As mentioned by Fry (2009), separating spirituality and religion will be a problem, especially in Eastern cultures. This chapter focuses on the local context of Indonesia. The unique blend of sustainability mindset, namely the systems perspective, spiritual intelligence, ecological worldview and emotional intelligence (Kassel, Rimanoczy, & Mitchell, 2016), is perfectly aligned with the religious/spiritual perspective of the Indonesian cultural heritage with the strong belief that human beings are created as vicegerents of God (Allah) to take care of the universe (Indrajaya, 2016).

Indonesia has a unique background of unity in diversity. Even though the majority of the population is Muslim, conflicts are rare, and other religious beliefs are given high tolerance and ample support. Islam as the majority religion does not promote proselytizing. In this chapter, the writer will illustrate the development of a sustainability mindset via experiential learning in a culturally diverse background. There are six major religious belief systems acknowledged by the Ministry of Religious Affairs in Indonesia: Islam, Christian, Catholic, Hindu, Buddhism and Confucianism. Hence, all of the experiential learning discussed in this chapter is designed for multiple religions and suitable for various cultural backgrounds.

The final project for the students in the course described in this chapter, titled "Outstanding Value: The Knowing, Being and Doing", is in the form of setting up their own startup business. In order to be able to implement the project, students go through several individual and team projects. Neal (2013), in her paper on Spirit at Work, refers to the four levels of spiritual development, which aims at developing within the students the ability to shift their paradigm and redefine the role of business. The first level focuses on Individual Development. In this phase it is critical to identify the students' and/or employees' passion in life and their self-purpose. The second level focuses on Team Development, where students and/or employees need to discover the skill to work with others from different cultural backgrounds and beliefs. The third level is Total System Development, which is intended to transform the way the students and/or employees will address a situation and/or a problem. The fourth level is the development of the ability to Redefine the Role of Business. In this step, students are able to understand the role of Business as an Agent of World Benefit and the flourishing impact it creates for society.

The following section describes the activities in the said course, designed for the undergraduate students of IPMI International Business School in Jakarta, Indonesia.

All of the activities are used in the experiential learning process of this course, which encompasses 32 sessions of 90 minutes each over one semester. The activities are implemented to support the learning process in addition to the content from the text book and case studies. Learning development is implemented in four areas: (1) Individual Development, (2) Team Development, (3) Total System Development, and (4) Redefining the Role of Business. The following diagram is the big picture of the learning development activities (Figure 8.1).

Understanding the big picture through Individual Development

Some authors propose that the human brain has the potential for multiple intelligences (Goleman, 2006). One conceptualization is that multiple intelligences can be seen as part of the three intelligences: IQ (Intellectual Quotient), EQ (Emotional Quotient) and Spiritual Quotient (SQ) (Agustian, 2001). IQ, EQ and SQ have been posited as intertwined and inseparable (Wigglesworth, 2013). Using an experiential learning approach to show the integration among the intellectual, emotional and spiritual approaches has been recommended instead of the traditional teaching pedagogies (Agustian, 2001).

Neal (2013) proposed that spiritual development is necessary to build the desire to transform an approach to business. The first level is thus focused on developing

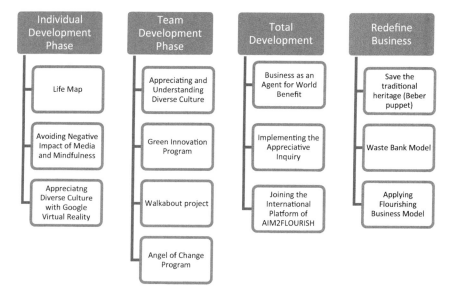

FIGURE 8.1   The Individual Development, Team Development, Total Development and Redefine Business phases conducted in IPMI International Business School, Jakarta, Indonesia

the individual. At this level, students are encouraged to see their life in a big-picture setting.

For the Individual Development phase, there are three exercises: Life Map, Avoiding Negative Impact of Media and Practicing Mindfulness, and Appreciating Diverse Cultures through Virtual Reality (VR) Google. Each section will be discussed as follows.

Life Map

The Life Map is used to understand the big picture in relation to the individual and is designed to focus on helping the students to foster self-reflection and understand more about their values, spiritual principles and sense of purpose. Such foci are basic necessities of the individual development phase, as posited by Neal (2013). The Life Map helps the students to become more aware of what might be their life purpose (Ibrahim, 2004). Figure 8.2 presents the template to implement the Life Map exercise.

1   Writing the identity base. In the birthday column, each student posts a note on their possible purpose. For example: On the 12th of December 2000, Wati was born to a proud couple: Bambang and Ita. Wati believes that her existence is for a noble purpose, which will be stated throughout the Life Map. (The map has all the years of life up to 70 and can be expanded.) Her spiritual principle is

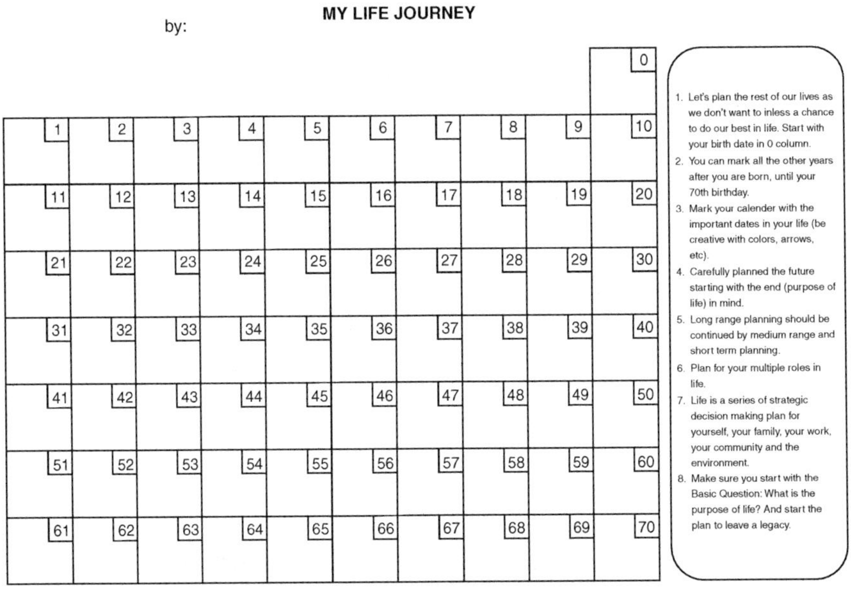

FIGURE 8.2   Life Map

to be an agent of change in serving the community, specifically in helping the farmers of Indonesia to be free of loan sharks by setting up an online system connecting the farmers and the consumers. In order to exercise her spiritual value, Wati will engage in spiritual practices to guide her in achieving the noble purpose. The spiritual practices will be in the form of a moment of silence and meditation according to her spiritual belief in Islam and joining Friday and Sunday activities in the mosque.

2   To facilitate the spiritual practice, the school could offer a prayer or meditation room and courses on spiritual practices and/or teachings, and might bring in speakers who instruct about spiritual development. Research shows that when people can discover and respond to their own "calling" or sense of purpose, they will be more creative, committed and service-oriented (Fry, 2003; Indrajaya, 2016; Neal, 2013).

3   The students envision the big picture of how they will see themselves in the future. The objective is to start with the end in mind (Covey, 2014) and conduct a self-reflection of how they see themselves in a variety of roles in life, such as son/daughter, businessman/woman, activist, social worker, change maker, etc. Students are encouraged to look at themselves through a variety of roles simultaneously in the future. The development of one role will not sacrifice the capacity for the other roles, as a zero-sum game is not applicable in this setting. The spiritual values enable the students to look at all of the simultaneous roles as equally engaging toward an integrated role of servanthood toward the Almighty. Work, as well as other purposeful human activities, including marital intimacy, are part of the act of worship (Beekun, 1997).

4   The students then answer the Heaven on Earth questions (Rutte, 2006). Incremental theory suggests that personal characteristics can be developed. Achieving one's dream is possible, if you are really committed and have a high level of resilience (Yeager, & Dweck, 2012). Rutte (2006) encouraged people to recognize their dreams in the form of Heaven on Earth questions, as follows:

- When have you experienced Heaven on Earth? Vividly recall what was going on.
- Suppose I gave you a magic wand and with it you can create Heaven on Earth. What is Heaven on Earth?
- What small, simple, concrete actions will you take in the next 24 hours to continue creating and enjoying Heaven on Earth? How would the future be?

Students can perform team reflections by asking questions reciprocally. The purpose of Heaven on Earth is to challenge students to think differently and purposefully while creating their Life Map. Working with the end in mind, students can carefully plan their mid-term and short-term goals.

This Life Map is an ongoing self-reflection and team-reflection exercise. The template (see Figure 8.2), and plans for the future, can be shared in small-group presentations.

Avoiding negative impact of media and practicing mindfulness

In Indonesia navigating the digital world is a big issue. Grammar school students are already exposed to the negative content in the media. In a research study of 1,346 junior high school students (grade 7), 100% are exposed to pornography through different forms of media. Seventy-three percent confess that currently they are continuously exposed to pornography contents up to the level of addiction (Indrajaya, 2016). The students need to be aware of the downside impact of media and digital industry in their lives. Media and digital literacy is a must in this overwhelming information era. Once addicted to the negative content of media, it is very hard to practice mindfulness and maintain a sustainability mindset. Students need to understand the threat of the addiction cycle. For example, digital pornography has been found to generate a cycle of addiction including escalation, desensitization and finally the loss of self-control (D'Orlando, 2009). Eventually, some of these addicts will conduct criminal acts to satisfy their addiction at any cost.

The media/digital addiction impact is not only fostered through access to pornography, but other self-destructive acts follow the same addiction model. For example, digital exposure to bullying follows a similar model. The addiction model for bullying, for example, can be seen through six main stages: blameless exposure, trying out, addiction, escalation, desensitization and exhibition (Owusu, 2014). Research conducted in a youth penitentiary found that addiction to pornography may lead toward youth delinquencies in which some kids are remanded to a facility (Indrajaya et. al, 2008).

In order to develop and maintain the balance of knowing, being and doing, in the Outstanding Value course, it is very important for the students to be aware of the issue of media/digital literacy. The spiritual dimension can explain the addiction model: if human beings were created with a holy mission of servanthood toward the One and Only One Creator (Naim et al., 2008), not following one's original purpose by attention to a competing self-oriented material goal, creates space for an addiction. The addiction process is comprised of: Addiction-Escalation-Desensitization-Acting Out (D'Orlando, 2009). In "escalation", the same dosage of addiction would not be sufficient to give the same level of satisfaction. In the "desensitization" phase, the increasing dosage leads to numbness, in which the individuals begin to ignore their conscience. In the "acting out" phase, self-control is compromised, and individuals feel lost and expelled from a sense of safety. In the process of losing touch with the spiritual side, one becomes a slave of greed toward material goals (Agustian, 2011).

All classroom sessions are designed as a two-way communication process. At the end of the session, the students describe the possible downsides of media/digital exposure and how to anticipate problems. For instance, manufactured demand is an impact of media brainwashing, in which people begin to believe they have a specific need, when it is actually manufactured by the corporation through the media channel, as mentioned in the "Story of Stuff" model (Leonard, 2010). After the session, the students are asked how they would avoid getting addicted to the media/digital world, with its new technology and stimulating, distracting games. With this new understanding, students are encouraged to engage in self-reflection and mindfulness as regular, life-long practices. At this point, the facilitator can offer one of a number of mindfulness activities, such as the moment of silence exercise described later.

In the Outstanding Values course, toward the end of each class the students are given some time to do self-reflection on the activities of the day. Students should be in a mood that is conducive to do self-reflection. A self-reflection learning diary can be useful, based on what has been achieved for the day, to enable self-appreciation.

Appreciative Inquiry, as proposed by Cooperrider and Whitney (2005), illustrates that collective strength does more than perform, it transforms. Therefore, the moment of silence should focus on the day's accomplishments, however minor they may appear. One option is to make an example of Thomas Alpha Edison: instead of looking at his 1,000 pre-success experiments as failures, he referred to it as an accomplishment of creating new knowledge of what does not work. Developing this type of self-appreciation will increase students' self-esteem. After appreciating what went well and what had been learnt, students can proceed to plan for how to improve for the future.

This learning diary can be assigned through Google classroom applications (https://classroom.google.com), as a weekly self-reflection of the learning process for the students.

Appreciating diverse cultures through VR Google

Thanks to technology, almost everyone has access to experience the global world without physically being there. This open information access to the world and curiosity about the global world helps to cultivate a global mindset (Gupta & Govindarajan, 2002), which supports the development of a sustainability mindset. The global mindset mirrors self-confidence by humility, generosity, flexibility and adaptability through collaboration and listening (Cseh, Davis, & Khilji, 2013). In order to accept and respect a diversity of beliefs and cultural backgrounds, now every student has the chance to experience virtually in a three-dimensional perspective how it feels to be inside a spiritual sacred place, regardless of one's belief. Students using the Google Virtual Reality (VR) device can experience a pilgrimage ritual while performing Hajj, the fifth principle of Islam (Hitchcock, 2014), conducted by millions of Muslims around the world in Mecca, Saudi Arabia. While performing Hajj, all pilgrims will go through the ritual of encircling the Kabah, which is known as the House of God. The movement is counterclockwise, a simulation of the movement of the universe. All of the galaxies are in their respective orbits, moving counterclockwise, each on their specific, exact, designated path. The simulation is designed to convey that humankind who follows the Celestial guidelines by following the righteous way will be on the safe path, but those who choose to go astray (going against the designated orbit) may become lost, as illustrated in the addiction process mentioned earlier.

The low-cost (occasionally sponsored entirely by Google) and self-made Virtual Reality cardboard enables the students to experience almost any VR sites available through the internet. The first step is to let each individual browse through several VR sites of sacred places. The students then conduct a self-reflection and contemplation to describe the feel of various holy places, and they are encouraged to be creative in finding high-quality VR sites for the locations on the internet. In a second step, students may pair up and share sacred place sites in VR, offering their partners the opportunity to experience the look and feel of a variety of the sacred places of different religions.

This VR exercise can be expanded to include all of the sacred places available on the internet. Students could explore their similarities in terms of ultimate purpose, discussing their understanding of the essence and meanings behind the rituals. The team reflection should encourage a conversation on the values behind religion-related sites and rituals. This teamwork will enable the students to share the core beliefs of their religion and explore the substance behind the spiritual rituals they perform in the context of their religious activities.

Team Development

The team-reflection (reflection with others) process is an important part of the Team Development phase (Neal, 2013). The sharing of VR sites explained previously can be a tool to support the team-reflection process.

Self-reflection activities are designed to build self-esteem and an understanding of the purposeful goals for each student on the individual level. In order to develop leadership abilities, students need to go through the Team Development phase. Kassel, Rimanoczy, and Mitchell (2016) posited that business schools need to develop leaders who utilize a strong sustainability mindset, and as such, schools would need a shift in the learning approach, in addition to developing a new set of behaviors, mindsets and leadership competencies. Some of these competencies include self-reflection and reflection with others. Management education institutions could conduct project-based programs as a proven means for developing the leadership competencies through collaborative teamwork and specific learning goals (Rimanoczy & Pearson, 2010). Many integrated leadership approaches also cover the spiritual side, such as "Authentic Leadership," "Leading with Soul," and "Spiritual Leadership" (Neal, 2013). All of these approaches share the concept of virtues, in which leaders are encouraged to apply spiritual values such as humility, trust, courage, integrity and faith to their work with teams (Neal, 2013). Transcendence, plasticity of the mind (flexibility), openness, having multiple frames of reference, mindfulness, curiosity and humility emerged as requirements of leading in the global environment (Cseh, Davis, & Khilji, 2013). The global leaders' learning journeys are characterized by informal learning during everyday work and life experiences, including learning from mistakes and from and with others. Self-reflection leading to the "awareness of otherness" as well as reflection with others were at the core of learning and developing a global mindset (Cseh, Davis, & Khilji, 2013). This pattern of learning could also be part of the students' activities in the classroom setting. While there is a myriad of ways to develop "team spirit" and "noble purpose", the following are some examples of the activities that have been conducted in the Team Development phase which have shown positive results.

Social and environmental impact projects

Reinhardt (1998) posited that leaders and managers in corporations need to go beyond the question of whether doing 'green' is beneficial to the firm, but should instead focus on how to innovate a business model where the environmental investments deliver benefits to the shareholders. This point of view will be supported once the students in a team setting conduct an assignment of reporting green innovation by corporations or small/medium enterprises. Students also need to be engaged in social impact projects to be able to develop empathy for, and understand the reality of life at, the bottom of the pyramid. The following examples are some of the team activities enabling the process of reflection with others.

Green innovation program

Students are assigned to report green innovations which have shown positive results and earned profits. Through this detective work, students investigate the specific green innovative business model and how the model inspires. One of the firms investigated by the author's students was a micro enterprise producing a Biopori, a tool to create small holes in the ground for storing water. The holes become an organic waste dumpster and flood prevention system.

The Biopori enables everyone to become a change-maker in their own area, as people build their own absorption holes with a multi-purpose function. Rainwater will be easily absorbed into the soil with biopori holes, and thereby that land will have enough water reserves during the dry season. Worms make their own version of biopori holes in the soil; by providing additional nutrition by the installation of biopori holes, we can help worms to aerate and condition soil, forming additional soil support and water reserves in the areas over time. The food is organic waste such as vegetables, food scraps, leftover fruits, grass cuttings or dry leaves.

Organic waste in the biopori hole will turn into compost. This compost can be harvested from the hole every three months. After harvesting the compost, the hole is refilled with new organic waste to feed the microbes in the soil. Thus, the biopori, in the form of a small hole 10 cm wide, offers many benefits: saving water, preventing flooding, making compost, conditioning the soil and reducing the waste stream.

In the case of IPMI, students went even further by initiating a competition to support the spread of Biopori through a campaign in their communities. They went to junior high schools and high schools in the neighborhoods and taught the students and teachers how to make their own Biopori holes in their neighborhoods. The story and process of making the Biopori was posted on social media as a campaign to promote green activities. Students gave away Biopori's tools with the IPMI International School's seal for the Biopori's cover and visited schools, offices and community housing in the neighborhood to promote the competition and the benefit of Bioporis. The students conducted their own fundraising to buy the Biopori packages. At the end of the project, they performed a final presentation showing how deeply they had learned about green innovation. First, the startup entrepreneur producing Biopori sold many packages and received free word-of-mouth advertising. Second, Biopori became a tool to conduct a green campaign, promoted awareness of ways to prevent flooding and to create an organic dumpster/composter. Third, by using Biopori, students became change-makers and conducted a campaign on the importance of installing your own Biopori in your backyard. Fourth, students initiated a competition project, where they invited high school students to send their Biopori-related activities video through YouTube. Through this competition, the students were able to create more change-makers.

Walkabout project: students can choose an experience of supporting/helping marginalized people

This is a program where the students spend at least one full day following and serving any occupation in the bottom of the pyramid. As a boutique business school, IPMI International Business school students come from the most affluent sections of the society. This task of experiencing the life of someone at the bottom of the pyramid becomes a life-changing event. One of the groups decided to join a scavenger. They almost could not complete it, since the scavengers walk long distances across the countryside collecting waste from the dumpsters. The students discovered that a whole day of collecting plastic waste could only be sold for Indonesian Rp 1000 per kilogram, which is $7 cents of a US dollar for two pounds of waste. During the presentation, the students showed the movie of the scavengers' compound and reported that they never buy shampoo or toothpaste, and that they have to share one toothbrush with 20 other people from their compound. The way the students presented the heartbreaking findings showed how they were transformed by this powerful learning experience of becoming a part of the marginalized people's world, which sadly comprises a large population in Indonesia. Once these students become corporate leaders, they may never look at the marginalized people in the same way as before, since they now have seen, first-hand, how it feels to be marginalized. The learning experience has the potential to create a significant commitment in their hearts to be change-makers and create a Business as a Force for Good.

Angel of change program

In this program, students are assigned to conduct an energy conservation campaign at their high school alma mater. Their challenge is to create more change-makers. They are equipped with posters and cards and tools from the Ministry of Energy and Energy Conservation. The high school students are encouraged to create their own energy conservation campaign. Some of the students currently still keep their mailing list of high schools' angels of change and maintain the network of doing good. The inspiring part of this program is to witness how creative these business school students are in designing their campaigns. Some use a theatrical approach, others use games and competition, and certainly all of them enjoy the opportunity to be change-makers, inspiring more angels of change.

In all of these group assignments, the team-reflection process is encouraged, and the learning diary completed during the moment of silence will reveal their group-reflection results.

Total System Development

A growing number of leaders and CEOs have become personally committed to creating organizations that nurture the human spirit. The positive spirit can therefore expand to all the stakeholders of the company: employees, customers, suppliers, vendors and other stakeholders. A number of new systemic approaches have been developed to help organizations transform to a higher level of spiritual values (Neal, 2013), and the purpose of these organizational development processes is to transform the way an organization views the business system by not just focusing on profits, but to also show a commitment to human development and make a positive contribution to society.

The Appreciative Inquiry approach can be brought into the classroom through a platform called AIM2Flourish. The students are invited to identify companies in their region that are profitable while supporting at least one of the Sustainable Development Goals, via a radical innovation. The students then interview the business leaders using the Appreciative Inquiry approach and get inspiration from interviewing the innovators. The process has been so motivating and transformative that comments from IPMI students were featured by AIM2Flourish as examples of how the students have developed a new way of thinking of business, as a Force of Good. This is a quote from Bernard Balroy, one of the 2016 IPMI International School MBA students involved in the AIM2Flourish platform (www.AIM2Flourish.com):

> Being a participant in your initiative (AIM2Flourish) is already a great achievement. Having an opportunity to conduct an interview and probe a particular innovation and flourishing story is a great learning experience for us. Our paradigms somehow shifted toward a sustainable direction of conducting business (in the future) wherein social innovation will form the nuclei of our business models. Writing the story highly inspired us. That in itself is already a huge reward for us. And, this was made possible through our enthusiastic and unselfish friend, mentor and guru, Ms. Amelia. We hope that you persistently continue your initiatives, sowing the seeds for future generations to nurture, grow and reap for the betterment of the earth (and the universe) we live.
>
> *(Student giving AIM2Flourish presentation, 2016)*

Appreciative Inquiry (AI) methodology, by itself, is already a different way of looking into a situation. Instead of focusing on the problems or challenges, AI focuses on what is working well, on the strengths exhibited by a team or organization. When we shift our focus toward the strengths, it transforms our perspective and unleashes the potential power from within (Laszlo et al., 2012).

Redefining the role of business

Finally, after focusing on the Individual, Team and Total System Development, business schools need to prepare graduates to be ready to face an ever-changing and uncertain world. At the same time, students need to develop a strong understanding of their cultural background. Given the many competing demands facing business schools, being both locally embedded and globally connected will form a strong and integrated way of thinking.

A new paradigm is emerging among a growing number of business leaders. They are committed to redefining the purpose of business as the solution to solving problems in society and around the globe, rather than being a contributor to the world's sustainability problems. The focus is on using the creative energy and talent of their employees, along with their vast capital resources and international reach, to truly make a positive difference in the world (Cooperrider & Whitney, 2005).

In IPMI the students' coursework is not complete by reporting stories on Flourishing Business through AIM2Flourish; they are required to create their own startup business. The school is involved in an entrepreneurship project by developing unique programs in terms of its values, vision and readiness for supporting the new paradigm of business.

In response to the Sustainable Developmental Goals of the UN Global Compact and the current business approach addressing sustainability issues, students now have a new way of understanding business. They redefine the way they understand how a business might be better modeled. This new model is more challenging and rewarding since it attempts to address world problems. This could be done by embedding the social and environmental issues into the business model. In order to leverage on this, our school offers a challenge to the students to develop a micro-business with only $30 USD of initial investment, which must be returned, with or without interest, by the end of the term. The requirement is that the sustainability mindset has to be embedded in the business model, and the project has to address at least one of the 17 United Nations Sustainable Development Goals. Beyond these requirements, the students have almost unlimited flexibility. This assignment model was developed by Henrietta Onwuegbuzie (Onwuegbuzie & Ugwuanyi, 2016; Onwuegbuzie, 2010) at the Lagos Business School in Nigeria, as part of the Entrepreneurship course for graduate students. The author adapted the idea to the local context of Indonesia. At IPMI we decided to start this project early, for undergraduate students. This decision was taken considering that the graduate students mostly are already business players and leaders with limited time. We considered that the startup project is more suitable for the undergraduates, who have the energy and the time to create an innovation.

The invitation to the undergraduate students to start up a business with only $30 USD, with sustainability mindset embedded in the model, was at first a surprising challenge for them. But as the assignment started, and they began designing the business model, their enthusiasm grew. The school acknowledged the effort and the impact made by the students, and this appreciative approach created more energy, promoting collaboration among the students, which felt to them different and better than the more traditional competitive approach. When they presented their business model, they illustrated their developing capacity to think out of the box, and they surprised the faculty with their genuinely innovative ideas.

One example of a business model launched by a student was focused on saving and preserving the cultural heritage in the form of "Save the Beber Puppet art", a traditional art heritage of Javanese culture. The students designed and facilitated a social campaign to develop awareness about the importance of preserving this national and cultural art heritage, a tradition dating back to 1244 AD, from being lost forever. Most of the youngsters are not even aware of this traditional cultural art tradition. Through the campaign, the students raised the awareness of the local wisdom and tradition, and the fact that without support, all of these traditional arts soon could only be found in history books.

In the endeavor to save the tradition, the students are selling miniatures of the Wayang Beber in order to raise the funds. The video campaign, social media exposure and the viral impact of patriotism of preserving the local wisdom have created a successful emotional and spiritual awareness campaign. Even though the hype of selling these miniatures might be temporary, the students get the message of "Doing Well by Doing Good". The more they do business selling the artwork, the more they are helping the traditional artists to make an income while preserving the traditional art culture.

Another example is the Waste Bank network with the local communities. Students have set up this network without any startup investment. They are implementing the Partnership for the Sustainable Development Goals (SDG 17) by setting up a collaboration between a corporation, Unilever, the local communities, and the Rumah Pelangi Foundation, an NGO working for sustainability issues. IPMI serves as the facilitating educational institution. The first endeavor was to set up an awareness campaign. Local champions were invited from the surrounding neighborhoods to participate in the awareness campaign. Speakers were invited from the ministry of Environment, Energy Conservation, and NGO green activists. The local champions were divided into smaller groups based on their respective areas. Every group had to go through a brainstorming session on their current environmental challenges and explore the possibilities to improve those conditions. The awareness presentations opened up their paradigm to look for a solution for their social/environmental problem. The NGO provided the answers to their quest by facilitating and supporting the community to build their own waste bank system.

Waste bank operations simulate the model of a bank, but instead of saving money, in this model homeowners save their waste at the waste bank. The challenge is to introduce and implement the system to classify every home's garbage and waste. Organic waste should be processed into compost with a simple composting method using the composting liquid. Plastics, cans and paper should all be classified and submitted to the waste bank. Unilever, as the corporate sponsor, usually helps by providing the manual book and the log book for each client of the waste bank. The log book has the record of how much waste each client is submitting to the waste bank. For example, plastic, paper and other forms of waste have their own value per kilogram. Hence every client has their own waste saving account book. The NGO experts become the partner to facilitate the process and help the community to set up their waste bank system of scales to weigh the waste. The waste is sold daily to the garbage collector, who pays cash to the waste bank. The clients usually save their money in the waste bank account until it reaches a substantial amount. Each waste bank also has its own composting facilities and upcycle product shop where they sell up-cycle products. The margin between the price paid by the garbage collector buyers and the price paid to the client plus the income from compost and upcycle products are the sources of income of the waste bank. The amount might not be much, but as the volume increases, the amount becomes more significant. And most importantly, the waste bank system has successfully reduced the amount of trash sent to the landfill. This is a tremendous help since in a large city like Jakarta, with a population of 12.7 million, one of the most pressing problems is the waste handling system.

Another group of students came up with the idea of an online business to sell cupcakes in a jar. They bake their own cupcakes and sell the premium Cup Cake in a Jar with the purpose of helping disadvantaged kids to go to school by donating part of the profit to buy school uniforms for the students. Government schools are free, but the children need to wear a school uniform, and this is where the students contribute through their "Cup Cake in a Jar" business. The online campaign of Cup Cake in a Jar is posted with the label of Food4Future. The customers can order the cupcakes through an online system and use it as a substitute for sending cards or presents for special occasions. The online campaign of cupcakes for a good cause has received a good response. Surprisingly, this simple business model is sustainable and currently still operating even though the class is over.

Another team launched the "Awareness Campaign", which sells premium quality organic blouses and T-shirts with quotes of wisdom. By supporting and wearing the Awearness product, customers become change-makers, since 50% of their profit goes to the Cancer Society. In two and a half months, they managed to gain revenues 10 times the initial investment. The assignment of creating a Business as a Force for Good has generated a lot of positive feedback from the students. All of the teams have been able to generate good returns by the end of the third month, and return their initial investment of $30 USD plus the dividend for the school cooperative.

Students learned a lot about triple bottom line impact through the hands-on experiential learning of running an innovative startup business with a social and environmental impact. They no longer talk only about reducing harm, or complying with regulations, or what they would get from making a social impact or a green investment. Now they are able to redefine the way they look at the business model. In the process, they are nurtured emotionally and spiritually through a whole new concept of Business as an Agent of World Benefit. This said, there are several challenges to be addressed still. For example, one is a legal consideration. Some of the students may be younger than 17 years old. Another issue is the tax obligations of these new enterprises. This problem has been addressed by setting up a cooperative system in the campus. The cooperative has its own tax system, and the businesses created by the students are part of the cooperative activities. Even though there are still some challenges to solve, the output of the project is highly motivating. Some of the groups have managed to get a revenue 10 times their initial investment of $30 USD in less than one semester.

Conclusion

This chapter presented examples of activities and initiatives introduced by the author with graduate and undergraduate students at IPMI, designed for the purpose of a more holistic development of socially and environmentally responsible leaders. Inspired by the cognitive, spiritual and action-oriented dimensions of the sustainability mindset model, the author provided new experiential learning opportunities supporting the SDGs and a new model of Business as an Agent of World Benefit. As a result, IPMI has started a Center of Sustainability Mindset and Social Responsibility (CSMSR IPMI).

In the future, IPMI, under the CSMSR, plans to host a startup incubator model for Business as an Agent of World Benefit. The triple helix of corporations, educational institution and the communities promises to be a rewarding and productive collaboration for community empowerment.

References

Agustian, A. G. (2001). *The Islamic guide to developing ESQ: Emotional spiritual quotient.* Jakarta: Arga Wijaya Persada.

Beekun, R. I. (1997). *Islamic business ethics.* IslamKotob: The International Institute of Islamic Thought.

Burns, J. M. (1978). *Leadership.* New York: Harper & Row.

Cooperrider, D. L., & Whitney, D. (2005). *Appreciative inquiry: A positive revolution in change.* San Francisco, CA: Berrett-Koehler Publishers.

Cooperrider, D. L., Whitney, D., &. Stavros, J. M. (2008). *The appreciative inquiry handbook: For leaders of change.* Brunswick, OH: Crown Custom Pub.

Covey, S. R. (2014). *The 7 habits of highly effective families.* New York: Golden Press.

Cseh, M., Davis, E. B., & Khilji, S. E. (2013). Developing a global mindset: Learning of global leaders. *European Journal of Training and Development, 37*(5), 489–499.

D'Orlando, F. (2009). The demand for pornography. *Journal of Happiness Studies*, *12*(1), 51–75. doi:10.1007/s10902-009-9175-0

Fry, L. (2009). Spiritual leadership as a model for student inner development. *Journal of Leadership Studies*, *3*(3), 79–82.

Fry, L. W. (2003). Toward a theory of spiritual leadership. *The Leadership Quarterly*, *14*(6), 693–727.

Goleman, D. (2006). *Emotional intelligence: Why it can matter more than IQ*. New York: Bantam Books.

Gupta, A. K., & Govindarajan, V. (2002). Cultivating a global mindset. *The Academy of Management Executive*, *16*(1), 116–126.

Hitchcock, J. (2014). The 5 pillars of Islam. *Verbum*, *2*(2), 43–50.

Ibrahim, M. D. (2004). *Mengelola hidup dan merencanakan masa depan*. Jakarta: MHMMD Productions.

Indrajaya, A. (2016). *Spirit at work: The Telkom experience of great spirit grand strategy*. Jakarta: Hasanah.

Kassel, K., Rimanoczy, I., & Mitchell, S. F. (2016, January). The sustainable mindset: Connecting being, thinking, and doing in management education. In *Academy of management proceedings* (Vol. 2016, No. 1, p. 16659). New York: Academy of Management.

Krishnan, V. R. (2008). Does management education make students better actors? A longitudinal study of change in values and self-monitoring. *Great Lakes Herald*, *2*(1), 36–48.

Laszlo, C., Brown, J. S., Sherman, D., Barros, I., Boland, B., Ehrenfeld, J. . . . Werder, P. (2012). Flourishing: A vision for business and the world. *The Journal of Corporate Citizenship*, *46*, 31.

Leonard, A. (2010). *The story of stuff: How our obsession with stuff is trashing the planet, our communities, and our health-and a vision for change*. New York: Simon and Schuster.

Mitroff, I. I., & Denton, E. A. (1999). A study of spirituality in the workplace. *Sloan Management Review*, *40*(4), 83.

Muttaqin, A. (2012). *Hybrid spirituality and religious efficacy of Yogyakarta spiritual centres*. Dissertation. University of Western Sydney, Australia.

Naim, A., Elmier, T., Farouk, F. (2008). *Badai Pornografi: Fenomena dan Penanggulangannya* [Pornography and the way to overcome the addiction to pornography]. Jakarta: Hasanah.

Neal, J. (2013). *Creating enlightened organizations: Four gateways to spirit at work*. New York: Palgrave Macmillan.

Onwuegbuzie, H. (2010). *Sustainable development strategy using indigenous knowledge and entrepreneurship*. Working Paper. Lagos, Nigeria: Lagos Business School.

Onwuegbuzie, H., & Ugwuanyi, I. (2016). Doing good is good business: Embedding ethics in teaching entrepreneurship and business venturing. In K. Ogunyemi (Ed.), *Teaching ethics across the management curriculum, Volume III: Contributing to a global paradigm shift*. New York: Business Expert Press, LLC.

Owusu, S. (2014). *Cyberbullying behavior: Characteristics, development, and prevention*. Baltimore, MD: University of Maryland.

Reinhardt, F. L. (1998). Bringing the environment down to earth. *Harvard Business Review*, *77*(4), 149–57.

Rimanoczy, I. (2014). A matter of being: Developing sustainability-minded leaders. *Journal of Management for Global Sustainability*, *2*(1), 95–122.

Rimanoczy, I. B. (2010). *Business leaders committing to and fostering sustainability initiatives*. Dissertation. ProQuest LLC.

Rimanoczy, I., & Pearson, T. (2010). Role of HR in the new world of sustainability. *Industrial and Commercial Training*, *42*(1), 11–17.

Rutte, M. (2006). *The Work of Humanity: project heaven on earth* citing Patanjali (in *Seeking the Sacred: leading a spiritual life in a secular world* (M. Joseph, Ed.). Toronto, Canada: ECW Press.

Sterling, S. (2011). Transformative learning and sustainability: Sketching the conceptual ground. *Learning and Teaching in Higher Education, 5*(11), 17–33.

Wigglesworth, C. (2013). Spiritual intelligence. In J. Neal (Ed.), *Handbook of faith and spirituality in the workplace: Handbook of faith and spirituality in the workplace.* New York: Springer Science.

Yeager, D. S., & Dweck, C. S. (2012). Mindsets that promote resilience: When students believe that personal characteristics can be developed. *Educational Psychologist, 47*(4), 302–314.

9

'I (DO NOT) CARE WHAT YOU THINK ABOUT MY IDEAS'

Navigating agripreneurship through sustainable learning processes from a cross-cultural perspective

Alexander Tetteh Kwasi Nuer

Introduction

The quest for alternative ways of learning, as well as inculcating cultural dimensions in 'sustainable agripreneurship' in many developing economics, have become prominent among both scholars and researchers (Dentoni & Bitzer 2015 Van Dijk, 2011). Interestingly, many developing and developed countries have begun to look for avenues to share their learning experiences with each other (Africa in Motion, 2013; www.africainmotion.nl). This has resulted in many initiatives whereby undergraduate students, especially from developed and developing world institutions, have been paired to jointly conduct various research studies within and among agriculture value chains and agribusinesses (www.africainmotion.nl). The aim of such joint collaborations is to co-create new forms of learning processes (www.africainmotion.nl), as well as sustainable curricula that could help change the mindset of practitioners, researchers and academics, as to how cross-cultural, multidisciplinary and agriculture-related issues could be tackled by co-creating joint learning and action research (Dentoni & Klerkx, 2015; Nuer, Rivera-Santos, Rufin & Van Dijk, 2014; Fang, 2004; Fang, Kang, & Liu, 2004).

The chapter highlights new insights that inform scholars, faculty and peers on the possibility to improve the core tenets of Being (background and core values of students that inform their passions to engage in cross-cultural learning). It also addresses the Knowing dimension (the focus and interests of students that guide their mindset and learning processes). The chapter also shows what emerged from the studies that informs faculty on new ways (system thinking) to conduct joint curricula development and action research (doing) by using appreciative inquiry. It again shows how the Sustainable Mindset model can be adapted for future joint-learning activities. The chapter further draws insights and inferences from systems theory, with a primary aim to highlight, and build its method of data collection, which leans towards a qualitative approach. The paper draws inferences to highlight student learning processes, appreciation and challenges encountered during the process of joint-learning that informed their thinking as well as mindset.

Sustainability mindset

The concept of the being, doing and thinking has become important to sustainability mindset scholars (Kassel, Rimanoczy & Mitchell, 2016; Rimanoczy, 2010). Such scholars argue that

> *Sustainability Mindset is a way of thinking and being that results from a broad understanding of the ecosystem's manifestations as well as an introspective focus on one's personal values and higher self, and finds its expression in actions for the greater good of the whole.*
>
> *(Kassel, 2014; Kassel et al., 2016, p. 8; Rimanoczy, 2014)*

The act of thinking in introspect, as well as retrospect, of doing something good or not for the greater good of the whole, helps to create a mindset that is likely to lead to extended benefits for a whole biosphere that humans may benefit from such good. The benefit of doing good for the greater number of people, planet and profit thus informs systemic thinking not only in organizational settings, but also such benefits translate to a form of feeling good for undertaking such a venture.

Scholars of sustainability mindset subscribe to system thinking, which argues that systems and institutions enable practitioners, as well as scholars, to be able to integrate many disciplines such as environmental studies, spirituality, management ethics, self-awareness and related others, into the context of being (values), thinking (knowledge) and doing (competencies). Systems thinking highlights the creation of an avenue to include feedback mechanisms in a given process. In the context of this chapter, systems thinking helps to develop a feedback mechanism that improves on existing process such as improvement on a school's curriculum, approaches of teaching and approaches to learning. It has become imperative to test how far the system thinking approach fits into business schools' curricula. This is more important in an era where many cross-border, multinational and multicultural-based businesses have been established to create value and impact across continents (Kassel et al., 2016; Rimanoczy, 2014; Cooperrider, & Srivastva, 1987).

Social shaping of mindset cannot only be located in institutions and structures that do add value to a person's personality and worldview (Kassel et al., 2016). This translates to arguments made by sustainability mindset advocates who suggest that for a general worldview to become inherent, it behooves future leaders to extend their thinking to cover geographical biosphere such as developing economies, emerging, as well as the diverse developed world. Social shaping of mindset helps scholars and practitioners to place importance on divergent views, such as on the way things are viewed, governed and managed, as well as benefits derived for people, planet and profit (Rivera-Santos, Holt, Littlewood & Kolk., 2014; Nuer et al., 2014; Van Dijk, 2011).

Traditional classroom versus field experiential learning impartation

Many scholars have suggested the need to digress from traditional classroom form of teaching as well as impartation of knowledge to students (Kassel et al., 2016). Advocates of this assertion suggest the inclusion on worldview of the person (i.e. the concept of '*I-We-Us-Them*') in the teaching and learning processes in the classroom. Whilst this suggestion has been adopted by many business-related and management scholars, it has become evident that not all scholars subscribe to this form of knowledge impartation. Interestingly, studies and topics that hover around sustainability (Kassel et al., 2016), cross-cultural, environment-related fields (Rufin & Rivera-Santos, 2013; Murphy, Perrot & Rivera-Santos et al., 2012 Van Dijk, 2011) and social entrepreneurship and impact investments (Nuer, Rivera-Santos, Rufin, & Van Dijk, 2016; Nuer, 2015) have almost cemented the bid to include practice-based knowledge sharing, as well as learning impartation, within business models and schools' curricula (Kassel et al., 2016).

The traditional era in which students within disciplines such as agriculture, engineering and related studies visit the field, to engage in hands-on learning practical work, have become appreciated among scholars. This is aside from the fact that not many field studies are engaged in due to funding and large size of class intake in many developing economies. A large segment of agribusiness scholars, as well as management-related cohorts, used to follow the traditional value chain in the area of marketing, value-addition packaging and sales of farm products at either the farm gate or the final market (Gereffi, Humphrey, & Sturgeon, 2005; Nuer et al., 2016; Van Dijk, 2011). Currently, many agribusiness and management scholars have further adopted the applied and shared knowledge approach, by following value chains that have cross-cultural tenets within business, marketing and entrepreneurship studies (Van Dijk, 2011; Fang, 2004; Fang, Kang, & Liu, 2004).

In the areas of sustainability and social well-being, many business schools seem to tackle examples from highest capital valuation corporate institutions (Van Dijk, 2011). This limits many graduates from business schools to have hands-on experiences, as well as core competencies, when it comes to doing business, as well as managing cross-cultural businesses in precarious environments (Rimanoczy, 2014; Rimanoczy, 2010).

Sustainability studies look at three cardinal points of social, economic and environmental tenets of worldviews. These areas should benefit current and future generations in building a robust sustainability mindset. It is noteworthy that many developing economies' paradigms are not fully perceived to have a contributing factor in building such insightful knowledge. There also seems to be limited knowledge shared or empirically documented from cross-cultural perspectives from the developing economies divide. The question as to who writes and tells the story of developing economies has become debatable in the last few decades as well (Van Dijk, 2011). A shared knowledge on how sustainability mindset issues are tackled across developed and developing economies divide, is perhaps a good way to help sustain the context of people, planet and profit.

Cross-cultural scholars such as Rivera-Santos et al. (2014) have recently studied how businesses thrive in developing economies, as well as how divergent business models and approaches inform our understanding of the reality on the ground (Rivera-Santos et al., 2014; Rivera-Santos, Rufin, & Kolk, 2012). These scholars further have looked at how various partnership arrangements are inducing changes in how business and management education are pursued. These scholars found a gap in knowledge sharing that limit investors, entrepreneurs and organization from advanced economies in taking the best option decision when it comes to investment in developing economies (Kolk, Rivera-Santos, & Rufin, 2013). These type of scholars have positioned their findings as 'wicked problems' (Dentoni et al., 2017; Kievit, 2011; Lai, Chan, Dentoni, Neyra, 2017; Van Tulder, 2016; Lem, Van Tulder & Geleynse, 2013).

The current trend has interestingly seen many corporate entities, donors, non-profits and related private actors to seek, pursue, as well as roll out new business models such as social entrepreneurship and impact investment in many developing economies. It is thus paramount that business and management scholars begin to turn their attention to how businesses thrive, as well as how faculty in business schools in these economies nurture and train their human resources such as employees and student graduates. Such an approach may go a long way toward helping management and business schools come to appreciate how systems and institutions thrive and work in developing economies (Cooperrider & Srivastva, 1987).

Connecting mindset with values

Many scholars of sustainability talk about the importance of values to not only be developed but also shared with leaders within organizations as well as business schools. To make this as an extension, the context of thinking, being and doing connects with activities that are naturally connected with a person's worldview (Rimanoczy, 2010). If business schools postulate to not only create formal business leaders, then it would be to their advantage to begin to inculcate into their pressure cooker syllabuses the call to connect with practice. What seems to be limited, as well as not fully explored, relates to how business schools from advanced and developing economies jointly co-create synergy in curricula developments that will factor in multicultural and transdisciplinary tenets that cuts across geographical boundaries. A joint-learning approach can be used, whereby students and faculty from north-south, studying similar courses, can be grouped together to conduct joint field studies. They share experiences that can help inform future leaders whose tasks and jurisdictional responsibilities cut across developed and developing economies (Kolk et al., 2013; Rivera-Santos, Rufin, & Kolk, 2012). This is a contribution of this chapter.

Whilst many field studies have focused on 'mono-impartation' tracks (i.e., when the focus of the field study is narrowed towards a particular theme or interest), it can be of multiple importance if a multidisciplinary knowledge impartation approach could be considered by faculty. Field experiments have been conducted and encouraged across borders and geographical boundaries. Interestingly, not many have focused on how students, who are future leaders, engage together in field research and studies that have Appreciative Inquiry (AI) and sustainability mindset as the core vision and that have sought to create synergies regarding their worldviews. The development of the sustainability mindset approach, it is suggested, could lead to insights that can inform scholars, practitioners and decision makers on how diverse worldviews are expressed, as well as experienced by students and faculty that are expected to co-create the next generation of world leaders. Insights from co-created joint learning effects can inform and improve decision making in business and management-related issues. Probably such studies can help influence and inform decision-making processes that confront leaders in current complex experiences they encounter when making decisions in a world now embedded with cross-national and multicultural business portfolios.

The task to make a difference, create a positive impact and create a better world by using our unique skills and capabilities (Rimanoczy, 2010) infers that future curricula that focus on sustainability should set, as part of its guidelines, a sustainability mindset paradigm, to spearhead the efforts among future leaders, management and organizations (Kassel et al., 2016).

Methodology

Research context

A study to explore how actors and investors help to enhance agriculture value chains, whilst identifying areas that faculty can co-create synergy in enhancing curricula used by the two business schools, was conducted in Zambia (Southern Africa) in 2011. A field trip was engaged by selected staff and students from the business school in Mulungushi University (MU), Kabwe, Zambia, and the Inter-College Business School (ICBS), Utrecht, The Netherlands in July 2011. Follow-up discussions were conducted in the last quarter of 2011, and a final questionnaire was sent to the students who took part in the field trip again in October 2016. Prior preparations were made with six Dutch students who were mentored and trained by faculty, investors, entrepreneurs, consultants and practitioners as well as by the lead researcher between January and June 2011 in The Netherlands and Mulungushi University Business School.

The dairy value chain, positioned within the context of co-creation and joint learning efforts by students from ICBS and MU, as well as to explore the role of social entrepreneurship, insurance and microcredit, in inducing changes in the value chain, was the unit of analysis for the study. To look for a way that will be different from traditional forms of conducting action research, students were paired based on their interests and study background via the courses they were pursuing within the two business schools.

FIGURE 9.1   Map of study area

Source: Google Maps.

One of the reasons for this approach was to study patterns of how the students could co-create their focus, as well as processes by which they surmount challenges they were likely to encounter. Also, the approach used in the field study was to identify forms of areas that students show and exploit their core competencies, whilst improving on their weaknesses.

Since the dairy value chain has common traits between The Netherlands and Zambia, the research team settled to study how the dairy chain was organized, as well as how social entrepreneurs could take advantage to invest in this particular chain. The study team followed Zambia's 'Rails' network, where dairy plays an important role in the livelihoods of individual farmers and cooperatives.

Three categories of dairy value chain segments were covered (i.e., smallholders, large-scale and emerging farmers). Processors and markets where farmers sell their end product (milk) were also targeted in the field study.

Whilst the primary interest was to explore how investors and entrepreneurs help to enhance changes in agriculture value chains (specifically, dairy), the underlying motive was to study how the combined categories could forge synergies, and to generate data that had dual and cross-cultural perspectives. The findings, expected to be shared and reflected on by the combined team, and on an individual basis, would become the input for future curricula development to be shared by the two business schools.

Action research

Action research has been one of the cardinal approaches used by experiential learning practitioners. Many scholars and practitioners subscribe to this method to study and understand how particular phenomena evolve (Dentoni, Waddell, & Waddock, 2017; Van Dijk, 2011; http://domenicodentoni.blogspot.nl/). In this study, students not only collected data in the field, but together with the lead researcher they also participated in informal activities within the communities and businesses they visited during the entire study period. Dutch and Zambian students were paired based on interest to follow a particular component of the dairy value chain: farming, processing, financing and retailing.

Appreciative Inquiry

Appreciative Inquiry (AI) as a method places researchers in the arena whereby they are able to follow change dynamics, as both participants and assessors, through experiential learning processes and context development. Initiators of AI argue that this form of action research 'represent a viable complement to conventional forms' as well as help 'to create the world we later discover' (Cooperrider & Srivastva, 1987).

AI focuses on the coevolutionary search for the best in people, their organizations and the relevant world around them (Cooperrider, Barret, & Srivastva, 1995). AI as a methodology ensures that the idea of social construction of reality is taken to its positive extreme. Its emphasis is on metaphor and narratives, as well as ways of knowing, language and how phenomena are viewed from diverse perspectives (Cooperrider, Barrett, and Srivastva, 1995; Cooperrider & Srivastva, 1987). AI helps the action researcher to study, to seek and to understand a positive change core that links the energy of this core directly to any change agenda and changes never thought as positive but democratically mobilized.

Students and faculty in this study reflected on the importance of joint learning and shared values. They identified their core competencies, weaknesses and jointly participated in solving challenges they encountered. These were there fore learning curves encountered and engaged in by students and faculty during the entire field study. This approach enabled the lead researcher to document shared insights and learning curves learned by the respondents during and after the field study.

Data analysis

Thematic content analysis, where emerging themes and constructs are grouped under themes, as well as member category analysis, where responses are placed in the level of categories, were used to analyse data for this chapter. As an example, responses generated from Zambian and Dutch students on the same questions were categorised as responses from the two main multicultural divides (Silverman, 2006; Yin, 1994; Yin, 2004). Data was transcribed and then coded under various themes in ATLAS.ti qualitative data software. This was then linked to a particular group. Specifically, responses were grouped into the three main types of participants that engaged in the field trip: 'Dutch Students', 'Zambian Students' and 'Zambian Scholar' (see Table 9.1).

Findings/results

Because this chapter is focused on developing sustainability mindset in management education, emphasis is on students' perspectives and experiences gained during the field study in Zambia. The findings further highlight the multicultural and regional perspectives that show that the concept of being within the context of "I-We-Us-Them" plays an important role in creating synergies and curricula that can be of importance to faculty and practitioners. The later results that inform this chapter are thus presented as follows.

TABLE 9.1 Respondents

Students	Male	Female	Remarks
Zambia	4	2	
Dutch	5	1	
Scholars / Mentors	Male	Female	
Zambia	2	–	These were professors who had divergent international as well as cross-cultural and business education core competencies.
Dutch	4	–	The lead researcher, though of African descent, was resident in the Netherlands and thus was captured as Dutch.

Appreciative Inquiry

The results of this study brings out how achievements, assets, unexplored potentials, innovations, strengths, elevated thoughts, opportunities, traditions, strategic competencies, stories, high-point moments, lived values, expressions of wisdom and insights into deeper corporate spirit or soul are expressed by students and faculty of the two business schools. Students and faculty in this chapter represented a viable complement to conventional forms and were able to create a new worldview they discovered during the field study.

Students were able to discover the "what is", "what might be" and "what should be" in their curriculum and syllabuses at their various schools. Again, the cross-cultural approach and synergies exhibited by both students and faculty helped to unravel differences and synergies that were appreciated due to the adoption of the action research approach. The search for meanings and understanding of how and why traditions, values and explored potentials of the two main categories of students could help initiate joint learning was brought to bear during the field action research. Another insight from the study brought out issues of empowerment, as well as how students and faculty were willing to learn, adjust and improvise to meet the study objective of their action. The question of "what should be the ideal?" approach to improve the field study and curricula development by the two schools brought out possible approaches students and faculty presumed could help enhance the theory and practice of teaching in the two business schools.

The following statements highlight students' appreciation of the joint field study conducted by the two business schools:

> *It was really interesting to get to know them and see how they work and study and live.*
> *(Dutch Student, 2011)*

Faculty members from the Mulungushi University had the following insights from the field study they participated in:

> *Students from ICBS had a better understanding of the subject matter than MU. They picked up the concept as the study progressed.*
> *(Zambian Scholar, 2011)*

> *It is a method MU students encountered for the first time but it was informative.*
> *(Zambian Scholar, 2011)*

> *Conducting practical work or study 'using a find-it- out-yourself method' – this tool is good for making students link theory and practice.*
> *(Zambian Scholar, 2011)*

Whilst both Dutch and Zambian students complemented each other, unique differences were also made explicit and shared by the two categories of students.

They, however, had a common opinion regarding what bonded them together during the field trip. The following statement is a summary from some respondents:

> *The Dutch Students that came were a very interesting bunch. They each had different characteristics. We all got along fine from the very first night we all met. They easily joined us Zambian students in conversation, laughter, and even a group dance.*
>
> *(Response from a Zambian Student, July 2011)*

Another observation that summed up how the students perceived themselves is further highlighted:

> *The Dutch maybe had a little more practical knowledge but overall I think they had the same skills.*
>
> *(Response from a Dutch Student, July 2011)*

These statements seem to suggest that both groups of students acknowledged their universal connectedness during the field trip. Divergent learning outcomes were, however, captured in the following statements.

From a systems perspective, data analysed revealed that whilst students could bring their knowledge to bear in following the dairy value chain, knowledge and experiences were shared among themselves in order to collect data for their assigned tasks. The feedback generated from this exercise was informative enough for the faculty from the two business schools to update and align their curricula to suit expectations from students. The following learning outcomes from the field study were seen by students and faculty as important to improve value chain curricula at Mulungushi Business School:

> *It (the purpose of the study) did fulfil (its objectives) because it covered the entire spectrum of value chain in dairy industry.*
>
> *(Zambian Scholar, July 2011)*

> *It dealt with six sections in the chain value, although some sections are not yet developed in Zambia.*
>
> *(Zambian Scholar, July 2011)*

Insights from new knowledge gained from the field study were further mentioned by faculty members who took part in the action research as follows:

New Knowledge/Insight Gained by Scholars

> *Developing the dairy industry requires the understanding of all the sections of value chain.*
>
> *(Zambian Scholar, 2011)*

For me, it aroused interest in the area of business incubation. The method to use in developing an incubation programme for dairy industry is to conduct a value chain study.

(*Zambian Scholar, 2011*)

Interestingly, students shared the following as knowledge and insights gained, and as further shared among them during evaluation of the entire co-created action research.

New Knowledge/Insights Shared by Students

I did find it useful that we split up, so every team could focus on one subject, but the negative about that was that you didn't get the whole picture and a lot of information wasn't shared well enough.

(*Dutch Student, July 2011*)

There was some level of equality [in the capability of the students to conduct the field research] although a few lapses were noticed, due to courses offered at first year. . . . It [the study approach] was a good one because it captured the purpose for the subject and any other questions [that we encountered].

(*Zambian Student, 2011*)

Cross-Cultural Perspectives (Biosphere)

The field study brought about insights from students' perspectives, as to ways by which curricula development and re-alignment can be of mutual benefit to the two business schools. Whilst business schools in The Netherlands have subjects such as business economics, social entrepreneurship and commerce as part of their curricula, this was an omission in the curricula of MU. Students and faculty from the two business schools opined that such subjects are important to be taught at both schools. This was evident in a comment by a Zambian student as follows:

Zambian business schools need Social Venturing Entrepreneurship as well as Business economics and commerce [to be included in their curricula].

(*Zambian Scholar, 2011*)

Multicultural Dimension in Complex Environments

Dutch students developed quite interestingly coping strategies that helped them to integrate into the local context. Whilst this was quite a challenge at the beginning, Zambian students appreciated the '*willing to learn to adapt characteristics*' exhibited by their Dutch colleagues. The following are summaries from data analysed:

The first Sunday, our visiting students went to their first Zambian church service and even though they couldn't understand the local language, they enjoyed the song and dance that came so naturally to the locals in the atmosphere of the church.

(*Observation from a Zambian Student, July 2011*)

Another student respondent observed the following:

> *Although there were many differences, the way they interacted amongst themselves reminded me so much of how my friends and I interact. This was what made it so much easier for me to feel comfortable around them. They managed to pick out a number of popular local phrases, and we shared the same sense of humour on many occasions. All in all, they are good people, very clever, and receptive to certain bits of the culture. Their direct approach to everything was a quality that I really appreciated.*
>
> *(Observation from a Zambian Student, July 2011)*

These comments reveal an interesting observation by Zambian students who had hitherto perceived their Dutch colleagues to be superior, due to the fact that they live and study in a developed economy.

Divergent Values and Thinking

An interesting observation that was also made by students was in the area of religion and socio-cultural values. Whilst the Zambian students were predominantly religious (Christians), only two out of the six Dutch students believed in the existence of God. The sharp contrast was further highlighted by the students, pointing to multicultural differences of the two groups of students and faculty. The following comment was captured:

> *Another difference was that whereas we are generally more careful about what we say and what conversations we have in the presence of our elders, the Dutch students always spoke their minds no matter who was present. One night during dinner in Livingstone, [Name withheld] and I were making a toast with our drinks when he mentioned how important it is to look into the eyes of the person you are toasting or else they would have seven years of bad sex. When he said this I couldn't help but laugh because on my left was Professor [name withheld], an elder; such topics are basically off bounds in front of elders, a taboo, but the Professor took it lightly and laughed as well.*
>
> *(Zambian Student, July 2011)*

> *. . . he (Zambian professor) calls me by the side to say it's not African to speak aloud when elders are around. His implication was the MU students to keep quiet, while the IBS (Dutch students) make noise! So not fair. . .*
>
> *(Zambian Student, July 2011)*

> *Nowhere in Africa would they allow smoking in a bus. The one-way hand-shake [where some Dutch students did not feel worried to smoke even in the presence of faculty] was obviously because of differences in culture.*
>
> *(Zambian Student, 2011)*

Whilst cultural differences were of paramount interest to the team, it was revealing to note that Zambian students were surprised their Dutch colleagues were not used to basic traits that local Zambian students exhibit. This is summarized as follows:

There are many differences between the two sets of students; from how their business degree takes three years to complete, instead of four, to how they have not used bar soap in years or have never hand washed their laundry.

(*Zambian Student, July 2011*)

Basically there is free attitude towards questioning with the ICBS (Dutch) students compared to MU (Zambian) students.

(*Zambian Student, 2011*)

In the context of religion, the following response was analysed from post-field interviews conducted as part of the experiential lessons gained by the students:

One thing that caught me by surprise, certainly something I'm not used to, was that the majority of them didn't believe in God. I think it was only [name withheld] that told me he was a Christian and that he even went to church every Sunday, and [name withheld] too was a believer.

(*Zambian Student, 2011*)

To talk to local people who live totally different than I live and still have the same values (like faith and dreams for the future) [was interesting to me].

(*Dutch Student, 2011*)

In the context of divergent settings of the research project's co-created educational curriculum and the joint action research, the following was a summary of students' observations:

Mono-Cultural/Cross-Cultural Educational Settings

I could tell that some of my fellow Mulungushi students got a little bothered by how much Dutch was spoken, automatically ruling them out of certain conversations. For me it was understandable. First of all, English isn't their first language and secondly I think it made them feel a little closer to home and not so far away. I surprisingly picked up a little bit of the Dutch language; if I paid close enough attention I could at least understand what the topic of the conversation was.

(*Zambian Student, July 2011*)

Reading culture was not all that at its peak [competency levels] by both [student] groups, and [students] strengths were the ability to work hand in hand [as a team].

(*Zambian Student, 2011*)

Both have a drive to get a good job later in life, and are willing to work hard for it.

(Dutch Student, July 2011)

[The Zambian Students] were very secure and serious about their job.

(Dutch Student, 2011)

For me it was about getting the experience to work in another country with opposite ways of doing business. And the project certainly fulfilled that target.

(Dutch Student, 2011)

Since one of the main objectives was to understand how students worked around challenges, as well as how they were able to jointly solve these challenges, the following responses were revealed:

Challenges

The long journeys travelled and uncomfortable gravel roads and difficulties in making visiting appointments [was challenging].

(Zambian Scholar, 2011)

Synthesis of different items into a coherent report that flows (was a challenge), poor team work.

(Observation by Zambian Scholar, 2011)

English writing skills.

(Observation by Zambian Scholar on Dutch students' main challenges faced during field trip and study)

Information, Communication and Technology (ICT skills), student-centered learning, and analytical skills.

(Observation by Zambian Scholar on Zambian students' main challenges faced during field trip and study)

Towards sustainability mindset paradigm shift in learning

Whilst these challenges revealed systemic, as well as institutional, issues associated with teaching and learning among the students, and were captured by both scholars and students, the study further revealed that there will be the need to have practitioners with field experience as part of the business school faculty. This was highlighted by students as follows:

Mostly the way in which business world is practically on the ground, a balance between practical and theory must be considered.

(Zambian Student, July 2011)

The need to use businessmen with experience to teach the students.

(Dutch Student, 2011)

More practical teaching and teachers that know business.

(Dutch Student, 2011)

• Future joint-learning activities

The respondents further had suggestions for areas that would need further improvement, that is, should such a learning approach be used to expose students to field action research studies:

If this could happen again, let the business school at MU prepare their students with adequate information. . . . Yes it's good to learn, but you learn more when you are prepared. Thank you!!

(Zambian Student, July 2011)

We should try to get the Zambian students to the Netherlands.

([Dutch Student, 2011)

Discussions and conclusion

Sustainable learning processes from cross-cultural perspective is one approach that business schools, scholars, practitioners and students can jointly co-create new avenues that can help address current world challenges with leadership and change in mindset (Kassel et al., 2016, p. 8).

Many studies have looked at sustainability-related issues from mono-cultural and quasi-cultural practices, yet current decision makers connected to business (and agribusiness) schools would be well advised to begin to actively and practically apply their business and teaching models to encompass a multicultural worldview. As evident in the results of this study, the worldviews of students and faculty as regards curricular development and teaching are important to improve sustainability thinking among scholars and practitioners. Capacity building in the area of joint development of field studies helps faculty and students to test, in a practical and applied manner, how their knowledge and experiences shape their worldview. This study reveals that cross-cultural perspectives present opportunities for students to not only explore and appreciate synergies and diversity, but also develop an enhanced mindset, as exhibited by the students and faculty in this study. Students are further able to appreciate their unique culture and that of others with which they may not be as conversant. This study also revealed the coping mechanisms exhibited by Dutch and Zambian students in order to help keep aligned with the field study mission (Fang, 2004; Fang, Kang, & Liu, 2004).

Furthermore, this study revealed that while students may graduate with similar certifications, their cultural, local and teaching approaches inform their thinking and to a very large extent their worldview when they enter leadership positions in organizations. It is therefore prudent to introduce sustainability mindset models to develop student and faculty thinking, as business schools develop their curricula to generate future leaders who can appreciate diversity in the management of their businesses in the foreseeable future.

References

Cooperrider, D. L., Barrett, F., & Srivastva, S. (1995). Social construction and appreciative inquiry: A journey in organizational theory. In D. Hosking, P. Dachler, & K. Gergen (Eds.), *Management and organization: Relational alternatives to individualism* (pp. 157–200). Aldershot, UK: Avebury Press.

Cooperrider, D.L., & Srivastva, S. (1987). Appreciative inquiry in organizational life. In *Research in organizational change and development* (Vol. 1, pp. 129–169). ISBN: 0-89232-4749-9

Dentoni, D., & Klerkx, L. (2015). Co-managing public research and development in Australian fisheries through convergence-divergence processes. *Marine Policy, 60*, 259–271.

Dentoni, D. & Bitzer, V. (2015). "Managing Wicked Problems in Global Agriculture: The Role of Universities in Multi-Stakeholder Engagements and Value Creation." Journal of Cleaner Production 106, 68-78. Special Issue on Building Bridges for a More Sustainable Future.

Dentoni, D., Waddell, S., & Waddock, S. (2017). Pathways of transformation in global food and agricultural systems: Implications from a large systems change theory perspective. *Current Opinion in Environmental Sustainability*.

Dijk, G.V. (2011). Social venturing and cooperative entrepreneurship-motives for entry and institutions for exit in developing countries. In F. v. d. Velden (Ed.), *New approaches to development cooperation*. Utrecht: Context, International Cooperation.

Fang, Z. (2004). Scientific literacy: A systemic functional linguistics perspective. In *Science education*. Wiley Periodicals Inc. 89:335–349, 2005.

Fang, F., Kang, S.-P., & Liu, S. (2004). *Measuring mindset change in the systemic transformation of education*. Paper presented at the National Convention of the Association for Educational Communications and Technology, Chicago, IL.

Gereffi, G., Humphrey, J., & Sturgeon, T. (2005). The governance of global value chains. *Review of International Political Economy, 12*(1), 78–104. http://dx.doi.org/10.1080/09692290500049805

Kassel, K. (2014). *The thinking executive's guide to sustainability*. New York, NY: Business Expert Press.

Kassel, K., Rimanoczy, I., & Mitchell, S. (2016). The sustainable mindset: Connecting being, thinking, and doing in management education. *Academy of Management Conference Paper*, Anaheim, CA.

Kievit, H. (2011). *Social venture entrepreneurship*. Een Plaatsbepaling. Dissertatie Nyenrode Business Universiteit. Bruekelen, Nederland. ISBN 978-90-817767-0-7.

Kolk, A., Rivera-Santos, M., & Rufin, C. (2013). Reviewing a decade of research on the "Base/Bottom of the Pyramid" (BOP) concept. *Business & Society.* 53(3), 338–377. doi:10.1177/0007650312472928

Lai, C., Chan, C., Dentoni, D., & Neyra, E. (2017). Measuring youth entrepreneurs' potential: The case of an out-of-school youth training program in Mindanao, Philippines. In C. Chan, B. Sipes, and T. Lee (Eds.), *Agri-entrepreneurship in conflict and transition regions* (pp. 72–88). London, UK: CABI.

Lem, M., Van Tulder, R. J. M., & Geleynse, K. (2013/June 2015). *Doing business in Africa. A strategic guide for entrepreneurs* (3rd ed.). Berenschot, Resource Centre, NABC.

Murphy, M., Perrot, F., Rivera-Santos, M. (2012). New perspectives on learning and innovation in cross-sector collaborations. Journal of Business Research, 65(12), 1700-1709.

Nuer, A. T. K. (2015). *Exit strategies for social venture entrepreneurs.* PhD Thesis, Wageningen University, Wageningen, NL. ISBN 978-94-6257-568-4

Nuer, A. T. K., Rivera-Santos, M., & Rufin, C. (2014, January). Maasai or Tanzania? Institutional Isolation/Integration of subsistence markets and business ventures. *Academy of Management Proceedings.* doi:10.5465/AMB.2014.15881

Nuer, A. T. K., Rivera-Santos, M., Rufin, C., & Dijk van, G. (2016). Leaving a social venture: Social entrepreneurial exit among the Maasai in Northern Tanzania. Africa Journal of Management, 2(3), 281–299. http://dx.doi.org/10.1080/23322373.2016.1206805.

Rimanoczy, I. (2014). A matter of being: Developing sustainability-minded leaders. *Journal of Management for Global Sustainability*, 2(1), 95–122.

Rimanoczy, I. B. (2010). *Business leaders committing to and fostering sustainability initiatives.* Doctoral dissertation. Teachers College, Columbia University.

Rivera-Santos, M., Holt, D., Littlewood, D. & Kolk, A (2014). Social Entrepreneurship in sub-Saharan Africa. Academy of Management Perspective. Vol.29. 172-9. Published online before print October 29, 2014, doi: 10.5465/amp.2013.0128.

Rivera-Santos, M., Rufin, C., & Kolk, A. (2012). Bridging the institutional divide: Partnerships in subsistence markets. *Journal of Business Research, 65*(12), 1721–1727.

Rufin, C., & Rivera-Santos, M. (2013). Cross-sector governance: From institutions to partnerships, and back to institutions. In A. Crane & M. M. Seitanidi (Eds.), *Social partnerships and responsible business: A research handbook* (pp. 125–142). London, UK: Routledge.

Silverman, D. (2006). *Interpreting qualitative data* (3rd ed.). London; Thousand Oaks; New Delhi: Sage Publications.

van Tulder, R. J. M. (2016). Solving wicked problems through partnerships. *RSM Discovery – Management Knowledge, 28*(4), 5–7. Retrieved from http://hdl.handle.net/1765/94708

Yin, R. K. (1994). *Case study research: Design and methods.* Thousand Oaks: Sage Publications.

Yin, R. K. (2004). *The case study anthology.* Thousand Oaks, CA: Sage Publications.

10

MAKING SENSE OF MINDFULNESS IN MANAGEMENT EDUCATION

Charlie Yang

Mindfulness, as a powerful tool for alleviating stress and chronic pain, has gained significant attention among academics and practitioners in recent years. The term "mindfulness" is an English translation of *sati*, which originally means "recalling to mind" or "memory" in Pali, the ancient Indian language (Sangharakshita, 2003). From the ancient Buddhist perspective, mindfulness is often defined as *a state of being* that facilitates the moment-to-moment nonjudgmental awareness of bodily sensations, emotions, and thoughts (Kabat-Zinn, 2005a). Conceptually, mindfulness as a mental state of presence to one's experience seems deceptively simple: essentially, it refers to paying undivided attention to the present moment in the here and now.

Meditation as a practice of mindfulness is an English translation of *bhavana* from Sanskrit, which means "to cultivate," and its Tibetan equivalent, *gom*, meaning "to become familiar with" (Ricard, 2017). According to Ricard (2017), meditation helps cultivate a clear and accurate way of seeing things and wholesome qualities such as empathy and compassion. Hence, meditation as a disciplined mental practice can enable us to become more attentive to passing thoughts and emotions without being engulfed by them. It enhances our capacities for concentration, deepened awareness, and insights in the silence and stillness (for a review of the Buddhist perspectives on mindfulness, see Williams & Kabat-Zinn, 2013).

Meditation is, however, not the only way to cultivate mindfulness. From a Western cognitive psychological perspective, mindfulness is defined as "an active state of mind characterized by novel distinction-drawing" (Langer, 2014, p. 11). From this perspective of mindfulness without meditation, mindfulness can be enhanced through developing an orientation in the present moment, openness to novelty, and attending to the variability of one's mental and physical states (Langer, 1990). Accordingly, we can maintain a heightened sense of awareness through practicing an open awareness of novel information through *noticing* differences and distinctions and cognitively *making* new categories out of our experiences. By noticing variations and differences among alternatives in the ever-changing flux of our experiences, we can liberate ourselves from the mental state of mindlessness, which is the consequence of automatic repetition of learned behavioral repertoire from the past. In this respect, the Eastern and Western approaches toward mindfulness are not mutually exclusive or incompatible; they are simply two "different ways to get to essentially the same place" (Langer, 2014, p. 10), where appreciating wholesome states of mind, such as paying attention, curiosity, and equanimity, is highly valued (for a review of the Western and Eastern approaches to mindfulness, see Ie, Ngnoumen, & Langer, 2014).

The positive effects of various mindfulness practices have been well documented. Mindfulness practices reduce mind wandering (Mrazek, Franklin, Phillips, Baird, & Schooler, 2013), strengthen attention (Jha, Stanley, Kiyonaga, Wong, & Gelfand, 2010), and help individuals to be more empathetic in interpersonal relationships (Shapiro, Brown, & Astin, 2011). It has also been reported that mindfulness prevents mindless impulses (Papies, Barsalou, & Custers, 2012) and increases compassion and the sense of community (Haynes, 2011), thereby enhancing a sense of well-being (Brown & Ryan, 2003; Shapiro, Oman, Thoresen, Plante, & Flinders, 2008). After having examined the effects of mindfulness in the workplace, Dane and Brummel (2013) reported that workplace mindfulness was positively related to job performance while negatively related to turnover intention. Hence, mindfulness tends to be positively related to overall life satisfaction (Brown, Ryan, & Creswell, 2007; Glomb, Duffy, Bono, & Yang, 2011).

Although mindfulness has gained much attention in the fields of management and leadership studies in recent years (Good et al., 2016), little is known about how management students actually make sense of mindfulness in the classroom. Although there has been an increasing need for "rebalancing" of three pedagogical pillars – "knowing," "doing," and "being" – in business and management education (Datar, Garvin, & Cullen, 2010), few have explored how mindfulness and its practices as pedagogical tools can actually cultivate the "being" mindset in the management classroom. By ignoring the "being" aspect of responsible management education, which emphasizes the cultivation of students' inner qualities for self-understanding, empathy, and compassion toward others (Rimanoczy, 2016a; Sunley & Coleman, 2016), apparently management education has been negligent in developing a well-balanced "whole person." Given that mindfulness helps us "become intimate with the vast wisdom of feelings" (Kozak, 2016, p. 6), mindfulness practices can be adopted to help students to become more familiar with the embodied basis of their mental life.

Therefore, the primary purpose of this study is twofold: first, this study explores how management students make sense of mindfulness as embodied experiences of (a) paying attention to the here and now (as generally understood from the Eastern Buddhist perspective) and (b) noticing novelty and the variability in the environment to make meaningful distinctions (as often conceptualized from the Western psychological perspective). Second, this chapter investigates how students describe and create meaning out of their experiences of mindfulness practices such as sitting meditation and art appreciation. The pedagogical implications of meditation and art appreciation as genuine experiences for personal meaning-making contributing to a sustainability mindset are further discussed in the context of responsible management education.

As the purpose of this chapter is to explore how management students make sense of mindfulness as a genuine way of being and how they create meanings out of their experiences, interpretative phenomenological analysis (IPA) (Smith, Flowers, & Larkin, 2009) is used to understand the "personal meanings" that the students form from their practice of meditation and art appreciation. IPA is "a qualitative research approach committed to the examination of how people make sense of their major life experiences" and is mostly "concerned with exploring experience in its own terms" (Smith et al., 2009, p. 1). IPA as a valid and useful theoretical lens allows me to make sense of the first-person narratives of the students on their initial emotional reactions and the processes of their meaning-making from the two mindfulness practices.

Mindfulness in the management classroom

> The faculty of voluntarily bringing back a wandering attention, over and over again, is the very root of judgment, character, and will. No one is *compos sui* [master of one's self] if he have it not. An education which should improve this faculty would be *the* education *par excellence*.
>
> (James, 1890/1950, p. 424, emphasis in original)

Given that instrumental knowledge and quantitative analysis have been the focus of management education since the late 1950s (Datar et al., 2010; Statler & Guillet de Monthoux, 2015), it is not surprising to find that management students hold very conventional expectations when it comes to appropriate content materials that should be taught and practiced in the management classroom. As Pavlovich (2010, p. 201) aptly put it, students primarily look for "'useful and relevant' externalized information regarding the what and how of business techniques." In this respect, mindfulness as a genuine experience of slowing down and paying attention to one's breathing must be quite a challenging task, especially for those students whose daily schedules are already filled with constant activities. Nowadays, college students work an average of 30 hours a week, while taking five or six courses at school (Rapacon, 2015). Their lives are already overscheduled and overwhelming. For example, one of my undergraduate students shared his experience by stating:

> I have been so caught up in my life that I haven't had the chance to take a step back and realize what is around me. I almost feel sorry for myself in that I don't even notice nature at this point. I'm *so focused on getting from point A to point B that I ignore what's around me* [emphasis added]. Being my age, and the

circumstances that I face day to day, I really don't have time. . . . I'm not a person to meditate. I know that sounds naïve, but I just have too much going on to take time to sit and try and focus on nothing. I am a very active person. *I need to be stimulated and stay active in order to feel a sense of accomplishment* [emphasis added].

Under these conditions of living and learning, with an overly structured and very fast-paced lifestyle, any genuine experience of slowing down is easily considered "something one doesn't need for success" as confessed by the aforementioned student. For instance, a majority of business students tend to consider art appreciation as irrelevant and out of their comfort zone. In the beginning of a semester, the author's full-time working MBA students are often skeptical about the worth of art appreciation for cultivating mindfulness by *pausing* for a few moments and *noticing* beauty in stillness and quietude. Given that those students have been rarely exposed to arts while they are taking other business courses, it makes sense that they are not fully aware of the potential of art museums as a different *place* for their learning of mindfulness.

It has also become clear that the majority of these students possess the mindset of constant "doing" rather than "being," because they want to accomplish so much in a short period of time. Without being fully aware of the purpose or reasons for their actions, they often think about what they need to do next so that they can remove items from their to-do lists, instead of focusing on the current task. However, as one of the students succinctly put it, "A to-do list is not self-reflection." In his book, *Art as Experience*, Dewey (1934/2005, p. 46) described this state of mind as follows:

> Zeal for doing, lust for action, leaves many a person, especially in this hurried and impatient human environment in which we live, with experience of an almost incredible paucity, all on the surface. No one experience has a chance to complete itself because something else is entered upon so speedily. *What is called experience becomes so dispersed and miscellaneous as hardly to deserve the name* [emphasis added]. Resistance is treated as an obstruction to be beaten down, not as an invitation to reflection. An individual comes to seek, unconsciously even more than by deliberate choice, situations in which he can do the most things in the shortest time.

Under the pressure of the constant tyranny of the urgent, students feel anxious and restless, as their sympathetic nervous system is constantly on alert and overstimulated, even when they are free from work. As a consequence, it is almost impossible to have a genuine experience about which "we say in recalling them, 'that *was* an experience'" (Dewey, 1934/2005, p. 37, emphasis in original).

This is the primary reason why I have intentionally incorporated mindfulness as a practice of optimal way of *being* into the management classes. For example, in the teaching of an undergraduate special topics course on *Mindful Leadership*, defined as the embodied practice of multiple ways of knowing, being, and doing (Rimanoczy, 2016a; Sinclair, 2007; Tideman, 2016), students attend eight sessions of ten-minute mindfulness meditation in class to enhance their capabilities for paying undivided attention, emotional awareness, and empathy/compassion. Specifically, with a conceptual overview of mindfulness and meditation, I have used guided meditation CDs (e.g., Kabat-Zinn, 2005b) and training video clips for in-class sessions. Given that the students have different levels of familiarity with mindfulness or meditation, this practice of using guided meditation audio/visual materials has helped reduce the emotional resistance felt by those who are not comfortable – at least initially – with the idea of "sitting still" in the classroom.

Besides the eight in-class meditation sessions, the students are assigned approximately ten practice sessions of sitting meditation (ten to fifteen minutes for each sitting) at home, in addition to keeping a meditation journal describing their experience of observing their minds. Encouraging students to write a meditation journal is especially helpful in terms of reinforcing the importance of practicing "presence," by making it a habit to ask a simple question such as "What's going on inside me at this moment?" Following are the general instructions for the meditation journal:

> Following the completion of each assigned practice of sitting meditation, take about ten minutes to jot down your reflections on your observation of your inner experience during the meditation session. However, do not actively think about your passing thoughts and emotions during your meditation, but try rather to stay fully attentive to your breath. The key point to remember is not to try to inhibit any bodily sensations, sensory experiences, thoughts or feelings that may arise, but acknowledge these and each time gently return attention to your breath. After completing the designated sitting meditation practice, write a brief reflection note, describing your observation of recurring thoughts, emotions, or bodily reactions.

Besides their meditation journals, the students are expected to respond to a set of four open-ended questions during the fourth week and again at the end of the semester. The first four questions include: (a) to what extent were you familiar with the notion of mindfulness before taking this course? (b) what was your first impression of mindfulness? (c) what is your current understanding of mindfulness? and (d) what changes have you noticed in your life over the past four weeks? The second four questions are: (a) upon having almost completed a special topics course on mindfulness, what is your most current understanding of mindfulness? (b) what has been the most difficult aspect for you in understanding the concept of mindfulness? (c) what has been the most difficult aspect for you in practicing mindfulness meditation? and (d) what changes have you noticed in your life over the past fifteen weeks? By answering these questions, the students have an opportunity to reflect upon their embodied practice of mindfulness meditation as a genuine experience of observing their mind and body so that they can be more open to their physical sensations as well as their thoughts and feelings.

As aforementioned, meditation is not the only tool for cultivating mindfulness in the classroom. I have often used visual arts – in particular, paintings and photographs – to enhance students' skills for visual discernment and their emotional intelligence (André, 2014; Morris, Urbanski, & Fuller, 2005). For example, photographs by Gregory Crewdson have been used, whose visual images are usually ambiguous and indeterminate, yet emotionally quite realistic. As a facilitator of students' visual learning, I often deliberately create a situation where students are encouraged to construct a plot based on their intuitive understanding of the emotional states of the characters in his snapshots. In order to do so, the students need to imagine the inner worlds of the characters to understand the meaning of his photographs empathetically.

In addition to this classroom activity, both undergraduate and MBA students are expected to visit two local art museums and send two postcards to me, briefly describing their aesthetic experiences in the art galleries. The students are also given a homework assignment to choose two objects of art (paintings or sculptures) and take photos of them. Then they are asked to provide specific and detailed answers for the following questions: (a) how would you describe your museum experience? (b) why have you chosen those specific works of art? what aspects of them have attracted you? (c) what were your initial reaction(s) when you first looked at them? (d) how would you describe your emotional and physical reactions when you first observed them? and (e) if you could have found some meaning(s) out of your chosen art works, how would you describe them? The purpose of this assignment is to provide an opportunity for the students to engage in *integrated awareness* (i.e., observing art objects externally and sensing mind-body reactions internally), which has been emphasized in both Western and Eastern conceptualizations of mindfulness (Greenhalgh, 2015; Langer, 2005). Art appreciation can also facilitate students to learn different ways of mindfulness through *walking slowly* in the galleries and seeing everyday objects from an artist's perspective. It is possible because, as Gadamer (1986, p. 26) described, "after going through a museum, we do not leave it with exactly the same feeling about life that we had when we went in."

Hence, art appreciation can provide an opportunity for honing students' perceptual and observational skills (Naghshineh et al., 2008), which are the essential components of authentic mindfulness practices:

> And yet even the least well-informed observer can take in the general atmosphere of a painting. What we observe should never be underestimated. Our reaction may appear naïve, even to ourselves, but it is always a valid response. The way we first react to an image, falling in love with it or rejecting it out of hand, depends to a large degree on the way that image defines reality. . . . *What matters is the ability to approach each work directly* [emphasis added], just as we might go and meet an individual without knowing his or her history in advance.
>
> *(Barbe-Gall, 2010, pp. 4–5)*

For instance, upon examining the painting, *Portrait of Mr. Van Amburgh, as He Appeared with His Animals at the London Theatres* by Edwin Henry Landseer (1846–1847), a graduate student explored the underlying themes of the painting based on his own observation:

> To look at the portrait further is to see the ugliness of power unchecked. If Mr. Van Amburgh was a brave man to be memorialized, he would have been portrayed defending someone from a pack of animals virtuously, rather than abusing a lion in captivity while a tiger, leopards, and lionesses appeared to be in horror, despair, or in the case of tiger almost asking a viewer to do something about this injustice. I think that *the best art doesn't just have meaning to us, but asks something of us* [emphasis added], whether it is a direct action or some introspection of our humanity that we may or may not like.

Mindfulness as an optimal experience for meaning-making practices

> What we cannot understand by analysis, we become aware of in awe.
>
> (Heschel, 2001, p. 3)

In order to explore how management students make sense of mindfulness and mindfulness practices, especially meditation and art appreciation, I analyzed the meditation journals and short essays on art appreciation, which were collected from my students enrolled in the undergraduate special topics course on *Mindful Leadership* (*n* = 50) and the MBA *Organizational Behavior* course (*n* = 88) from the Spring of 2015 to the Spring of 2017. Therefore, personal narratives from the students' meditation journals and their reflections on the works of art are the two major sources of material that I read and reread to make sense of their meaning-making practices from the perspective of interpretative phenomenological analysis (IPA) (Smith et al., 2009).

In terms of students' *first* impressions of mindfulness, the two most frequently mentioned responses of the undergraduate students were (a) something culturally foreign and weird and (b) the apparent irrelevancy of the practice:

> It felt weird to sit up straight and to just breathe, letting my thoughts come and go. It was very difficult for me to just let time pass and to become more aware of my breathing. My first reaction was that I could be using this time more wisely.
>
> What does being mindful have to do with becoming a manager? I thought it was silly and could not possibly be something that I could or would ever use in my daily life. I believed that I would never have time for this and that it is a waste of time.

However, contrary to the initial skepticism and mildly negative attitudes toward mindfulness, the students usually learned quickly, after a couple of sessions of meditation practices in class and at home, that they experienced better affective regulation, a reduced level of stress, and an increased awareness of their bodies ("I can actually feel my body," "There is more to your body than just being in good physical shape"). They also experienced enhanced focus and attention, empathy, and compassion ("I am a little more understanding of others," "I do forgive those that have hurt me or may not have my best interests at heart") and improved social relationships. Their eating habits also changed ("When I eat food, I try and focus more on the actual taste and savor it," "I have been eating my meals much slower and tasting every bite"). Regarding their enhanced skills for affective regulation and managing social relationships, an undergraduate student described his experience as follows:

> I have been using substances much less to counter my high levels of stress. I have had anger issues and it wasn't uncommon for me to break things or lose my temper and yell. Now when I am feeling this way, I try to *step back and think* [emphasis added], "Is this really the problem that is leading to this amount of anger?"

Despite having signed up to this class as an elective, in the beginning of the course, the undergraduate students have often faced some challenges in making sense of mindfulness as a concept and meditation as a practice. One of the most difficult aspects of mindfulness concerns dealing with the two conflicting mindsets, the "doing versus being" modes (Williams & Penman, 2011). Given the greater emphasis put on the "driven and goal-oriented" mindset of a successful entrepreneur – often tacit and widely cherished – at business schools, the students at first felt quite confused with the notion of "being mindfully present" and maintaining focused attention on their breathing. For example, an undergraduate student expressed his confusion by stating:

> My personality is based on the state of "doing," my values encompass action and accomplishment, and for me, to embrace this concept [of mindfulness] would challenge every aspect of my life, a thought nearly impossible. How can we actually keep our stream of consciousness focused only on breathing for extended periods of time?

In terms of the difficulties for actually doing meditation, maintaining a non-judgmental attitude ("what does it mean to have a non-judgmental focus towards our emotions?") and becoming a persistent practitioner ("the hardest part is staying with the meditation because when you first start you don't see a difference") turned out to be quite challenging for the students. It was also not easy to find the time for practice ("being okay with using my time to meditate and only meditate by canceling out any interruptions").

In addition, the students had difficulty in dealing with intruding thoughts while they were sitting still, mainly because they knew that they couldn't "control" the disturbing thoughts and emotions without feelings of inadequacy. Students often felt that their meditation didn't work. It seemed that they had some preconceived notions of what "successful" meditation should be, and ironically, it was revealed as the major source of their frustration, as they knew that they couldn't meet their expectations. It became clear that most of the students had a strong need for "control" of their own wandering mind.

By the end of the fifteenth week, however, approximately 92% of the undergraduate students enrolled in the *Mindful Leadership* class reported that they had overcome the initial obstacles and reached a more wholesome understanding of mindfulness. One student shared his insight by saying that mindfulness is "an ongoing part of every aspect of life, *a simple state of being* [emphasis added]." They also became more positive ("I have become much more positive about life in general"), calmer ("I began exploring on my own and performing more walking meditation. I feel so at peace"), and more aware of their bodies ("I have been much more aware of the things that I do to my body"). The students' meditation journals also revealed that meditation encouraged them to acquire the attitude and the skill of *decentering*; instead of believing in *a reality* of "I can't do anything right about meditation," they learned to say that they had just *a thought* of "I can't do anything right about meditation." Thus, sitting meditation helped students to maintain some *psychological distance* in order to be better attuned to the state of mindful awareness. As they became more awake and perceptive to their own emotions and their interactions with others in a more compassionate manner, the quality of their relationships with others also improved.

Art appreciation, as another way of practicing mindfulness through *walking slowly* in art museums, also helped the students to *notice* unexpected novelties and to become more empathetic through paying close attention to the distinctive forms and colors of works of art. When art really works, our deepest passions and imaginations are awakened and aroused, while our typical instrumental and calculative mindset is deliberately silenced. Furthermore, aesthetic experience often facilitated the students to make their visual experiences more meaningful by incorporating their own life experiences into a work of art and by exploring their own reactions. By engaging in the visual tasks, it became clear that they learned how to put themselves into the paintings and sculptures empathetically. It is quite interesting to find out how quickly full-time working students overcome their initial reluctance and appreciate the benefits of slowing down from a single visit to the art gallery. In fact, quite a few students often expressed their willingness to revisit the art museums soon after the completion of the course. The two MBA students, who were initially very doubtful about the purpose of art appreciation, described their new insights by stating:

> After visiting the museum, my perception has changed. When I walked into the museum, I was first *overtaken by the silence and atmosphere of admiration*

[emphasis added] that everyone portrayed while viewing each piece of art work.

As I walked through the rooms, there was a great feeling of appreciation for the assignment and for the beauty of each art piece. . . . You never know what the true beauty is *unless you apply your attention to it* [emphasis added].

Some students further articulated that the museum experience seemed like an exercise in mindfulness. For instance, upon having appreciated the art work, *Mandala of the Sacred Name of the Kasuga Deities*, created during the Muromachi period in Japan (1336–1573), a graduate student wrote:

It attracted me because I like to practice meditation and this would have been the perfect place to meditate. . . . Instantly, I *felt warm* [emphasis added] on the inside, and I felt at peace like all my troubles and worries went away in that moment. *I felt infinite* [emphasis added]. In that moment nothing else mattered, as I had said I felt a sense of peace and harmony. I really wanted to meditate there to be able to have that *experience as a spiritual encounter* [emphasis added] as well.

These authentic experiences were possible because an art museum as a contemplative space offered the students the opportunities to experience the power of *place* and the different quality of *time*, as poignantly described by Gadamer (1986, pp. 41–42):

Two fundamental ways of experiencing time seem to be in question here. In the context of our normal, pragmatic experience of time, we say that we "have time for something." This time is at our disposal; it is divisible; it is the time that we have or do not have, or at least think we do not have. In its temporal structure, such time is empty and needs to be filled. . . . There is in addition, however, a totally different experience of time which I think is profoundly related to the kind of time characteristic of both the festival and the work of art. In contrast with the empty time that needs to be filled, I propose to call this "fulfilled" or "autonomous" time.

It should also be emphasized that the process of art appreciation is not solely cerebral; it is rather a genuine experience of meaning-making engaged in by one's whole being. As Dewey (1934/2005, p. 77) succinctly pointed out, "there are *values and meanings that can be expressed only by immediately visible and audible qualities* [emphasis added], and to ask what they mean in the sense of something that can be put into words is to deny their distinctive existence." The appreciation of an art work is also universal, as it can "continuously inspire *new personal realizations in experience*" (Dewey, 1934/2005, p. 113, emphasis added). For example, upon having appreciated the painting *Cityscape* by Elmer Bischoff, an undergraduate student articulated his visual experience as follows:

> I just stared at the painting for about 30 seconds in disbelief, because this painting actually represented me.... I say this because this picture represented me as a whole, and what I mean by that is my life, all of the ups and downs that I have been through. This picture represents New York City and those days and nights where I felt like giving up; being able to step outside and look over the balcony was a huge help.

Discussion

> When we dwell upon the work [of art], there is no tedium involved, for the longer we allow ourselves, the more it displays its manifold riches to us. The essence of our temporal experience of art is in learning how to tarry in this way.
>
> (Gadamer, 1986, p. 45)

> Instructions for living a life: Pay attention. Be astonished. Tell about it.
>
> (Oliver, 2008, p. 35)

The phenomenological exploration of the students' meditation journals and reflection essays, which emphasizes "personally lived meanings and experiences" (Morley, 2012, p. 586), has shown that the students' initial meaning-making tended to be focused on their immediate and direct emotional reactions. Later on, they gradually incorporated their reflections on their felt experiences into a more meaningful personal narrative. Yet, this doesn't imply that the meaning-making process through meditation and art appreciation necessarily follows a straightforward and simple linear sequence. On the contrary, meditation and art appreciation are *dynamic* and *layered* experiences, as we can be aware of and reflect upon our own thoughts, emotions, and physical sensations simultaneously. Accordingly, engaging in both meditation and art appreciation would be better understood "as a complex, non-linear practice involving somatic, affective, perceptual, cognitive changes and more" (Kornfield, 1979, p. 57).

Specifically, as meditation practices deepened, the students seemed to be more aware of the subtle movements of their strong emotions – constantly arising and passing away – and to perceive the constant flux of changes in their social environments. It should also be noted that the enhanced capabilities for self-awareness and the emotional regulations are the important dimensions of emotional intelligence, which is one of the key components of a sustainabiltly mindset (see Chapter 1, in this book). In fact, by letting go of the passing mental events and their intentions to control them, they noticed that their bustling inner voices were gradually silenced. Regarding the heightened awareness through meditation, Patrick (1994, p. 49) wrote,

> Even though this kind of heightened awareness experience is primarily perceptual, it does not exclude reflective thoughts about the experience itself....

Thus even though one's attention is engrossed in perception, one is able to reflect upon the altered nature of the experience and judge it as a heightening of awareness. There is a quality of surprise (at least for the beginning practitioner) in this reflective acknowledgement that the heightened awareness experience is truly different from the vast majority of perceptual experiences; one is rather awe-struck at the peculiar nature of the experience; one even wonders how the experience is possible at all.

It became thus clear that the students enrolled in the courses explored here might not be able to articulate what they had come to know, but they felt that they had gained some insights about the inner workings of their own minds. At least, they felt assured that their minds were capable of having some *inner freedom* from their own thoughts and emotions. Thus, meditation helped them to be attuned to the real sense of "being." An undergraduate student reported that:

> Recently I have been battling with anxiety. I was put on medicine but I like to look at the natural point to everything. Meditating has 100% helped me with my anxiety. It has given me a comfort zone. When times get rough I know that if I meditate, *I won't feel like I'm going to drown in my thoughts* [emphasis added]. I am a much calmer person and this is how I felt today after my practice of meditation.

Some might be skeptical about the fact that only several weeks of practicing mindfulness actually helped the students experience the positive benefits of meditation with an increasing sense of inner peace. Yet, it has been reported that *within a day*, meditating for eight hours on mindfulness and compassion actually reduced the expression of pro-inflammatory genes (Kaliman et al., 2014), which implies that meditation can alter neural and biochemical processes among experienced meditators. In practical terms, meditation can be adopted as a three- to ten-minute experiential activity in the management classroom by teaching students "to secure the *feelingful experience* [emphasis added] that slowed perception makes possible" (Eisner, 2002, p. 24).

In terms of meaning-making through art appreciation, initial reactions toward great works of art are – not infrequently – a non-verbal sense of wonder and awe, which are apparently very similar to what Patrick (1994) described about the heightened awareness experience. In the beginning of an aesthetic encounter with a specific art work, the meaning-making process can be therefore characterized by non-conceptual and subjective "good" feelings or dim awareness of some truth. This subtle and nuanced process is well described by de Bolla (2001, pp. 12–13):

> It is certainly the case that I may learn from these experiences – intense moments of aesthetic experience feel as if they are in the orbit of knowing, as if something has been barely whispered yet somehow heard. . . . One way of putting this is to note that these experiences often may help me to identify what it is I already know but have yet to figure to myself as knowledge. They

point toward the limit of my knowing that, make visible what is unknown or unknowable. And when this happens I project into the object this unknown or unknowable knowledge: I sense the artwork as containing something I strive to uncover or appropriate.

According to Sullivan (1960), meaning-making through the arts is not necessarily or even primarily dependent on the power of our conceptual and analytical mind. Instead, the actual process seems to be more like perceiving our whole organic aesthetic experiences as directly as possible with much *curiosity* and a sense of *awe*. Hence, from the Langerian psychological approach toward mindfulness (Langer, 1990; Weick & Putnam, 2006), art appreciation can function as an important practice for enhancing mindfulness, as it confers the ability to think flexibly, to explore the possibilities, and to invent wide ranges of *choices*. Furthermore, as a valuable process to introduce the question of life purpose and meaning, which are key to develop a sustainability mindset, the appreciation of an art work seems to *accelerate* individuals' search for meaning, given the strong emotions and sensations that ensued from the appreciation of beauty (Dewey, 1934/2005). This is also why art appreciation as "the refined and intensified forms of experience" (Dewey, 1934/2005, p. 2) provides even a secular mode of spiritual experience of being present:

> To the being fully alive, the future is not ominous but a promise; it surrounds the present as a halo. It consists of possibilities that are felt as a possession of what is now and here. . . . Because of the frequency of this abandonment of the present to the past and future, the happy periods of an experience that is now complete because it absorbs into itself memories of the past and anticipations of the future, come to constitute as esthetic ideal. Only when the past ceases to trouble and anticipations of the future are not perturbing is a being wholly united with his environment and therefore fully alive. *Art celebrates with peculiar intensity the moments in which the past reenforces the present and in which the future is a quickening of what now is.*
>
> *(Dewey, 1934/2005, p. 17, emphasis added)*

To put it differently, when art objects evoke a response in us or stir us up, we know immediately that we are realizing a special moment of the superior organization of our − often fragmented − consciousness (Sullivan, 1960). From *noticing* some distinctive features of a Cubist painting, or even *sensing* subtle irregularities in our mundane daily experiences, which usually receive less or no attention, we can reach a very mindful moment of awakening or a new insight, which is significant for personal integration and meaningful actions (Humphries, Casey-Cox, & Dey, 2016). This is what art appreciation as a genuine practice of mindfulness can make us capable of:

> The work of art transforms our fleeting experience into the stable and lasting form of an independent and coherent creation. It does so in such a way that

we go beyond ourselves by penetrating deeper into the work. That "something can be held in our hesitant stay" – this is what art has always been and still is today.

(Gadamer, 1986, p. 53)

As an example, upon having examined an Urhobo sculpture titled *Maternity Figure*, created by unidentified Nigerian artist, a graduate student decribed how the work helped her appreciate and celebrate her womanhood more deeply:

> I derived meaning from the statue because of my strong maternal instincts and my desire to become a mother one day. Prior to having read a brief description of the art work, I had already derived meaning of the figure. . . . Then after having read some information about the statue, I learned more about the figure and its purpose: it was to be used as a shrine, safeguarding the wellbeing of the community and honoring the founding ancestors. So she was not only a mother, but also the mother, my mother.

This is also probably what happened when the aforementioned undergraduate student was standing in front of the painting *Cityscape* at the art gallery. He must have revisited his past emotional experiences, as his appreciation of the painting had stirred up "a store of attitudes and meanings derived from prior experience" (Dewey, 1934/2005, p. 68). The specific work of art had gently induced him to integrate them into his self-identity and strengthened his evolving self in the present.

Therefore, based on the phenomenological exploration of the students' subjective experiences, mindfulness and its practices through meditation and art appreciation are suggested not only to have positive instrumental value (e.g., stress reduction) but also to be meaning-making practices through which the students can enhance their self-awareness, empathy, and compassion. Especially when developing responsible leaders who address their future work with a sustainability mindset, it is important to develop social sensitivity and compassion, for which these mindfulness practices seem appropriate instruments.

Generally speaking, the meaning-making through meditation and art appreciation seem to share the dynamic flow of a two-step process: the immediacy of perceptual awareness of a whole person with cognitive, emotional, and bodily reactions from meditation and/or art objects, followed by gradual conceptual integration of one's reflections on the felt experiences. As the key outcome of the two meaning-making practices, the embodied insights gained about the habits of one's mind, emotions, and somatic reactions are the germinating seeds of practical wisdom of being in the present moment. As aforementioned, students often feel perplexed and uncomfortable in the beginning of a semester, as most of them are not familiar with mindfulness and its practices. It is also because their initial experiences with meditation and aesthetic appreciation rarely fit with their preconceptions or preexisting meaning structures about the nature of management knowledge and the proper learning activities in the management classroom. Hence, it is very plausible that the two mindfulness practices create the situation of "a disorienting dilemma," where the unconscious habits of mind are made conscious, revisited, and challenged for authentic transformative learning (Mezirow, 2000).

This process is especially important for the transformative learning of a sustainability mindset, which is defined as "a way of thinking and *being* [emphasis added] that results from a broad understanding of the ecosystem's manifestations, from social sensitivity, as well as *an introspective focus on one's personal values and higher self* [emphasis added], and finds its expression in actions for the greater good of the whole" (Kassel, Rimanoczy, & Mitchell, 2018; Chapter 1 in this book). As Reason (2007) perceptibly wrote, the current crisis of sustainability is "a crisis of mind and thus a challenge for management education" (p. 27). This is also why active engagement within aesthetic and spiritual practices may enable us to see beyond "the purposive consciousness" (Bateson, 1972), which can be characterized as seeking short-sighted and immediate satisfaction of our almost hardwired desires and needs, leading us into ecological peril.

Bateson (1972) further argued that "mere purposive rationality unaided by phenomenona such as art, religion, dream, and the like, is necessarily pathogenic and destructive of life" (p. 146) and offered "an account of how humans can and should *make* art and *live* aesthetically *within* nature" (p. 306, emphasis in original).

Hence, I cautiously claim that the aforementioned two mindfulness practices have some potential to cultivate *phrónêsis* (the Greek term for practical wisdom) in management students, through which they can enhance their self-awareness, emotional skills, and their relationships with others and even with our planet Earth. Based on the well-documented positive effects of mindfulness (Brown et al., 2007; Glomb et al., 2011; Good et al., 2016; Hölzel et al., 2011), I suggest that in more responsbile management education, various mindfulness practices should be more seriously considered as innovative pedagogical tools for enhancing practical wisdom, which entail virtuous character development, along with aesthetic sensibility and spiritual discernment (Case, 2013; Coutu, 2006; Culham, 2013; Rimanoczy, 2016b). This suggestion is also relevant from the perspective of implementing the Principles of Responsible Management Education (PRME), especially the third principle regarding method, in that educational frameworks, educational materials, and processes should be continuously developed and refined to help design more innovative and effective learning experiences for responsible leadership (Sunley & Leigh, 2016).

Conclusion

The primary purpose of this paper is to explore how management students make sense of the increasingly popular concept of mindfulness and the two methods of its practice, designed to enhance their mindfulness. Considering that business educators have relatively overlooked the need for developing students' self-awareness and their reflective mindset (Datar et al., 2010; Dyllick, 2015; Mintzberg, 2005), I hereby suggest that the two mindfulness practices have the potential as innovative pedagogical tools to enhance management students' capability for embodied learning of practical wisdom (Küpers & Pauleen, 2013), which incorporates a sustainability mindset that enables us to take a more ecologically sound and systemic perspective toward responsible management education.

Considering the increasing demand by employers for business graduates with soft skills, and the apparent gaps in the business curriculum in terms of cultivating soft skills (Boyatzis, Stubbs, & Taylor, 2002; Navarro, 2008; Robles, 2012), I also propose that various contemplative practices (Barbezat & Bush, 2014), including meditation and art appreciation, need to be more seriously considered and to be skillfully adopted to *complement* "the traditional logico-rational paradigm (way of knowing)" (Nissley, 2002, p. 27) or "Logical Empiricism, Rational Choice, Agency Theory [LERCAT] paradigm" (Statler & Guillet de Monthoux, 2015, p. 3) that still shapes much of management education today. These practices should be more actively adopted in order to enhance the students' "meta-competencies," which can be understood as the overarching competencies that facilitate flexibility and adaptation in a wide range of work settings (Heery & Noon, 2008).

It is fortunate that mindfulness and arts-based teaching and learning have gradually received more attention in recent years (Adler, 2015; Hunter & Chaskalson, 2013; Katz-Buonincontro, 2015; Marques, 2014; Purg & Sutherland, 2017). The mindful approach to the cultivation of embodied wisdom among management students will create more personally meaningful management education as well. The embodied practical wisdom of being in the present moment should not be understood as merely a poetic idea. We all need to remember that mindfulness as a learned life skill does not come naturally. As the key stakeholders of responsible management education, we are all encouraged to practice mindfulness in order to be more aware of the consequences of our mindful (and mindless) actions.

References

Adler, N. J. (2015). Finding beauty in a fractured world: Art inspires leaders-leaders change the world. *Academy of Management Review, 40*(3), 480–494.

André, C. (2014). *Mindfulness: 25 ways to live in the moment through art.* London, UK: Rider.

Barbe-Gall, F. (2010). *How to look at a painting.* London, UK: Frances Lincoln.

Barbezat, D. P., & Bush, M. (2014). *Contemplative practices in higher education: Powerful methods to transform teaching and learning.* San Francisco, CA: Jossey-Bass.

Bateson, G. (1972). *Steps to an ecology of mind.* San Francisco, CA: Chandler.

Boyatzis, R. E., Stubbs, E. C., & Taylor, S. N. (2002). Learning cognitive and emotional intelligence competencies through graduate management education. *Academy of Management Learning & Education, 1*(2), 150–162.

Brown, K. W., & Ryan, R. M. (2003). The benefits of being present: Mindfulness and its role in psychological well-being. *Journal of Personality and Social Psychology, 84*(4), 822–848.

Brown, K. W., Ryan, R. M., & Creswell, J. D. (2007). Mindfulness: Theoretical foundations and evidence for its salutary effects. *Psychological Inquiry, 18*(4), 211–237.

Case, P. (2013). Cultivation of wisdom in the Theravada Buddhist tradition: Implications for contemporary leadership and organization. In W. Küpers & D. J. Pauleen (Eds.), *A handbook of practical wisdom: Leadership, organization and integral business practice* (pp. 65–78). London, UK: Gower.

Coutu, D. (2006). Ideas as art. *Harvard Business Review, 84*(10), 82–89.

Culham, T. E. (2013). *Ethics education of business leaders: Emotional intelligence, virtues, and contemplative learning.* Charlotte, NC: Information Age.

Dane, E., & Brummel, B. J. (2013). Examining workplace mindfulness and its relations to job performance and turnover intention. *Human Relations, 67*(1), 105–128.

Datar, S. M., Garvin, D. A., & Cullen, P. G. (2010). *Rethinking the MBA: Business education at a crossroads.* Boston, MA: Harvard Business Press.

De Bolla, P. (2001). *Art matters.* Cambridge, MA: Harvard University Press.

Dewey, J. (1934/2005). *Art as experience.* New York, NY: Penguin.

Dyllick, T. (2015). Responsible management education for a sustainable world. *The Journal of Management Development, 34*(1), 16–33.

Eisner, E. W. (2002). *The arts and the creation of mind.* New Haven, CT: Yale University Press.

Gadamer, H-G. (1986). The relevance of the beautiful: Art as play, symbol and festival. In R. Bernasconi (Ed.), *The relevance of the beautiful and other essays* (pp. 1–53). Cambridge, UK: Cambridge University Press.

Glomb, T. M., Duffy, M. K., Bono, J. E., & Yang, T. (2011). Mindfulness at work. *Research in Personnel and Human Resources Management, 30*, 115–157.

Good, D. J., Lyddy, C. J., Glomb, T. M., Bono, J. E., Brown, K. W., Duffy, M. K. . . . Lazar, S. W. (2016). Contemplating mindfulness at work: An integrative review. *Journal of Management, 42*(1), 114–142.

Greenhalgh, W. A. (2015). *Mindfulness & the art of drawing: A creative path to awareness.* East Sussex, UK: Leaping Hare Press.

Haynes, D. J. (2011). Mindfulness and contemplative practice in art and religion. In J. Simmer-Brown & F. Grace (Eds.), *Meditation and the classroom: Contemplative pedagogy for religious studies* (pp. 223–226). Albany, NY: State University of New York Press.

Heery, E., & Noon, M. (2008). *A dictionary of human resource management.* Retrieved from www.oxfordreference.com/view/10.1093/acref/9780199298761.001.0001/acref-9780199298761-e-774?rskey=wpwRZX&result=1024

Heschel, A. J. (2001). *I asked for wonder: A spiritual anthology.* New York, NY: Crossroad.

Hölzel, B. K., Lazar, S. W., Gard, T., Schuman-Olivier, Z., Vago, D. R., & Ott, U. (2011). How does mindfulness meditation work? Proposing mechanisms of action from a conceptual and neural perspective. *Perspectives on Psychological Science, 6*(6), 537–559.

Humphries, M., Casey-Cox, A., & Dey, K. (2016). Choosing food yet consuming plastic: Learning to notice the difference in management education. In R. Sunley & J. Leigh (Eds.), *Educating for responsible management: Putting theory into practice* (pp. 52–70). Sheffield, UK: Greenleaf.

Hunter, J., & Chaskalson, M. (2013). Making the mindful leader. In H. S. Leonard, R. Lewis, A. M. Freedman, & J. Passmore (Eds.), *The Wiley-Blackwell handbook of the psychology of leadership, change, and organizational development* (pp. 195–219). Hoboken, NJ: Wiley-Blackwell.

Ie, A., Ngnoumen, C. T., & Langer, E. J. (Eds.). (2014). *The Wiley Blackwell handbook of mindfulness* (Vol. 1). West Sussex, UK: Wiley & Sons.

James, W. (1890/1950). *The principles of psychology* (Vol. 1). New York, NY: Dover.

Jha, A. P., Stanley, E. A., Kiyonaga, A., Wong, L., & Gelfand, L. (2010). Examining the protective effects of mindfulness training on working memory capacity and affective experience. *Emotion, 10*(1), 54–64.

Kabat-Zinn, J. (2005a). *Full catastrophe living: Using the wisdom of your body and mind to face stress, pain, and illness.* New York, NY: Bantam Dell.

Kabat-Zinn, J. (2005b). *Guided mindfulness meditation Series 1* [CD]. Louisville, CO: Sounds True.

Kaliman, P., Alvarez-Lopez, M. J., Cosin-Thomas, M., Rosenkranz, M. A., Lutz, A., & Davidson, R. J. (2014). Rapid changes in histone deacetylases and inflammatory gene expression in expert meditators. *Psychoneuroendocrinology, 40*, 96–107.

Kassel, K., Rimanoczy, I., & Mitchell, S. (2018). A sustainability mindset model for management education. In I. Rimanoczy & K. Kassel (Eds.), *Sustainability mindset development in management education*. New York, NY: Routledge.

Katz-Buonincontro, J. (2015). Decorative integration or relevant learning? A literature review of studio arts-based management education with recommendations for teaching and research. *Journal of Management Education, 39*(1), 81–115.

Kornfield, J. (1979). Intensive insight meditation: A phenomenological study. *The Journal of Transpersonal Psychology, 11*(1), 41–58.

Kozak, A. (2016). *108 metaphors for mindfulness: From wild chickens to petty tyrants*. Somerville, MA: Wisdom.

Küpers, W., & Pauleen, D. J. (Eds.). (2013). *A handbook of practical wisdom: Leadership, organization and integral business practice*. Surrey, UK: Gower.

Langer, E. J. (1990). *Mindfulness*. Cambridge, MA: Da Capo Press.

Langer, E. J. (2005). *On becoming an artist: Reinventing yourself through mindful creativity*. New York, NY: Ballantine.

Langer, E. J. (2014). Mindfulness forward and back. In A. Ie., C. T. Ngnoumen, & E. J. Langer (Eds.), *The Wiley Blackwell handbook of mindfulness* (Vol. 1, pp. 7–20). West Sussex, UK: Wiley & Sons.

Marques, J. (2014). *Leadership and mindful behavior: Action, wakefulness, and business*. New York, NY: Palgrave Macmillan.

Mezirow, J. (2000). *Learning as transformation: Critical perspectives on a theory in progress*. San Francisco, CA: Jossey-Bass.

Mintzberg, H. (2005). *Managers not MBAs: A hard look at the soft practice of managing and management development*. San Francisco, CA: Berrett-Kochler.

Morley, J. (2012). Phenomenological psychology. In S. Luft & S. Overgaard (Eds.), *The Routledge companion to phenomenology* (pp. 586–595). New York, NY: Routledge.

Morris, J. A., Urbanski, J., & Fuller, J. (2005). Using poetry and the visual arts to develop emotional intelligence. *Journal of Management Education, 29*, 888–904.

Mrazek, M. D., Franklin, M. S., Phillips, D. T., Baird, B., & Schooler, J. W. (2013). Mindfulness training improves working memory capacity and GRE performance while reducing mind wandering. *Psychological Science, 24*(5), 776–781.

Naghshineh, S., Hafler, J. P., Miller, A. R., Blanco, M. A., Lipsitz, S. R., Dubroff, R. P. . . . Katz, J. T. (2008). Formal art observation training improves medical students' visual diagnostic skills. *Journal of General Internal Medicine, 23*(7), 991–997.

Navarro, P. (2008). The MBA core curricula of top-ranked U.S. business schools: A study in failure? *Academy of Management Learning & Education, 7*(1), 108–123.

Nissley, N. (2002). Arts-based learning in management education. In C. Wankel & R. DeFillippi (Eds.), *Rethinking management education for the 21st century* (pp. 27–61). Greenwich, CT: Information Age.

Oliver, M. (2008). *Red Bird: Poems*. Boston, MA: Beacon Press.

Papies, E. K., Barsalou, L. W., & Custers, R. (2012). Mindful attention prevents mindless impulses. *Social Psychological and Personality Science, 3*(3), 291–299.

Patrick, L. E. (1994). Phenomenological method and meditation. *The Journal of Transpersonal Psychology, 26*(1), 37–54.

Pavlovich, K. (2010). Educating for conscious awareness. *Journal of Management, Spirituality & Religion, 7*(3), 193–208.

Purg, D., & Sutherland, I. (2017). Why art in management education? Questioning meaning. *Academy of Management Review, 42*(2), 382–396.

Rapacon, S. (2015). *More college students are working while studying.* Retrieved from www.cnbc.com/2015/10/29/more-college-students-are-working-while-studying.html

Reason, P. (2007). Education for ecology: Science, aesthetics, spirit and ceremony. *Management Learning, 38*(1), 27–44.

Ricard, M. (2017). *Why should I meditate?* Retrieved from www.lionsroar.com/why-meditate-september-2010/

Rimanoczy, I. (2016a). A holistic learning approach for responsible management education. In R. Sunley & J. Leigh (Eds.), *Educating for responsible management: Putting theory into practice* (pp. 159–184). Sheffield, UK: Greenleaf.

Rimanoczy, I. (2016b). *Stop teaching: Principles and practices for responsible management education.* New York, NY: Business Expert Press.

Robles, M. M. (2012). Executive perceptions of the top 10 soft skills needed in today's workplace. *Business and Professional Communication Quarterly, 75*(4), 453–465.

Sangharakshita. (2003). *Living with awareness: A guide to the Satipatthāna sutta.* Birmingham, UK: Windhorse.

Shapiro, S. L., Brown, K. W., & Astin, J. (2011). Toward the integration of meditation into higher education: A review of research evidence. *Teachers College Record, 113*(3), 493–528.

Shapiro, S. L., Oman, D., Thoresen, C. E., Plante, T. G., & Flinders, T. (2008). Cultivating mindfulness: Effects on well-being. *Journal of Clinical Psychology, 64*(7), 840–862.

Sinclair, A. (2007). *Leadership for the disillusioned: Moving beyond myths and heroes to leading that liberates.* Crows Nest, Australia: Allen & Unwin.

Smith, J. A., Flowers, P., & Larkin, M. (2009). *Interpretative phenomenological analysis: Theory, method and research.* Thousand Oaks, CA: Sage.

Statler, M., & Guillet de Monthoux, P. G. (2015). Humanities and arts in management education: The emerging Carnegie paradigm. *Journal of Management Education, 39*(1), 3–15.

Sullivan, J. W. N. (1960). *Beethoven: His spiritual development.* New York, NY: Vintage Books.

Sunley, R., & Coleman, M. (2016). Establishing a foundational responsible learning mind-set for business in the 21st century. In R. Sunley & J. Leigh (Eds.), *Educating for responsible management: Putting theory into practice* (pp. 28–51). Sheffield, UK: Greenleaf.

Sunley, R., & Leigh, J. (Eds.). (2016). *Educating for responsible management: Putting theory into practice.* Sheffield, UK: Greenleaf.

Tideman, S. G. (2016). *Business as an instrument for social change: In conversation with the Dalai Lama.* Saltaire, UK: Greenleaf.

Weick, K. E., & Putnam, T. (2006). Organizing for mindfulness: Eastern wisdom and western knowledge. *Journal of Management Inquiry, 15*(3), 275–287.

Williams, M., & Kabat-Zinn, J. (Eds.). (2013). *Mindfulness: Diverse perspectives on its meaning, origins and applications.* New York, NY: Routledge.

Williams, M., & Penman, D. (2011). *Mindfulness: An eight-week plan for finding peace in a frantic world.* New York, NY: Rodale.

11

HOLISTIC EDUCATION, TRANSFORMATIVE LEARNING AND SUSTAINABILITY MINDSET IN A BUSINESS SCHOOL

A case study of a Brazilian Jesuit university

Soraia Schutel, Janaína Pimenta Lemos Becker and Janaina Franciscatto Audino

Introduction

Over the past several years, Brazil has faced massive economic, social and environmental problems. On November 5, 2015, the breakdown of a dam owned by Samarco, a joint venture between Brazilian Vale and Anglo-Australian BHP Billiton, in Mariana, state of Minas Gerais, discharged 60 billion liters of iron mining tailing along more than 500 kilometers in the Rio Doce basin, the fifth largest river in Brazil. This was the biggest ecological disaster in Brazil's history.

The country that has hosted the Earth Summit in 1992 and Rio+20 in 2012 shows that it is still far from reaching a condition of sustainable development. In this crisis context, it's important to emphasize the role and impact of organizations. For Kevany (2007), corporations are quickly becoming the highest force in society; businesses have replaced the prominent role held by religious institutions in the past due to their power over financial and technological resources, their political ability and their ability to coordinate people. For the author, "the lack of sustainable practices reveals ubiquitous value-action gaps" (Kevany, 2007, p. 109).

The sustainability problem is related to the destabilization of societal value orientations or worldviews (Egmond and Vries, 2011). For Egmond and Vries (2011), the worldview is defined as a combination of a person's value orientation (the question about the importance of certain things and themes over others; they are subjective and refer to a certain chosen quality of life) and his or her view on how to understand the world and the capabilities it offers, the lens through which the world is seen.

To reach sustainable development, we may need a mindset shift, including a change of values, attitudes and behaviors (Leiserowitz, Robert e Thomas, 2004; Garrity, 2012). For Kevany (2007, p. 116), "if corporate leaders remain uneducated about sustainable development, progress toward sustainable development will be thwarted. Higher education is vital to equip current and future business leaders with insights and skills essential for their pivotal positions in society."

Education can play a crucial role in changing the next generation's values and mental models. Given that the current growth model is no longer benefiting humanity (Garrity, 2012), new competencies are required to encourage learners to act as responsible citizens who operate with self-awareness, mutual respect and social responsibility within the global context (Kevany, 2007). Blake, Sterling, and Goodson (2013, p. 5348) state that "the role of higher education in shaping the leaders of tomorrow and nurturing graduates equipped to act in future scenarios is arguably one of the central issues facing the sector."

Among the various strategies that business schools might mobilize to educate future managers, the pedagogical approach of transformative learning operates at deeper levels of knowledge (Sterling, 2011; Blake et al., 2013), which aims to foster individual, organizational and social changes. It is therefore appropriate to develop more sustainable practices and a new mentality (Blake et al., 2013).

A sustainability mindset is increasingly vital in today's world. It offers a systemic approach that goes beyond technical knowledge and focuses instead on a broader understanding of the overall ecosystem and society (Van Lopik, 2013). A sustainability mindset can contribute to a new style of management education: one that incorporates ethics and prosperity into our economic, social and natural living system (Akrivou & Bradbury-Huang, 2015).

Following Kumar (2015), we must recover a sense of wholeness when it comes to education, to ensure our integral development as human beings. We believe that holistic education, which integrates hands (doing), head (thinking) and heart (being) (Kumar, 2015), is vital to developing future sustainable leaders.

This book chapter analyzes a business administration undergraduate program, called GIL (*Gestão para Inovação e Liderança* – Major in Management for Innovation and Leadership), which is offered at *Universidade do Vale do Rio dos Sinos* (UNISINOS), a Jesuit university in southern Brazil. The program aims to develop a sustainability mindset among students, via interaction with various stakeholders. This chapter explores the program as a case study, aiming to answer the research question, "How to develop the sustainability mindset among management students, using holistic education and a transformative learning pedagogical approach?" To answer this question, we studied the differences of the pedagogical approach from the management education mainstream, as well as the competencies and sustainability mindset that were developed in management students as a result.

This chapter is structured as follows. First, we present and discuss the concepts of a sustainability mindset and of holistic education. Next, we explore transformative learning as applied in management schools, including its aim to change students' worldviews by exposing them to new values. This is followed by a presentation of the methodology that has been used in this research. Last, we discuss the results of our findings and the implications for future studies.

Sustainability mindset and holistic education

The success of an organization is related to its engagement with the environment in which it operates. It is important to consider the well-being of the organization's employees, the financial status of its customers, the strength of the communities in which it operates and which it serves, and the health of the biosphere involved (Kassel, 2014).

Meadows (2006) points out that the revolution toward sustainability must be guided by the vision of a sustainable society, of networks of people with shared values, of speaking the truth, of learning and of love for humanity and nature. Knowing this, it is crucial to develop in future leaders a profound holistic mentality that considers each management decision in terms of its social and environmental impact: a sustainability mindset.

The sustainability approach to learning goes beyond technical knowledge and leads to an understanding of the ecosystem and society that is simultaneously broad and deep (Van Lopik, 2013). With its deeper perspective, the sustainability mindset is a new way to think about the social and environmental aspects of the world around us, through the development of social sensitivity, self-awareness and connection with purpose (Kassel, Rimanoczy, and Mitchell, 2016).

For Kassel, Rimanoczy, and Mitchell (2016, p. 8), a sustainability mindset is

> a way of thinking and being that results from a broad understanding of the ecosystem's manifestations as well as an introspective focus on one's personal values and higher self, and finds its expression in actions for the greater good of the whole.

According to Rimanoczy (2014), one of the factors that motivates leaders to act from a sustainability mindset is spirituality. For the author, the sustainability theme in management education too often focuses on processes and rational facts, while forgetting to consider the spirituality and values that motivate sustainable actions. Rimanoczy's 2010 research found that spiritual elements are crucial factors that drive the personal mission and social sensibility of leaders.

In terms of the personal mission, spirituality – especially in secular terms – drives the need to act, to make a personal contribution, to achieve life dreams and to make a difference. When it comes to social sensibility, spirituality is related to awareness about "their lives, their contribution to the problem, and their role" (Rimanoczy, 2014, p. 105). Spiritual intelligence is thus a key factor to help us face the essential theme of sustainability in this century (Stead & Stead, 2010; Rimanoczy, 2014).

For Zohar (2005), great leaders are those we can appreciate intellectually, emotionally and spiritually. Besides the financial capital to create sustainable enterprises, Zohar (2005) believes that leaders need two other forms of capital: social and spiritual. Spiritual capital is for Zohar (2005) a new paradigm that requires a radical change of mindset about "the philosophical foundations and practices of leadership in business. . . . I mean the power a leader can unleash in individuals or organizations by evoking people's deepest meanings, values, and purposes" (Zohar, 2005, p. 46).

Spiritually intelligent leadership can be fostered by applying 12 principles:

> *Self-Awareness*: Knowing what I believe in and value, and what deeply motivates me;
>
> *Spontaneity*: Living in and being responsive to the moment;
>
> *Being Vision and Value-Led*: Acting from principles and deep beliefs, and living accordingly;
>
> *Holism*: Seeing larger patterns, relationships, and connections; having a sense of belonging;
>
> *Compassion*: Having the quality of "feeling-with" and deep empathy;
>
> *Celebration of Diversity*: Valuing other people for their differences, not despite them;
>
> *Field Independence*: Standing against the crowd and having one's own convictions;
>
> *Humility*: Having the sense of being a player in a larger drama, of one's true place in the world;
>
> *Tendency to Ask Fundamental "Why?" Questions*: Needing to understand things and get to the bottom of them;
>
> *Ability to Reframe*: Standing back from a situation or problem and seeing the bigger picture; seeing problems in a wider context;
>
> *Positive Use of Adversity*: Learning and growing from mistakes, setbacks and suffering;
>
> *Sense of Vocation*: Feeling called upon to serve, to give something back.
>
> *(Zohar, 2005, p. 47)*

Educating future leaders for spiritual intelligence is part of holistic education and seems to be one important root for the sustainability mindset. The spiritual dimension of education dates from the ancient Greek civilization through the Paideia model (Jaeger, 2013). This educational model was based on spiritual and historical dimensions of the human being, which allowed the influence of Greeks throughout the centuries. For Jaeger (2013), Paideia was the education of arts recognized as philosophy, poetry, eloquence, being thus the capacity to foster the human being in his genuine and perfect form, the true human nature. The Greeks' understanding of nature has its origin in the spiritual constitution, where the parts belong to a whole organized by the living connection, in and through which everything gained connection and meaning (Jaeger, 2013).

Satish Kumar is the founder of one of the main contemporary educational references on sustainability, Schumacher College (Blake et al., 2013), located in Totnes, UK. For Kumar (2015), education should integrate the spiritual dimension, to develop new leaders and to advance beyond the outdated role of getting students to pass exams so they can find jobs and earn money. "The meaning of the word 'education' is to bring out what is already there, the potential of every student.

Every soul has its own built-in intelligence. Knowledge and wisdom are intrinsic to soul" (Kumar, 2015, p. 111).

Demajorovic and Silva (2012) note that management programs are usually focused on combining resources to achieve maximum productivity and profitability. Paulo Freire, one of the most influential pedagogy thinkers of the 20th century (Gerhardt, 1996), denounces the predominance of "banking education" that aims to deposit knowledge in students while canceling or minimizing their creative power, stimulating naivete and an uncritical viewpoint (Moreira, 2014).

According to Kumar (2015), we must recover a sense of wholeness when it comes to education, to ensure our integral development as human beings. "Education should be about training head, heart and hands, developing the power of thinking, feeling and doing. . . . Education is about finding out who you are and becoming your true self" (Kumar, 2015, p. 114).

In terms of "hands," Kumar emphasizes that our educational system has given exclusive value to working with ideas, theories and concepts. He likewise highlights that intellectual occupations provide only a limited number of jobs, and advocates for a return to "hand skills." The heart dimension, in education, is to learn "to be respectful, grateful, compassionate, generous, and caring. Furthermore, learning to deal with your emotions, feelings, anxieties and uncertainties" (Kumar, 2015, p. 119). To contribute to a holistic education, per Kumar, students must learn from nature. Universities and schools could thus be built in open fields and forests, surrounded by nature and bringing students outside of the classrooms.

Holistic education in business schools goes beyond mainstream contents, considering the integral dimensions of human beings, and connecting students to other areas of knowledge. Closs, Aramburu, and Antunes (2009) suggest that new themes and expertise could be integrated into management education such as the value of subjectivity; contextualization of information that makes sense; importance of philosophy and history, among other humanities, such as culture and art; reflections on social responsibility and sustainable development; constancy of uncertainty; solidarity, in order to generate possibilities for survival; and ethics. According to the authors, it is necessary to look for new educational models and methods that allow the transformation of the thinking and treatment of the ethical, political, social and environmental dimensions.

In response to this challenge, the pedagogical approach of transformative learning can be helpful in building the sustainability mindset, amplifying students' worldviews through the expansion of consciousness, as it acts on the deepest levels of knowledge (Mezirow, 1994).

Transformative learning in education for sustainability

Education for sustainability aims at developing students' decision-making skills that consider environmental, social and economic implications within a holistic approach. It is a new perspective, based on critical thinking and reflection of human aspects, as a path to help students act and change (Sidiropoulos, 2014).

The pedagogical model addressed in this chapter's case study is transformative learning, an interactive method of teaching and learning to develop an understanding and respectful relationship with nature (Kevany, 2007). It offers a theoretical approach that contributes to the creation of a new education for sustainability (Blake et al., 2013; Lange, 2004).

Introduced by Mezirow in 1978, transformative learning became a foundational theory of learning in adult education (Groen, 2010). Mezirow points out that transformation can occur when an individual critically recognizes that his perspective is no longer functional and decides to appropriate a new, more valuable perspective. The individual then reorganizes the way she looks at herself and her relationships, enabling her to change the situation by her own initiative (Mezirow, 1978).

Transformative learning helps us to critically question and reflect on our own actions and beliefs. Essentially, it is a rational process in which we recognize that our worldview is limited, is ineffective to explain new experiences, and does not fit anymore. "Transformative learning takes place when this process leads us to open up our frame of reference, discard a habit of mind, see alternatives, and thereby act differently in the world" (Cranton and King, 2003, p. 32). The essence of transformative learning is a fundamental change in how people see themselves and the world.

Experiences that can help promote transformative learning include living in community and group dynamics, a diversity of pedagogies, learning and co-creation, and spaces that allow for moments of epiphany or inspiration. Among the pedagogical methodologies are field work and use of the external environment, questions and discussions, lectures, group work, experiential work, audiovisual support, art and craft activities, games/simulations, individual investigations and theater (Blake et al., 2013).

Sterling (2011) observes the importance of the main influencers of transformation: the educator, who is oriented to transform the apprentices' worldview, the student, and the learning environment. The student is an active agent in this pedagogical approach, since the openness and preparation of learners to participate in this internal change and transformation is propaedeutic. The learning environment goes beyond the classroom walls, aggregating experiential methods and bringing about a new concept of the world for students. "Transformative learning arises from the interaction between the state of readiness of the learner and the quality of the learning environment to yield a particular learning experience as an emergent property of that interaction" (Sterling, 2011, p. 27).

To develop a sustainability mindset, students should interact with collaborative projects as an opportunity to develop social sensitivity, self-awareness, ecoliteracy and connection with purpose, as well as to discover the satisfaction and self-confidence that can emerge from meaningful work. Individuals develop their skills to work in teams, and their self-confidence is enhanced as they see how they are able to become proactive at shaping a better world (Kassel et al., 2016). The "hands" dimension connects the students with real-world circumstances, exposing participants to the social dimension of humankind. According to Marquardt (2000), action learning puts learners in front of real problems, brings commitment to action, developing the leadership skills that are required for the 21st century as systems thinker, change agent, innovator, servant, polychronic co-ordinator, teacher-mentor and visionary.

Considering the aims of education for sustainability, the transformative learning approach uses projects, techniques and tools to help students question and reflect on their own beliefs and values. Sterling (2011) noted that learning can take place at different levels of knowledge and meaning, and transformative learning acts in the deepest levels, not always conscious, influencing ways of thinking, knowing and acting.

The first level of learning does not interfere with the value system and is related to the external objective world. The second level of learning is more challenging, concerned with doing better things, and generates a critical examination of the learner. This level of learning may change beliefs, values and assumptions, and thus is considered a deeper level of learning. The third level of learning relates to epistemic learning, which generates a change in epistemology: how the person knows and thinks, generating a shift in the worldview (Sterling, 2011). Thus, to change the worldview, an epistemic transformative learning is necessary. Sterling (2011) points out that the levels are cumulative: the second order of learning changes the thought and action, while the third order changes all levels of knowledge.

Lange (2004) notes that transformative learning is not just an epistemological process that involves changing a learner's worldview and thinking. It is also an ontological process, where participants expand their sense of self and identity and change their position of being in the world, establishing a new way of relating with their material, social and environmental reality, becoming active citizens with social responsibility. Changing students' worldview – through new values that impact their thinking, doing and being – lies at the core of the transformative learning approach.

This chapter analyzes an undergraduate program in business administration, with an emphasis on innovation and leadership, offered at a Jesuit educational institution guided by humanist values. This program aims at developing a sustainable mindset in management students and a comprehension of leadership in business that goes beyond the mainstream, embracing the roots of the Jesuit culture. Leadership, in the Jesuit philosophy, is characterized by four pillars: self-awareness, ingenuity, love and heroism (Lowney, 2015).

Self-awareness is the ability to reflect on one's own worldview, values, strengths and weaknesses, in order to constantly improve and learn. Ingenuity is the consideration of new possibilities, while self-reflection allows us to contact our inner fears, motivations and attachments that can influence and control our decisions and actions. Ingenuity is "a mix of boldness, adaptability, speed and good judgment" (Lowney, 2015, p. 128).

Lowney (2015) goes on to state that love is manifested in actions, and encourages the engagement of others through a positive attitude. The principle of love allows us to "create environments bound and energized by loyalty, affection, and mutual support – places marked by 'greater love than fear'" (p. 42). It also allows us to seek to "see the talent, potential and dignity of every person" (p. 182).

The Jesuit concept of heroism is not restricted to the idea of a lonely "leader-hero." Rather, it emphasizes the role of leaders as active agents to shape the future and help develop the "unique links that unite a team" (Lowney, 2015, p. 191). The leader's overarching role is to "influence those who cause the greatest impact on society" (p. 227).

A knowledge of the principles that guide Jesuit philosophy on leadership is fundamental to understanding the institutional culture that serves as a backdrop to the pedagogical approach studied here. To develop a sustainable mindset through a change in students' worldview, it's also important to understand the values of the educational institution and ensure coherence with its pedagogical philosophy. In the next section, we will describe the methodological procedures that have guided our research in the management program and its results.

Methodology

As noted, this chapter explores the case study of a pedagogical approach to develop a sustainability mindset in students at UNISINOS, one of Brazil's largest private universities. Our analysis focuses on the pedagogical approach used in an under-graduate program on business administration, called GIL (*Gestão para Inovação e Liderança* – Major in Management for Innovation and Leadership).

A case study, per Yin (2001), is carried out through the direct observation of the study object and through a systematic series of interviews. We applied a participa-tory action research method, where the respondents are both subjects and collabo-rative participants in the research (Kemmis & McTaggart, 2007; Thiollent, 2005), to answer the main question of this study: "How to develop the sustainability mindset among management students, using a holistic education and a transformative learn-ing pedagogical approach?"

For this case study, we interviewed students, professors and other stakeholders, including: (1) JAMA Institute, focused on the sustainability of third sector organi-zations and (2) *Primeiro Saque* Social Project ('First Serve' Social Project), an NGO oriented toward child education in high-vulnerability areas. Interviewees involved in the process of the educational approach implementation are identified as E1 (professor), E2 (program coordinator), E3 (manager of social project) and E4 (man-ager of JAMA Institute). Interviewees E5 to E14 are students who have participated in GIL's pedagogical approach. Institutional documents and the program's websites were analyzed in the data research.

The data analysis was based on Bardin's (1994) perspective and on Kumar's (2015) three dimensions of holistic education: head (thinking), hands (doing) and heart (feeling). To Bardin (1994), there are three levels of data analysis: (1) pre-analysis (e.g., preparation of material for analysis); (2) material exploration (e.g., data codification to achieve a content representation); and (3) treatment of results, inference and interpretation (e.g., statistical operations and the use of test results with theoretical and pragmatic purposes, or the orientation of these results to a new analysis).

Results

In this section, we share the results of the data analysis through the description of the pedagogical approach implemented in the management program, the competencies and sustainability mindset developed in the students, and the perceptions of those involved in the educational process as students, professors and stakeholders.

The pedagogical approach implemented in the GIL management program

GIL is one of 81 undergraduate courses offered at UNISINOS and taught by UNISINOS Business School (one of six schools at the university). More than 30,000 students currently take undergraduate, graduate and continuing education programs at UNISINOS.

The GIL program started at the São Leopoldo campus in the first semester of 2003. After eight years, it is now also offered at the campus in Porto Alegre, the largest city in Brazil's southeastern state of Rio Grande do Sul. Fonseca and Daudt (2007) assert that "the launch of GIL represented an important effort for UNISINOS to become a reference in some areas (including Management)" (p. 3). Nearly 200 students have now graduated from GIL's program and are working in various sectors of the national and international industry.

The program's distinguishing features cover different areas: curricular exchange programs (graduates study for a semester at a foreign university, in countries like Canada, USA, Germany, Portugal, South Korea, and Spain); English language training; emphasis on communication and expression; technological resources; integration with companies; investigative approach; continuous updating of the knowledge involved; and its process for the assessment of students in the program, individualized monitoring and career planning.

GIL's learning environment also differentiates it from all of the other major programs at the university. At GIL, small groups of around 15 students study together in a full immersion program. They meet for classes and study for the first two years in both the morning and in the afternoon. This is different from other management programs in Brazil, in which classes are held only once a day, in the morning or evening. The class configuration focuses on working groups, and teachers are enabled to change the layout of tables and chairs to best serve their pedagogical purpose. Teachers are also encouraged to organize activities outside of the classroom. Students visit companies as real-life case studies, participate in important events and conferences and may be in contact with entrepreneurs from Brazil and abroad, all with the support of the program coordinators.

To develop a sustainable mindset in management students and to create opportunities to learn beyond the classroom with entrepreneurial leaders, GIL develops partnerships with organizations from different economic sectors. Since January 2016, GIL has an institutional partnership with JAMA Institute, which counts among its founders a major telecommunications entrepreneur from southern

Brazil, who is partner and emeritus president of RBS (*Rede Brasil Sul*) Group: Jayme Sirotsky.

For several years, Sirotsky had developed a personal practice of helping young people to go to university, through scholarships and donations. In 2009, he saw the need to professionalize this and to monitor the process of donations, as well as to measure the sustainability of benefits in the social projects he supported. For this purpose, Jayme Sirotsky, along with his wife and three sons, founded the JAMA Institute. JAMA is a non-profit association, which seeks to help children and young people in gaining access to good education, both in primary and secondary school and at the university level. Since its inception, the Institute has invested around R$ 1,000,000 per year (approximately US$ 350,000) in social projects. Among the initiatives developed and supported by the Institute, there is a project developed in partnership with GIL. The partnership includes the yearly donation of R$ 20,000 (equivalent to US$ 5,000) to support the interaction of management students with an NGO focused on civic education for children.

The NGO that was chosen by JAMA Institute for interaction with students of GIL is *Primeiro Saque* Social Project ('First Serve' Social Project). It was founded by the professional tennis player Matheus Triska and, through sports, promotes the social inclusion of children living in vulnerable conditions in the city of Canoas, district of Niterói (also in the state of Rio Grande do Sul). Since April 2015, the NGO has offered tennis, yoga, mindfulness practice, cultural workshops and counseling to children. The project serves 40 children between 6–12 years and focuses on objectives like strengthening self-esteem, as well as fostering a sense of belonging and personal responsibility.

The NGO's work to promote children's empowerment is based on the values of love, compassion, discipline, freedom, respect and autonomy – aiming to develop and value the potential of every child. For this to happen, the management of the third sector organization needs to be evaluated systematically. With this purpose, JAMA Institute indicated *Primeiro Saque* to partner with GIL. Non-profit organizations often lack technical support in financial management; thus, this partnership provides both students and the NGO with an important opportunity to exchange knowledge and practical advice in a real-world situation.

Among the objectives of the partnership is to allow GIL students to approach management theory in practice by contributing to *Primeiro Saque*'s management, as well as to develop socio-emotional skills that are needed for a sustainable mindset and for social and environmental responsibility.

The GIL courses that interact with these two different stakeholders – JAMA Institute and *Primeiro Saque* – on this innovative pedagogical approach are 'Learning to Learn' (which we followed in the first semester of 2016) and 'Social Project' (which we followed in the second semester of 2016). The two classes are coordinated by the same professor and each carry a workload of 30 hours. It's important to highlight that these disciplines are offered in the first year of the program, and that management students are usually 17–18 years old.

The program of the first semester, 'Learning to Learn,' aims to awaken in students the importance of continuous learning and their individual responsibility in this process, as well as understanding the ways of learning, developing their self-awareness and learning in action. The 'Social Project' discipline, in the following semester, aims to introduce the concepts of social entrepreneurship, social innovation and the management and funding of third sector projects.

Due to the flexibility of the program, which is one of GIL's differentiating characteristics, the classes of the 'Learning to Learn' discipline on the first semester were organized as one meeting per month, for a full day. This allowed students to visit the third sector organization, which is located 20 kilometers from the university, and to interact with the children beneficiaries of the social project. In the second semester, students from GIL and the social project travelled to another city, Florianópolis, financed by the partnership with the JAMA Institute. Located 500 kilometers away from the university, Florianópolis is considered the capital of social innovation in Brazil. Table 11.1 presents the schedule for the teaching plan and the actions that were implemented on both disciplines.

Through this teaching plan and the actions of the pedagogical approach implementation, it's important to note the role of the teacher of the disciplines, who acts beyond the classroom; the role of stakeholders, who are engaged in the process of teaching and learning; and the role of the GIL's coordinator, who is personally involved in the process. Thus, the pedagogical approach is implemented with the contribution and engagement of all participants and stakeholders, creating an innovative learning environment in accordance to Sterling (2011), who notes the importance of the main influencers of transformation: the educator, the student, and the learning environment. Students' contact with real-world situations, action and experiential learning, reflection on all meetings, and contact with different entrepreneurs and leaders also stand out in this methodology. The next section will analyze the characteristics of the pedagogical approach, according to students, professor, program coordinator and other stakeholders.

Characteristics of the pedagogical approach to develop a sustainability mindset

The first dimension of this research was the characteristics of the pedagogical approach applied in GIL. According to students, professor, program coordinator and stakeholders, the main aspect of the pedagogical approach is the connection of theory and practice. For student E7: "with this methodology we learn beyond theory, we learn through practice." E8 says that "we have the opportunity to learn hands-on." For E9, "the interaction with the social project enables the development of competencies which wouldn't be possible in the theoretical dimension alone."

In fact, all students confirmed that one of the main differentials of business schools is when theory is allied with practical experiences, building bridges with the real world. "Study and acquire knowledge in a more dynamic and efficient way" (E14). "It's necessary to learn from theory and from living experiences, where we

TABLE 11.1 Teaching plan and actions implemented on 'Learning to Learn' and 'Social Project' disciplines

First semester 'Learning to Learn' discipline

January 2016	First visit by the teacher of 'Learning to Learn' discipline to *Primeiro Saque* social project, in order to establish a first contact, understand the project needs, establish the first academic ties and plan initial actions. The teacher was able to observe the activities of the social project with children: arts, meditation and tennis lessons. The first bonds with the social project manager and team leaders were formed as a result of this visit.
February	Alignment meeting of 2016 first semester with the manager of JAMA Institute and the manager of the *Primeiro Saque* Project.
March *First and second classes*	First meeting with management students, who were introduced to the concept of 'learning to learn' in leadership and management and the importance of self-awareness. Different group dynamics and readings of philosophical texts (Seneca's "Learning to Live") were implemented in this meeting, to stimulate reflection.
April *Third and fourth classes*	Meeting of management students with managers of social project and JAMA Institute, where they presented their organizations and cases. In the afternoon, GIL students visited the *Primeiro Saque* headquarters, learning about the main difficulties in different areas of management (human resources, financial, pedagogical) through a diagnosis. Students suggested improvements and feasible actions, with the teacher's support. Thus, students in the first semester of the program are encouraged to develop their diagnostic skills, socio-emotional skills such as empathy and collaboration, and to learn by doing in contact with reality. Start of the fund-raising and crowdfunding project.
April	Visit to the Guga Kuerten Institute in Florianópolis by the GIL instructor, the manager of the JAMA Institute and the manager of the *Primeiro Saque* Project. The purpose of the visit was to do a benchmarking against one of the main social organizations in Brazil that educates children through sports, and to plan the study travel of GIL students and children of the social project in October 2016.
May *Fifth and sixth classes*	Meeting of management students with children of the social project. GIL students had to organize the interaction with children through the theme 'learning to learn.' Different activities were implemented, such as creating a sustainable garden using PET bottles, experiencing sowing seeds. In the afternoon, GIL students, accompanied by the manager of the *Primeiro Saque* social project, visited a third sector organization with more than 30 years of existence and a vast experience on management on education for children living in vulnerable areas. Benchmarking and a case study were done on this visit.

June *Seventh and eight classes*	Seminar presentation by GIL students. In groups of two, management students had to present (after reading a biography and papers) the case of entrepreneurs and leaders through the lens of 'learning to learn' and investment in social projects. In the afternoon, GIL students hosted children of the social project at the university, and did a tour of UNISINOS together, as well as other activities. They visited the technological park, the library, the sports center, and did group dynamics for integration.
June *Ninth class*	Visit to the RBS Group and meeting with JAMA Institute founder, Jayme Sirotsky.
July	Meeting among the professor of the disciplines, the coordinator of GIL program and the manager of JAMA Institute to plan the second semester. Meeting with the professor of the disciplines, the manager of JAMA Institute and the manager of *Primeiro Saque* social project to plan the second semester.

Second Semester 'Social Project' discipline

August	Visit to Florianópolis by the professor of the disciplines, the coordinator of GIL program and manager of JAMA Institute, in order to plan the study travel and to contact social business and social entrepreneurs that will interact with GIL students.
September *First class*	Introduction of concepts of sustainability and sustainable development, social business, social responsibility, social entrepreneurship, new capitalism.
September *Second class*	Presentation of documentary seminars by management students, aiming to develop a deep reflection on the themes around sustainability.
September *Third class*	CANVAS workshop: strategic planning of *Primeiro Saque* social project.
October *Fourth Class*	Seminar 'Social Business around the World.' Students present, in a seminar, research done on two cases of social business situated in different countries and continents (Brazil and other countries of South America, Central America, North America, Europe, North Africa, South Africa, Oceania, Russia and countries of the Ex-Soviet Union, Asia).
October *Fifth to eight classes*	Visit from GIL students to the business and social projects in Florianópolis. Visit of children of the social project to the "Guga Kuerten Week", a huge tennis festival. They had the possibility to meet Gustavo Kuerten, one of the most recognized tennis players in the world.
October *Ninth class*	Visit to *Escola Ayni*, a social and educational project managed by a young leader that aims to contribute to a new education.
November *Tenth class*	Presentation of the *Primeiro Saque* project's strategic plan, performed by GIL students, to all stakeholders involved in the pedagogical process.
November *Last meeting*	Event organized by students where they show the results of the pedagogical approach to the university community (professors, other students, parents, etc.).

can put into practice what we learn. This is the best way to really learn something" (E12). Learning by doing is seen, by all interviewees, as a differential of the pedagogical approach that resonates with the holistic education proposed by Kumar (2015), for whom one of the pillars is 'hand' learning. In addition, E4 believes that learning is improved when it is pleasurable. "Students demonstrate a thirst for knowledge. They are interested and proactive and they want to put their hands to work." In this way, the role of the students changed; they are not forced to sit in the classroom, but are instead engaged with the purpose of the project.

Students saw case studies as another differential, whether they studied through reading books or by visiting the case studies in person. For E9: "the methodology brought case studies from successful entrepreneurs from different areas, and all of them invest in social projects, which makes it more interesting for the students." In addition, E11 said "the opportunities of socializing with the children of the social project and entrepreneurs with extensive experience are the main differences of the methodology, because we were face to face with challenges and opportunities of a different type of learning."

For the program's coordinator, "the partnership between GIL and JAMA institute strengthened the 'learning in practice' by the students' empowerment" and "the students, even if they are in the first year of the program, planned and carried out actions which led to the development of important management competencies." According to the professor, E1: "The differential is in the transformative learning approach, which works at the deepest levels of knowledge and puts students constantly in touch with practice and with the real world."

Beyond that, E1 saw that action learning and social learning were efficient tools that contributed to transformative learning, as are the engagement of the professor, the connection with other disciplines and the support of the program coordinator to implement this pedagogical approach. This is in accordance with Sterling (2011), who highlights the importance of different influencers in the learning process. Stakeholders see the differences of the pedagogical approach mainly in the engagement of all the partners that are involved in the experiences and activities.

E4 talked about the role of professors and managers of the program: "It's important to highlight the humility of the professors and managers of the program, being open to listen to stakeholders, and to learn. By doing so they become a reference to students." In addition, E4 emphasized the openness of the University: "Other universities identify the importance of innovating their pedagogical processes, but not all have a culture open to this kind of partnership. According to E4, "UNISINOS, through the management program GIL, has a differentiated and practical curriculum, and also a culture of innovation that has facilitated the implementation of this different methodology." Thus, beyond the openness of those that are directly involved in the partnership, the culture of the educational institution contributes to the implementation of innovative pedagogical approaches. Being a Jesuit university, the values and philosophy of the institution contribute to an open culture, with a new view of leadership (Lowney, 2015).

According to E4: "If Brazil and other countries need new leaders, it's necessary to change the traditional education to follow this new world that changes every day." To meet this challenge, E4 believes that it's necessary that different stakeholders join forces for the purpose of education. It's important to observe that partnerships were built not just with external stakeholders, but also with internal stakeholders, such as other disciplines of the program.

For the professor and the program coordinator, E1 and E2 respectively, there were many impacts and influences of the new pedagogical approach on other disciplines. E1 considered this new methodology as a "catalyst of interdisciplinary relations" and said: "in the second semester, for example, we have interactions with an English workshop using theoretical texts related to social entrepreneurship, social innovation and social business, to support the activities of the semester, as well as with the discipline of Business Strategy to propose a strategic plan to the organization that students are interacting with." For E2, "the pedagogical experience gave the courses 'Learning to learn' and 'Social project' a more central role, connecting with other courses." E1 added that, to build interdisciplinary aspects into the program, it's necessary also to build relationships among professors with similar values.

Stakeholders, such as JAMA Institute and *Primeiro Saque*, have seen an impact on their organizations since the project started. Thus, a pedagogical approach that brought different partners together with the purpose of education created a learning environment for everyone. E4 observed that all stakeholders learned together in the process: "we learn, teach and share, because knowledge is only meaningful when shared." E3, the manager of the social project, noticed the impact on the motivation and behavior of the children in the social project, which also touched their families and schools, and was a contribution to the management of the third sector organization, in the domains of marketing, fund-raising and human resources. E3 underlined that the decisions are taken horizontally, which shows that there is not a hierarchy, and each stakeholder develops its own leadership.

For the manager of JAMA Institute (E4), "the partnership with the University is fundamental for systematization of knowledge for further research and identification of good practices. . . . the results can serve as a future reference in the training of students." In addition, the interviewee said: "The contact with different realities (UNISINOS and *Primeiro Saque*) was innovative in our partnership. The Institute is the bridge between these different worlds and, in this partnership, everyone wins when each one contributes their expertise." Thus, to build innovation in education, the role of bridging organizations is important as a stimulator to 'connect the dots' between those organizations that are really engaged in the purpose of the partnership – that is, to develop future leaders with a sustainable mindset and with an amplified worldview.

In fact, via the pedagogical approach, students realized the impact on their worldview when they were at the center of the process of learning, as protagonists of this process. E5 said "it was extremely important to change our worldview as a result of facing a different reality. We developed an ethical awareness and an obligation to help the transformation of the world for the better." Student E12 added: "It was possible to watch closely the social reality of our environment, also to see the importance of a virtuous individual and the impact it makes on the society." The contact of young people with a different reality – the reality of a children's social project – results in the development of ethical awareness. Students recognized the importance of virtuous people, as well as their impact on society.

The change of the worldview is intrinsic to transformative learning (Sterling, 2011; Cranton and King, 2003). For E1:"Transformative learning provides students transformation through the change of worldview and new values." According to E4, the manager of the Institute that invests in the partnership, one of the main differentials on changing worldviews is to bring students to experience another reality. "The methodology provides opportunities for the students to know the social realities which go beyond the classroom. . . . together, the students get involved in a social cause, were they can learn, exchange experiences and teach." Being in front of the reality of social vulnerability leads students to reflection, both about their own reality and about their future role as managers. Another dimension of holistic education appears: the thinking dimension, or the 'head,' according to Kumar (2015).

Student E12 affirmed: "meeting the children of the project amplified my horizon, creating a more realistic vision of the world. And I think that this will be very useful in our future life as managers, especially knowing from up-close how the management of a third sector organization works." Students also perceived that being in contact with reality led them to understand that third sector organizations need management, just like for-profit organizations. For E7, "it was important to learn that third sector organizations use a methodology of management as profit organizations do." For the student E12, "it was possible to obtain a more systematic and practical vision of how an organization really works." For the student E13, it was important "to perceive that the third sector organization needs good management. Thus, we did a brainstorming to solve some questions of the *Primeiro Saque* project. In addition, we will create a strategic plan for the project, which for sure will add to our learning as future managers." Thus, management is also learned in the field, putting students in front of the challenges of the third sector organization.

The characteristics of the pedagogical approach led to the development of competencies that contributed to a sustainability mindset. The next section will describe the findings on these topics.

Competencies and sustainability mindset developed through transformative learning and holistic education

Different competencies were developed in the students during the implementation of the pedagogical approach. Improved critical thinking was observed in students' presentations. One of the pillars of transformative learning is to develop the learners' critical thinking; Mezirow (1978) asserted that transformation can occur when an individual critically recognizes that his perspective is no longer functional and decides to appropriate a new perspective as being more valuable. According to student E6, "through discussions about books and articles I could improve my critical thinking and position on different issues." Student E9 said: "the ability to judge what is best for the project through critical thinking was developed in students and in project managers." For E12, " experiencing how an organization works allowed me to develop critical thinking."

E1 affirmed that critical thinking was stimulated, especially rethinking socio-economic conditions and using philosophical authors like Seneca to bring up discussions about the meaning of life. The students' presentations showed their ability to reflect both profoundly and critically on different topics, including, for example, organizational issues and questions about the meaning of life. Learning from theory, allied to practice, contributed to the improvement of critical thinking in the learners.

Openness to innovation was another skill that emerged in this research. Student E8 affirmed that "we had to seek innovative alternatives at different occasions during the project, because we had fewer resources." According to E13, "regarding the aspect of innovation, in all meetings through lectures, classes, talks and debates, it was possible to have insights and understanding that small ideas can turn into great solutions. For that reason it's necessary to put your hands to work." Bringing action learning to the pedagogical approach facilitated students' openness to innovation, which corroborates Kumar's (2015) proposal of holistic education and the importance of learning by doing.

Another competency developed was that of communication. E9 said, "Throughout the semester, the number of interactions with different stakeholders forced us to develop our communication skills. . . . For a manager who wants to become a leader, the ability to teach, express and communicate clearly is fundamental." Student E12 said: "this discipline gave us a great opportunity to express our feelings." For student E13: "all these activities have given us a greater ability to communicate." Students thus recognized the development of their communication skills, for the exercise of management and for leadership.

Leadership and entrepreneurship were other competencies that emerged through this pedagogical approach. E7 affirmed that "leadership and entrepreneurship were being developed in every meeting with the social institutions, through many activities that we had to perform and to plan, also in the fundraising that we engaged." E9 observed the importance of acting as a leader but also of learning how to be led. For E12, this competency was facilitated not only through the interaction with the social project but also via contact with leaders (i.e., the president of JAMA Institute, one of the main entrepreneurs of the south of Brazil), and by reading leaders' biographies that were proposed during the course 'Learning to Learn.' For E14, "I developed empowerment and self-confidence during this course." According to professor E1, leadership and entrepreneurship were stimulated, helping the students to take more responsibility for the learning process.

Another developmental goal that was stimulated through the pedagogical approach was self-awareness. For student E5: "Through working with people in a different reality, having to pass some knowledge to them and reading about people who have actually achieved success in life, we know ourselves better, our strengths and weak points and where we want to go." This is aligned with Lowney's (2015) self-awareness principle of Jesuit leadership, as the ability to self-reflect regarding one's worldview, values, strengths and weaknesses in order to improve and learn constantly.

In addition, student E7 said: "since the first class, self-awareness was considered very important for our personal development. Knowing myself helped me to understand what moves me in this life." Self-awareness, beyond knowing our strengths, thus has a role in defining our life mission. E13 highlighted the importance of self-awareness that was elicited by the pedagogical approach: "to be a good leader, first of all it's necessary to know yourself." According to E1, the professor of the program: "Self-awareness is a goal of the pedagogical interactions." For the students, sharing knowledge with the children of the social project and analyzing the cases of successful leaders in the workshop were the principal reasons for their improved self-awareness.

Self-awareness is the essence of holistic education. According to Kumar (2015), education means to bring out the potential of every student, and it is about finding out who you are and becoming your true self. Transformative learning enables us to change our worldview. It touches as well on the ontological dimension, where participants expand their sense of self, their identity, and change their way of being in the world (Lange, 2004).

Platonic love emerged as a topic in the students' interviews, including love for the children of the social project, love for self, and love that developed from the interactions with other management students and with leaders. For E6, "after one week in the program our class became a family, and we could transmit these feelings to the children of the project, which enriched our souls." E9 talked about the meeting with the founder of the institute that finances the partnership: "it was interesting to see that a man 80 years old with a large fortune still works with love every day." E13 emphasized the way the manager of the social project relates with children: "the love and affection that he puts into the social project and relates with children is what really moves everything."

For professor E1, "love permeates the whole process of teaching and learning; especially from the relationship of the teacher with education itself, building bonds of love between student and knowledge." Love is fundamental to holistic education. The heart dimension of education is to learn "to be respectful, grateful, compassionate, generous, and caring. Furthermore, it is learning to deal with your emotions, feelings, anxieties and uncertainties" (Kumar, 2015, p. 119).

Love awakens students' social sensibility. For student E9, "the contact with a third sector organization and the knowledge of social actions in practice allows many students to develop their humanitarian sense." Contact with a different social and economic reality led students to reflect on their own situations and responsibilities, highlighting the 'heart' dimension of holistic education.

Love is implicit in social awareness. As noted, in the principle of Jesuit leadership, love is manifested in actions and encourages the engagement of others through a positive attitude. The principle of love allows us to "create environments bound and energized by loyalty, affection, and mutual support" (Lowney, 2015, p. 42), seeking to "see the talent, potential and dignity of every person" (p. 182).

Among other competencies that emerged, according to E3, manager of the social project, the students "gained more confidence to have autonomy." All of those interviewed agreed that empathy was one of the main socio-emotional skills developed by the students in the program. Humility, respect and collaboration were other skills and ethical values mentioned in the interviews. Other competencies were "teamwork, patience, calmness" (E5); "persistence" (E6); "proactivity, improvement of interpersonal relations" (E10); "compassion" (E12); "resilience, self-confidence, determination, admiration, empowerment, friendship" (E14).

This research shows that students developed individual competencies, such as self-awareness, communication skills and critical thinking. Yet, most of all, their social sensibility was strengthened through their relationship with different realities; they developed greater empathy, collaborative skills, humility and compassion. Global awareness was also stimulated in students. E8 said: "the sense of collectivism and the perception of the world as a whole is essential for the sustainability of a business. We have developed this capability through knowledge and direct contact with the children involved in the project."

The altruistic vision was reinforced through the pedagogical approach, creating a stronger collective attitude and a less individualist behavior in the students. These are fundamental components of a sustainability mindset. E6 affirmed that to make decisions it's necessary to have a broader vision: "decision-making goes through a process of analysis of an entire context. . . . it's necessary to measure what will be the social and environmental impacts that these decisions would generate." For E11, "before the interaction with the third sector organization, the concern with sustainability was not on my mind. The world where we live in is far from perfect and if we have the opportunity to do something, it must be done." For E13, a work proposal or a business model should aim to be more humanistic and sustainable while providing a financial return. The students' interviews showed a clear comprehension of the different dimensions of sustainability (economic, environment and social).

From the viewpoint of the professor and coordinator: "the student understands that management goes beyond economic results, considering the socio-environmental results" (E1). Regarding the pedagogical goal, it was possible to see "the development of the awareness that it is imperative to mobilize all resources (people, organizations and the world) as best as possible" (E2).

In the other stakeholders' vision, "this approach encourages a sense of responsibility in students. It facilitates the development of a more sustainable consciousness" (E3). For the interviewee E4: "Looking at the social problems promotes co-responsibility, teamwork, respect for the differences and for diverse ways of thinking."

E8 asserted that "it is possible to do the 'impossible' with few resources." This shows a shift in management worldview toward one in which it's not necessary to have a lot of financial, human or other resources to create an organization and impact a community. E14 observed the importance of investing in education; profit should not be the center of interests when aiming at a better society in the long term. Spirituality emerges here, again, as a necessary element in the sustainability mindset that brings about an awareness of "their lives, their contribution to the problem, and their role" (Rimanoczy, 2014, p. 105).

As noted, various competencies were developed among the students at an individual and collective level, and pointed toward an emerging sustainability mindset. In the next section we present the final considerations and implications for future studies.

Conclusion

A sustainability mindset is a new way to think about the social and environmental aspects of our world, including the development of social sensitivity, self-awareness and connection with purpose (Kassel et al., 2016). This mindset is more and more crucial as we educate future managers and leaders, and we can make a massive contribution to the economic, environmental and social problems that humanity currently faces. Transformative learning is a pedagogical approach that helps in developing a sustainability mindset, due to its impact on the deepest levels of knowledge, including on the worldview of learners (Sterling, 2011) and on the ontological level (Lange, 2004). Allied to transformative learning, holistic education – which aims to integrally develop human beings through the dimensions of hands (doing), head (thinking) and love (being) – can contribute to the development of a sustainability mindset.

In this chapter we presented a case study of an innovative pedagogical approach oriented towards developing a sustainability mindset in management students in the GIL program at UNISINOS. To answer the research question ("How to develop the sustainability mindset among management students, using a holistic education and a transformative learning pedagogical approach?"), we interviewed the management students, the professor, the program coordinator and other stakeholders about the differentials of the pedagogical approach, as well as the competencies that were developed in management students, in terms of the sustainability mindset.

The differentials of the pedagogical approach emerged in the research at the methodological, individual and organizational levels. On the *methodological* level, the differentials are the transformative learning approach; action learning and social learning; case studies, whether studied in books or by visiting entrepreneurs and leaders in person; and methodology allied to practice, which allowed students to build bridges between theory and the real world. On the *individual* level, differentials included the openness of the professor and program coordinator to learn with the process and to listen to stakeholders; interdisciplinary relations in the management program between faculty with a correspondence of personal values; the contribution and engagement of all participants and stakeholders; the change in the students' worldviews when they are at the center of the process of learning; and students' empowerment. On the *organizational* level, differentials included the educational institution being based on a culture of innovation; the role of bridging organizations; impacts and influences of the new pedagogical approach on other disciplines; and learning about the hands-on management of third sector organizations.

The management students developed greater social and emotional competencies, which are necessary for the sustainability mindset. The competencies that emerged from the research included critical thinking, openness to innovation, communication skills, leadership and entrepreneurship, self-awareness, platonic love, social sensibility and global awareness. Other competencies, and also ethical values, appeared: greater self-confidence, autonomy, empathy, humility, responsibility, respect, collaboration, teamwork skills, patience, calmness, persistence, proactivity, improvement of interpersonal relations, compassion, resilience, determination and empowerment.

The altruistic vision was reinforced in this pedagogical approach, creating a stronger collective attitude and less individualistic behavior in the students, corresponding to Kassel et al.'s (2016) conceptual model, where collaborative and innovative action is at the center of a sustainability mindset. All of these competencies helped to develop a sustainability mindset, in which students start to think through the different dimensions of sustainability (economic, environment and social).

It's clear that the deeper purpose of this pedagogical approach as applied to a management program, beyond developing social and emotional competencies, is to develop spiritual intelligence. Kumar argues that true education integrates the spiritual dimension, to integrally develop new leaders. "Every soul has its own built-in intelligence. Knowledge and wisdom are intrinsic to soul" (Kumar, 2015, p. 111).

Research shows that this pedagogical approach can be applied only because all participants (professor, program coordinators and other stakeholders) are embedded in education as a life mission – understanding education not just as a way of building a student's understanding of the content, but as a way to transform people and create a better world. Without this comprehension and without being personally involved, it's not possible to develop a sustainability mindset through management education. To create a new kind of education, and new management practices, it is essential to consider the spiritual dimension.

For future studies, continuous and longitudinal research is recommended, to follow these students and their future practices as managers over several years. This could be a way to confirm the maintenance of the results that were seen due to the implementation of this pedagogical approach. Other research could explore transformative learning practices, as applied in different educational institutions and different organizational cultures, to see the effectiveness of their impact on innovative pedagogical approaches.

Note

1 www.unisinos.br/noticias/universidade/unisinos-e-tri

References

Akrivou, K., & Bradbury-Huang, H. (2015). Educating integrated catalysts: Transforming business schools toward ethics and sustainability. *Academy of Management Learning & Education*, *14*(2), 222–240. doi:10.5465/amle.2012.0343

Bardin, L. (1994). *Análise de conteúdo* (3rd ed.). Lisboa: Edições 70.

Blake, J., Sterling, S., & Goodson, I. (2013). Transformative learning for a sustainable future: An exploration of pedagogies for change at an alternative college. *Sustainability*, n. 5, pp. 5347–5372.

Closs, L. Q., Aramburu, J.V., & Antunes, E. D. D. (2009). Produção Científica sobre o Ensino em Administração: uma Avaliação Envolvendo o Enfoque do Paradigma da Complexidade. *Revista Eletrônica de Gestão Organizacional*, *7*(2), pp. 150–169.

Cranton, P., & King, K. (2003). Transformative learning as a professional development goal. *New Directions for Adult and Continuing Education*, *98*, 31–37.

Demajorovic, J., & Silva, H. C. O. (2012). Formação interdisciplinar e sustentabilidade em cursos de administração: desafios e perspectivas. *RAM, Rev. Adm. Mackenzie*. São Paulo, *13*(5), Out.2012.

Egmond, N. D., & Vries, H. J. M. (2011). Sustainability: The search for the integral worldview. *Futures*, 43, 853–867.

Fonseca, M. J., & Daudt, S. I. D. (2007). Mantendo a inovação: o processo de revisão curricular do Curso de Graduação em Administração – Gestão para Inovação e Liderança, da UNISINOS. In: ENCONTRO DA ANPAD, 31, 2007, Rio de Janeiro. *Anais eletrônicos*. Rio de Janeiro.

Garrity, E. J. (2012). Tragedy of the commons, business growth and the fundamental sustainability problem. *Sustainability*, *4*, 2443–2471.

Gerhardt, H.-P. (1996). Paulo Freire (1921–27). *Prospects: The Quarterly Review of Comparative Education*, *23*(3/4), 1–16.

Groen, J., & Hyland-Russell, T. (2010). Humanities professors on the margins: Creating the possibility for transformative learning. *Journal of Transformative Education*, *8*(4), 223–245.

Jaeger, W. (2013). *Paideia: A formação do homem grego* (6th ed.). São Paulo: Martins Fontes.

Kassel, K. (2014). *The thinking executive's guide to sustainability*. New York, NY: Business Expert Press.

Kassel, K., Rimanoczy, I., & Mitchell, S. (2016). The sustainable mindset: Connecting being, thinking, and doing in management education. *Academy of Management 2016 Annual Meeting*, Anaheim, CA.

Kemmis, S., & McTaggart, R. (2007). Participatory action research. In N. K. Denzin and Y. Lincoln (Eds.), *Handbook of qualitative research*. London: Sage Publications.

Kevany, K. D. (2007). Building the requisite capacity for stewardship and sustainable development. *International Journal of Sustainability in Higher Education*, *8*(2), 107–122.

Kumar, S. (2015). *Soil, soul, society: A new trinity for our time*. Lewes, UK: Leaping Hare Press.

Lange, E. A. (2004). Transformative and restorative learning: A vital dialectic for sustainable societies. *Adult Education Quarterly*, *54*, 121.

Leiserowitz, A. A., Robert, W. K., & Thomas, M. P. (2004). Sustainability values, attitudes, and behaviors: A review of multi-national and global trends. *CID Working Paper*, no. 113. Cambridge, MA: Science, Environment and Development Group, Center for International.

Lowney, C. (2015). *Liderança heróica*. Rio de Janeiro: Edições de Janeiro.

Marquardt, M. J. (2000). Action learning and leadership. *The Learning Organization*, *7*(5), 233–241. doi:10.1108/09696470010352990

Meadows, D. L. (2006). Tools for the transition to sustainability. In M. Keiner (Ed.), *The future of sustainability* (pp. 161–178). Springer: Netherlands.

Mezirow, J. (1978). Perspective transformation, *Adult Education, 28*(2), 100–110.

Mezirow, J. (1994). Understanding transformation theory. *Adult Education Quarterly, 44*(4), 222–232. doi:10.1177/074171369404400403

Moreira, M. A. (2014). *Teorias de Aprendizagem* (2nd ed.). São Paulo: E.P.U.

Rimanoczy, I. (2014). A matter of being: Developing sustainability-minded leaders. *Journal of Management for Global Sustainability, 2*(1), 95–122.

Rimanoczy, I. B. (2010). *Business leaders committing to and fostering sustainability initiatives. Doctoral dissertation.* Teachers College, Columbia University.

Sidiropoulos, E. (2014). Education for sustainability in business education programs: A question of value. *Journal of Cleaner Production, 85,* 472–487.

Stead, J. G. & Stead, W. E. (2010). Spirituality and sustainability: co-evolutionary perspective. Management, Spirituality & Religion Conference Paper Abstracts. Academy of Management Annual Meeting Proceedings, August: 1–17, doi: 10.5465/AMBPP.2010.54503765.

Sterling, S. (2011). Transformative learning and sustainability: Sketching the conceptual ground. *Learning and Teaching in Higher Education*, (5), 17–33.

Thiollent, M. (2003). *Metodologia da Pesquisa-Ação.* São Paulo: Cortez.

Van Lopik, W. (2013). Learning sustainability in a tribal college context. In P. F. Barlett & G. W. Chase (Eds.), *Sustainability in higher education: Stories and strategies for transformation* (pp. 107–114). Cambridge, MA: MIT Press.

Yin, R. K. (2001) *Estudo de caso: Planejamento e Métodos* (2nded.). Porto Alegre: Bookman.

Zohar, D. (2005). Spiritually intelligent leadership. *Leader to Leader, 38,* 45–51.

12

DEVELOPING A SUSTAINABILITY MINDSET THROUGH SERVICE LEARNING

Mario Vázquez Maguirre and Consuelo García de la Torre

Service learning has been a useful tool for education and community development. It has proven to increase the level of student engagement and assimilation of concepts (Centro Latinoamericano de Aprendizaje y Servicio Solidario, n.d.). Service learning can be defined as "service performed by students, aimed at attending to a real need of the community, and oriented in an explicit and planned way to enhance the quality of academic learning" (Nieves Tapia, Gonzalez, & Elicegui, 2006, p. 68). This tool can be oriented towards developing the capabilities required to promote a sustainability mindset. This book chapter describes how a service-learning project has been implemented in a Mexican university that is a signatory of the Principles for Responsible Management Education (PRME), in order to generate a sustainability mindset in the participating students. Experience regarding teaching sustainability in this university indicates that students of management-related careers have difficulties interiorizing the benefits of sustainability practices. Therefore, at the end of a core course on sustainability and corporate social responsibility (CSR), a substantial number of them disregarded the advantages of implementing sustainable practices in organizations. In order to develop a sustainability mindset, students need to evaluate, first-hand, the benefits of sustainability practices in business and non-governmental organizations (NGOs). This involves taking theoretical classes combined with conducting interviews with people who have succeeded and failed in implementing these practices. Once they relate sustainability practices with the theoretical concepts, students develop projects to promote sustainability in entities that are not familiar with the concept. As a result, the university contributes to community development while consolidating the new mindset not only in students but also with practitioners. This effort would be difficult to achieve in a one-semester class; therefore, this project has a transversal focus, lasting up to eight semesters. Vividly understanding the benefits of sustainability and how it can be implemented in organizations through service learning represents a novel approach to promote a sustainability mindset in higher-education students.

Drivers of Change, created by Universidad de Monterrey (UDEM) with mentoring from Elon University in 2016, is a selective, multidisciplinary program that seeks to address different problems regarding how sustainability is taught in the university. UDEM was born when different Catholic congregations and a group of businesspeople from the region decided to create a university that provided a comprehensive preparation to students under the premise that the realization of the individual is only possible through service to others. Therefore, the university has always sought innovative ways to bring students' attention to social and environmental issues.

UDEM's business division is no exception, as every program includes classes on Ethics, Social Responsibility and Sustainability, and Social Entrepreneurship. These courses emphasize sustainability and how crucial it is for organizations seeking survival, lower risks, and long-term returns. However, the scope of the courses is somehow limited. On the one hand, students at the end of the classes recognize the issue of sustainability, its main components, and its importance within organizations. On the other hand, most of them lack the capacity to develop sustainable projects or establish processes that seek to forward sustainable development. An initial diagnosis might suggest that students need to take more classes that more deeply explore the issue of sustainability. Another alternative would be to find more creative ways to formulate and implement sustainable projects for students. Drivers of Change emerges in this context, as a program that seeks to develop students' ability to address social issues through sustainable social innovation.

Sustainability is a multifaceted discipline that should permeate virtually every aspect of business organizations; therefore, a four-year project was proposed to achieve such a challenging task. This is the longest range the university could afford, since most undergraduate programs last nine semesters and one semester is needed to recruit each Drivers of Change generation. The objective of this chapter is to describe this project as a novel approach to generating a sustainability mindset in management students. The first section provides Latin America's social context and how universities in the region have responded to the more urgent problems and challenges. The second section explores service learning and how it can help student learning processes. The third section describes the project and its dimensions. The discussion section compares Drivers of Change with the sustainability mindset model. Finally, the concluding remarks section examines the opportunities and challenges that this kind of project poses on universities, especially management education.

Social context in Latin America

Latin America has undergone a process of irregular and uneven economic development. Welfare states that developed in the middle of the twentieth century brought a degree of prosperity to the region, but the neo-liberal policies that followed affected most countries, boosting inequality between countries and within them (Hofman, 2000). The end of the welfare state had a negative impact on the working classes, which had historically relied on state subsidies for food, health, housing, education, etc. This scenario became more complex with globalization. The world became flat, as Thomas Friedman (2005) argued in his famous book, and competition from abroad became stronger for companies in Latin America. Few corporations circumvented this obstacle, and the region turned into a world supplier of raw materials and a manufacturer of cheap products. Cheap labor was one of Latin America's main competitive advantages.

Government instability was also a problem that inhibited growth and development, bringing high levels of corruption and difficulty in managing ventures. Later, some countries went bankrupt, and the austerity policies that came as a condition of loans from international organizations like the International Monetary Fund (IMF) brought social unrest and greater challenges in regard to how to address social issues. The emergence of an organized civil society that would respond to the most pressing problems facing cities and rural areas of Latin America was urgent.

Universities responded to this call, opening the debate on the effectiveness of traditional education systems and what alternatives could make education more effective while contributing to alleviating social issues. In this sense, evidence in Latin America suggests that educational projects that combine solidarity practice and formal learning are more effective in reaching the four main pillars of UNESCO's education: learning to know, learning to be, learning to do, and learning to live together. Many universities started programs to create social welfare in their communities while experimenting with innovative forms of meaningful learning for students. Service learning became one of the most successful tools to achieve both goals (Centro Latinoamericano de Aprendizaje y Servicio Solidario, n.d.).

Service learning

Service learning is a new pedagogical method which is spreading rapidly in some countries. It has three fundamental characteristics (Centro Latinoamericano de Aprendizaje y Servicio Solidario, n.d.):

1   Activity of solidarity to attend real needs of the community
2   Planned and integrated into the students' curricula
3   Performed by the students

Service learning promotes desired social behavior among students. It also tends to promote the civic and moral development of students (Umpleby & Rakicevik, 2008). This can be seen as a preventive strategy as it directs young people away from anti-social behavior that sometimes degenerates into violence and school dropout. A service learning experience should be meaningful and beneficial to the community; learning objectives should be clearly identified, and students should be involved in selecting and designing the service activity. Other characteristics of service learning are the need for a theoretical base, and the integration of the service experience with the academic curricula and opportunities for student reflection (Furco & Shelley, 2002). Regarding the outcomes, Eyler, Giles, Stenson, and Gray (2001, p. 1–4) summarized the research on service learning in higher education:

- Service learning has a positive effect on the student's personal development such as sense of personal efficacy, personal identity, spiritual growth, and moral development.
- Service learning has a positive effect on interpersonal development, the ability to work well with others, and leadership and communication skills.
- Service learning has a positive effect on reducing stereotypes and facilitating cultural and racial understanding.
- Service learning has a positive effect on the sense of social responsibility and citizenship skills.
- Students and faculty report that service learning has a positive impact on students' academic learning.
- Students and faculty report that service learning improves students' ability to apply what they have learned in the "real world."
- Service learning participation has an impact on such academic outcomes as demonstrated complexity of understanding, problem analysis, critical thinking, and cognitive development.
- Students engaged in service learning report stronger faculty relationships than those who are not involved in service learning.
- Service learning improves student satisfaction with college.
- Students engaged in service learning are more likely to graduate.
- Faculty using service learning report satisfaction with the quality of student learning. They report commitment to research. They increasingly integrate service learning into courses.
- Colleges and universities report that community service positively affects student retention and enhances community relations.
- Communities report satisfaction with student participation and enhanced community relations.

Service learning is different from other initiatives that also involve work in the community. Fieldwork, for example, requires students to visit a place in order to appreciate the object of study; however, it does not expect to modify the reality. There is learning involved, but not service in this initiative. Nonsystematic solidarity initiatives seek to attend an urgent need in the community (Centro Latinoamericano de Aprendizaje y Servicio Solidario, n.d.). They don't usually transcend the assistance perspective, and they generate spontaneously, rather than being planned in advance. They allow students to learn basic concepts of management. Meanwhile, the institutional community service goes one additional step in its attempt to solve a social or environmental problem, not departing that much from the assistance perspective.

The main difference with service learning is that those initiatives are usually not part of the student's curricula. In this sense, service learning promotes an active role of the beneficiaries, intends to provide solutions to structural problems, develops capabilities and resources in the stakeholders, and is sustainability-oriented (Centro Latinoamericano de Aprendizaje y Servicio Solidario, n.d.).

Drivers of Change

The Drivers of Change program is divided into five pillars (theoretical training, experiential learning, research, human-centered, and sustainability) that seek to improve the service-learning experience for the students at the same time that it expands the positive impacts of the projects for every stakeholder involved. Each Drivers of Change generation is led by a mentor, who is in charge of guiding the students through these pillars during the four years. The program's recruiting process involves the staff working during the first semester in promoting the program (usually through making a five-minute presentation in the classrooms), and selecting the appropriate team of students through two interviews (led by a mentor and an administrative coordinator), conducting an attitudes test, composing a curriculum vitae, and evidence from social work the candidates have done so far. The program admits an average of 35 students every year. The mentor is also recruited in the first semester based on her credentials: quality research on social issues, full-time or part-time professor at UDEM, and experience developing sustainable projects that address social issues.

At the end of the first semester, the official kickoff takes place with a full day at UDEM's leadership center, where they have collaborative activities intended to boost teamwork. After that, the students have a general orientation about the program, the university and its resources, and how to manage time efficiently. The program starts in the second semester.

Theoretical training

The program has a theoretical pillar consisting of training on issues related to sustainable management projects. At first, the Sustainable Development Goals (SDGs) are reviewed, along with the results of the Millennium Development Goals, the concept of sustainability, corporate social responsibility, and other ways in which private enterprises can address social problems, such as the Bottom of the Pyramid (BoP) or inclusive business. The concepts of social innovation and frugal innovation are also reviewed. After that, the students review issues related to planning and project management, social business models, attracting funds, cases, etc. It is important to note that training is not only held in the classroom; there are four ways to achieve this pillar:

- Theoretical classes led by the mentor, who shares the key elements and theory that must be the base of practical knowledge

- Case methodology to review stories of success and failure
- Experiential lessons taught by a social entrepreneur who seeks to inspire students while developing a specific issue
- Visits to NGOs, foundations, social enterprises, and civil associations where students can see first-hand how some concepts and theories are applied. This part requires a major effort to develop a network of organizations that can help the program in each theme.

The program also requires students to take five mandatory classes that are part of their curricula: leadership in organizations, global competencies, social thinking of the church, compared international contexts, and academic writing. These five courses are adapted to the requirements of the program: mainly a deep emphasis on issues regarding business ethics, sustainability, and social value creation.

Experiential learning

Meaningful learning through service learning occurs only when students are actively involved in the development and implementation of projects (Centro Latinoamericano de Aprendizaje y Servicio Solidario, n.d.). One of the main changes in how the students learn sustainability consists in leaving the classroom and putting their hands to work. In this pillar, it is also important to highlight the issue of students' leadership. Every cohort must democratically decide what SDGs it wants to address, in order to align most projects to that cause. In the same way, they must decide which projects to be involved with and which NGOs or associations to collaborate with. The different types of projects are as follows:

- *Single-semester projects led by an NGO or social enterprise that requires the participation of some students.* This type of project is very specific, seeks to develop a particular topic, and may not require the effort of the entire cohort. Each semester students can choose to get involved in one of these projects to consolidate theoretical knowledge. These projects are usually led by NGOs who are seeking more sustainable operations, and Drivers of Change students support the organization with planning, implementation, impact measurement, innovative business model, social innovation, etc.
- *Projects by semester or by year led by an NGO or social enterprise that require the participation of the entire cohort.* Before proposing a sustainable project, students should participate in every stage of a project that promotes sustainability in addressing a social problem. These efforts are usually led by large NGOs with the scale to include every student of the cohort. UDEM has been working with local NGOs since its foundation, developing a vast network of organizations.
- *Projects that last more than a year are led by Drivers of Change where other organizations may be involved.* It is mandatory that students develop two sustainable projects during the four years of the program. Both projects must be aligned

to one of the SDGs and must meet a social need while minimizing negative impact on the environment and also creating mechanisms to make the project self-financing. These two projects will also mostly measure the student's skills throughout the program.

While students receive theoretical training and visit NGOs and social enterprises, they are involved in a variety of projects to apply new knowledge, creating more meaningful learning. The program opens a call for projects for NGOs and other organizations to submit initiatives that require the expertise of the students. Thus, every cohort has a wide variety of options to choose from. One of the main requirements of the projects is the pursuit of sustainability, which means that the social, environmental, and economic areas must be considered in the planning and implementation of each project.

Research

Research is another important pillar of the program. One of the main goals is to strengthen research skills so students will be able to analyze the context surrounding the problem they want to solve. Students research and diagnose the main problems afflicting Mexico and Latin America, issues such as poverty, insecurity, business run under informality schemes, social exclusion of minority groups, poor education system, pollution, overexploitation of natural resources, inequality, corruption, etc.

Students also investigate the context surrounding the projects they will develop. They familiarize themselves with the economy of the community or neighborhood, the history of the settlement, their welfare statistics, and in general, all the secondary information that provides insights to plan an intervention. Likewise, the students document every project in order to develop case studies and other research that will help future students of this program, and also to provide evidence of the capabilities generated by the students. To this end, the program includes modules where quantitative, qualitative, and mixed research is explained, along with research strategies, and the most common data collection instruments: questionnaire, interview, focus group, observation, and experiments.

One of the secondary objectives of the program is that the students are encouraged to publish their cases in research journals. To this purpose, the student must also be able to investigate the different theories that may explain the involvement of the private sector in addressing social issues: corporate social responsibility, inclusive business, social entrepreneurship, base of the pyramid, philanthropy, etc.

Human centered

One of the pillars of the program is the intrinsic recognition of the human being and the individual's central role in the economy related to social welfare, where the ultimate goal is human well-being. The term *sustainability* already involves components that enable future generations to enjoy the same resources that their predecessors had, putting the pursuit of welfare and quality of life for all people as the central elements of this effort.

One of the purposes of Drivers of Change is that the students recognize that this is part of a larger effort; a group of students together can accomplish great things that otherwise individually might be practically impossible. Teamwork abilities are essential in this program. Literature (Timmons & Spinelli, 2007; Wright & Vanaelst, 2009) suggests that the entrepreneurial team is one of the most important variables when starting an organization, and that synergies are necessary to increase the probability of success.

The program includes a series of activities to promote unity and teamwork. The first semester is key to this objective, and so are the three main events through which unity is accomplished: camping activities, regular informal meetings, and sessions at UDEM's center of leadership. The role of the mentor is crucial here, because he must identify each student's strengths and how they can benefit the group. Eclecticism is one of the reasons the students apply to Drivers of Change, because they want to develop sustainable projects with students from other disciplines who share their own interests.

At the end of the four years, the intention is that the students become not only change makers but also develop a strong network to promote sustainable social ventures. Students may support each other to start new projects and to become increasingly involved in social innovation projects, which are desperately needed in this region. The students that finish the program get a certificate in social innovation.

Sustainability

As mentioned in the introduction, the motivation behind Drivers of Change is to prepare students with more tools to bring sustainable solutions through social innovation. The different social work programs at UDEM promote that its graduates have a social sensitivity that drives them to get involved in social problems mainly through philanthropic acts, but very few seek to develop sustainability-minded organizations. This is one of the reasons why sustainability is one of the pillars of the program: it necessitates that students develop new capabilities to be agents of change, not just social philanthropists.

This emphasis on sustainability initially involves the implementation of projects that are not sustainable yet. Students support NGOs, which finance their operations mainly through donations, making these organizations dependent on a third party. The objective of the student involvement in these projects is twofold: to learn by doing (service learning), and to understand that these efforts are limited (at least financially), and they do not represent a lasting solution to most social issues. Therefore, this represents the first step towards convincing the student that economic sustainability is the only way to solve this kind of problem permanently. The student then also understands that the economic constraint is not the only problem to solve, since many of the projects have negative environmental impacts. As the students reach their second year in the program, the training focuses on preparing them to do a baseline analysis of each project, and then set the social, economic, and environmental indicators that may bring sustainability to the ventures they will create. To this end, students need a systems thinking approach in terms of relationships, connectedness, and context. They need to understand the relationship within the elements of the ecosystem if they aspire to find a long-term solution to the issues at hand.

One way to achieve this is through projects in indigenous communities. In Mexico, 10% of the population is indigenous; they share a unique cosmovision that honors and cooperates with nature in order to preserve their land and resources (Vázquez-Maguirre, 2012). As the students get involved with projects within these communities, they come to understand the indigenous perspective on the interconnectedness of the different elements in nature, including humans, and how to protect the entire ecosystem.

Drivers of Change and the sustainability mindset model

The values (being) dimension of the Systemic Perspective for a sustainability mindset focuses on developing a sense of interconnectedness (Kassel, Rimanoczy, & Mitchell, 2016). Although cultures in the western-northern hemisphere tend to privilege individualization, this dimension seeks the opposite, a sense that we as individuals are part of a larger ecosystem that we can easily change with our decisions. As such, people's decisions around us also might affect us, thus the need to cooperate and work towards a common goal.

Developing a sense of interconnectedness is primary for Drivers of Change. The idea of a cohort that is going to work together for four years, while cooperating with different social organizations, seeks to develop the "being" dimension in the student. The values involved in Drivers of Change are teamwork, tolerance, honesty, respect, interdependence, co-responsibility, resilience, democracy, participation, and empowerment. These values point to a student who develops a global ethic that recognizes every ecosystem in the world as a relevant one. These values do not neglect the individuality of each person, but rather ask for everyone's sense of self-awareness in order to recognize his or her motivations, limitations, moods, and emotions, and how they can affect others.

The early theoretical classes that focus on the Sustainability Development Goals, Millennium Development Goals, Global Compact, etc., seek to develop the sense of urgency to shift from an individualistic paradigm to an interconnected one. This also creates the conditions to work more effectively as a group. Interconnectedness not only includes present agents and ecosystems but also future ones, which is why students need to develop a long-term perspective of how projects are managed and measured. This perspective represents an important departure from traditional short-term business decision making in Latin America. Therefore, students' interaction with all stakeholders becomes critical to create long-lasting solutions, turning students into agents of social, environmental, and economic change towards sustainability.

The competencies (doing) dimension that seeks engagement with all of the relevant stakeholders is the primary shift of this project from traditional in-class education. This includes stakeholders that promote healthy environmental practices. As students engage in projects led by themselves or an external organization, there should be an urgency to account for negative externalities.

Although a socially oriented project usually has well-defined metrics of the target population, beneficiaries, expected outcomes, and a budget, the environmental dimension is not always that evident and is sometimes neglected in these initiatives. Students need to make sure the three aspects are well balanced in each venture. Thus, there is the need to convince different stakeholders that tend to privilege the social or economic dimension about the urgency to develop a biospheric orientation in each project. In this sense, there also should be a special consideration about the cultural impacts generated, which involve changes to the norms, values, and beliefs of individuals that guide and rationalize their perception of themselves and their society (Burdge & Vanclay, 1996).

The knowledge (thinking) dimension, which incorporates concepts related to systems theory, was a major challenge in this program. How to train students to accept and navigate chaos and uncertainty, under changing circumstances? How to design a venture that meets the demands of every element of the ecosystem? In order to address these issues, the students are trained as social entrepreneurs: individuals who strive to achieve social value creation through the display of innovation, sustainable operations, risk management, and proactive behaviors (Weerawardena & Mort, 2006).

Social entrepreneurs pursue sustainable solutions to problems of neglected positive externalities under conditions of uncertainty (Santos, 2012). This involves a high level of awareness and being able to manage different approaches to a problem knowing that each intervention will have a different path to success. There are different methodologies designed to exemplify what it is like to manage under chaotic circumstances. One of them is the lean startup model, designed to create a new customer-centric product or service under conditions of extreme uncertainty by providing tools to test the product continuously and incorporate new learning (Ries, 2011).

Every mentor has the freedom to incorporate methodologies that might be more appropriate to solve the issues each cohort chooses to address, but the objective remains unaltered. Because one of the goals of every cohort is to address a social issue through a sustainable and innovative solution, the organizational venture that is more likely to emerge is a social enterprise.

These entities have a higher chance of establishing inter-organizational alliances to achieve their goal (Seelos & Mair, 2007; Werhane, Kelley, Hartmann, & Moberg, 2010). In addition, they follow an empowerment logic that seeks to provide the stakeholders with the necessary resources and capabilities to achieve higher levels of well-being (Santos, 2012). In this sense, managing the creation of a social enterprise may help the students to develop the knowledge dimension of the sustainability mindset.

Concluding remarks

The challenge of developing a sustainability mindset in undergraduate students poses the opportunity and urgency to generate new teaching-learning mechanisms. This chapter describes a program that seeks to combine service learning and social innovation to generate the idea that sustainability should be a way of thinking in every aspect of the student's life. Drivers of Change rely on five pillars to achieve this goal: theoretical training, experiential learning, research, human centered, and sustainability. Through service learning, the students are involved in a series of projects that are focused on making a contribution to the community. As the complexity of the projects increases, the students also develop the three dimensions of the sustainability mindset model: values, competencies, and knowledge (Kassel, Rimanoczy, & Mitchell, 2016).

The challenges of a multidisciplinary program like Drivers of Changes are numerous: First, there needs to be a significant level of coordination among academic, social, administrative, and financial areas within the university. A program of this nature needs funding, since the magnitude of the projects may require seed money; therefore, the board and dean should be in agreement that each cohort needs time and resources to develop a sustainability mindset. Drivers of Change needs a vast network of organizations that help the student learn by doing: NGOs, foundations, social enterprises, corporations with CSR programs, crowdfunding organizations, and universities. Coordination between the program's needs and every partner is also a challenge.

Value creation in the community is also an important outcome of the program. Mexico is currently facing social disturbances as a result of higher criminality rates (drug cartels), corruption, half the country living under poverty conditions, marginal GDP growth, and a government with a highly constrained budget. Universities and other social actors need to take a more proactive role to address the challenges society faces, especially minorities and marginalized groups. In this sense, service learning offers a win-win situation. Other organizations are also taking on the protagonist role in these efforts, so the possibilities for alliances and synergies are huge.

Although Drivers of Change is still in an early stage (initially more than 80 applications were received, and the first generation of 35 students started in fall 2016; at the time of this writing, the staff of the program are starting to recruit the second cohort), the interest generated by the program suggests that the students are aware of the importance of the subject. Also, students demand more innovative, interdisciplinary methods to learn while making a positive contribution to their community.

References

Burdge, R. J., & Vanclay, F. (1996). Social impact assessment: A contribution to the state of the art series. *Impact Assessment, 14*(1), 59–86.
Centro Latinoamericano de Aprendizaje y Servicio Solidario. (n.d.). *Centro Latinoamericano de Aprendizaje y Servicio Solidario*. Retrieved from www.clayss.org.ar/04_publicaciones/PaSo_Joven_Completo.pdf

Eyler, J. S., Giles, D. E., Stenson, C. M., & Gray, C. J. (2001). *At a glance: What we know about the effects of service-learning on college students, faculty, institutions, and communities, 1993–2000: Third edition.* Retrieved from www.mnsu.edu/cetl/academicservicelearning/Service-Learning.pdf

Friedman, T. L. (2005). *The world is flat: A brief history of the twenty-first century.* New York: Farrar, Straus and Giroux.

Furco, A., & Shelley, H. B. (2002). *Service-learning: The essence of the pedagogy.* Greenwich, CT: Information Age Publishing.

Hofman, A. A. (2000). *The economic development of Latin America in the twentieth century.* Northampton, MA: Edward Elgar Publishing.

Kassel, K., Rimanoczy, I., & Mitchell, S. F. (2016). The sustainable mindset: Connecting being, thinking, and doing in management education. *Academy of Management Conference,* Anaheim, CA.

Ries, E. (2011). *The lean startup: How today's entrepreneurs use continuous innovation to create radically successful businesses.* New York, NY: Crown Business

Santos, F. M. (2012). A positive theory of social entrepreneurship. *Journal of Business Ethics, 111*(3), 335–351.

Seelos, C., & Mair, J. (2007). Profitable business models and market creation in the context of deep poverty: A strategic view. Academy of Management Perspectives, 49–63.

Tapia, M. N., González, A., & Elicegui, P. (2006). Service-learning in Argentina schools: A descriptive vision based on the projects presented to the "Presidential Service Learning Award" (2000–2001). In K. McKnight, G. Davidson, S. H. Billig, & N. C. Springer (Eds.), *Advancing knowledge in service-learning: Research to transform the field.* Greenwich, CT: Information Age Publishing.

Timmons, J. A., & Spinelli, S. (2007). *New venture creation, Entrepreneurship for the 21st century.* Boston, MA: McGraw-Hill/Irwin.

Umpleby, S., & Rakicevik, G. (2008). Adopting service-learning in universities around the world. *Journal of the World Universities Forum, 1*(2), 39–48.

Vázquez-Maguirre, M. (2012). *Indigenous social enterprises in subsistence economies.* Monterrey, México: Tecnológico de Monterrey.

Weerawardena, J., & Mort, G. S. (2006). Investigating social entrepreneurship: A multidimensional model. *Journal of World Business, 41,* 21–35.

Werhane, P. H., Kelley, S. P., Hartmann, L. P., & Moberg, D. J. (2010). *Alleviating poverty through profitable partnerships: globalization, markets, and economic well-being.* New York, NY: Routledge.

Wright, M., & Vanaelst, I. (2009). *Entrepreneurial teams and new business creation (The International Library of Entrepreneurship).* Northampton, MA: Edward Elgar Publishing.

PART III

Integrating sustainability mindset in programmatic learning goals

13

CONSCIOUSNESS-BASED EDUCATION

Cultivating sustainable minds

Dennis Heaton and Colin Heaton

Sustainability mindset for a sustainable world

A number of writers in the field of managing for sustainability in various ways have identified "mindset" or "consciousness" to be a key factor in addressing the global sustainability crisis. Kassel, Rimanoczy, and Mitchell (2016) have called for the development of a sustainability mindset, which they describe as "the internal state of the leader, her mindfulness, emotional intelligence, and deeper questions about purpose" (p. 10), in order to realize "a shift that is foundational to all substantively sustainable initiatives" (p. 3). In an issue of the *Academy of Management Review* devoted to sustainability, Cooperrider and Khalsa (1997, p. 335) quoted Albert Einstein: "We cannot solve the problems that come with the world we have made thus far from the same level of consciousness at which we created them." Laszlo (2008) explained that whether or not leaders understand that business value can be created through ameliorating negative stakeholder outcomes is a function of their mindset or hidden beliefs. And Senge, Smith, Schley, Laur, and Kruschwitz (2010) argued that a mind which can comprehend whole systems and not simply fix isolated problems is necessary to create a sustainable world.

Changing mindset entails something more than providing business decision makers with new scientific information such as models and measures relating business impacts to climate change. What is called for is some transformation of the underlying level of mental development through which one constructs knowledge about oneself, others, and the environment. Such transformational learning has been described by developmental psychologist Robert Kegan as not just "a new set of skills to be 'put in' but a new threshold of consciousness" (Kegan, 1994, p. 165). Loevinger's (1976) research identified a sequence of stage-like shifts in the cognitive, interpersonal, and moral structures through which people make meaning of their lives. These stages of development are "maturational differences in the way individuals make sense, experience and act upon reality through the lens of various stages of consciousness" (Boiral, Baron, & Gunnlaugson, 2014, p. 365). Research using a measure of Loevinger's developmental stages has linked differences in sustainability practices to stages of consciousness development in leaders (Boiral et al., 2014; Brown, 2011).

Introducing consciousness-based education at Maharishi University of Management

An approach which has shown evidence of promoting the kind of consciousness development which can be foundational for valuing, understanding, and enacting sustainability is the Consciousness-Based Education[1] (CBE), which we have experienced at Maharishi University of Management (MUM). MUM is an accredited university which offers degree programs in a variety of fields at the bachelor, masters, and doctoral levels.[2] It is located in Iowa in the United States. CBE combines experiential, intellectual, pedagogical, and environmental features all aimed at developing students' consciousness of connectedness with his or her own deepest self and, through that, connectedness with others and with nature. This consciousness approach has been presented as a model of spirituality in management education (Schmidt-Wilk, Heaton, & Steingard, 2000) and a foundation for realizing the aims of responsible management education (Heaton, Schachinger, & Lazslo, 2016).

Figure 13.1 (from Pearson, 2011) illustrates three components of knowing: knower, known, and process of knowing. Any education entails all three components: there is something to be known, there is someone to know it, and there is a process of learning connecting the knower and the known. In CBE each of these three components are handled in distinctive ways which contribute to cultivating a more holistic mind. With reference to the knower, CBE include daily practice of

FIGURE 13.1   Three facets of knowledge: knower, process of knowing, and known

Source: Reprinted from "Introduction to the Series," by C. Pearson. In D. Heaton, J. Schmidt-Wilk, & B. McCollum (Eds.), *Consciousness-Based Education: A foundation for teaching and learning in the academic disciplines, 8, Consciousness-Based Education and Management* (pp. 2–14). Fairfield: M.U.M. Press. Copyright 2011 by Maharishi University of Management. Reprinted by permission.

the Transcendental Meditation® (TM) program, which has been found to positively affect a number of cognitive and personality characteristics (Nidich et al., 2010; Schmidt-Wilk et al., 2000). The known, the body of knowledge in any discipline at MUM, is made more profound and more unified by reference to a theoretical framework of unifying principles which are connected to one's personal TM experiences. This framework of unifying principles is the Science of Creative Intelligencem which is explained in the section "The Known – Universal Principles and Specific Knowledge."

With reference to the process of knowing, CBE uses teaching and learning methodologies that cultivate comprehension of how specific parts of knowledge connect with other parts of knowledge and with one's self in a holistic context. The sections which follow discuss how each of these three aspects of CBE – knower, known, and process of knowing – contributes to developing a sustainability mindset.

Developing higher consciousness in the knower

Knowledge depends fundamentally on the mental maturity of the knower, which frames how each individual makes sense of his or her world and own self. Empirical research by Loevinger identifies a sequence of ego development stages, which are also referred to as action logics (Rooke & Torbert, 2005) or stages of consciousness development (Boiral et al., 2014). As explained by Loevinger and Wessler (1970), each stage has characteristic differences in impulse control, character development, conscious preoccupations, cognitive complexity, and interpersonal style.

The post-conventional range of development encompasses stages which Loevinger called Individualistic, Autonomous, and Integrated. At the Individualistic level, there is recognition that the world one sees is constructed from one's own point of view and that others may be framing their own varied interpretations. The Autonomous stage has a high toleration for polarity, complexity, and multiple facets, and the Integrated stage reconciles conflicting opposite which are found within oneself.

Among adult managers who have been tested with a version of Loevinger's test, only 15% scored at post-conventional action logics (Rooke & Torbert, 2005). Managers who score at post-conventional action logics respond to situations with solutions that are more proactive, solution-oriented, participative, systemic, and transformative (Merron, Fisher, & Torbert, 1987).

Kassel et al. (2016) describe *both-and* logic as an aspect of a systemic perspective in a sustainability mindset. Such embrace of differences appears to correspond with characteristics of Loevinger's post-conventional Autonomous and Integrated stages. In other words, development of psychological maturity may be a foundation for a sustainability mindset. Boiral et al. (2014) explained that the skills of both sustainability leadership and the upper stages of consciousness development "include a broader and systemic perspective, long-range focus, integration of conflicting goals, collaboration with stakeholders, complexity management, collaborative learning" (p. 363). Similarly, Brown's (2011) dissertation discusses characteristics of post-conventional development which may contribute to effective execution of sustainability management; these include the capacity to take a systems view on reality, integrate ideas, create long-term visions with profound purposes and build truly collaborative relationships.

It appears therefore that educational practices which could cultivate developmental transformations could serve to help develop a sustainability mindset. Longitudinal research on graduates from CBE at MUM (Chandler, Alexander, & Heaton, 2005) found that they had grown to exceptionally high levels of mental and personality development, as indicated by Loevinger's (1970) Sentence Completion Test of ego development, Rest's (1987) Defining Issues Test of principled moral reasoning, and McAdams' (1982) measure of Intimacy Motivation. Ten-year longitudinal data indicated that MUM subjects increased markedly in ego development in contrast to three control groups matched for gender and age over the same time period. At post-test 53% (N = 34) scored at post-conventional levels, of which 38% (13 of 34) scored at or beyond the Loevinger's Autonomous level versus 1% of controls ($p <$ .001). MUM subjects also increased to very high levels of principled moral reasoning and intimacy. These unique developmental outcomes are attributed principally to practice of the TM technique and are consistent with other evidence that TM promotes psychological development, as reviewed in Orme-Johnson (2000).

Transcendental meditation for consciousness development

Transcendental Meditation technique is a key practice for development of the knower in CBE. TM is normally practiced for 20 minutes twice daily sitting quietly with the eyes closed. In this technique a specific sound or *mantra* – utilized for its sound value without reference to meaning – is used to shift attention away from its habitual outward direction. During meditation the mantra is experienced at progressively deeper and finer levels until the mind settles down to a state of quiet self-awareness beyond thought (Roth, 1987). This experience is described as a state of "pure consciousness" because it is wakefulness as its essential nature, unmixed with images, thoughts, feelings, or any other objects of perception; and as "Transcendental Consciousness" because it transcends time, space, and all relative, changing experience.

According to Shear, the TM technique makes the experience of transcendental consciousness accessible through a practice that is "independent of all matters of belief and affiliation" (2006, p. 47). This technique has been taught in a consistent manner around the world and thus has lent itself to scientific study on the effects on mind and body during meditation and on the stabilization of those effects outside of meditation as the result of repeated practice. The extensive research on this specific meditation technique includes randomized clinical trials, single-blind studies in which the experimenter was blind to group membership, and the use of active controls so that expectancy effects would be similar in treatment and comparison groups.

During the practice of the TM technique, there are reductions in heart rate and oxygen consumption and increased electroencephalographic (EEG) coherence indicative of a state of profound restful alertness, distinct from eyes–closed relaxation or sleep (Dillbeck & Orme-Johnson, 1987; Gaylord, Orme-Johnson, & Travis, 1989; Travis, 2002; Travis, Tecce, Arenander, & Wallace, 2002).

The state of restfulness gained during the practice of the TM technique is said to dissolve the stress in the mind and the body. TM practice is reported to decrease the effects of previous stressors and help an individual function better in stressful situations. A series of randomized controlled trials on the effects of TM practice on prevention and treatment of cardiac heart disease (CHD) reported reductions in hypertension, atherosclerosis, left ventricular mass, and CHD morbidity and mortality in high-risk, multi-ethnic populations practicing the TM program, compared to controls (Castillo-Richmond et al., 2000; Schneider et al., 1995; Alexander et al., 1996).

The TM technique has been associated with improvements such as decreased anxiety (Eppley, Abrams, & Shear, 1989), reduced health insurance utilization (Orme-Johnson, 1987; Herron, Hillis, Mandarino, Orme-Johnson, & Walton, 1996), decreases in overall incidence of diseases (Orme-Johnson & Herron, 1997), improvements in ego development and moral reasoning (Chandler, Alexander, & Heaton, 2005), self-actualization (Alexander, Rainforth, & Gelderloos, 1991), creativity (Travis, 1979; So & Orme-Johnson, 2001), flexibility in concept learning (Dillbeck, 1982), fluid intelligence, constructive thinking, and reaction time (So & Orme-Johnson, 2001; Cranson, Orme-Johnson, Gackenbach, Dillbeck, Jones, & Alexander, 1991). Alexander, Rainforth, and Gelderloos (1991) completed an exhaustive statistical meta-analysis of all existing studies (42 treatment outcomes) on the effects of the TM program and other forms of meditation and relaxation on self-actualization. The effect size, in standard deviation units, of the TM program on overall self-actualization (ES = .78) was approximately three times as large as that of other forms of meditation (.26) and relaxation (.27), controlling for duration of treatment and strength of experimental design (p < .0002).

An additional future area for research can be to examine performance measures of sustainability in relation to the types of changes in brain functioning found in student assessment research at MUM. The Brain Integration Scale (BIS) is part of MUM's system of assessment of psychological and physiology effects of CBE (Maharishi University of Management, 2016). Brain integration refers to the degree to which individual modules of the brain are working as an integrated whole. BIS measures patterns of ordering between different parts of the brain (Travis, Tecce, Arenander, & Wallace, 2002; Travis, 2002). Travis and Arenander (2006) reported evidence of concrete effects of the TM technique on students' brain functioning at MUM. They found that frontal coherence is achieved during TM practice even in beginning meditators, and also that the result of TM practice is growing frontal coherence not only during meditation but also during activity. Higher levels of brain integration correlate positively with higher emotional stability, higher moral reasoning, and more openness to experience, and correlates negatively with anxiety (Travis, Arenander, & DuBois, 2004).

Schmidt-Wilk et al. (2000) reviewed studies on students practicing TM in projects at five universities other than MUM, with positive outcomes on EEG coherence, self-concept, anxiety, creativity, perception, and academic performance. For example, Travis et al. (2009) reported changes in EEG coherence and power in university subjects who were randomly assigned to TM practice, compared to eyes-closed rest. Such studies suggest that the results of Consciousness-Based Education, which have been demonstrated at MUM, merit further investigation in other university settings.

Higher states of consciousness for sustainability

The Science of Creative Intelligence (SCI) course at MUM (Maharishi Mahesh Yogi, 1972) explains that knowledge is different in different states of consciousness. States of consciousness include the familiar three states of sleeping, dreaming, and waking consciousness and also a progression of what are called in SCI higher states of consciousness. Development of higher states of consciousness unfolds the potential for an increasing sense of oneness and interconnectedness, which has been identified as a fundamental aspect of a sustainability mindset (Heaton et al., 2016; Kassel et al., 2016; Laszlo et al., 2014).

The first of these higher states of consciousness is Transcendental Consciousness, a state of quiet inner wakefulness when thought is transcended. The founder of MUM, Maharishi Mahesh Yogi, (1995, p. 271 fn.), identifies this inner state as the spiritual essence of life: "eternal silence, which is pure wakefulness, absolute alertness, pure subjectivity, pure spirituality." In Maharishi's analysis, rooted in traditional Vedic knowledge, this transcendental level of the mind is identical to the unified field underlying and interconnecting all phenomena. Therefore, through the experience of this higher state of consciousness, the human mind can grow in the ability to function like nature:

> The functioning of transcendental pure consciousness is the functioning of natural law in its most settled state. The conscious human mind, identifying itself with this level of nature's functioning, gains the ability to perform in the style with which nature performs its activity at its most fundamental level.
> *(Maharishi Mahesh Yogi, 1986, p. 31)*

Steingard, Fitzgibbons, and Heaton (2004) argued that experience of transcendental consciousness overcomes the division of man and nature, and they hypothesize that development of higher states of consciousness in the knower leads to more sustainable business practice. Herriott, Schmidt-Wilk, and Heaton (2009) found that entrepreneurs who were long-term practitioners of TM reported experience of a pervasive sense of being part of a larger wholeness and that these experiences were related to adopting more universal values: going beyond individual interests to the wider interests of employees, community, or environment as a whole.

Development of consciousness is said to progress ultimately to unity conscious-ness – in which one appreciates one's own identity and all objects of perception in terms of one unified, universal reality, "a completely unified view of self and the environment traditionally known as 'enlightenment'" (Hagelin, 1987, p. 59). Such a development endpoint was theoretically described by developmental psychologist Robert Kegan, who has theorized:

> The ultimate state of development would have to do with some way in which the self has become entirely identified with the world. It would be the recognition essentially of the oneness of the universe, which is something we have heard over and over again in wisdom literatures of the East and West
> *(in Debold, 2002, p. 2)*

By cultivating self-awareness, inner stability, relaxed alertness, and a connected brain, the knower component of CBE broadens and deepens awareness as a foun-dation for more sustainable thinking and behavior. Such broadened awareness may be more sensitive and conscientious about the environmental and social impacts through a product life-cycle, such as resource depletion in the sourcing of materi-als or potential health hazards in the disassembly of components for reuse. The two other components of CBE – the known and the process of knowing – also cultivate growing wholeness of awareness.

The known – universal principles and specific knowledge

In Kassel et al.'s sustainability mindset model, the content area of Ecological World-view "encompasses a broad understanding of the manifestations of ecosystems . . . a basic conceptualization of how the natural world works and of the human inter-action with the planet's natural ecosystems (2016, p. 15). CBE can help further Ecological Worldview by making connections to transdisciplinary principles for understanding how nature functions in our lives and in the world around us.

In CBE, the Science of Creative Intelligence (SCI) course® (Maharishi Mahesh Yogi, 1972) explores the nature of creative intelligence as it manifests throughout nature and as it grows in our lives through the practice of Transcendental Medita-tion. SCI provides a scaffolding on which each individual discipline in university education can find connections to common underlying principles. The applica-tion of familiar principles makes new content familiar, while the content of the discipline gives concrete examples which make these common principles clear and relevant to the students. By seeing that the same principles can be meaningful in a variety of academic fields, the student can grow to appreciate that nature is not compartmentalized into fragmented disciplines but is a unified whole. In this way, the known aspect of CBE contributes to the type of integrative understanding of nature that is helpful for sustainability.

Table 13.1 enumerates a subset of 16 principles of SCI. Goldstein (2015) has applied these principles in his teaching of entrepreneurship at MUM. Efficiency is

TABLE 13.1 Sixteen principles of the science of creative intelligence

1. The nature of life is to grow.
2. Order is present everywhere.
3. Life is found in layers.
4. Outer depends on inner.
5. Seek the highest first.
6. Rest and activity are the steps of progress.
7. Enjoy greater efficiency and accomplish more.
8. Every action has a reaction.
9. Purification leads to progress.
10. The field of all possibilities is the source of all solutions.
11. Thought leads to action, action leads to achievement, and achievement leads to fulfillment.
12. Knowledge is gained from inside and outside.
13. Knowledge is structured in consciousness.
14. Harmony exists in diversity.
15. Whole is contained in every part.
16. The whole is greater than the sum of the parts.

Source: Adapted from Maharishi University of Management Faculty Resources.

one of the principles of nature's function that has been observed in various phenomena in physics. Reflecting on personal growth through the practice of TM provides evidence of one's own life growing to efficiently do less and accomplish more. This suggests that through TM life is growing to be more in accord with natural law, leading to the reduction and elimination of waste and the improvement of flourishing.

The principles that "life is found in layers" and "seek the highest first" inform the practice of sustainability to leverage the deepest layers rather than operating only at the level of surface symptoms of problems. The principles "The nature of life is to grow" and "purification leads to progress" guide us to rely on nature's own intelligence, which spontaneously takes a direction toward happiness and toward the removal of impurities which block the natural expression of creative intelligence. Knowledge of SCI, then, can be seen as contributing to ecoliteracy, which Kassel et al. (2016) explain can enable us to "cooperate with nature's inherent ability to sustain life" and bring us "closer to achieving the goal of sustainable communities" (p. 18).

Parallels can be observed between Maharishi's principles of the Science of Creative Intelligence (Table 13.1) and another expression of transdisciplinary principles in Ken Wilber's (2000) 20 tenets. Wilber's 20 tenets represent, in his words "what we might call 'patterns of existence' or 'tendencies of evolution' or 'laws of form'" (2000, p. 40) that are present in the realms of matter (physics), life (biology and biological evolution), and mind (history and psychology). The first of Wilber's tenets is that the universe is composed of neither parts nor wholes but of holons that are simultaneously both wholes and parts. Holons are comprised of parts and together comprise larger wholes. This corresponds to the SCI principles, which state that the whole is greater than the sum of the parts and the whole is contained in every part.

The SCI principle "outer depends on inner" means outwardly expressed symptoms are the result of internal causes at deeper levels. This principle is consistent with the systems literature, in which a distinction is made among symptoms, stimuli, and causes. For example, when we are sick, we perceive symptoms such as coughing and sneezing. An example of the stimuli would be bacteria that take up residency in our bodies, and the cause would be that our body chemistry is providing a healthy ecosystem in which pathogens can take residence.

In addition to principles which describe the functioning of creative intelligence, SCI also articulates qualities of the nature of creative intelligence that can be observed in physical and social systems. Fifty qualities of creative intelligence are presented in pairs of contrasting, yet complementary qualities (Maharishi International University, 1974). An example of paired qualities are stable and adaptable. Stability implies constancy, whereas adaptability implies openness and movement. All living systems are structures that maintain a constant form, even while matter and energy are constantly flowing through (Capra, 2004, p. 13). Other complementary pairs include gentle and strong, dynamic and restful, harmonizing and diversifying.

A set of five qualities of creative intelligence has been presented together as the five fundamentals of progress (Maharishi Mahesh Yogi, 1978). This set of qualities – stability, adaptability, purification, integration, growth – has been used to explain the dynamics of cultural integrity, as follows. By virtue of the quality of stability, change influences from outside are not able to overthrow the integrity of the system. An influence from outside will be spontaneously purified, so that the system will naturally adapt to and integrate what will be useful to its growth. These same five fundamentals have been applied at MUM in other diverse subjects such as human physiology, cell biology, ecology, organizational change, cross-cultural management, and information systems, illustrating the transdisciplinary power of SCI principles. Making connections to SCI throughout the curriculum cultivates Ecological Worldview through intellectual familiarity with principles of natural law, which students also see in multiple fields of knowledge and growing in their personal lives.

Structuring wholeness through the process of knowing

CBE aims to design the process of knowing to facilitate learning of the academic disciplines and strengthen the capacity to think in comprehensive, systemic terms. We describe some of the pedagogical practices of CBE here and then discuss their value in light of education theories of other educational scholars. The general purpose of the practices described here is to enable the learner to appreciate any specific knowledge with reference to wholes in which it is nested and to the ultimate nature of the learner's own Self. The cultivation of this kind of systemic cognition helps develop the mental competencies for sustainability, which requires comprehending the ecology of interrelatedness in human systems and the natural environment.

A profound rationale for these pedagogical methods is explained by MUM in terms of intellectually promoting the development of higher consciousness, enlightenment for the knower. In faculty development materials provided to teachers at MUM (Maharishi University of Management, 2010), the founder Maharishi explains:

> Enlightenment is the goal of our study. Therefore we teach the whole, then show how the whole generates the parts. We teach each part thoroughly, see where the parts fit, then step back from all the parts to their common basis, bringing the parts into the mainstream, and the mainstream into the ocean of the Self. All knowledge is made Self-referral by the teacher in every class.

By "Self-referral" here Maharishi means that all knowledge is with reference to the transcendental Self, which is experienced in Transcendental Consciousness as silent, unbounded pure consciousness that is at once knower, known, and process of knowing – without reference to outside objects. In Unity Consciousness, Self-Referral means that all objects of knowledge are appreciated as expressions of the one pure consciousness that is the transcendental knower, the Self. This enlightened state is described in Vedic literature as "To see the Self (Ātmā) in all Beings and all Beings in the Self" (Bhagavad-Gita chapter 6, verse 29).

Teachers at MUM participate in faculty development seminars in which they gain practice in constructing and utilizing a number of tools for curriculum design and instruction (Maharishi University of Management, 2010). These tools are based on educational guidelines from Maharishi Mahesh Yogi, the founder of the university. One tool for cultivating the capacity to connecting parts and wholes is called the Unified Field Chart – a visual illustration of the structure of knowledge of a particular discipline. Specific parts of the discipline are organized in a display which shows the relationship of different parts to each other. Vertically the knowledge is in layers from the most subtle underlying causes to the most manifest and applied aspects of the discipline.

At the most basic level of every discipline is the field of transcendental consciousness, which in CBE is regarded as the common source of all streams of knowledge and is equated with the notion of unified field from theoretical physics (Hagelin, 1987). Figure 13.2 is a simplified version of the Unified Field Chart developed by Professor John Hagelin at MUM for teaching physics. The left side of the chart models the progressive unification of physical forces and points to an ultimate unification at the level of the unified field. The Transcendental Meditation side of the chart shows that the mind, like the physical world, has progressively more subtle, powerful, and unified levels culminating in the experience of pure consciousness, which is identified with the unified field, the ground of both physical and psychological realities.

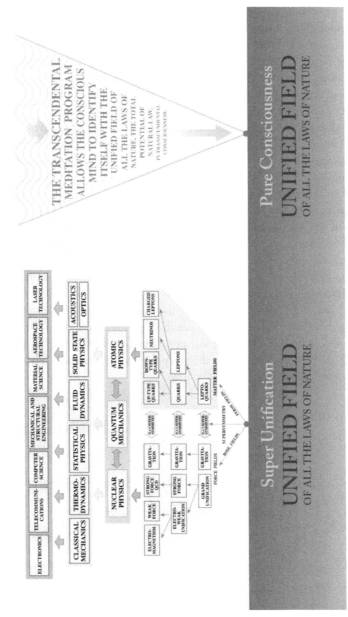

FIGURE 13.2 The unified field at the basis of mind and matter

Source: John Hagelin. Used with permission.

Figure 13.3 is part of a Unified Field Chart depicting a model showing consciousness of connectedness (level 1) as being at the basis of the achievement of sustainability outcomes (level 4). This model is used at MUM to explain how the inner development cultivated through the TM technique can give rise to outer expressions of responsible management. Note how this visual model encompasses the SCI principles (Table 13.1) that "life is found in layers" and "inner is the basis of outer."

Unified Field Charts are referred to in each lesson in order to situate the topic of the day within a greater context and also to intellectually present the notion that all aspects of the discipline have roots in a common unified field. Through seeing multiple Unified Field Charts across various disciplines of study, the student gains a sense that all branches of knowledge are connected to a unifying basis and that the basis of all knowledge is accessible within one's own mind.

By participating in the construction of such Unified Field Charts to map some area of knowledge, students in CBE exercise their capacity to focus on specific details while simultaneously making connections to a larger context. In this way, CBE contributes to the type of integrative understanding of nature that is helpful for sustainability. Furthermore, by actively participating in designing a model of a field of knowledge, learners come to appreciate how ideas are not fixed entities but living human constructions.

The use of Unified Field Charts within CBE can be related to a dimension of Spiritual Intelligence, which the sustainability mindset has called "Oneness with all that is" (Kassel et al., 2016, p. 29). Indeed, the pedagogy of CBE aims to converge with the experiential dimension of meditation practice to develop the "student's consciousness of unity – a sense of interconnectedness with his or her own complete self, the social environment, the physical environment and, ultimately, the entire universe" (Heaton et al., 2016, p. 218).

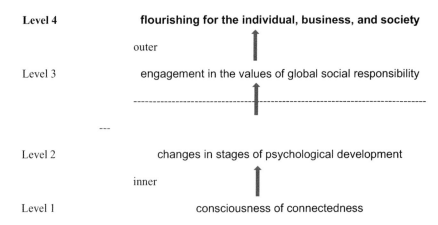

FIGURE 13.3 From inner development to outer responsible management

Source: From Heaton, D., Schachinger, E. & Laszlo, C. (2016). Consciousness-development for responsible management education. In R. Sunley & J. Leigh (Eds.), *Educating for responsible management: Putting theory into practice* (pp. 211–232). Sheffield, UK: Greenleaf.

Another CBE tool for cultivating a holistic mindset is called the Main Point Chart. There are two elements in the chart. The first element is to express the three most significant points of the lesson, in one or two sentences for each point. A second part is to relate each main point to some aspect of consciousness or creative intelligence (Maharishi University of Management, 2010).

The Main Point Chart serves to organize the content of the lesson. Each main point is elaborated with supporting logic, evidence, and detailed explanation, and then restated so that the main idea is clear and easy to remember. The Science of Consciousness points are intended to make the knowledge more relevant by connecting to the inner life of the learner. Students can also be assigned to construct main points along with corresponding consciousness points for readings, to help them consolidate and deepen their own understanding.

The following are examples from Main Point Charts in a course on socially and environmentally responsible management at Maharishi University of Management (Heaton, 2016):

> As stakeholders' expectations are shifting to accept less negative societal and social impacts (value destruction), shareholder value will be lost unless business strategies evolve toward sustainable value which is positive for stakeholders as well as shareholders. Collective consciousness is evolving toward more positive and holistic values in alliance with the total potential of natural law.

This sample main point first brings out a key idea about a shift in business management – that societal expectations for responsible management are shifting and are having an increasing influence. This evolutionary trend in society is then related to a phenomenon called *collective consciousness*, which is the prevailing consciousness of a society as a whole. The point argues that collective consciousness is evolving toward more healthy and holistic values. In elaborating on this main point, the MUM course forecasts that a general trend in collective consciousness is toward less destructive, more regenerative business impacts as more individuals are accessing their own Transcendental Consciousness, which is conceived of as the unified field of natural law.

Another main point from this course concerns a tool for gaining a better understanding of environmental impacts so that they can be ameliorated:

> Life Cycle Assessment (LCA) systemizes the measurement, analysis and improvement of environmental and societal impacts throughout the whole system of a product's life, from raw material acquisition through production, use and disposal or reuse.

This is the first part of the main point: summarizing the technical tool called LCA. Then the second point of the main chart connects LCA to an SCI principle about natural law:

> Within the functioning of nature, parts work together in synergy: the whole is more than the combination of parts.

This part of the main point inspires us that we can function as nature functions and that practices such as LCA can be seen as natural law functioning through us. Stu-dents in CBE are growing in the broad comprehension and compassionate spirit to make improvements through the life cycle, so subjective development and objective tools become complementary in the execution of responsible management.

A prominent application of tools like LCA is the Walmart Sustainability Index (Walmart, 2016). Walmart is a powerful downstream stakeholder for tens of thou-sands of global suppliers. Walmart recognizes that for products sold in its stores, the bulk of environmental impacts are made upstream by its suppliers. It therefore has been working with its suppliers to eliminate greenhouse gas (GHG) emissions from the supply chain. Walmart is sharing information with its suppliers about sustainability management. By requiring sustainability measurements from its sup-pliers, Walmart is leveraging its buying power to promote shifts towards its three aspirational sustainability goals: (1) to be supplied 100% by renewable energy; (2) to create zero waste; and (3) to sell products that sustain people and the environment. Walmart has reported that the company's sustainability efforts have led to 40 mil-lion metric tons of CO^2 emissions avoided since 2005, compared to business as usual. These sustainability advances by Walmart substantiate that stakeholder expec-tations and consequently business practices are evolving as collective consciousness is evolving.

Main point charts, including related consciousness or SCI points, are displayed as posters on the wall during a particular lesson and are left there for reference during subsequent classes – when connections can be drawn between what is happening in class and main points from prior lessons, as selected by the faculty. An exercise can be for learners to bring to class their own main points and cor-responding SCI points of assigned readings. This puts the learner in a purpose-ful frame of mind to get more meaning out of the reading by asking learners to articulate the deepest or most significant points. MUM Professor John Collins assigns students to create main points of their own during class. He will present his main points again at the lesson and invite students to challenge his main points or the corresponding SCI principle, thus sparking debate, active engagement, and critical reflection.

In their landmark 1995 article, "From Teaching to Learning: A New Paradigm for Undergraduate Education," Barr and Tagg describe the learning paradigm, which they contrast to the teaching paradigm. Educators in the teaching para-digm conceptualize educational content as discrete particles, objects of knowing that can be transmitted from a source, such as a book, or a lecture, directly into the memory of students where it is later recalled and made useful. It is education which puts the emphasis on what is known, where the learning paradigm is more cognizant of the process of knowing. Barr and Tagg sound the call for educators to recognize that all students learn differently and that the lecture is but one of many tools available to the teacher. The role of the teacher, in the learning paradigm, is to maximize the learning of each student "by whatever means work best." CBE, particularly when carried out in a way that involves learners in the active analysis and synthesis of knowledge, provides specific methodologies for implementing the learning paradigm.

CBE and generative learning

Main Point Charts, Unified Field Charts, and other CBE methodologies used at MUM can also be understood as strategies to promote generative learning. According to generative learning theory, the learner is not a passive recipient of information but an active generator of knowledge (Grabowski, 2004). Through connecting new stimuli, information, and experiences to previous experiences and understanding, the learner generates new knowledge, new understanding (Wittrock, 2010). The knowledge generated by the learner in any situation will be dependent upon the context in which the stimuli is presented/experienced, the state of consciousness of the learner (emotions, clarity of mind, level of psychological maturity), the learner's previous knowledge, and the objectives of the learner. The goal of generative learning is increased retention, comprehension, and transferability of knowledge by the learner, in short, "learning with understanding" (Wittrock, 2010). To promote generative learning, the teacher may offer explanations, metaphors, analogies, flow charts, paraphrases, main points, advanced organizers, and activities.

Harvard educational psychologist Howard Gardner (1991, p. 3) has found such generative learning to be far too uncommon in education. As Gardner makes clear, our educational system encourages rote memorization of information and knowledge but does not encourage genuine understanding:

> In schools – including "good" schools – all over the world, we have come to accept certain performances as signals of knowledge or understanding. If you answer questions on a multiple-choice test correctly, or carry out a problem set in a specified manner, you will be credited with understanding. No one ever asks the further question "but do you *really* understand?" because that would violate an unwritten agreement: a certain kind of performance shall be accepted as adequate for this particular instructional context. The gap between what passes for understanding and genuine understanding remains great.

Beyond genuine understanding which grasps the principles that underlie and guide observed properties and behaviors, according to Ackoff and Greenberg (2009) is wisdom. Wisdom is qualitatively different from data, information, knowledge, and understanding, which are all concerned with efficiency, with maximizing the probability of achieving an objective while minimizing the expenditure of resources, without considering the value of what is being pursued. Wisdom is examined understanding, it is concerned with doing the right thing.

Human beings, according to Ackoff and Greenberg, are incredibly intelligent and creative and can usually achieve anything that they put their minds to; the problem is that, for the most part, we put our minds to achieving the wrong things. In fact,

Ackoff and Greenburg contend that the most serious social and environmental problems we are currently facing as a species are the result, not of doing things wrong, but of doing the wrong things. An educational program which focuses on maximizing learning of knowledge, and even understanding, will only increase our capacity for doing things right.

To illustrate an example regarding wisdom, let's consider the case of farming in the U.S. Midwest. Large-scale agriculture production has become efficient in creating commodity outputs, which yield short-term profit in comparison to input costs. But wisdom in food production (and consumption) adds considerations about long-term economic, environmental, and health impacts, which may lead to different decisions in the food sector.

Creating the sustainable world we want will require that we create the conditions for our citizens to develop wisdom and begin doing the right things. Pedagogical tools of CBE are an intellectual approach which integrates with the experience of the Transcendental Meditation technique to promote development toward unity consciousness – in which one knows one's own identity and all objects of perception in terms of the same one universal intelligence. This level of consciousness enables the most natural wisdom to do what is right for oneself, others, and the environment.

Conclusion: transformative pedagogy for sustainability

We have presented three aspects of a Consciousness-Based Education approach to cultivating capabilities for comprehending the wholeness of the natural order so that the effects of our actions are naturally regenerative rather than contributing to unsustainability. Student development toward a sense of a unified consciousness about oneself and one's relationship to others and the environment is supported by each of three integrated streams of MUM's CBE pedagogy. The knower aspect of CBE, stimulating brain integration and higher stages of human development, supports a growing capacity to think comprehensively about social and environmental impacts of business for present and future generations. The process of knowing aspect involves specific instructional methods for constructing meaning through connecting parts and wholes. The known component explores transdisciplinary principles for gaining holistic understanding of natural and social systems.

The aspirations of CBE align with Systemic Perspective, Spiritual Intelligence, and Ecological Worldview content areas of Kassel et al.'s (2016) sustainability mindset model. From its founding, the goal of MUM has been the enlightenment of the students and the generation of wisdom through higher education for higher consciousness. Wisdom, as defined by Ackoff and Greenberg (2009), is the capacity to apply understanding of the principles and relationships that underlie observable behavior and properties of systems in order to select the right course of action to get the result we truly want. The framework of Consciousness-Based Education as applied at Maharishi University of Management facilitates the development of wisdom because it is transformative (changes the student's level of consciousness), transdisciplinary (integrative, universal, spiritual), and generative (educating for understanding by making connections and drawing relationships).

Notes

1 The Transcendental Meditation®, Consciousness-Based Education, Science of Creative Intelligence course®, and Maharishi University of Management are protected trademarks and are used in the U.S. under license or with permission.
2 www.ncahlc.org/Directory-of-HLC-Institutions.html

References

Ackoff, R., & Greenberg, D. (2009). *Turning learning right side up: Putting education back on track.* Upper Saddle River, NJ: Pearson Prentice Hall.

Alexander, C., Barnes, V., Schneider, R., Langer, E., Newman, R., Chandler, H., Davies, J., & Rainforth, M. (1996). Randomized controlled trial of stress reduction on cardiovascular and all-cause mortality in the elderly: results of 8 year and 15 year follow-ups. *Circulation,* *93*(3), 19–27.

Alexander, C., Rainforth, M., & Gelderloos, P. (1991). Transcendental meditation, self-actualization, and psychological health: A conceptual overview and statistical meta-analysis. *Journal of Social Behavior and Personality,* *6*(5), 189–247.

Barr, R., & Tagg, J. (1995, November/December). From teaching to learning: A new paradigm for undergraduate education. *Change,* 13–25.

Boiral, O., Baron, C., & Gunnlaugson, O. (2014). Environmental leadership and consciousness development: A case study among Canadian SMEs. *Journal of Business Ethics,* *123*(3), 363–383.

Brown, B. C. (2011). *Conscious leadership for sustainability: A study of how leaders and change agents with postconventional consciousness design and engage in complex change initiatives.* Doctoral dissertation. Fielding Graduate University, Santa Barbara, CA. Retrieved from http://integralthinkers.com/wp-content/uploads/Brown_2011_Conscious-leadership-for-sustainability_Full-dissertation_v491.pdf

Capra, F. (2004). *The hidden connections: A science for sustainable living.* New York: Anchor.

Castillo-Richmond, A., Schneider, R. H., Alexander, C. N., Cook, R., Myers, H., Nidich, S. . . . Salerno, J. (2000). Effects of stress reduction on carotid atherosclerosis in hypertensive African Americans. *Stroke,* *31*(3), 568–573.

Chandler, H. M., Alexander, C. N., & Heaton, D. P. (2005). The transcendental meditation program and post conventional self development: A 10-year longitudinal study. *Journal of Social Behavior and Personality,* *17*(1), 93–121.

Cooperrider, D. L., & Khalsa, G. S. (1997). The organization dimensions of global environmental change. *Organization & Environment,* *10*(4), 331–341.

Cranson, R., Orme-Johnson, D. W., Gackenbach, J., Dillbeck, M. C. Jones, C. H., & Alexander, C. (1991). Transcendental meditation and improved performance on intelligence-related measures: A longitudinal study. *Personality and Individual Differences,* *12,* 1105–1116.

Debold, E. (2002, Fall/Winter). Epistemology, fourth order consciousness, and the subject-object relationship, or . . . how the self evolves with Robert Kegan. *What Is Enlightenment,* *22,* 143–154.

Dillbeck, M. C. (1982). Meditation and flexibility of visual perception and verbal problem solving. *Memory & Cognition,* *1*(3), 207–215.

Dillbeck, M. C., and Orme-Johnson, D. W. (1987). Physiological differences between Transcendental Meditation and rest. *American Psychologist,* *42,* 879–881.

Eppley, K. R., Abrams, A. I., & Shear, J. (1989). Differential effects of relaxation techniques on trait anxiety: A meta-analysis. *Journal of Clinical Psychology, 45*(6), 957–974.

Fisher, D., Merron, K., & Torbert, W. (1987). Human development and managerial effectiveness. *Group &Organization Studies, 2*(3), 257–273.

Gardner, H. (1991). *Unschooled mind.* New York, NY: Basic Books.

Gaylord, C., Orme-Johnson, D., & Travis, F. (1989). The effects of the Transcendental Meditation Technique and progressive muscle relaxation on EEG coherence, stress reactivity, and mental health in black adults. *The International Journal of Neuroscience, 46*(1–2), 77–86.

Goldstein, H. (2015). *Entrepreneurship and Maharishi's science of creative intelligence – 16 Principles.* Retrieved from http://meditatingentrepreneur.com/entrepreneurship-and-the-16-principles-of-maharishis-science-of-creative-intelligence/

Grabowski, B. (2004). Generative learning contributions to the design of instruction and learning. In D. H. Jonassen (Ed.), *Handbook of research on educational communications and technology* (pp. 719–743). Mahwah, NJ: Lawrence Erlbaum.

Hagelin, J. S. (1987). Is consciousness the unified field? A field theorist's perspective. *Modern Science and Vedic Science, 1*(1), 59.

Heaton, D. (2016). An innovative approach to cultivate responsible next generation leaders: Transcendental Meditation in management education. In S. Tiwari and L. Nafees (Eds.), *Innovative management education pedagogies for preparing next-generation leaders* (pp. 139–160). Hersey, PA: IGI Global.

Heaton, D., Schachinger, E., & Laszlo, C. (2016). Consciousness-development for responsible management education. In R. Sunley & J. Leigh (Eds.), *Educating for responsible management: Putting theory into practice* (pp. 211–232). Sheffield, UK: Greenleaf.

Herriott, E., Schmidt-Wilk, J., & Heaton, D. P. (2009). Spiritual dimensions of entrepreneurship in Transcendental Meditation and TM-Sidhi Program practitioners. *Journal of Management, Spirituality and Religion, 6*(3), 195–208.

Herron, R. E., Hillis, S. L., Mandarino, J. V., Orme-Johnson, D. W., & Walton, K. G. (1996). Reducing medical costs: The impact of the Transcendental Meditation Program on government payments to physicians in Quebec. *American Journal of Health Promotion, 10*(3), 206–216.

Kassel, K., Rimanoczy, I., & Mitchell, S. F. (2016, August). *The sustainable mindset: Connecting being, thinking, and doing in management education.* Paper presented at the Academy of Management Conference, Anaheim, CA.

Kegan, R. (1994). *In over our heads: The mental demands of modern life.* Cambridge, MA: Harvard University Press.

Laszlo, C. (2008). *Sustainable value.* Stanford, CA: Stanford University Press.

Laszlo, C., Brown, J. S., Ehrenfeld, J., Gorham, Barros-Pose, I., Robson, L., Boland, B. . . . Werder, P. (2014). *Flourishing enterprise: The new spirit of business.* Stanford, CA: Stanford Business Books.

Loevinger, J. (1976). *Ego development: Conceptions and theories.* San Francisco, CA: Jossey-Bass.

Loevinger, J., & Wessler, R. (1970). *Measuring ego development.* San Francisco, CA: Jossey-Bass.

Maharishi International University. (1974). *Science of creative intelligence for secondary education: Three year curriculum.* Livingston Manor, NY: Maharishi International University Press.

Maharishi Mahesh Yogi. (1972). *The science of creative intelligence: Knowledge and experience (Lessons 1–33). [Syllabus of videotaped course].* Los Angeles, CA: Maharishi International University Press.

Maharishi Mahesh Yogi. (1978). *Enlightenment to every individual and invincibility to every nation.* West Germany: MERU Press.

Maharishi Mahesh Yogi. (1986). *Life supported by natural law.* Washington, DC: Age of Enlightenment Press.

Maharishi Mahesh Yogi. (1995). *Maharishi University of management: Wholeness on the move.* Vlodrop, Holland: Maharishi Vedic University Press.

Maharishi University of Management. (2010). *Faculty development seminar, May 8, 2010: Creating effective Maharishi Science of Consciousness points in the Main Points Chart.* Fairfield, IA: Maharishi University of Management.

Maharishi University of Management. (2016). *Brain integration progress report.* Retrieved September 10, 2016, from www.mum.edu/academics/research-institutes/center-for-brain-consciousness-and-cognition/brain-integration-report-card

McAdams, D. P. (1982). Intimacy motivation. In J. A. Stewart (Ed.), *Motivation and society* (pp. 133–171). San Francisco: Jossey-Bass.

Merron, K., Fisher, D., & Torbert, W. R. (1987). Meaning making and management action. *Group and Organization Studies, 12,* 274–286.

Nidich, S. I., Rainforth, M. V., Haaga, D. A., Hagelin, J., Travis, F., Gaylord-King, C. . . . Schneider, R. (2010). A randomized controlled trial on effects of the Transcendental Meditation Program on blood pressure, psychological distress, and coping in young adults. *American Journal of Hypertension, 22*(12), 1326–1331.

Orme-Johnson, D. W. (1987). Medical care utilization and the Transcendental Meditation Program. *Psychosomatic Medicine, 49*(5), 493–507.

Orme-Johnson, D. W. (2000). An overview of Charles Alexander's contribution to psychology: Developing higher states of consciousness in the individual and society. *Journal of Adult Development, 7*(4), 199–215.

Orme-Johnson, D. W., & Herron, R. E., 1997. An innovative approach to reducing medical care utilization and expenditures. *The American Journal of Managed Care, 3*(1), 135–144.

Pearson, C. (2011). Introduction to the Series. In D. Heaton, J. Schmidt-Wilk, & B. McCollum, (Eds.), *Consciousness-based education: A foundation for teaching and learning in the academic disciplines, 8, consciousness-based education and management* (pp. 2–14). Fairfield: M.U.M. Press.

Rest, J. R. (1987). *Guide for the defining issues test.* Center for the study of ethical development. Minnesota: University of Minnesota.

Rooke, D., & Torbert, W. R. (2005, April). Seven transformations of leadership. *Harvard Business Review,* reprint, 1–11.

Roth, R. (1987). *Transcendental meditation.* New York, NY: Donald I. Fine.

Schmidt-Wilk, J., Heaton, D. P., & Steingard, D. (2000). Higher education for higher consciousness. *Journal of Management Education, 24*(5), 80–611.

Schneider, R. H., Staggers, F., Alexander, C. N., Sheppard, W., Rainforth, M., Kondwani, K. . . . King, C. G. (1995). A randomised controlled trial of stress reduction for hypertension in older African Americans. *Hypertension, 26*(5), 820–827.

Senge, P., Smith, B., Kruschwitz, N., Laur, J., & Schley, S. (2010). *The necessary revolution: Working together to create a sustainable world.* New York, NY: Crown.

Shear, J. (2006). Transcendental meditation. In J. Shear (Ed.), *The experience of meditation: Experts introduce the major traditions* (pp. 23–48). St. Paul: Paragon House.

So, K.-T., & Orme-Johnson, D. W. (2001). Three randomized experiments on the longitudinal effects of the Transcendental Meditation technique on cognition. *Intelligence, 29*(5), 419–440.

Steingard, D., Fitzgibbons, D., & Heaton, D. P. (2004). Exploring the frontiers of environmental management: A natural law based perspective. *Journal of Human Values, 10*(2), 79–97.

Travis, F. (1979). The Transcendental Meditation technique and creativity: A longitudinal study of Cornell University undergraduates. *The Journal of Creative Behavior, 13*, 169–180.

Travis, F. T. (2002). Development along an integration scale: Longitudinal transformation in brain dynamics with regular Transcendental Meditation Practice. *Psychophysiology, 39*, S81.

Travis, F. T., & Arenander, A. (2006). Cross-sectional and longitudinal study of effects of Transcendental Meditation practice on frontal power asymmetry and frontal coherence. *International Journal of Neuroscience, 116*(11), 1519–1538.

Travis, F. T., Arenander, A., & DuBois, D. (2004). Psychological and physiological characteristics of a proposed object-referral/self-referral continuum of self-awareness. *Consciousness and Cognition, 13*(2), 401–420.

Travis, F. T., Haaga, D., Hagelin, J., Tanner, M., Arenander, A., Nidich, S., ... Schneider, R. H. (2009). A self-referential default brain state: Patterns of coherence, power, and eLORETA sources during eyes-closed rest and the Transcendental Meditation practice. *Cognitive Processing, 11*(1), 21–30.

Travis, F. T., Tecce, J., Arenander, A., & Wallace, R. K. (2002). Patterns of EEG coherence, power, and contingent negative variation characterize the integration of transcendental and waking states. *Biological Psychology, 61*, 293–319.

Walmart. (2016). Spotlight on the sustainability index. Retrieved September 12, 2016, from http://corporate.walmart.com/2016grr/enhancing-sustainability/spotlight-the-sustainability-index

Walmart. (2017). 2017 Global responsibility report. Retrieved January 11, 2018, from https://corporate.walmart.com/2017grr

Wilber, K. (2000). *Sex, ecology, spirituality* (2nd ed.). Boston, MA: Shambala Publications.

Wittrock, M. C. (2010). Learning as a generative process. *Educational Psychologist, 45*(1) 40–45.

14

LEAPFROGGING TO THE FOURTH MISSION IN HIGHER EDUCATION

A new Ghanaian college creates sustainability approaches and community engagement

Helen Akolgo-Azupogo, Roland Bardy and Arthur Rubens

Introduction

Historically, the primary mission for universities and other higher education institutions has focused on education since the founding of the earliest recorded university in Bologna in 1088. This mission and total focus on education was largely unchanged until the 19th century, when what has been called the 'first academic revolution' was put forward, where 'research' was integrated into the universities' core activities (second mission). This model of conducting applied research can be traced to the early agricultural extension programs at that time, which encouraged faculty to conduct research that could be translated into practice (Anders, 1992). Since the 1980s, a new mission, or 'second academic revolution', has occurred with universities', where economic development was incorporated into the core mission of many universities (Etzkowitz, 1998).

Prior to the second academic revolution or emergence of a third mission, educational institutions, departments and faculty regarded their mission and responsibilities as teaching, research and service. This triad could be regarded as a three-legged stool where teaching and research were the dominant legs of the stool and were regarded as key to the mission, with teaching being the first mission and research being the second mission. Service, the third leg of the stool, primarily focused on university service (serving on committees, etc.), with some select faculty being engaged on community boards or associations. However, in the 1980s this started to change: faculty and departments started to recognize that their responsibilities go beyond service to the university or college to the communities they served. Correspondingly, communities surrounding the universities started to recognize the human capital and assets that resided within educational institutions and requested their support and help. However, most significant, financial and economic constraints led to university colleges and departments recognizing the need to partner with businesses in the surrounding communities. In addition, universities were faced with an increased accountability due to political and financial pressures from local governments and others to show their contribution to their communities and the economy. This second academic revolution has brought about the advent of what has been called the "entrepreneurial university" (Clark, 1998; Anders, 1992).

More recently, a fourth mission is starting to emerge with a focus on sustainable development. The focus started within universities through varied programs and activities (Lopez, 2013; Kurland, 2011; Krizek et al., 2012) and has spread to outside of the university through a variety of programs in the university community (Laninga, Austin, and McClure, 2011; Molnar et al., 2011). This fourth mission, as Gregory Trencher has said (Trencher et al. 2013), finds universities collaborating with government, industry and civil society to advance sustainable development and create sustainable transformation in these industries and communities. The model of the "triple helix" approach (Amaral, Ferreira, and Teodoro, 2011) has emerged: public, private, partnerships. These partnerships are evolving to what could be called a "quadruple helix model" of public-private-people-professor partnerships, where universities, faculty, departments, and so on are networking and working with living labs in their community and beyond. These transformations and transition to this fourth mission are happening at varied educational institutions throughout the world to varying degrees. For example, universities worldwide are adding sustainability programs and/or sustainable development into their curriculum and into their university mission (Khalaf-Kairouz, 2012; Vincent and Focht, 2009; Cole and Fieselman, 2013; Cook and Cutting, 2014; Figueredo and Tsarenko, 2013; Chhokar, 2010; Madeira Carravilla, Oliveira, J. F., and Costa, 2011). Although not as frequent as university campus–based sustainability programs, there are examples of universities being the impetus and driver of sustainable development programs in the university's surrounding communities (Xypaki, 2015; Molnar et al., 2011; Laninga, Austin, andMcClure, 2011). Universities are also investigating different strategies to achieve greater success with these programs. For example, Cebrián, Marcus, and Humphris (2013) explored varied theoretical frameworks to better understand and improve the effectiveness of the organisational change processes towards sustainability in universities. They found that employing an integrated framework could provide the best results for embedding sustainability in the core activities of the university (Cebrián, Marcus, and Humphris, 2013). Collins and Gannon (2014) proposed a "four-type" sustainability action model to empower students, faculty, and staff to be active environmental change agents on their campuses and local communities.

However, interest and focus on sustainability and sustainable development is not only being carried out in universities and other institutions of higher education, but is also being called for in local communities on a global level. The Education for Sustainable Development (ESD) Program at the United Nations University Institute for the Advanced Study of Sustainability (UNU-IAS; see https://ias.unu.edu/en/) has created a global network of more than 100 Regional Centers of Expertise (RCEs) on ESD worldwide. The RCEs provide a framework for strategic thinking and action on sustainability by creating diverse partnerships among educators, researchers, policymakers, scientists, youth, leaders within indigenous communities and throughout the public, private and nongovernmental sectors. Due to the RCEs' diverse network of partners and their wealth of local knowledge and resources, these groups and networks have the potential to transform the approach to traditional knowledge and biodiversity issues. Globally, RCEs have launched a number of groundbreaking ESD initiatives that address some of the greatest challenges we face in safeguarding biodiversity and traditional knowledge (see, e.g., Wade, 2013). Connecting to colleges in the developing world has proven to be a major challenge for UNU-IAS because historically many universities and colleges are often funded for, and tied to, their primary objectives of their first and second missions only. However, it has been found that colleges that have a long history of embeddedness within their communities have many opportunities to develop this fourth mission through a wide variety of activities ranging from community-based research projects to service learning activities, community-based training programs, and different shared programs with the community (Hunter, 2013; Khalaf-Kairouz, 2012; Russell and Flynn, 2001). An example of this can be drawn from the developing nation of India (this is a case where Western universities and colleges can learn from a developing nation): India's highest court has mandated environmental education at all levels of formal education, which includes a compulsory undergraduate course. Yet, there have been challenges in implementing this requirement, primarily because inter-disciplinary competence among staff is not sufficient in all schools of this vast country, and traditional methods of assessment still prevail in higher education. Nevertheless, India has provided many examples of successful community-based initiatives, and many efforts to develop learning opportunities in this field have emerged primarily from academic and student interests and priorities rather than from formal policy initiatives (Banga Chhokar, 2010).

In order for the third and fourth missions to be successful, it requires a careful balancing of university and community partnerships. These partnerships can be laden with multiple tensions and conflicts due to the diverse expectations of the respective groups. Roni Strier (2014) refers to the university–community partnerships as a "field of paradox" fraught with conflict, which can impact the collaboration among the various partners. Strier indicates that this paradox arises from issues such as top-down institutional presence vs. grassroots orientation, unequal power relationships, trust, goal differences, and so forth. By contrast, the grassroots aspect is shared by all partners if a school starts all anew, if it embraces community relations from its very beginning and if goals are developed jointly through the new faculty, community leaders and the wider stakeholders in the community. This is precisely the case with Regentropfen College, where the fourth mission was envisioned by its founders when they formed the idea, the vision and the strategic planning for the new higher education institution. The case study of this new college will present the implementation of their vision, its repercussions and the first achievements that have become visible.

Regentropfen College's vision, strategies and deployment

Regentropfen College is built upon a theme and premise of growth. *Regentropfen* is the German word for rain drops, and rain is a scarcity in the area where the new college is located – if rain falls or, to extend the metaphor, if irrigation brings water to farming activities, then green pastures will develop. Irrigation is one major theme for the rural population to achieve self-sufficiency – through technological support, but even more through capacity building, and so is the issue of building a new educational institution in a region that is underserved with teaching and dissemination of knowledge. This new venture will provide self-sufficiency for the region with regard to training and professional development. In addition, it could easily become a model for other ventures in similar regions. It is from this conception that Regentropfen was born.

The college's full name is Regentropfen College of Applied Sciences (ReCAS). It is located in Kansoe Namoo, a village near Bongo, which is the capital of one of the districts of Ghana's Upper East Region. The Upper East Region of Ghana with a population of about 1 million people is one of Ghana's ten regions and lies in the northeastern corner of the country, bordered by Burkina Faso to the north and Togo to the east. The region's economy is based on agriculture, cattle and cereals like millet, sorghum and rice. The region is also known for its handicrafts, which are sold at the markets in Bolgatanga, which is the primary center for trading to other regions in Ghana, as well as the center for export to other countries in the continent and beyond. Transport to the north into Burkina Faso and to the south toward the seaports at Accra has a long tradition. Burkina Faso is land-locked, and almost all export and import require this connection. The ancient trans-Saharan trade route from Mali, which passed through Burkina Faso, is joined in Bolgatanga by a second route from northern Nigeria. Currently there is no airport in Bolgatanga. The closest air travel would be in Tamale, which is approximately 160 miles (257 kilometers) to the south. Tamale is the capital of the bordering region and houses the University of Development Studies, which oversaw Regentropfen College's accreditation process.

The main occupations in the Upper East Region are agriculture and related work (65.9%), production and transport equipment work (14.5%), and sales and service work (13.4%). The substantial lack of formal sector and office-based bureaucratic activities in the region is reflected in the fact that only 1.7% of the economically active are engaged in administrative, managerial, clerical and related work (Ghana Statistical Service, 2013, p. 487). Most of those working in these areas live and work in and around Bolgatanga, which has a population of 70,000 (Ghana Statistical Service, 2013, p. 228). Much of the outreach programs, third and fourth mission activities of Regentropfen College, will be disseminated within this vicinity and population.

Table 14.1 shows the region's location in the northeast of Ghana and gives a few details on the area which it shares with two other regions.

Specifically, the Upper East Region (Figure 14.1) was initially part of the Upper Region (Upper East and Upper West), which on 1 July 1960 was itself carved out of

TABLE 14.1 Characteristics of the three regions of Northern Ghana

Northern Region
- Size: 70,384 sq km (29.5% of total Ghana)
- Population: 1.8 million people with two major ethnic groups: Mole-Dagbon (52.2%)
- Vegetation: Vast areas of grassland, some savannah woodland, drought-resistant trees
- Education: Illiteracy rate, 78%
- Occupation: Agriculture, hunting and forestry (71.2%)

Upper West
- Size: 18,478 sq km
- Population: 0.7 million people with four major ethnic groups: Mole-Dagbon (75.7%)
- Vegetation: Savannah vegetation
- Education: Illiteracy rate, 73.4%
- Industry: Agriculture, hunting and forestry (71.2%)

Upper East
- Size: 8,842 sq km
- Population: 1 million people with four major ethnic groups: Nabdam (30.5%) and Kusasis (22.6%)
- Vegetation: Savannah woodland
- Education: Illiteracy rate, 77%
- Industry: Agriculture (72%) and sales (13%)

Source: Adapted from Ghana Statistical Service (2013).

Note: In all regions, the proportion of the population that has never attended school is 60.4%.

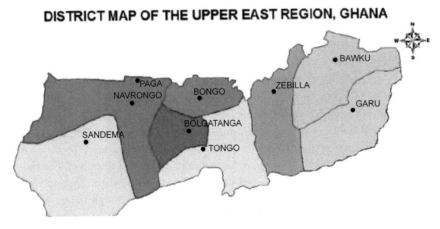

FIGURE 14.1 District map of the Upper East Region

Source: Adapted from Ghana Statistical Service (2013).

what used to be the Northern Region. In 1983 the Provisional National Defence Council (PNDC) divided the Upper Region into Upper East and Upper West Regions. The Region is administered politically from Bolgatanga and is headed by the Regional Minister. The map in Figure 14.1 displays the districts in the region, and it can be seen that Bongo, where Regentropfen College is located, neighbors the Municipal District of Bolgatanga, the region's capital.

In the Upper East Region, as per the census of 2010, more than half of the population (52.6%) is less than 20 years old, with people who are between the ages of 0–14 years representing 41.5% and those between 15–19 years constituting 11.1%. The elderly population (65 years and older) make up only 6.8% of the Region's population. Gender wise, there are more females (51.6%) than males (48.4%) in the region, which is very similar to what is found in the national population (females, 51.2%).

In the region, there are about 54 government agencies and approximately 110 non-governmental organizations (NGOs) which are registered with the Social Welfare. Almost all communities in the region have basic education facilities. There are 632 primary schools, 330 junior high schools and 37 senior high schools in the Region (Ghana Statistical Service, 2013). In addition, there are a few private educational institutions, but these are mostly found in the urban centres.

The 2010 census data also revealed that the population aged 6 years and older who are currently in school are 38.0%, which is higher than what was seen in the past (16.2%). However, the rate of 60.4% of those who have ever attended school (age 6 years and above) is lower than the national rate, which is 76.5% as per the 2010 census. The explanation for the low attendance is that there was a policy by the colonial government to deliberately delay the introduction of education and literacy programs in the northern part of Ghana, which includes the Upper East Region. Even when it was introduced, education for the north was limited to primary sixth grade for all and primary seventh grade for only the best out of the population. It was only in 1951 that the first secondary school was opened. Other contributory factors that would have to be considered are social, cultural and economic (Bening, 1990).

Although the region has three teachers' colleges and several nursing schools, there is a dearth of higher education institutions in the region. Economic opportunities are limited in the region, thus many young people seeking higher education training do not have the necessary financial resources to pay for fees, accommodation, food and books at an institution outside of the area, and they ultimately end up either terminating their academic ambitions or obtaining a menial job to earn a living. As a result of this, the region loses invaluable human resources. For those who are financially able to leave and pursue education elsewhere, they move to other regions of the country and frequently don't return. Although there is a definite demand and need for tertiary education in the Upper East Region, historically there has been no outlet for these individuals. The establishment of Regentropfen College helps to address the needs and growing demand by the region's population at several levels. First and foremost, the creation of a tertiary institution will give opportunities to underprivileged youths to have scientific and professional training. Second, Regentropfen College will create a 'Special Education Unit', thus people with disabilities, such as sight or hearing impairment, inside and outside of the region, will have an opportunity to learn and acquire practical academic training and certifications.

The primary mission of the college is to provide students with knowledge that can be practically applied and to make opportunities available to get on-campus training. For example, in pursuit of responding to the primary industry of the region and providing applied education and continuing opportunity, it is establishing a small experimental farm for the agriculture students, as well as establishing a primary and a secondary school on campus (this is something that is not found in other teaching colleges in the country). The latter (primary and secondary school on campus) provides a chance for praxis, as opposed to theories, to students who pursue a career in teaching. In addition, this educational center will be used as a benchmark and model of excellence in education. The focus on these centers will not only be to produce great teachers for the children of the region but also to serve as a model for retraining and continuing education for teachers within the region and beyond. Also, the physical vicinity to the experimental farm can help teachers demonstrate how caring for the soil and the crops prudently contributes to better cultivation – one step toward developing a mindset that is aware of sustainability.

The college's curriculums started in May/July of 2016, beginning with programs and courses on education of teachers, business administration, accounting, computer science and agriculture. Following this, programs in ethics will be created. As with the departments of education and agriculture, there will be a focus on 'applied, experiential' learning. In order to enable graduates of Regentropfen to very quickly and easily integrate themselves into the labor market, a Business and Career Development Center (BCDC) was built. The BCDC's primary focus and mission will be to integrate graduates into the labor market. Also, fund-raising campaigns are under way in order to attract high-caliber (former) CEOs and qualified professionals to be incorporated as part of the business programs.

In addition to the BCDC, a second specialty center has been developed: the Center for Cross-Cultural Ethics and Sustainable Development (CCCESD). The CCCESD's primary focus will be to integrate the sustainability focus, together with a focus on ethics. It was felt that, from the onset, both sustainability and ethics must be priorities in the teaching and practice for graduates of the college. This focus is extremely important due to the diversity of people, culture and language in the region. For example, the cultural background of people from Burkina Faso and Togo, which neighbors Ghana's Upper East Region, is French, with French being the official language in these other two countries. In addition, there is also a large diversity of ethnicities with their own languages, as well as diverse religious cultures (Catholic, Evangelical and Muslim). Finally, there is also great diversity among local bureaucratic institutions in the capital, Bolgatanga, their local employees, as well as the large rural population in the surrounding area. The College and the CCCESD will work to blend these multicultural groups together.

The CCCESD will provide a comprehensive view on ethics while specific topics like business ethics, educational ethics, agriculture ethics and so on will be dealt with within the various curricula of the college's departments. Similarly, this same process will apply to the topic of sustainable development.

In the African rural environment, people are much closer to and dependent on nature than they are in the Western world, and thus they have a practical understanding of the essence of sustainable development: "meeting the needs of the present without compromising the ability of future generations to meet their own needs" (U.N. General Assembly, *Our Common Future*, Chapter 2: Towards Sustainable Development, p. 43). From an applied perspective, the population can readily see how achieving human development goals is closely coupled with maintaining the natural systems, which ultimately provide the resources and ecosystem services upon which the economy and society depend. One could say that there is an inherent 'mindset for sustainability' which is engrained in the subconscious of the population. However, as with any mindset, there is a need to 'awaken' it. It is our belief that this awakening must begin with the young people within the region. Two of the authors of this study gave a presentation to the Youth Group of Kansoe where the college is located (for some of these presentations an interpreter was needed to facilitate communication as some of the youths' command of English was poor). Following the presentation, a rich and fruitful discussion ensued, in which most of the young attendees gave stunning insights into how they personally feel, the extent to which sustainable development affects their daily lives and what each of them can contribute. The sensitivity and basic judgment given by the participants far exceeded anything that was seen by the authors in presentations and lectures given to Western students on the importance of sustainability and sustainable development. In contrast, in Europe, many young people when asked about sustainable development would primarily refer to issues of climate change (of which none of them is personally affected at present, cf.: Kagawa, 2007). Conversely, the discussants here referred to topics like improving access to water and sanitation, enhancing self-sufficiency in food production, increasing mobility and security on the roads, and raising the effectiveness of public institutions – all of which influence their daily lives and areas which they can alter and change by their own actions.

From its inception, in the first deliberations among the faculty and with representatives of the community, the CCCESD was designated to increase sensitivity and judgment and to build knowledge and skills in all areas of sustainable development. The Mission Statement of Regentropfen College clearly spells this out as follows:

CCCESD Objectives are:

1 **To Create Sensitivity**: Ethics sets the values and rules that govern interaction between people. One substantial prerequisite is to make people aware. Sustainable development also requires a status of awareness. The CCCESD will organize seminars and workshops that are tailored to

enlightenment of the actors and users of development projects, in order to bring about ethical and efficient use of resources as well as to the need to cultivate maintenance culture.

2 **To Build Knowledge:** Most people are conscious of what is ethical/good and unethical/bad in human interactions and in activities that affect natural environment. The CCCESD will put this knowledge into theoretical and practical perspective. The focus will be on applicability, which will be achieved through the provision of courses of academic and professional character to students and interested parties such as governmental organisations, NGOs and Business.

3 **To Provide Soft Skills:** The CCCESD aims at providing soft skills to its students, its clients/customers and the public in general through interactive seminars, field trips and workshops.

4 **To Enhance Judgement:** Based on sensitivity and knowledge in the topics of ethics and sustainable development, students will be led to develop their own judgements. This will be supported with field work and case studies.

5 **To Strengthen Ability:** Even with good judgment the ability to perform good actions both in the ethical and the sustainable fields will often be barred by constraints. Therefore, a strategy will have to be developed to conquer the constraints. The programs of the CCCESD will provide learning tools in this matter.

6 **To Raise Will-Power:** Arriving at a successful execution of programs/projects in ethics and sustainable development is often very demanding. Perseverance and will-power are needed to overcome the many obstacles. These include the will to make uncomfortable decisions. The students will learn the processes that are needed to approach this issue.

This mission statement clearly shows that the founding intention and purpose of the CCCESD is to create a 'center of excellence' for teaching, training and research and to produce expertise and experts in this field, in Ghana and in West Africa. The eventual long-term goal of the CCCESD is to build a nucleus of research and consultancy that offers expertise and knowledge for ensuring the practice of ethics in economic and social business. Through its unique embeddedness in the (rural) African environment and culture, the CCCSED of Regentropfen College will be able to become a hub that propagates a different narrative to many other colleges and universities around Africa (and potentially the world). The program is situated in, and is part and parcel of, the global process of transformation. Therefore, skills and tools taught need to be adequate to conceptualize the large system change which draws on the United Nations Sustainable Development Goals (SDGs) from which their mission and architecture is derived. Although it goes without saying that understanding the concept of the large system change is too much to ask for from students in their first semesters in a new academic program, this mindset will be present from the onset. In addition, a substantial part of the SDGs will be in the implementation process worldwide at the time when the first bachelor's students will graduate in 2019. Thus, the CCCESD could potentially be a model for the role which business schools perform in this transformation and how management could be taught and inspired to develop a passion toward the public good and collective interest.

Reviewing the literature on third and fourth mission

As previously noted, the emergence of the third mission in the 1980s was the beginning of the 'second academic mission' and a turning point of universities' roles in society. The notion of a second academic mission and the entrepreneurial university was first conceptualized by Etzkowitz (1998). In this model, the university enters in 'triple-helix partnerships' (Etzkowitz and Leydesdorff, 2000), with industry and government contributing to innovation-driven strategy aimed at regional or national economic growth strategy (Yarime et al., 2012). While in principle, third mission activities would refer to the bundle of activities that generate, use, apply and exploit knowledge and other university capabilities outside of academic environments (Molas-Gallart et al., 2002) – essentially encompassing all activities that are not covered by the first and second missions –this social contribution is mainly promoted as an economic contribution (Trencher et al., 2014a, 2014b).

The concept of a fourth mission of sustainable development is closely connected to social entrepreneurship education. By providing education and training, incubator space, mentoring, networking opportunities and even seed funding, universities exert an impact on local business activity and employment. Supporting student entrepreneurship provides an alternative strategy for those colleges that lack expansive infrastructure – they use this alternative to promote local economic activity. While social entrepreneurship education holds the possibility for reinvigorating attention to the universities' role in addressing social problems, the focus, so far, seems to be on market and market-like mechanisms – on economic contribution (Kretz & Sá, 2013).

The view of a main economic contribution appears to be too narrow when dealing with transversal and complex issues such as that of sustainability, whose challenges encompass social, economic, political, cultural and environmental considerations. This issue is so broad and ambitious that concrete solutions necessarily need to be co-created by multiple actors, such as universities, local government, communities, economic actors and civil society (Trencher et al., 2014a). In order to contribute to sustainability, it is necessary to engage in place-based, multi-stakeholder partnerships that are able to solve real-world issues. Trencher et al. (2013, 2014a, 2014b) state that a new function is emerging for universities: that of co-creation of sustainability. In this new function, the model passes from entrepreneurial to transformative university, conceived as a multi-stakeholder platform engaged with society in a continual and mutual process of creation and transformation, as per Table 14.2.

TABLE 14.2 Time line of universities four mission model

Mission Focus	First	Second	Third	Fourth
	Education	Research	Economic	Sustainability
Prototype	Université de Paris	Humboldt Universität Berlin	MIT, Stanford	ETH Zürich, Oberlin College
Triggering Event	Expansion of Catholic Church	Humboldtian Reform	Knowledge Economy	Sustainability Crisis
Time Line	1150–70	1810	1980	2010–on

Source: Adapted from Trencher et al (2014). "Beyond the third mission: Exploring the emerging university function of co-creation for sustainability." Science and Public Policy 41.2 (2014): 151–179.

TABLE 14.3 Definitions of third and fourth missions

Betts & Lee (2004) (Third Mission)	Trencher et al. (2013) (Fourth Mission)
University as a trainer: university's role in providing to local economy an ample supply of skilled young graduates.	**Scientific advisor/communicator role**: university actors seek to influence local governance structures and development trajectories by communicating results of pilot or research project and advising an appropriate course of action.
University as innovator: generation and commercialization of academic knowledge.	**Inventor/innovator role:** Hard dimension: creation and diffusion of cutting-edge technologies and innovative ideas. Soft dimension: how university actors and partners innovate with policies or social entrepreneurialism.
University as partner: provision of technical know-how.	**Revitalizer/retrofitter role**: working with external developers and authorities to improve existing buildings, spaces and infrastructures rather than pursuing new development. **Builder/developer role**: new development, infrastructure and construction.
University as regional talent magnet: the presence of a university increases the attractiveness of the region to talented academics, entrepreneurs, engineers.	**Director/Linker role**: academics create a grand vision for the future and seeks its materialization by leveraging other partners' assets and know-how. They mobilize other actors by creating networks into which they feed intelligence and guidance.
University as facilitator: facilitate networking between private and public sector.	**Facilitator/Empowerer role**: university attempts to unleash change by empowering key community stakeholders to self-diagnose problems and creating conditions that will lead to a self-realized transformation.

Source: Adapted from Betts & Lee (2004) and Trencher et al. (2013) by Rinaldi et al. (2018).

"Co-creation for sustainability" represents a radical paradigm shift in the academy. The academy does not only contribute to economic and social development via technology transfer and entrepreneurialism, but it also collaborates with different stakeholders with the aim of materializing sustainable development (Trencher et al., 2013). In Table 14.3, we see how the literature defines the third and fourth missions (Betts and Lee, 2004; Trencher et al., 2013) and how the universities' roles over time have evolved together from the framework of third mission economic-driven activities to more sustainability-driven activities.

Applying the insights from literature and outside experience to ReCAS

None of the publications that were reviewed in Table 14.3 referred to the green-field project of actually creating a new college in a geographic region that lies very far from centers of academic tradition and that intends to serve a community of learners and stakeholders who have an indigenous rural background. In reviewing the literature, the authors could find just one report by Van Lopik (2013) on learning sustainability in a tribal college context. However, the content and concepts put forward in the literature can be directly transferred to what ReCAS stands for. For example, the college is talking about these things but "walking the talk" (Collins & Gannon, 2014) and plans to assume the role of an incubator for ethics and sustainable development projects. In addition, ReCAS has an audience that is eager and ready to use all the new opportunities ReCAS brings to the region. The region's population possesses an intrinsic understanding of their ecosystem and how it could be improved for shifting the level of well-being, thus no "marketing" of the idea or buy-in is needed. Adding to this is the valuable body of traditional knowledge that ReCAS has on its doorsteps. This can be systemically used to develop a mindset that goes beyond the intellectual and the technical and that makes use of what traditional and indigenous knowledge contribute to supporting biodiversity conservation and its sustainable and equitable use.

Traditional and indigenous knowledge related to biodiversity is central to elucidating its status and to developing community participation with regard to the way biodiversity is conserved and used. In a region like the Upper East of Ghana, this knowledge can be combined with appropriate technology (not "state-of-the art") to cut back soil erosion and increase the availability of water. This will enhance biodiversity-dependent services such as provision of food and fiber, purification of water and air. ReCAS is not only aware of the tactical knowledge but also poised to spread and incorporate this as part of the cultural and spiritual values that are key to human well-being and sustainable development. This integration of knowledge, culture and values concurs precisely with the main assertions in the mission statement of the UNESCO-wide Biodiversity Initiative. The UNESCO report on traditional knowledge contributions for innovation in learning systems for sustainability states the following:

> *Learning about biodiversity, about how traditional and indigenous holders of biodiversity-related knowledge cope with biodiversity, how this knowledge is used to effectively manage biodiversity and to maintain ecosystem services at various scales, as well as which are the most appropriate approaches to promote education and raise further awareness on these issues – all of this has been part and parcel of the mission.*
>
> *(Unnikrishnan and Fadeeva, 2013, p. 3; see also*
> *Fadeeva and Mochizuki, 2010)*

ReCAS is actively taking up this mission. The college has the opportunity to make a difference because it is building common grassroots experience in its activities.

'Common experience' has been practically applied in many ventures on sustainability that include colleges and the community. Developing and cultivating a common intellectual conversation across the campus and fostering a sense of togetherness across the campus and extended community connects and inspires people from diverse backgrounds. This contributes to changing behavior and policies, building scientific understanding, connecting local environmental issues to academic themes, and reshaping values – components that are crucial to sustainability education (López, 2013; Molnar et al., 2011).

Local environmental issues and social issues in the community have induced ReCAS to start with developing programs not just for academic purposes, but those that can be applied and incorporated into the community. As seen from the CCCESD that commenced with an outreach to the community before the academic program, the college in essence has aimed at strong engagement with stakeholders from the very beginning. For example, the CCCESD, while the accreditation process for the college's new ethics department was still waiting to be conducted, prepared an array of short courses that could be offered to the communities of the Upper East Region. In pursuit of this, an initial study was conducted regarding which topics would receive the best and highest interest – ranging from ethics in labor relations and community relations to diversity management and sustainable development in agriculture and infrastructure. To corroborate the findings, interviews were held with key stakeholders in the region: business owners, business managers, assembly members, heads of government authorities, civil service personnel, directors of education, school teachers, health service personnel, religious leaders and heads of NGOs. They were asked, among other questions, which (additional) course content they would suggest and for which or whom it should be applied. From this series of interviews came four interesting outcomes: (1) over-population, (2) codes of conduct for law enforcement, (3) ethical conduct in business, and (4) dealing with the mainly small Chinese foreign enterprises which illegally exploit banks of streams and rivers for mining gold. Apart from a culture clash, there seems to be a potential for conflict in this regard that could be solved through persuasion, dialogue and consensual developing of solutions to the problem.

Awareness of conflicts is nothing new in the population of Ghana's Upper East, as in many other African regions which have a long history of hostility among tribes, with foreigners and migrants from other regions (Miller, Vandome, and McBrewster, 2009). For overcoming conflicts, it is essential that the local populace respect each other. With this in mind, the programs of ReCAS are designed to support students and the community stakeholders to reflect on their own personal beliefs, passion and ethos and at the same time on those of others. This stresses the logic of ethical theory. Beyond providing knowledge and skills, there is an emphasis on developing civic leadership for collective impact. Ethical and sustainable development starts with reflecting on one's own mindset and contributing to organic change of the society one lives in. The platform offered by ReCAS focuses on combining academic research with practical training. The CCCESD will provide topics, concepts and solutions which are applicable to all situations in everyday life and in all professional and societal environments. From this logic, the teaching content of the CCCESD is connected to the other departments of ReCAS, and the CCCESD shares its program with them through interdisciplinary work and exchange of lecturers.

Interdisciplinary work is imperative when forging alliances not just between the departments of the college but with stakeholders in the community as well. The common denominator is ethics and sustainable development. Striving for improved standards in ethics and sustainable development is of high value, and it relates closely to the high aspirations of the sustainability mindset framework applied through the Principles of Management Education Sustainability Mindset Working Group (PRME SM Working Group) (Rimanoczy, 2013), which is the overarching topic of this book. Systemic thinking, spirituality, ecological concern and emotional intelligence, which are ingredients of the framework, are all in the spirit of the CCCESD program. This spirit creates a sense of sensitivity, builds knowledge, provides soft skills, enhances judgement and raises will-power for ethical and sustainability concerns as per the six objectives of the CCCESD in the mission previously displayed. This concurs with the objectives as described in the sustainability mindset framework of the UN PRME SM Working Group. This framework notes three dimensions that need to be employed for attaining these objectives. They are values, knowledge and competency, connected in a sequence: values, which are manifested (e.g., in the ecological perspective of sustainable development, by biospheric orientation), evolve into knowledge (e.g., ecoliteracy), and on this, competency is built (e.g. protective/restorative action) (Kassel, Rimanoczy, and Mitchell, 2016).

The PRME SM Working Group's concept stands out from the other frameworks that connect to the notion of sustainability mindset that can be found in the literature and online. Briefly, the first area is in the concept of a "Matrix Map" developed by Zimmerman and Bell (2014), which mainly addresses non-profit sustainability, offering non-profit professionals a step-by-step guide to move their organization towards the intersection of exceptional impact and financial viability. While the concept engages leadership in setting a non-profit organization's strategy, it does not attempt to disperse the elements of the mindset beyond this leadership group. The focus is on implementing a strategic tool and on measuring impact (Zimmerman and Bell, 2014, pp. 164–166). The impact measurement tool, however, is restricted to monetary terms, which is certainly important for an organization that needs to render accounts to stakeholders; ReCAS and the CCCESD will unquestionably have to take this up in due course. For the time being, impact measurement has to aim at non-financial outcomes of the programs and projects as will be set forth later.

The other notion of the term "sustainability mindset" comes up in a post on the Project Syndicate Opinion Page (www.project-syndicate.org) by Nobel laureate Michael Spence. Spence argues that for many people sustainability is associated with finite natural resources and the environment and the fear that the planet's natural resources and recuperative capacities will not withstand the pressure. For this to be reverted, Spence says, it makes no sense trying to change the existing economic growth model globally, as there is no alternative at present to which we can all switch. The only solution lies with inventing a new growth model over time, step-by-step, for which the two key ingredients are education and values. If sustainability is to triumph, it must be predominantly a bottom–up process, driven by and driving local innovation, altering lifestyles, and shifting social norms and business behavior (Spence, 2012). This is exactly what ReCAS attempts to do: helping to create improvements for the local society by efforts endeavored by this society on its own. But Spence's argumentation does not provide the tools for achieving a shift of values and of what would follow from this shift. It is the PRME SM Working Group framework that indeed provides pathways to both.

The pathways pointed out by the PRME SM Working Group framework follow from the sequence of the three dimensions on which it has been developed:

Values: (being) => Knowledge (thinking) => Competency (acting).

The authors of the framework proceed very carefully, taking account of the high potential of categorization among these dimensions – like inclinations such as a sense of *interconnectedness, oneness with all that is*, and *biospheric orientation*, which may superficially appear to overlap, as might *systems theory* and *ecoliteracy* (Kassel, Rimanoczy, and Mitchell, 2016, p. 29). This viewpoint strengthens the framework's validity, because all of these inclinations and their relations to each other occur in practice. If we just take the limited "biosphere" of the community around ReCAS, we find interconnections (e.g., between upholding family cohesion and caring for nature) that apply to the values (maintaining indigenous tradition), knowledge (applying indigenous wisdom) and competency (implementing newly acquired skills and technology without sacrificing tradition). A good framework is applicable on all levels, as is the case with the PRME SM Working Group: This can be seen if we move from the level of the community surroundings of ReCAS to the level of the World Business Council for Sustainable Development (WBCSD). There we would find that the sequence of values => knowledge => competency embraces the many interlinkages between the nine pathways of which the WBCSD outlines that they could ultimately lead to a more sustainable world. They are "values and behaviors", "human development", "economy", "agriculture", "forests", "energy and power", "buildings", "mobility" and "materials" (World Business Council for Sustainable Development, 2010, p. 10). On both the small scale and on the large scale, multi-dimensionality and interconnectedness are the predominant features of sustainable development.

The direction of thought that is pursued by the PRME SM Working Group concurs with what has been set up to be the relevant skills for education on sustainable development by the *Partnership for 21st Century Learning* ("P21", a coalition bringing together the US business community, education leaders, and policymakers; see www.p21.org):

- Ways of thinking. Creativity, critical thinking, problem-solving, decision-making and learning.
- Ways of working. Communication and collaboration.
- Tools for working. Information and communications technology (ICT) and information literacy.

P21 has called this "Skills for living in the world" (Bell, 2016, p. 56). Skills for living in the world is precisely what ReCAS intends to provide to its community. The founders of ReCAS feel that there is a demand for the wide area of knowledge that the CCCESD inspires and that this demand goes beyond the boundaries of the District of Bolgatanga and the Upper East Region: the academic program that will follow up on the outreach agenda of the CCCESD will complement many of the programs offered throughout the educational system of Ghana ReCAS and the CCCESD, which were built with a comprehensive approach which is not present in other schools. Currently, ReCAS has a co-operation with the University of Development Studies in Tamale. However, ReCAS, as a small establishment, must continue to develop more partnerships and co-operations. Further joint ventures will be sought with universities and Ethics Centers in Ghana and abroad. Potential target groups from outside the academic world are any professionals or laypeople who want to acquire knowledge and skills for building ethics and social responsibility programs, for managing sustainable development projects and/or for becoming specialists in the field.

Attempting an early assessment

ReCAS had planned a large event including a number of key stakeholders and high-profile personalities for the initial launch of its outreach program. In preparation for this, a communal decision on what to offer, and when, was established with the principal stakeholders that had been identified as addressees. Information about the center was also given through radio interviews and meetings with some of the public. The original idea was to promote the program by giving a first set of short courses for free to a specific group of people (police officers, health workers, government officers), but this idea was rejected because it turned out that both the employers and the participants were willing and ready to pay a fee for this training. This being a region of very low incomes, the willingness to pay right away can potentially be seen as a first positive result: the offer was clearly valued. However, some of this could perhaps be attributed to the expectation that it would boost the individual's career development. As of this writing, registrations were expected for the following ten short courses:

Short Course Topics on the Initial Launch of the University

1	Transparency and Accountability in the Public Service
2	Ethics in the Workplace
3	Sustainable Development and Sustainability Management
4	Conflict Resolution Management (Three Modules)
5	Conflicts/Moral Dilemmas in Sustainable Development
6	Practicing Business Ethics and Corporate Social Responsibility
7	Cultural Identity and Consciousness
8	Cultural Diversity/Cross Cultural Issues
9	Human Rights
10	Social Inclusiveness

In order to connect the short courses to the academic program in ethics that would start in 2017/18, incentives for participants were given that allowed the participant to upgrade or apply the qualifications they received in the short courses to a designated degree program.

Additionally, the surveys conducted with the local communities uncovered that there is a demand for assistance from the CCCESD in solving problems that exist in specific areas. The CCCESD thus offered to provide expert knowledge as well as support in project management for the following:

Topics for Project Support Given by the CCCESD to Resolve Community Needs

1	Community–Corporate partnerships for infrastructure development projects
2	How to develop concepts for sustainable development projects
3	Maintenance culture for enhancing sustainable development
4	Food security and appropriate infrastructure for sustainable development

The impact of the courses, the workshops and the projects will largely depend on the success of not only transmitting what the mindset should be for changes and progress in ethical and sustainability issues, but of also ensuring that the mindset does indeed adapt to what people are recognizing to be new requirements. We use the term "adapt" because along the lines explicated above, there has always existed a positive inclination in the population of the region (as is the case in most African rural regions) to take up biodiversity themes and of topics that improve how they live together in their communities. A checklist to be applied for measuring the impact could be taken from Ross (2010):

Are there outcomes that. . .

- demonstrate responsiveness to the region's historical, political, social and economic circumstances and priority needs;

- clearly integrate social development, empowerment, partnerships with grass-roots organizations and non-professionals as well as citizen participation;
- prioritize commitment to serving vulnerable communities and taking a stand against social injustice, inequality, oppression and marginalization;
- display sensitivity to local cultural values and practices;
- place an emphasis on and foster communal and community-based networks;
- are holistic in approaching all features of the "person-in-environment";
- are delivering appropriate theories, teaching materials, curricula and authentic procedures that correspond to what is rooted in local systems.

This list of impacts sets the bar very high for all endeavors to promote ethics and sustainable development anywhere – not just in ReCAS. ReCAS has established an outcome assessment program for the academic programs, and as soon as there is sufficient data for a representative number of CCCESD projects, impact assessments to be conducted. The founders of the college are dedicated to uncovering and discovering any areas that will help determine how to move forward.

In the short run, it might appear attractive to conduct assessments on the direct activities presently provided by the Center. However, there is a cautionary note to conducting short-term assessments: focusing only on the measurement of activities can lead to concentrating on issues of which their ultimate outcomes cannot be detected (Molas-Gallart et al., 2002). Thus, in assessing short-term goals, the CCCESD will focus on activities that can at least be connected to certain objectives. This (primary) assessment, which has been used by educational institutions for their "third mission activities", should be prudently applied. A good methodology presented by Molas-Gallart et al. (2002) suggests to examine the capabilities that lie beneath activities. The method distinguishes between the exploitation and use of existing capabilities (for teaching and research) and of those that are developed for the specific purpose of the additional mission.

However, to start the process, the CCCESD must first identify which are the essential capabilities (e.g., physical capabilities like infrastructure and knowledge capabilities). In an area like the Upper East Region, facilities such as faculty libraries, test rigs and computer centers, and more rooms and buildings for teaching and workshop programs will always remain a challenge due to funding and logistics. The CCCESD might also need more off-campus training and workshop rooms, as well as transportation to the off-campus facilities. In the region where the CCCESD is located, venues would need to be provided to facilitate the process of conducting surveys in the community (for which personal interviews are needed in most cases) and to have a center to connect with other institutions. These two examples demonstrate the contrast between Northern Ghana and regions which have a well-developed logistics infrastructure.

In regard to knowledge capabilities, there will be processes which will capture different forms of "knowledge stock", from the tacit knowledge and skills embodied in the faculty to codified knowledge as represented by reports and publications, software, procedures, business methods, and research methods and techniques.

316 Helen Akolgo-Azupogo et al.

A special emphasis, then, must be on how these capabilities are employed to shape and influence the relationship between the college and the society in its environment, as well as the storing and capturing of this knowledge for future employees and operations.

Conclusion

ReCAS is a new college in a previously underserved area. Ultimately, employing all capabilities to shape and influence the relationship between ReCAS and the society in its environment will be the key to the success of ReCAS. A key advantage of ReCAS and its CCESD is that the principal persons to direct operations and activities are locals and thus closely intertwined with the social network of the constituency – they in essence have a long and established vested interest and understanding, unlike other faculty that needed to be brought in from competing colleges at other institutions. Other factors that will be important for the success of ReCAS and the CCCESD are "broadcasting" the CCCESD's programs and results. Although the region lacks the traditional means to promote programs such as newspapers or journals, having indigenous members of the community as the key players in the operation provides a word-of-mouth network.

A distinct advantage that ReCAS has in its new venture, which is often a decisive success factor in sub-Saharan Africa, is what is termed the 'non-individualistic character' of this culture, for example, by Jesse N.K. Mugambi, renowned Kenyan theologian and ethics professor, who said: "*Community is the cornerstone in African thought and life*" (Stückelberger and Mugambi, 2007, p. vi). This perspective gives the most hope for the ReCAS initiatives on cross-cultural ethics and sustainable development.

For universities and other institutions to achieve success with their sustainability programs and create a sustainability mindset, they must incorporate it into every aspect of their operation and development. In the case of ReCAS, this mindset has been integrated into the thinking and operations from the onset. ReCAS challenges, as well as its distinct success, lies in its ability to weave this thinking and perspective into the prevailing cultures of the region and people. In already established institutions and universities in particular, there is a need to incorporate this thinking and actions into their mission and establish means to implement it (e.g., service learning, internships, operating procedures, new building, etc.). All participants within a university or organization must consider the impact on sustainability in all of its decisions and operations.

References

Amaral, M., Ferreira, A., & Teodoro, P. (2011). Building an entrepreneurial university in brazil: The role and potential of university-industry linkages in promoting regional economic development. *Industry and Higher Education, 25*(5), 383–395.

Anders, G. (1992). The changing role of the public university in local economic development. *Economic Development Review, 10*(4), 76–79.

Banga Chhokar, K. (2010). Higher education and curriculum innovation for sustainable development in India. *International Journal of Sustainability in Higher Education, 11*(2), 141–152.

Bell, D.V. (2016). Twenty-first century education: Transformative education for sustainability and responsible citizenship. *Journal of Teacher Education for Sustainability, 18*(1), 48–56.

Bening, R. B. (1990). *A history of education in northern Ghana, 1907–1976.* Accra: Ghana Universities Press.

Betts, J. R., & Lee, C. W. B. (2004, February). Universities as Drivers of Regional and National Innovation: An Assessment of the Linkages from Universities to Innovation and Economic Growth, Paper presented at the Conference "Higher Education in Canada", John Deutsch Institute Conference, Queens University, Kingston, Ontario, Canada, 1–59.

Cebrián, G., Marcus, G., and Humphris, D. (2013). Organisational learning towards sustainability in higher education. *Sustainability Accounting, Management and Policy Journal, 4*(3), 285–306.

Chhokar, B. K. (2010). Higher education and curriculum innovation for sustainable development in India. *International Journal of Sustainability in Higher Education, 11*(2), 141–152.

Clark, B. (1998). *Creating entrepreneurial universities: Organizational pathways of transformation.* Oxford, UK: IAU Press and Pergamon.

Cole, E. J., & Fieselman, L. (2013). A community-based social marketing campaign at Pacific University Oregon. *International Journal of Sustainability in Higher Education, 14*(2), 176–195.

Collins, D., & Gannon, A. (2014). Walking the eco-talk movement: Higher education institutions as sustainability incubators. *Organization & Environment, 27*(1), 16.

Cook, R., & Cutting, R. (2014). "Low-impact communities" and their value to experiential education for sustainability in higher education. *Journal of Adventure Education and Outdoor Learning, 14*(3), 247–260.

Etzkowitz, H. (1998). The norms of entrepreneurial science: Cognitive effects of the new university – industry linkages. *Research Policy, 27*, 823–833.

Etzkowitz, H., & Leydesdorff, L. (2000). The dynamics of innovation: From national systems and "Mode 2" to a triple Helix of University-Industry-Government relations. *Research Policy, 29*, 109–123.

Fadeeva, Z., & Mochizuki, Y. (2010). Roles of regional centres of expertise on education for sustainable development: Lessons learnt in the first half of the UNDESD. *Journal of Education for Sustainable Development, 4*(1), 51–59.

Figueredo, F. R., & Tsarenko, Y. (2013). Is "being green" a determinant of participation in university sustainability initiatives? *International Journal of Sustainability in Higher Education, 14*(3), 242–253.

Ghana Statistical Service. (2013). *2010 population and housing census: Regional analytical report.* Retrieved from www.statsghana.gov.gh/docfiles/2010phc/National_Analytical_Report.pdf

Hunter, C. P. (2013). Shifting themes in OECD country reviews of higher education. *Higher Education, 66*(6), 707–723.

Kagawa, F. (2007). Dissonance in students' perceptions of sustainable development and sustainability: Implications for curriculum change. *International Journal of Sustainability in Higher Education, 8*(3), 317–338.

Kassel, K., Rimanoczy, I., & Mitchell, S. (2016). *The sustainable mindset: Connecting being, thinking, and doing in management education.* Submission #16659 to the 2016 Academy of Management Annual Meeting.

Khalaf-Kairouz, L. (2012). Education for sustainable development at Notre Dame University – Louaize: Environmental science curriculum – a pre-phase to the Rucas Project on Education for Sustainable Development. *Discourse and Communication for Sustainable Education, 3*(1), 121.

Kretz, A., & Sá, C. (2013). Third stream, fourth mission: Perspectives on university engagement with economic relevance. *Higher Education Policy, 26*(4), 497–506.

Krizek, K. J., Newport, D., White, J., & Townsend, A. R. (2012). Higher education's sustainability imperative: how to practically respond?. *International Journal of Sustainability in Higher Education, 13*(1), 19-33.

Kurland, N. B. (2011). Evolution of a campus sustainability network: A case study in organizational change. *International Journal of Sustainability in Higher Education, 12*(4), 395–429. doi:http://dx.doi.org/10.1108/14676371111168304

Laninga, T., Austin, G., & McClure, W. (2011). Community-university partnerships in small-town Idaho: Addressing diverse community needs through interdisciplinary outreach and engagement. *Journal of Community Engagement and Scholarship, 4*(2), 5–17.

López, O. S. (2013). Creating a sustainable university and community through a common experience. *International Journal of Sustainability in Higher Education, 14*(3), 291–309.

Madeira, A. C., Carravilla, M. A., Oliveira, J. F., & Costa, C. A. V. (2011). A methodology for sustainability evaluation and reporting in higher education institutions. *Higher Education Policy, 24*(4), 459–479.

Miller, F. P., Vandome, A. F., & McBrewster, J. (Eds.). (2009). *History of Ghana.* Saarbrücken, Germany: Alphascript Publishing

Molas-Gallart, J., Salter, A., Patel, P., Scott, A., & Duran, X. (2002). Measuring Third Stream Activities: Final Report of the Russell Group of Universities, SPRU Science and Technology Policy Research Unity, University of Sussex.

Molnar, C., Ritz, T., Heller, B., & Solecki, W. (2011). Using higher education-community partnerships to promote urban sustainability. *Environment, 53*(1), 19.

Rinaldi, C., Cavicchi, A., Spigarelli, F., Lacché, A., & Rubens, A.(2018). Universities and smart specialization strategy: From third mission to sustainable development co-creation. *International Journal of Sustainability and Higher Education, 19*(1), 67–84.

Rimanoczy, I., (2013). *Big bang being: Developing the sustainability mindset.* Sheffield Greenleaf Publishing.

Ross, E. (2010). African spirituality, ethics and traditional healing – implications for indigenous South African social work education and practice. *South African Journal of Business and Law, 3*(1), 44–51.

Russell, J. F., & Flynn, R. B. (2001). Setting the stage for collaboration. *Peabody Journal of Education, 75*, 1–5.

Spence, M. (2012). The sustainability mindset. *Project Syndicate.* Retrieved from www.project-syndicate.org/commentary/the-sustainability-mindset

Strier, R. (2014). Fields of paradox: University-community partnerships. *Higher Education, 68*(2), 155–165.

Stückelberger, C., & Mugambi, J. N. (2007). *Responsible leadership. Global and contextual ethical perspectives.* Geneva: Globethics. Net/World Council of Churches Publications.

Trencher, G., Bai, X., Evans, J., McCormick, K., & Yarime, M. (2014b). University partnerships for co-designing and co-producing urban sustainability. *Global Environmental Change, 28*, 153–165.

Trencher, G. P., Yarime, M., & Kharrazi, A. (2013), Co-creating sustainability: Cross-sector university collaborations for driving sustainable urban transformations. *Journal of Cleaner Production, 40*–55.

Trencher, G., Yarime, M., McCormick, K. B., Doll, C. N., & Kraines, S. B. (2014a). Beyond the third mission: Exploring the emerging university function of co-creation for sustainability. *Science and Public Policy, 41*(2), pp. 151–179.

U.N. General Assembly. (1987). *Our common future: World commission on environment and development*. Oxford: Oxford University Press.

Unnikrishnan, P. M., & Fadeeva, Z. (2013). *Innovation in local and global learning systems for sustainability: Traditional knowledge and biodiversity – learning contributions of the regional centres of expertise on education for sustainable development*. Yokohama: United Nations University Institute of Advanced Studies.

Van Lopik, W. (2013). Learning sustainability in a tribal college context. In P. F. Barlett & G. W. Chase (Eds.), *Sustainability in higher education: Stories and strategies for transformation* (pp. 107–114). Cambridge, MA: MIT Press.

Vincent, S., & Focht, W. (2009). US higher education environmental program managers' perspectives on curriculum design and core competencies. *International Journal of Sustainability in Higher Education, 10*(2), 164–183.

Wade, R. (2013). Regional Centres of Expertise (RCEs). In S. Sterling, L. Maxey, & H. Luna (Eds.), *The sustainable university: Progress and prospects* (pp. 89–109). Abingdon, UK: Routledge.

World Business Council for Sustainable Development (WBCSD). (2010). *Vision 2050: The new agenda for business*. Geneva: WBCSD.

Xypaki, M. (2015). A practical example of integrating sustainable development into higher education: Green dragons, city university London students' union. *Local Economy, 30*(3), 316–329.

Yarime, M., Trencher, G., Mino, T., Scholz, R. W., Olsson, L., Ness, B., & Rotmans, J. (2012). Establishing sustainability science in higher education institutions: Towards an integration of academic development, institutionalization, and stakeholder collaborations. *Sustainability Science, 7*(1), 101–113.

Zimmerman, S., & Bell, J. (2014). *The sustainability mindset: Using the matrix map to make strategic decisions*. San Francisco: Jossey-Bass.

15

DEVELOPING THE ABILITIES FOR TOMORROW

What liberal arts can contribute to management education

Mary Grace Neville

Introduction

Business continues to rise in popularity as a preferred college major among undergraduate students worldwide. Industry recruiters and parents alike want colleges and universities to ready young people for first jobs, thus universities face market pressure to increase the number of pre-professional degree programs they offer. However, our complex, multicultural, and rapidly changing world increasingly needs professionals who can think critically, anticipate multigenerational outcomes, and reason through uncharted circumstances. Technology, geo-political complexity, systemic environmental issues, and booming populations continue to challenge society, and therefore challenge businesses within society. But undergraduate business education programs too often concentrate on teaching tools and frameworks, without companion thinking skills. It is a chronically siloed approach often devoid of the human caring dimensions that are crucial for addressing ethical problems in society (i.e., Adler, 2002; Bennis & O'Toole, 2005; Donaldson, 2002; Ghosal, 2005; Giacalone, 2004; Mintzberg, 2004; Mitroff & Swanson, 2004; Navarro, 2008). Unfortunately, one study even found that average American undergraduate business majors emerged from college less ethical than when they entered (Lamp, 1997). Undergraduate students of all majors (traditionally 18–23 years old) are at a sensitive cognitive development level where they are primed for either: expanding their awareness of others, their agility at entertaining multiple paradigms simultaneously, and their ability to draw on philosophy, science, literature, and history as a means for imagining new possibilities; or truncating their ethical reasoning, which accentuates their preference for self at the expense of other and fails to cultivate curiosity for that which is yet to be defined (Neville & Godwin, 2011). Therefore, educators and institutions must change how we do our business, the business of undergraduate business education.

Students, parents, and legislators alike seek near-term, quantifiable, and financial-centric metrics for assessing a college education's value. Yet many societal issues – citizenship, practice of democracy, eco-sustainability, courage – exist on long-term horizons. Rather than institutionally competing on short-term reductionist dimensions (those things that can be measured quickly, such as job-placement rate within six months of graduation, or course offerings addressing the latest market fad), colleges and universities need to reconsider who education serves. If higher education were to re-conceptualize the customer not as students today but as the larger society of tomorrow, then business educators would have to shift what educators deliver today in service of who students will actually become as citizens of tomorrow. Clearly, doing so would require a change of consciousness. Cost-benefit analysis of a college degree would not be based on salary after graduation, but instead on levels of integrity and engaged citizenry in society. Collectively, the evaluation metric for business education could eventually become global social well-being fostered for future generations.

Indeed, a "liberal arts" philosophy of education already advocates today's experience for tomorrow's well-being (Christenson & Eyring, 2011; Colby, Ehrlich, Sullivan, & Dolle, 2011; Neville & Godwin, 2011; Giacalone, 2004). The Association of American Colleges and Universities defines "liberal arts" as an education

> that prepares us to live responsible, productive, and creative lives in a dramatically changing world. It is an education that fosters a well-grounded intellectual resilience, a disposition toward lifelong learning, and an acceptance of responsibility for the ethical consequences of our ideas and action.
>
> *(AAC&U, 1998)*

Therefore, designing and delivering undergraduate business education through a liberal arts lens has the potential to appease the fear-based need for a "practical" degree while also honoring the larger world's need for imaginative and integrity-driven citizen-leaders across increasingly interdependent and realistically interconnected realms of the world. The theory makes sense, but making the requisite consciousness changes to implement the theory presents enormous challenges.

This chapter profiles a seven-year, multi-stakeholder inquiry into the question: What 'ought' we teach at the undergraduate business level in order to cultivate high-integrity citizen-leaders of tomorrow? Far beyond content literacy, findings suggest that educators can approach students in terms of capacity building. The approach builds on liberal arts education philosophies and objectives, and requires a shift in priorities.

What goes into a college education?

No one seems to disagree that education is important; however, perceptions about the type and purpose of that education vary significantly. At one end of the continuum is the assertion that young adults benefit most from technical training for job readiness. This approach is reflected in most technical colleges, in certificate programs, and in high-school equivalency degrees. At the university level, a Bachelor of Science (BS) and Bachelor of Business Administration (BBA) degree tend to emphasize technical skills. Given that business (aggregating the wide varieties of business and management majors) continues to rise as the most popular among college majors, tomorrow's world is heavily influenced by who comes through the business education pipeline today. Therefore, accrediting agencies began ensuring that students had some exposure to broader concepts than their major by instituting general education distribution requirements (Khurana, 2007; Neville, Godwin, Senchack, & Parks, 2007). For believers in time-to-job-market as the best metric for a "good" business education, this combination can appear to be a compromise.

However, at the other end of the continuum is the philosophy that 18–23-year-olds need to develop their abilities to absorb, critique, compare, and imagine. The most extreme is the study of Great Books (e.g., Plato and Dante studied in full text), literature, music, and art, deemed central to a culture's traditions. Through the experience of a Great Books curriculum, small group discussions, and faculty-directed tutorials, students build a reservoir of understanding and wisdom, which they then apply by attending professional training programs such as law school or medical school after graduation. In ancient Greece, this approach was the origin of liberal arts education, one that prepared the elite for leadership roles in politics, law, science, medicine, and business. Modern versions of American liberal arts colleges are concentrated in the country's Northeast, are residential and located in rural or suburban areas, have religious origins, offer small class sizes, tout low student-to-teacher ratios, and offer only theoretical (not applied) majors. For example, economics is considered theoretical and business is applied; math is theoretical and engineering is applied; chemistry and biology are theoretical, nursing or medicine is applied. The most traditional liberal arts college graduates receive a Bachelor of Arts (BA) degree, which refers to the breadth of courses (including languages, humanities, arts, social, and natural sciences) complemented by depth in one area. Therefore, finding business programs granting BA degrees within liberal arts colleges is quite rare; more common is the granting of a Bachelor of Science (BS) degree, one with fewer liberal arts courses and more technical courses. This makes sense when realizing that students "consider liberal arts courses, such as foreign language and political science, as simply 'filler' courses until they begin to take the business courses that they view as important after graduation" (Martinez, Padmanabhan, & Toyne, 2007, p. 42). Yet, these very same liberal arts courses would arguably expand the capacities discussed earlier that 21st-century business claims to want (Colby, Ehrlich, Sullivan, & Dolle, 2011; Neville et al., 2007; Neville & Godwin, 2011). This discouraging reality fits with historical and contextual trends, which Christensen and Eyring (2011) and Khurana (2007) trace in business education's changes over time. At best, faculty offer bridges to others' courses; at worst, students perceive their general education requirement as boxes to be checked (Chew & McInnis-Bowers, 2004).

Two colleagues and I joined a liberal arts college in the American South in order to reinvent the business major, a popular applied program among students and yet ironically embedded in the theoretical Department of Economics within the social science division of the college. There was no business "school." The small program had historical roots in BBA philosophy, training students for accounting and management careers while ensuring that they had exposure to small courses. We three believed that instead of training, these young adults would be better served in the near and long term by expanding their full human potential – not just towards doing but also towards deepened concepts of being that would include systems intelligence, emotional intelligence, and spiritual intelligence. In fact, we were seeing the critical need for the expansion of capacities we would years later learn about as "sustainable mindset" (Rimanoczy, 2014). At the time, 2004, we only knew the potential of a "liberal arts" philosophy that encourages thinking across content domains, critically inquiring into what is presented as truth and reasoning abilities to imagine and design new alternative realities. These abilities appeared to us as critical for enriching tomorrow's world, not just among political scientists and art historians, but also among students choosing to enter business. In 1998 the Association of American Colleges and Universities (AAC&U) had defined "liberal arts" broadly enough that business could not only belong in a BA curriculum, but that business *needed* to be approached from the liberal arts roots.

Therefore, we opened the strategic question among ourselves – what "ought" we be teaching and doing at the undergraduate level? We hoped we could simply benchmark our program against others' who had presumably asked and answered our same questions and begin delivering this future-oriented experience, but we found only a few innovators and faint threads of academic questioning. In fact, we found philosophical resistance to our ideas even among our own college's faculty, especially among humanities colleagues who traditionally perceived their disciplines as pure and central content. But more than content needed to change. The fundamental way in which higher education operates needed to be re-examined.

Seven-year inquiry: what "ought" to be

We designed an iterative, action-research approach using appreciative inquiry principles (Cooperrider & Whitney, 2001). The multi-year, multi-stakeholder dialogue generated the model that our small program began to use as our lens for curricular design, for in-class conversations with students about all of their courses, and for prospective students (and their parents) to understand the difference between our program and the larger, cheaper, more technically focused programs nearby.

Our **discovery phase** extended over nearly a year. We combed literature for philosophical and historical thinking and initiated conversations with every business–liberal arts champion we found. (For in-depth discussions of liberal education, see Kimball, 1996, 2003; for emergent innovations of liberal arts thinking applied to business curricula, see Colby, Erlich, Sullivan, & Dolle, 2011; for pedagogical approaches that build on Colby et al.'s framework, see the 2015 Special Issue of the *Journal of Management Education*; for foundational insights about blending liberal arts philosophy and business education, see McInnis-Bower & Chew, 2008, and

Nesteruk, 2005; for more general discussion of education philosophy applied to management, see Beatty, Leigh, & Dean, 2009.) Simultaneously, we convened focus groups with stakeholders including students and parents; alumni, both young and experienced; employee representatives, including recruiters and executives from diverse economic sectors; and interested colleagues from traditional liberal arts fields (e.g., philosophy, languages, literature, natural sciences). We also conducted an in-depth virtual survey of 53 teacher-scholars in colleges nationwide, people who were experimenting with various educational innovation projects. We analyzed these data in order to build a portrait of our status quo, including beliefs and values, curricular objectives, existing and emergent activities, and obstacles to systemic change.

That conceptual portrait became the content platform for a three-day, face-to-face design summit with a sub-group of the nationwide stakeholders involved to date (Godwin & Neville, 2008). The summit began by designing an ideal of what every college graduate "ought" to know or be able to do, and then began to tailor the ideas for business majors in particular (Neville et al., 2007). Colleague-researchers and I then worked iteratively on the design findings for two years in order to build a model for delivering the concepts to our current and future students.

We sought to understand emergent themes in the context of our experiences – as teachers and as former corporate managers. We built themes following a narrative analysis research approach. Then we returned to the literature to enrich our definitions and understanding of the themes. In addition, we drew on what CEOs were advocating both in the popular press and in academic research. In this way, we built the resulting Capacity Map (see Figure 15.1), a framework of four dominant capacity domains that is reliable when reviewed both with stakeholders and in light of secondary research. The capacities were consensually validated and deepened through conference presentations, discussion, and feedback, including an 18-month dialogue convened by the Aspen Institute and centered on the Carnegie Foundation's Business, Entrepreneurship, and Liberal Learning project.

Ultimately, we found overwhelming reasons to conceptualize student learning in the form of various *capacities*, not just traditional knowledge, skills, and abilities. The capacity approach aligned with a 2007 AAC&U study indicating that workers today need to fully understand problem solving, teamwork and team skills, oral and written communications, systems thinking, critical and analytical thinking, and global issues and perspectives. The integrative capacity approach is congruent with the more recent articulation of our world's need for people with a sustainability mindset (Rimanoczy, 2014), in that the goal of educating for the future is to ready young adults for a reality that "presents paradoxes, ambiguities, uncertainty, lack of data, and a welter of complex variables" (Kassel, Rimanoczy, & Mitchell, 2016, p. 2).

Capacities and competencies

Corporations have increasingly used competency models because such models can make explicit performance criteria and promotion hurdles. Alternatively, capacity

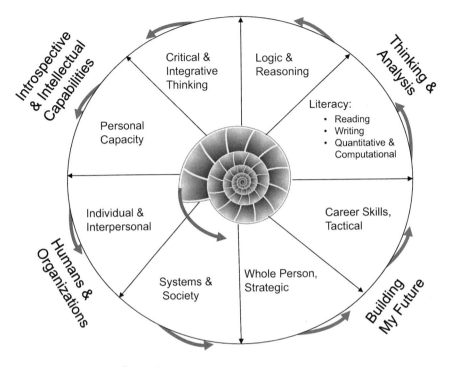

FIGURE 15.1 Personal capacity map

refers to potential that might be developed. Metaphorically, a student might have the capacity to earn high marks in a course if he applied himself, yet only demonstrate average competency on a test if he does not study the materials. (Note: Evers, Rush, and Berdrow (1998) define competencies as knowledge an employee can accomplish at different levels, like mobilizing innovation and change, managing people and tasks, communicating, and managing self. Chyung, Stepich, and Cox (2006) describe competencies as effectiveness towards a performance outcome.) Therefore, we intentionally began using the word *capacity* (rather than competency) to represent our undergraduate objectives – we sought to expand students' capacity for becoming high-integrity citizens of tomorrow, with our secondary objective being the same students' ability to demonstrate defined competency levels at graduation.

Capacities are non-hierarchical; they are interdependent and can create a variety of outcomes depending on strategic choices about how much of which one to emphasize at any given time. Building a sustainability mindset requires that young leaders learn content and also build capacity for life-long adaptive learning. Capacities represent *potential*.

Our study found an explicit call for domain literacy, but little to no consistency on which content elements, which domains, and what proficiency levels of which content mattered (Neville et al., 2007). Ironically, before 2004 when we began inquiring, our business students had only been measured on their mastery of content (even though stakeholders could not agree in 2006 on what levels of mastery they believed would represent an "effective" education). Then we heard themes that led to naming potential capacities. Stakeholders acknowledged the power of social and psychological development, including various forms of sense-making and reasoning. Others called for defining capacity as an intrinsic ability to perceive ideas in relationship to a continuously emerging self-identity. These abilities depended on meta-cognition, the ability to know what one knows, and to accurately and effectively become capable of analyzing and adapting one's mental models towards understanding in new situations. Analyzing what one knows in order to adapt also requires active reflection, a student's ability to intentionally and continuously reflect on and integrate advancing imaginative new possibilities. When pragmatic job-readiness themes kept appearing too, we represented on our map the tension between employability (i.e., ability to get a job) and development of "transferrable" skills (Wilton, 2008). And then, we noted the high degree of interdependence among our themes – no capacity could exist independent of others. Therefore, an effective education would require students to build their agility at shuttling among concepts and courses. We could build blended experiences and attempt interdisciplinary courses, but we were dependent on students choosing to take up the challenge of genuine, paradigmatic changes.

Ultimately, we codified a two-dimensional representation of the complexity we saw. We depended on the assumption that our purpose as educators was to build human capacity, not just transfer content. In fact, the main difference between technical training for what currently is and whole-person development for a sustainable world is a contextual – rather than fragmented – presentation of substance. And so we made explicit the case for approaching undergraduate business from a perspective of liberal arts (Neville & Godwin, 2011). A liberal arts paradigm may not be a panacea for business education woes, but it reliably established a place for my colleagues and me to begin.

Liberal arts capacity map

Approaching business education from a liberal arts mindset depends on educators' beliefs that (a) existing knowledge is insufficient for the challenges of the next generations; (b) human capacity for moral imagination exceeds what we can fathom even though evidence may not yet exist; and (c) real wealth depends on holistic vibrancy at all levels of system (e.g., micro, meso, macro; see Bronfenbrenner, 1979), not just on one's near-term financial profit maximization. From that mindset, business educators have a professional obligation to expand our own approaches to design and deliver disciplinary content in the context of whole-society phenomena, not as fragmented courses to be completed. That obligation requires us to actively engage colleagues *across* disciplinary, industry, and economic sectors, to heighten our own understanding, and thus to more elegantly blend messages we implicitly and explicitly convey to our students. These expectations challenged us; they required us to live beyond our comfort zones, to put future interests that we may never experience ahead of immediate competing metrics and demands, and to become activists for change within our college and classrooms.

The map facilitated our educators' thinking about curricular choices, course design, and content presentation. It helped students to see their general education requirements as integral rather than as boxes to be checked in their degree plan. And it allowed curious, prospective students and parents to see beyond what our industry currently champions – a fast-to-market degree.

The map is intended to be read from the center outwards. It assumes that everyone enters a learning process in a novice state, the center, and with high potential for development, as the spiral pattern moves outwards. The map implies life-long learning as individuals or systems develop beyond the map's outer ring. The four highest-order domains are artificially two-dimensional and assumed to be highly interdependent. Capacity for performance in these domains expands iteratively with theory, experience, and intentional reflection (see Kolb, 1984, for extensive discussion about experiential learning theory). Domains one through three – Thinking and Analysis, Introspection and Intellect, and Humans and Organizations – reflect abilities within the emerging leadership paradigm, sustainability mindset (Rimanoczy, 2014). Domain four repositions the demand for job-readiness training as a capacity for initiating a self-directed discovery, an entrepreneurial spirit. Rather than have students relying on a marketplace to provide them with a job, the domain encourages students to practice taking responsibility for building their own careers.

Domains are portrayed in equal proportion, but that does not imply that all domains should be equally weighted in a course or curricular design. Appropriate weighting depends on an institution's or program's mission and objective.

Domain 1: Thinking and analysis

Traditionally, building literacy has been education's dominant objective. Yet our discussions of what "literacy" meant became increasingly complex through critical reflection. For example, from one perspective, being literate in sustainable management meant understanding biology and ecology; from another perspective, it meant the ability to make responsible and strategic choices within constraints. Therefore, faculty researchers opened the dialogue about literacy to include not only information acquisition but also information comprehension; the domain now named "Thinking and Analysis" includes literacy and logic reasoning. Faculty researchers most frequently identified thinking and analysis as important.

Literacy

Disciplinary literacy includes the vocabulary and conceptual understanding of a specific discipline's concepts, as well as the reading, writing, and numerical skills that enable thinking and innovation. Management and leadership in particular depend on literacy across many business disciplines that are often taught in silos such as marketing, operations, accounting, and finance concepts. Beyond literacy in traditional business function's concepts though, managers benefit from becoming literate in contextual disciplines such as history, literature, philosophy, economics, sociology, psychology, and environmental science. These disciplines expand how people look at the world, and therefore expand how people discern meaning from events and experiences. Twenty-first-century complexity – geopolitically, commercially, socially, environmentally – demands an increased level of moral imagination (the ability to imagine solution possibilities that meet the needs of self and other in responsible ways; see Godwin (2015) on developing moral imagination).

Literacy can be approached in blended ways. For example, one might teach management, literature, philosophy, and history through the Shakespeare play *Othello* (see Hjorth, 2007; Stein, 2005). Short and Ketchen (2005) use Aesop's Fables to teach "timeless truths through classic literature" (p. 816). "Story telling can be an effective device in strategic management education because stories help communicate multidimensional concepts in a concise manner" (p. 817). Bumpus and Burton (2008) introduce a litany of ways teacher-scholars use classic prose in entrepreneurship courses. In addition, Kohn (2013) shifts to history and political life through interpretations of American Founder James Madison's Federalist lessons for teaching management. These are examples of blending multiple constructions of "literacy," which deepen students' experience of the rich interdependencies in the world as well as in content fields.

Technology and information literacy increasingly challenge our world. A survey by the AAC&U (2007, p. 89) reported:

> 82% of employers thought colleges and universities needed to place more emphasis on 'concepts and new development in science and technology,' a fraction similar to those urging greater attention to traditional business concerns, such as teamwork (76%), communication (73%), critical thinking (73%), or global issues (72%).

Balotsky and Christensen (2004) emphasize the importance of technology, both because of the onset of our "information era" and because organizations comprise distance work; they argue that students need to reconcile learning and working. Information literacy requires "determining the information needed, knowing how to access this information, being able to critically select and evaluate the relevant information and sources, and applying this information to the situation at hand" (Henninger & Hurlbert, 2007). A study by Conley and Gil (2011) validates that information literacy is in fact valued in the workplace, although most executives surveyed did not initially know what it was, as the term is not used in business (p. 221). Of the executives, once they understood the concept, 96% agreed (58% strongly agreeing and 38% agreeing) that "an employee's ability to recognize when information is needed as well as have the skills to locate, retrieve, evaluate, and use information ... was of high value in their workplace" (ibid). And 98% of respondents agreed that information literacy was necessary for professional development and promotion (ibid). Frequent reports of "plagiarism, poorly cited information sources, and over-reliance on non-authoritative Web-based sources, however, indicate that more needs to be done to improve the information seeking behavior and utilization of information by students" (Long & Shrikhande, 2007, p. 357). Gilinsky and Robinson (2008) propose concentrating activities on students' information identification and analysis abilities, as well as their research abilities to define and then find useful information. Though these studies refer to individuals' ability to identify and integrate secondary information, our inquiry process participants generally agreed that literacy also includes some form of ability in research methods beyond finding relevant and interpreting secondary information.

Numeracy, which means a comfort with numbers including calculations and quantitative analysis, varies by discipline, but every college graduate should have a basic ability to recognize relationships between numbers (percentages, ratios, significant versus precise numbers, probability, multiples, combinations, etc.). Such skills enable problem solving including the ability to define problems, develop solutions, analyze results, and interpret findings. For example, statistics at a basic level might mean calculations; at an advanced level, it can include the ability to apply a statistical approach to raw data and then to analyze the results with reasonable interpretations and implications. On a basic level, computational literacy means understanding statistics and ratios and the purpose each serves. At a moderate to advanced level, numeracy includes understanding

- why a ratio conveys what it does about a business's financial health or change,
- the implications of a ratio in comparison to benchmarks or industry trends, and
- the potential limitation to a given decision made through numeric analysis alone.

The ability to incorporate judgment into assumptions builds on quantitative analytics, thereby differentiating a student's ability from just being numerically astute. In a study by Holtzman, Stockton, and Kraft (2010), employers reported that "budgeting, financial accounting, project management, and forecasting were most common quantitative skills required *(for promotion).*" Crain and Ragan (2012) even offer an approach to integrating liberal arts into a finance course. Integration can happen across every business arena.

Writing across disciplines matters, too, as a skill as well as a tool to build thinking-literacy. Clear writing requires clear thinking. A student needs to learn to express herself by arranging her ideas in relationship to others' ideas. When accuracy and truth are at issue, students (and professionals) must be able to critically examine and to defend a source's reliability; information literacy therefore is increasingly important. Students also need to construct clean theses and appropriately elaborate on assertions to make the theses intelligible for others. At a more mature level of writing, a student also needs to anticipate objections that other readers might raise and address those objections and must even identify the limitations in her own argument. Knight (1999) offers a survey of programmatic practices. To implement these practices though, institutions must shoulder the responsibility for providing and rewarding continuous development among faculty in order to deliver such needed approaches.

Logic and reasoning

Literacy enables logic and reasoning, the second capacity group within the larger thinking and analysis domain. Logic, the ability to construct reliable inference using systematic reasoning either deductively or inductively, requires analytical reasoning, the ability to synthesize information and integrate it into knowledge. Both logic and reasoning require components of literacy and contribute to one's ability to deepen and extend acuity through reflection over time. Logic and reasoning can contribute to a researcher's ability to design a question and gather and analyze data to inform an answer. Logic contributes significantly to informed perspective taking, which is not just having an opinion but also articulating one's own perspective in the context of others' perspectives. I have observed in my 14 years of experience teaching undergraduate liberal arts that students struggle with logic and reasoning. Students are increasingly able to either recite information or hold a personal opinion; much less common is the student who can hold an opinion, then articulate the assumptions underlying his opinion, question his own assumptions, inquire into alternative perspectives, and then create a substantiated perspective while comparing that opinion with that of others. (See Neville and Godwin (2011) for an in-depth discussion of developmental stage theories as applied to teachers attempting to navigate their undergraduate business students differently from MBA students.) Bloom's 1956 *Taxonomy of Learning* offers seminal progression of abilities in these areas.

Using logic to work through an issue develops problem-solving abilities. According to MacPherson (2002), "Generally, problem solving is discussed in the literature as part of the wider topic of the nature of thinking" (p. 6). There has been much debate on the structuring of thinking skills and the hierarchy, but there is agreement that problem solving and reasoning are "higher-order" operations, and that undergraduates need to develop "higher-order" thinking skills (ibid). This helps students to stop seeing every issue as purely white and black and instead to see the areas of gray – a cognitive progression from dualistic to both-and thinking, which is foundational to sustainability mindset. Why does both-and thinking matter? In one study, students who gave answers that were "dualistic," indicating their black/white perspective, had lower overall problem-solving scores (p. 18). Bosco, Melchar, Beauvais, and Desplaces (2010) advance analytical reasoning while building systems and societal awareness as they teach business ethics content. Regardless of the subject matter, college students need to make meaning out of history and need to address contemporary business issues in anticipatory ways (meaning, not just taking a long-term perspective, but also thinking forward to a desired outcome and then logically reasoning backwards to the present in order to construct choices or decision pathways that might best lead to the desired state).

Numeracy affects logic, too. "Quantitative reasoning refers to the student's ability to solve problems through basic mathematical and statistical manipulations" (Amin & Amin, 2003, p. 547). When business students learn to interpret basic applied math and statistical concepts such as mean, standard deviation, variance, interest rate, rate of return, and issues of sampling distribution, the students are also learning to logically reason from a signal data point to a conceptual implication. Clearly, literacy and thinking abilities co-inform each other in significant ways.

Domain 2: Introspection and intellect

This domain bridges externally constructed (out-there) knowledge, which combines awareness and understanding of the world we see, with intra-psychic (in-here) awareness of one's own possibilities, biases, and mental models. Central to fostering a sustainable mindset, such bridges empower learners to go beyond eco-literacy. Through introspection and integration, learners go beyond simply knowing more into shifts of being in and engaging with the world. Traditional undergraduate education models tend to stay focused on knowing rather than also emphasizing the process of becoming (see Hunt, 1999, for exploration of learning from the inside out).

Critical and integrative thinking

Conceptually, critical thinking means taking an intellectual and disciplined approach to analyzing and understanding data or evidence in order to guide beliefs or decision making. According to Amin and Amin, analysis, integration and synthesis, and critical attitude make up critical thinking (2003, p. 543). However, the word "critical" in non-academic language implies disapproving judgment. Therefore, while teachers can face a complex challenge in building students' abilities at thinking and reasoning, the challenge also requires explicitly analytical understandings of "critical thinking" itself. When students demonstrate increasing mastery of critical thinking, they can draw sound conclusions from data, even potentially or superficially conflicting data. The capacity requires the ability to synthesize complex ideas, to articulate multiple positions, to identify and define key issues embedded in data or perspectives, and to reconcile data-supported knowledge with either common sense or anecdotal experiences. Glaser (1941) emphasizes the need for persistent examination of the data, especially in light of evidence that refutes or complicates what a person knows, believes, or is told. Advancing literacy and thinking abilities increases the likelihood that such analysis of conclusions will occur. Martin (2007) advocates the same capacity's significance in 21st-century leadership, while Quinton and Smallbone (2005) highlight the difficulty students have with generalizing and synthesizing. Institutions and educators need to chart better paths to get students where the world needs them to be.

Integrative thinking challenges people to create a new perspective in light of two seemingly contradictory realities. The Rotman School of Management describes integrative thinking as "the ability to constructively face the tensions of opposing models, and instead of choosing one at the expense of the other, generating a creative resolution of the tension in the form of a new model that contains elements of the individual models, but is superior to each" (Rotman website). Whether building an exhibit design for Disney in a way that honors heritage, reengineering a highway in Accra without inadvertently polluting scarce water sources, or maximizing a high-performance team at Google without fueling material consumption patterns in consumers, integrative thinking creates the possibility that one plus one can equal three or more. Such innovation is central to holistic sustainability within business. Rotman continues (ibid), stating that

> [integrative thinkers'] models capture the complicated, multi-faceted and multidirectional causal relationships between the key variables in any problem. Integrative thinkers consider the problem as a whole, rather than breaking it down and farming out the parts. Finally, they creatively resolve tensions without making costly trade-offs, turning challenges into opportunities.

Martin (2007) of Rotman popularized the value of integrative thinking in *The Opposable Mind*. Critical and integrative thinking are hallmarks of the liberal arts philosophy of education. Such capacities are central to fostering a world of sustainably minded leaders.[1]

Introspection: personal capacity

Memorizing and using a framework resides in literacy; understanding the strengths and limitations of a particular structural framework for an ambiguous situation resides in this personal capacity. A student's whole-person development depends upon their ability to self-reflect, to integrate knowledge into their own use of self as an instrument of citizenship, leadership, and change. Colby et al. (2011) allude to this capacity group as "reflective exploration of meaning." They suggest this group "lies at the heart of interpretation" (p. 65) and is therefore a differentiating experience from instrumental learning if we expect professionals to cultivate good judgment. Students learn here how to ask

> what difference does a particular understanding or approach make to who I am, how I engage the world, and what it is reasonable for me to imagine and hope? As such, it helps learners confront uncertainty amid conflicting understandings to arrive at commitment to purposes adopted with reflective awareness.

(ibid)

Internalized, individual, and interpersonal content can lead to questions:

- Who am I as an actor in the world?
- What is my impact on others?
- How do others impact me?
- What are my strengths and how can I apply them?
- Where am I most comfortable in the balance between leadership, followership, and citizenship?
- How do I see the imaginative and collaborative potential beyond the transactional solutions to a problem?

These questions are complex and responses evolve. Building the cognitive agility to adapt and making habit of our individual curiosity to stay curious over time matter when fostering sustainable mindsets.

Aware adults – ones this book explores as having a "sustainable mindset" – report experiencing cognitive dissonance in mainstream business, a confusion between espoused values and the actual choices or actions one sees himself and herself making on daily bases (Rimanoczy, 2010). In fact, the awareness of dissonance appears to have catalyzed new and progressive action among sustainably minded executives (Rimanoczy, 2014). Standing present in ambiguity requires self-awareness, mental self-regulation (emotional intelligence) toward improved decision making (cognitive reflection), behavioral and perceptual complexity to identify theory patterns and to diagnose plausible interventions (practical reasoning), and the ability to create a variety of approaches to solve unstructured problems. These abilities are intrinsic in "Introspection: Personal Capacity" and align with findings about how business leaders learn to invent solutions to new problems in innovative ways (Rimanoczy, 2014) often associated with entrepreneurship.

Interpersonal and influence skills enter here, too. The capacity also includes the courage and confidence to take a reasoned stand on an issue. For example, Gentile (2010) advocates the critical need for building students' ability at voicing their values and staying present through ensuing tensions; this extends most business ethics approaches that only emphasize literacy and reasoning abilities. Business students might learn tools and frameworks for making strategic marketing choices. However, the "smartest" students often dominate a work group's assignment, applying such frameworks, deducing possible outcomes, and refining their recommendations of a right solution. Without having the personal capacity to see a framework's benefits and limitations for a variety of circumstances and from other people's perspectives literacy mastery may easily be insufficient for that student to advance a group's outputs. At the highest level of organizing, business schools often teach group and team dynamics but fail to intrinsically value the area's significance in cultivating "whole" people sufficiently agile for multiculturalism or for complexity. Ironically, sustainably minded executives describe knowing that they need to connect with others and advocate, share, inform, and foster collaborative action in order to be effective (Rimanoczy, 2010). Sustainable effectiveness requires collaboration.

Personal capacity requires the ability to communicate, internalize good interpersonal skills, and critically reflect on and integrate insights about culture and politics within groups and organizations. To do this, one must learn to move between and among a variety of paradigms (i.e., integrative thinking). For example, a leadership course can be a theoretical understanding of characteristics and traits of outstanding leaders. However, for a student to build personal capacity skills in leadership, that student must internalize the theory and examples, model the selected behaviors, and adapt styles in response to his own awareness of different cultures or political dynamics.

As a teacher-scholar, I make explicit with students the difference between what I call "Big L leadership," the people we study, the ones hierarchically in charge, and "little l leadership" – each individual's responsibility for integrating knowledge, setting an example for others, and mindfulness. Through that lens, even the most timid students experience themselves as leaders in society, critical for the world's future stability. Building personal capacity for influencing situations toward an objective or a collective good (i.e., building one's ability as a "little l leader") requires acting with compassion for others, having the courage to act when others' behaviors compromise the objective or common good, and finding effective solutions by honestly entertaining holistic perspectives. These abilities (acting with compassion, taking courage in the presence of others, finding holistic solutions) can be coached but not memorized or recited. Educational philosophies vary about how to teach business and management (see Beatty, Leigh, & Dean, 2009, for a survey of philosophies embedded in business education over time). However, this capacity in particular benefits from choosing experiential approaches to learning from within such that students seek to intentionally integrate head and heart forms of knowing (see Neville, 2007, for theory and a pedagogical approach to building introspective capacity through dialogue). When we as educators seek to increase students' likelihood of perceiving themselves as foundational to how tomorrow's world unfolds, we choose to make sustainable mindset central to our designs.

Literacy, knowing concepts and frameworks, is a beginning. Deepening literacy towards an ability to understand functionality, limitations, and potential requires a student to integrate information into her intrapsychic reservoir, and that deeper literacy can give birth to complex thinking. Therefore, personal capacity manifests itself when a student uses reflective thinking by (a) listening deeply to the environment itself in order to identify strategic opportunities or challenge; (b) diagnosing a situation effectively because of theories, concepts, and frameworks studied; and (c) accurately reading the culture, politics, and design of an organization in order to effectively formulate a viable recommendation.[2]

Perhaps introspection is one of the least honored capacities, especially in business education, because it is beyond the quantitatively measurable intelligence that academia values. Quantitative methods, metrics, and assessments still trump qualitative analysis and insights. Greenberg, McKone-Sweet, and Wilson (2011) build on

Van Maanen (2011), lamenting, "until management disciplines learn to embrace and value qualitative social science methods, we do not expect that management students will find many learning opportunities that will enable them to investigate a corporate or industrial context through a contextual lens" (p. 189). This illustrates the complexity and systemic nature of the consciousness changes needed – from a priority on quantitative thinking to a respect for healthy balance between qualitative and quantitative perspectives. Such a shift appears needed in business education and therefore also in business itself.

Domain 3: Humans and organizations

"Humans and Organizations" comes from an interdisciplinary assumption about the world as highly interrelated and as wholes inextricably dependent on parts. Systems thinking, a core component of a sustainability mindset, shares this assumption that parts are interdependent and mutually influencing. Sustainability mindset depends on people having the agility to – what I describe to students as – telescope out to see events and choices in expansive contexts as well as microscope in to explore a phenomenon. Colby et al. (2011) label this educational objective as "multiple framing." Interestingly though, business disciplines have historically been treated as siloed fields of study rather than what Daft and Weick (1984) characterized as nested systems. Seen as nested systems, the world must be explored through multiple frames of perception in order to appear whole. For example, biology sheds light on environmental thinking differently from chemistry, and yet the study of environmental sciences depends upon students' ability to see through both lenses. Similarly, musical notes inform the larger symphonic performance; human behavior informs how culture and society can be interpreted; and art informs how history gets analyzed and portrayed. Therefore, the Humans and Organizations capacity domain concentrates on building students' capacity to shuttle among various frames of reference.

Individual and interpersonal

The individual and interpersonal capacity explicates relationships between animate units or concepts at relatively micro levels of analysis. For example, having introspective capacity builds upon literacy with content, and then relies on one's ability to cognitively reflect on the content in ways that encourage an individual's consciousness to notice, question, and imagine new possibilities. A specific classroom incident would occur if – while delivering data and theory about water scarcity – a teacher asked students to reflect upon what water scarcity means for each student individually. That form of question encourages students to practice what I describe as "microscoping in" to see water scarcity at a micro level. This type of question creates the potential for a "disorienting dilemma" (Mezirow, 1991), one that forces conscious attention onto incongruous choices.[3] Someone's ability to provoke and to reconcile disorienting dilemmas requires mental agility across levels of analysis and across traditionally siloed content arena.

Interpersonal skills – ones people use to make sense of each other such as verbal and non-verbal communication skills, behaviors, listening to words and meanings, etc. – have become an increasing success factor in multi-generational workplaces. Hershatter and Epstein (2010) find this particularly true in the early 2000s because of complex blends of assumptions and work ethics of three distinct population segments referred to as Millennials, Baby Boomers, and Gen Xers). For example, Dean and Fornaciari (2014, p. 18) found that,

> our Gen Y students have experienced unparalleled levels of externally provided psychological protection and safety. This means they are often ill equipped to handle ambiguity. We have seen this repeatedly with students who want to maximize certainty by asking for ever more directions or for sample assignments.

As undergraduates, "They look to us for structure to close every loophole because they have little experience navigating the ambiguity inherent in college work" (ibid). Yet navigating ambiguity is increasingly necessary. Compounding this, self-motivation and perseverance through difficulty, also known as 'grit,' matter in students' (Duckworth, Peterson, Mathews, & Kelly, 2007) and teacher's (Duckworth, Quinn, & Seligman, 2009) effectiveness. People need enormous grit, or perseverance, in order to become positive change agents in our ambiguous times.

Systems and societies

Telescoping out from individuals and interpersonal levels of analysis, the Capacity Map draws student attention to disciplines that consider society's macro levels of study such as economics or anthropology. We call this area "Systems and Societies." Significant fields at this macro level include governance studies, corporate social responsibility nationally and internationally, market and industry dynamics, and global sustainability. Global studies, social justice themes, cross- and inter-cultural and diversity issues, and multiculturalism are taught and learned at this level. But Musil (2009, p. 55) noted in reference to a large-scale Mellon Foundation study,

> while institutions claim that global learning is an essential component for a twenty-first-century college education, the Mellon study revealed that there is little evidence that students are provided with multiple, robust, interdisciplinary learning environments at increasing levels of engagement to ensure that they acquire the global learning professed in [a college's] mission statement.

This caution reinforces this chapter's intention of seeing the Capacity Map as a framework made coherent through reflection. Similarly, the Map and dependence on reflection suggests to educators that all levels of a university's curricular design and deployment need continuous and intentional integration.

According to Henninger and Hurlbert (2007, p. 5),

> business schools and programs that integrate cultural experiences and activities into business classes help prepare students to function in a multicultural business world and society while allowing them to practice their information literacy [and] research skills, writing, speaking, and critical thinking.

Professionals increasingly need to employ integrative and systemic thinking (Atwater, Kannan, & Stephens, 2008; Thurston, 2000). Undeniably, these skills can be used in one's career, but Wick and Phillips (2008, p. 24) lament,

> students no longer view our general education program as the core, or foundation, of a liberal education that will empower them with the knowledge, skills and values for personal enrichment, lifelong learning, civic engagement, and social responsibility. Instead, they view general education as a disconnected set of requirements to meet, or obstacles to remove, so that they can 'get to what matters'.

This pervasive attitude prevents students – especially pre-professional students – from exploring and developing an abstracted regard for the aforementioned data and phenomena. They do not build the capacity to see patterns across individual behaviors; rather, students often emerge from college still looking at individuals as distinct behavioral entities.

Domain three of the Capacity Map amplifies the need for seeing bi-directional influences. A proficient student should be able to notice similarities and differences between situations that might appear unrelated. This ability to see connections requires holistic and abstract thinking. Students should have the capacity to find the central issue in a complex situation, graphically represent (or interpret a representation of) a systems view of that situation, and effectively construct metaphors or analogies to explain it. Internalized as a personal capacity, a student could then effectively analyze large-scale complexities based on theoretical frameworks from studying systems and societies. This integration could emerge from activities such as civic engagement, service learning, or studies abroad. It could easily be found in content domains such as sociology, social psychology, race and ethnic studies, and environmental studies. Interestingly, modern languages and literature programs often extend students' ability to integrate and distill. The outcome of domain three is an ability to think critically from different perspectives.

If we want to make tomorrow's business practitioners more ethical, then they must see their technical abilities and training in the context of societies' needs. Future practitioners become aware of their own integral relationship to our global society as they engage in curricula, classes, and integrated college experiences based on implications of this model. In today's demand-centric reality, though, curricular designers and faculty too often perpetuate what has been done in the past: job training. I will set aside for a moment the discussion about curricular innovations – returning to it in the tactical and in the Implications sections – in order to explicitly address the job-training side of the dilemma identified above and named below as "Building My Future."

Domain 4: Building my future

Students, parents, and recruiters consistently speak to the importance of college as a readying process for a graduate to get a professional or career-oriented job. Yet, faculty, deans, and presidents consistently speak to the foundational role a college experience has in equipping students for life-long learning and discovery. And programs abound which promote their enrollees' rapid time-to-market. Therefore, domain four attempts to mediate what today's market demands and what tomorrow's society needs. "Building my future" represents both the skills and approaches effective for landing jobs – whether a first job or entering a career progression over time – and the capacity for leaning into self-directed development and discovery and manifestation of one's calling or vocation.

Colleagues and I choose, in collaboration with our multi-stakeholder inquiry, to assign primary responsibility for this domain to the individual students themselves. We sought to identify specific assignments that encourage students to build a professional network, to experiment with various existing jobs, and to develop their entrepreneurial potential; however, we consistently told students that getting a job and building a career were explicitly their responsibility. The university's career center was available to help, but the responsibility for making themselves employable and translating for recruiters the value of whole-person development rests with them. By doing so, and by simultaneously keeping the domain prominent in the map, we effectively confronted the significance of the introspective capacity and the profound significance of grit and courage that students will need for a lifetime. They can see their personal responsibility for becoming little-l leaders through the presence of this domain on their map; students hold responsibility for building their future – their future jobs are not something a college gives to them by virtue of the classroom experience alone.

How to position this domain in a university's curriculum or marketing strategy will depend on the university's objectives and mission. Some colleges approach education as a factory metaphor, producing job-ready graduates at the end of a highly calibrated assembly line; other colleges approach education as a developmental opportunity for opening young minds. The tension between today's demand for job readiness and tomorrow's need for morally imaginative citizenry cannot be over-emphasized.

Whole person, strategic

At the most conceptual level, whole person refers to the process by which students can become informed citizens about culture and the world. Tactically, this includes ways in which students take responsibility for their learning beyond what is required by a teacher and assessed towards a grade. For example, listening to or reading the daily news, discussing current events with others, staying informed about civic and political issues, actively engaging in community organizations, and choosing to read cultural or historic literature all serve to build this strategic cultivation of self. The experience, reflection, and formation of a rationale for otherness or behavior and choices outside of one's home environment cultivate a student's ability to engage our rapidly changing and increasingly complex world.

Building My Future includes both a strategy and tactics. Strategically, faculty can integrate the "outside world" into classroom discussions. Faculty should extrapolate from classroom activity and the college community (e.g., class projects, sports teams, activity groups) to skill sets, thinking, and behaviors that appear in jobs and careers beyond the classroom (e.g., "the real world"). Students can be asked to build learning portfolios or personal development plans at the beginning of a course or program of study, and then to revisit the portfolio at the end. Rimanoczy (2016) describes this approach as personal learning goals (p. 100), which students might design, a pedagogical strategy for educators to move the locus of ownership away from teacher-as-expert and towards students as empowered champions of their own learning. These activities reflect a faculty member's engagement with a student's need for post-college direction, but without taking on the educational responsibility for programming paths to specific jobs.

The capacity domain requires students to think (or imagine) forward about what life choices they might value and then to reason back to the present in order to inform their choices in college. A student who is interested in the global world might choose to major or minor in a language if educating herself towards whole-person development ideals; however, such a choice may not appear prudent if valuing college from the short-term financial perspective of return on investment (Lechtenberg, 2014). A student interested in environmental management would be wise to take chemistry and philosophy as well as environmental science courses. A student interested in being a capital-L leader would benefit from holding formal leadership roles in campus activities or student government. Learning organizational citizenship behaviors, those things someone does in service of being part of a larger team rather than because such behaviors have specific extrinsic rewards, matters too. Allison, Voss, and Dryer (2001) find that people who consistently demonstrate organizational citizenship behaviors enhance their own career effectiveness over time. Students can proactively cultivate their citizenship skills through what D'Abate (2010) calls "developmental interactions," such as internships, mentoring, and collaborative projects, even if a college does not award credit for doing so. D'Abate's study of recent graduates three to five years out of school found those experiences to be very helpful in preparing students for the work world (2010). Communications capacities – listening, articulating complexity, and engaging in difficult and necessary conversations – apply here too. And every student will benefit from engaging in informational interviews with alumni and other professionals in order to better understand correlations between college and post-college life.

Career skills, tactical

Job definitions and entry-level skill expectations change as rapidly as the business world. During the four years at a traditional college when a student concentrates on a baccalaureate degree, the job market will have continued to evolve at the pace of technology. Therefore, this tactical capacity group may be the most difficult for faculty to address. With that said, faculty can explicitly bridge classroom content and pedagogy with references to the work world. Most American colleges and universities have some form of career services program. Such programs generally provide students with tactical skills such as résumé building, interview training, internship locators, and even networking events. Faculty can encourage use of career services programs and even periodically require participation in a career services event.

Note that this choice to move "Building My Future" out of the teacher's responsibility and into the students' out-of-class responsibility is based on my American college experience. During my experience teaching in a developing country, I learned that students faced systemic obstacles to gaining needed access, experience, and professional development through their own internships or through companies' abilities to provide on-the-job-training. In that circumstance, I found that I chose to more heavily facilitate students' development in domain four than when I was making curricular choices within the American economy and context. Therefore, colleges in developing countries may benefit from addressing this capacity domain far more explicitly than colleges in post-industrial countries, especially if their graduates are emerging from college with professional capabilities that exceed what they encounter in a dominant portion of an existing economy or marketplace.

In an advice column for undergraduate liberal arts students, the Phi Beta Kappa society's newsletter *Corcodilo* (2009, p. 10) said,

> If you have a liberal arts background and have never applied it to business, it's up to you to figure it out for yourself . . . your success in fact depends on shoe-horning, forcing, pounding and otherwise mapping your skills into the jobs you want.

The author goes on to reinforce that businesses need liberal arts capacities such as defining problems and tasks, planning and executing research, organizing ideas and solutions, and writing and communicating, in addition to developing an open mind, disciplined work habits, and a critical eye and ear; "however, they're useless unless you know what to do with them" (ibid). Students need to take on the responsibility for how they want to engage with the curriculum and design their own individual capacities to focus on their own strengths. None of us can be excellent at everything.

Tactical ways to use the framework

Abilities to read, write, and be quantitatively and digitally literate allow students to move through daily life as we know it. Beyond information, though, students need cognitive abilities to structure unstructured problems, analyze complexity, extrapolate from experiences in reasoned ways, and synthesize multiple views or data into a coherent perspective. Deepening one's cognitive abilities requires intentional interaction between the learner and the world, both through the heart and through the head. The depth, accentuated by reflection, experience, and curiosity, builds what educators refer to as a whole person. The Capacity Map framework articulated in this chapter provides my colleagues and me with an effective tool for three different and on-going conversations.

First, the Map's domains offer faculty peers within and beyond business a common language for discussing university programs, majors, and specific course approaches. Therefore, we can evaluate the pros and cons of curricular designs with strategic, not just operational thinking. For example, business faculty at Southwestern University discovered that their curriculum was a metaphoric brick walkway, where each course was a stepping stone.

Figure 15.2 emerged as their visual starting point for curricular re-design conversations. Figure 15.3 then created a common way to discuss course progressions from introductory through to a senior capstone.

Figure 15.4, a sample course planning tool, helped faculty imaginers to consider which courses would best address basic "literacy" versus "mastery" levels of

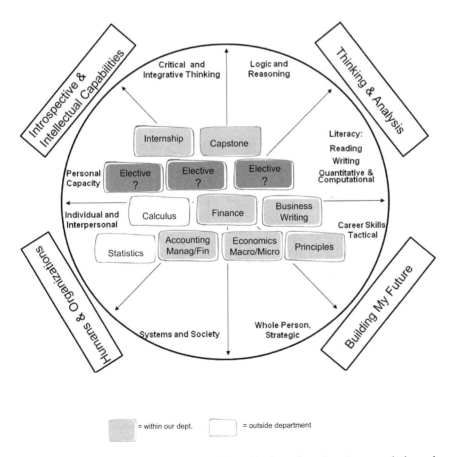

FIGURE 15.2 Example of courses as building blocks rather than integrated through capacity thinking

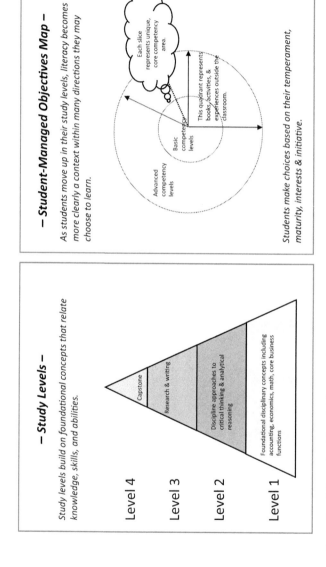

FIGURE 15.3 Example of Capacity Map thinking to discuss curricular design across disciplines

Study Level	Course	Analytical Skills Development		Humans & Organizations		Personal & Intellectual Capacity	
		Numeracy	Logic & Reasoning	Interpersonal Individual	Systems & Society	Personal Capacity	Critical & Integrative Thinking
1	Principles of Business		Low	Low	Low	Low	Low
1	Macro economics	Low	Low		Low		Low
1	Financial accounting	Low	Low				
2	Leadership perspectives			Med	Med	Low	Low
2	Financial statement analysis	Med	Med		Med		
2	Business ethics		Med		Med	Med	Med
3	A level-2 course adapted to include mjr research paper	Course dependent	Course dependent	Course dependent	Course dependent	Med	Med
4	Capstone	Med	Med	Med	Med	Med	Med

FIGURE 15.4   Sample course planning tool combining Capacity Map and competency thinking

development in the general business major. Figures 15.5 and 15.6 offered examples for discussing potential assignment implications with colleagues inside and outside of the business program. Colleagues university wide, from humanities and sciences to arts and business, were able to have shared conversations about aligning objectives even though their course content varied substantially (see Neville, 2015, regarding the power of dialogue, contrasted with positional debate, towards organizational innovation).

Second, my colleagues and I consistently improved our ability to explain to prospective students and parents the power of studying business through a liberal arts lens as we explained our small college's curriculum by using the Capacity Map. As faculty in a small college, we found it important to articulate to prospectives what our program offered – and indeed what our faculty expectations were for student engagement – especially because our small college competed with the larger universities' technical-functional degree programs. Technical-functional degrees can seduce students and recruiters who try to match fresh graduates with immediate industrial needs. However, our larger and emerging societal needs require the

Map's sector		Literacy (define & describe)	Mastery (integrate & understand implications)
Analytical Skills Development	**Numeracy**	• Calculate a regression	• Understanding implication of regressions
	Logic & Reasoning	• Articulate a position	• Compare and contrast to others' positions
Humans & Organizations	**Individual/ Interpersonal**	• Recognize behavioral temperaments	• Articulate effect of temperament on dyad or small group
	Systems & Society	• Identify organization's environmental components	• Understand bi-directional influence
Personal & Intellectual Capacity	**Personal Capacity**	• Avoid getting "voted off the island"	• Facilitating group success
	Critical & Integrative Thinking	• Understand implications in isolation (e.g., a particular situation)	• Identify & understand "mega-trends"

FIGURE 15.5   Example of KSAs for student-managed objectives map

whole-person abilities that a liberal arts education aims to build. As prospective students and parents begin to grasp the potential for holistic wealth and long-term global and social well-being, we find that students who are ripe for changing the world's paradigm from near-term to sustainability gravitate to our liberal arts college for a business program.

Third, we use the Capacity Map framework in every business course as a visual reminder for students about the power and potential of intentionally "showing up" in their educational experience rather than just approaching coursework as a box-checking requirement. We find that students' mantra, "when will I ever use this [content] in the 'real world'?" actually decreases, and their acceptance of learning to learn – beyond just retaining content for a test – increases, as we explain the course rationale through the framework (Neville et al., 2007). Liberal arts philosophy matters, and how educators manifest that philosophy matters, too.

Curricular innovation improves through strategic reflection and holistic action. Therefore, every conversation about what to do needs to be informed both through tactical and differentiated pedagogical ideas emerging in this book and its authors' references, as well as through broader dialogues for systemic changes. For example, Neville and Godwin (2011) call for differentiated pedagogies for undergraduate students than for MBA students.

"Building My Future"		Literacy	Mastery
Whole Person, Strategic	**Great Books reading list**	• Read daily/weekly news • Read classics	• Discuss current events • Recommend particular classics to others with rationale for why
	Civic engagement	• Be informed and vote • Join a community service project	• Be politically active • Actively engage in community organization
	Global-social citizenship & international awareness	• Study abroad • Minor in a language • Take environmental science courses	• Live abroad • Become fluent in a language • Organize students to pledge sustainability after graduation
Career Skill, Tactical	**Curricular areas of interest to career directions**	• Law school: lower level courses in political science, history, philosophy	• Law school: upper level courses in same and business law
	Communication	• Explain course skills to employer • Learn table manners	• Explain liberal arts ed to employer • Design and host a networking event
	Career development	• Attend career services programs • Network with family, friends, peers	• Do multiple internships • Maintain network beyond industry

FIGURE 15.6   Sample KSAs for career-focused map sector

Table 15.1 abstracts the authors' stage-theory argument indicating an example of abilities exhibited by adolescents, youth, and adults. Then Table 15.2 suggests tactical implications for faculty seeking explicit and capacity-centric approaches to meeting students where the students are – rather than simply covering content historically ascribed to a specific course (see Neville & Godwin, 2011, for an extensive discussion of development and stage-theory implications for business education).

These examples serve to stimulate readers' imagination and curiosity about ways to use frameworks and theory as tools for collaboration among faculty. No one model or tactic will ensure the changes needed; however, staying attentive to the range of possibilities is a critical first step toward influencing even more powerful models of learning for the future we most want to create.

TABLE 15.1 Sample indicators for identifying students' developmental levels

Developmental Area	Sample Capacities	Example Abilities Exhibited by Level of Development		
		Adolescent	*Youth*	*Adult*
Cognitive and Moral	• **Decision making** • **Ethical reasoning ability** • **Cognitive complexity**	• Decisions are based on self-interested, short-term needs; guided by "How does this impact me right now?" • Believes ethical actions are those that benefit self, what is 'right' is what is best for self • Belief that their own experience is the 'truth', accepting of what is, not yet curious about alternative perspectives	• Decisions are based on self-interested short- and long-term needs; guided by "How might this impact me now and in the future?" • Believes ethical actions are those that comply with rules and norms, what is 'right' is what is best for peer group • Recognition of multiple perspectives, but holds the belief that absolute truths are known or knowable	• Decisions are based on both the short-term and long-term costs/ benefits to self and others; guided by "How might this impact me and others now and later?" • Ability to identify and apply more universal moral values regardless of current rules or laws, what is 'right' depends on situation/issues • Belief that multiple "truths" may exist; able to hold one's own perspective as an object for subjective reflection
Psychosocial	• **Meaningful philosophy of life** • **Tolerance of difference** • **Emotional intelligence**	• Not yet considered • Difference seen as "other", often stereotypical characteristics are imposed without consideration • No emotional filter applied; felt emotions become enacted emotions	• Personal identity grounded in others and society; aware of likes and dislikes • Difference is perceived as "other", but begins to see exceptions to stereotypes on a case-by-case basis • Emotional filter driven by social codes for "appropriate" behavior in public; will meet anger with anger	• Able to construct personal identity separate from and in relationship with others • Differences not seen as threatening to self, accepted as potential for enhancing what is perceived or known • Stable emotional filter developed; can transcend negative emotions like anger and respond appropriately across settings

Skills and Abilities			
• **Quantitative reasoning**	• Can solve equations using a given formula	• Can choose the right equation/formula for solving a stated situation	• Can evaluate solutions and recommend implications for strategic action and further analysis
• **Literacy (reading, numeracy, domain knowledge)**	• (Reading) Understands reading at face-value, literal interpretation of ideas presented; (Numeracy) Does not understand what a regression is	• (Reading) Able to understand symbolism and broader themes in readings; (Numeracy) Can calculate a regression	• (Reading) Able to make connections across multiple readings and see multiple interpretations of works; (Numeracy) Understands the implication of a regression for planning
• **Critical thinking**	• Ability to agree or disagree with an argument based only on existing beliefs	• Ability to follow an argument from multiple points of view and distinguish between the perspectives if guided	• Ability to evaluate whether an argument is strong (both important and directly related to the question) or weak, can construct and evaluate arguments from different points of view on own
• **Reflective thinking**	• Does not differentiate opinions and beliefs from facts	• Can determine the significance or salience of one dominant theme among multiple themes	• Ability to distinguish between and weigh differently opinion from fact, assumes that an idea rests not only on its own merit but also that rationale for an idea is significant

Source: Abstracted from Neville, M. G., & Godwin, L. (2011). Returning to a holistic management education and the tradition of liberal education. In Wankle, C., & Stachowicz-Stanusch, A. (Eds). *Management education for integrity: Ethically educating tomorrow's business leaders*. UK: Emerald Group Publishing Limited.

TABLE 15.2 Example tactics for differentiating pedagogical format to support student developmental needs

	Typical developmental levels for traditional undergraduate students		Typical developmental level for MBA students
	Potential Format for "Adolescent" Level of Development	Potential Format for "Youth" Level of Development	Potential Format for "Adult" Level of Development
Case Studies	Case presented with possible solutions, including one solution that is 'best'; students told which solution is 'correct'.	Case presented with various possible solutions; no one best answer is obvious, students debate merits of each.	Case presented with no solutions; students are facilitated to develop their own solution, analyzing costs/benefits of their ideas.
Team Projects	Teams are assigned by faculty, work is done primarily in class under faculty supervision and guidance.	Teams are assigned, work is done inside and outside of class with regular updates provided to faculty to monitor process.	Teams are self-selected, work is done outside of class with faculty serving as a resource and intervening only if needed.
Service-Learning/ Applied Experiences	Project is explicitly defined by faculty, work is completed in a supervised setting and reported back to the organization.	Project is well-defined by the faculty, task is more complex requiring work both inside and outside the classroom, including participation within the organization.	Project is collaboratively defined by the students and participating organization, work is done primarily within the organization independently from the class, with faculty a resource as needed.

Source: Abstracted from Neville, M. G., & Godwin, L. (2011). Returning to a holistic management education and the tradition of liberal education. In Wankle, C., & Stachowicz-Stanusch, A. (Eds.), *Management education for integrity: Ethically educating tomorrow's business leaders*. UK: Emerald Group Publishing Limited.

Implication for higher education

The call for learning and development beyond lectures is not new. In 1953, Harry Wells, then vice president of Northwestern University, wrote a book arguing for liberal arts education, including experiential and interactive education, as central to the American "schema" in which farmers, factory workers, and managers alike deserve the right to free knowledge and participation in society (p. 64). He acknowledged the rapidly increasing specialization of professions, the pressures educational institutions face for cost control, and the centrality of a free society's dependence on broadly educated populations. By 1959, the Ford Foundation and the Carnegie Corporation published extensive critiques of American business education, condemning the narrowness of undergraduate curricula (Gordon and Howell, 1959; Pierson, 1959). Two more books emerged in the 1980s (Johnston, 1986; Useem, 1989), but no significant changes had occurred (Herrington & Arnold, 2013). In 2007, Khurana issued another focal call detailing shifts in the 20th and early 21st centuries that have led education to now produce "hired hands" instead of people who aspire to "higher aims." In 2007, the AAC&U issued the Liberal Education & America's Promise report explicitly calling for 21st-century college students' education to include knowledge of human cultures; physical and natural worlds; intellectual as well as practical skills; personal and social responsibility; and integrative and applied learning. In 2011, the Carnegie Foundation again released a nationwide report, now calling for broadening how business educators approach undergraduates (Colby et al., 2011). The Foundation highlighted business, and this time extrapolated education innovation implications to other popular professional programs (i.e., nursing and engineering) as needing to emphasize students' ability to frame situations from multiple perspectives, to analyze situations, and to reflect on the implications for self and others (p. 60). Despite these broad studies and continued calls for change, reductions in funding and increases in tuition cost, political pressure for economic stimulation through college training in job-ready skills, and an assessment culture that is still driven by short-term quantifiable snapshots, all complicate institutions' willingness to fund experimentation toward innovation. Collectively, we as educators face a wicked problem as we attempt requisite, systemic, interdependent changes necessary to improve students' ability to navigate the fractured world they find upon graduation (Waddock, 2007).

While education activists continue to call for systemic change, faculty individually need to attend to fostering change among our peers. Wick and Philips (2008, p. 22) write:

> as faculty and staff members committed to the purposes of higher education, we must move away from protecting and defending our specialized areas of expertise, whether in academic disciplines or in co-curricular areas. We must all become liberal educators who hold our students and ourselves accountable for the desired outcomes of a liberal education.

The Capacity Map is one example of fostering consciousness changes in small programs or even in one classroom at a time. Discussing the model with students opens conversations about self-awareness, reflection, motivation, local and global engagement, values, interdependencies, and Neville's (2004) concept of business relevance across "multiple generations of time." Each capacity (literacy, logic and reasoning, critical and integrative thinking, personal capacity, individual and inter-personal, system and society, whole person strategic, and career skills) functions in a fluid and interdependent way with others. The capacities themselves – essentially the philosophical intention of liberal arts – create value in content. Whether a student majors in political science, history, English, or business, the cognitive abilities learned through a liberal arts process correspond to the needs of high-functioning leaders for our complex, ambiguous, and changing 21st-century world.

Disruptive changes will come to business education. Those changes are already coming into business itself. This chapter attempts to empower business educators to actively shift the education paradigm from an individualistic training mindset to a futuristic developmental mindset. By approaching our content, students, and colleagues as if we are each responsible for stewarding the future, not just accountable for course completion this semester, we collectively pave the way for the academic system to change as well. "We can't teach courage," an economist colleague insisted, but we do each create classroom environments in which more or less courage is required. Find ways to structure engagement so that students learn to navigate ambiguity, to thoughtfully question what erodes public goodwill, and to lead with integrity in the face of complacency. In these ways, we build the mindfulness necessary for sustaining our world tomorrow. Collectively, we are accountable for that.

Notes

1 Note: Specific pedagogical interventions and classroom assignments can be found in education journals such as the *Journal of Management Education* and *Teaching in Higher Education* for teacher-scholars who are interested in being intentional about how they integrate these capacities into their courses.
2 Teachers could choose to build this skill through a one-semester dialogic seminar towards questioning dominant paradigms (see Neville, 2007) or a four-course sequence towards sociological imagination (see Hibbert, 2013).
3 Notice that academic domains such as neuroscience, developmental psychology, human biases in cognition (from "blinders" to "group-think"), multiple intelligences, motivation theory, interpersonal and group dynamics, theories of power and influence, team and project management, dimensions of diversity, moral imagination, and communication theory will naturally appear as content within this capacity area.

References

Adler, P. S. (2002). Corporate scandals: It's time for reflection in business schools. *Academy of Management Executive, 16*(3), 148–149.
Allison, B. J., Voss, R. S., & Dryer, S. (2001, May 01). Student classroom and career success: The role of organizational citizenship behavior. *Journal of Education for Business, 76*(5), 282–288.

Amin, M. R., & Amin, N. A. (2003). Benchmarking learning outcomes of undergraduate business education. *Benchmarking: An International Journal, 10*(6/7), 538–558.

Association of American Colleges and Universities (AAC&U). (1998). *Statement on liberal learning.* Adopted by the Board of Directors of the Association of American Colleges & Universities, October. Retrieved from www.aacu.org/About/statements/liberal_learning.cfm

Association of American Colleges and Universities (AAC&U). (2007). *College learning for the new global century: A report from the national leadership council for liberal education and American's promise.* Washington, DC: Association of American Colleges and Universities. Retrieved from www.aacu.org/leap/documents/GlobalCentury_final.pdf

Atwater, B., Kannan, V., & Stephens, A. (2008). Cultivating systemic thinking in the next generation of business leaders. *Academy of Management Learning & Education, 7*(1), 9–25.

Balotsky, R., & Christensen, E. W. (2004). Educating a modern business workforce: An integrated educational information technology process. *Group & Organization Management, 29*(2), 148–170. doi:10.1177/10596011032621353

Beatty, J. E., Leigh, J. S., & Dean, K. L. (2009). Philosophy rediscovered: Exploring the connections between teaching philosophies, educational philosophies, and philosophy. *Journal of Management Education, 33*(1), 99–114.

Bennis, W., & O'Toole, J. (2005). How business schools lost their way. *Harvard Business Review, 85*(5), 96–104.

Bloom, B. S. (1956). *Taxonomy of educational objectives: The classification of educational goals. Handbook 1; Cognitive domain.* New York: David McKay Co. Inc.

Bosco, S. M., Melchar, D. E., Beauvais, L. L., & Desplaces, D. E. (2010). Teaching business ethics: The effectiveness of common pedagogical practices in developing students' moral judgment competence. *Ethics and Education, 5*(3), 263–280.

Bronfenbrenner, U. (1979). *The ecology of human development: Experiments by nature and design.* Cambridge, MA: Harvard University Press.

Bumpus, M. A., & Burton, G. (2008). Chapters in the life of an entrepreneur: A case study. *Journal of Education for Business, 83*(5), 302–308.

Chew, E. B., & McInnis-Bowers, C. (2004). Blending liberal art and business education. *Liberal Education, 90*(1), 56–63.

Christenson, C. M., & Eyring, H. J. (2011). *The innovative university: Changing the DNA of higher education from the inside out.* San Francisco, CA: Jossey-Bass.

Chyung, S. Y., Stepich, D., & Cox, D. (2006). Building a competency-based curriculum architecture to educate 21st-century business practitioners. *Journal of Education for Business, 81*(6), 307–314.

Colby, A., Ehrlich, T., Sullivan, W., & Dolle, J. (2011). *Rethinking undergraduate business education: Liberal learning for the profession.* San Francisco. Jossey-Bass.

Conley, T. M., & Gil, E. L. (2011). Information literacy for undergraduate business students: Examining value, relevancy, and implications for the new century. *Journal of Business & Finance Librarianship, 16*(3), 213–228, doi:10.1080/08963568.2011.581.562

Cooperrider, D. L., & Whitney, D. (2001). A positive revolution in change. In D. L. Cooperrider, P. Sorenson, D. Whitney, & T. Yeager (Eds.), *Appreciative inquiry: An emerging direction for organization development.* Champaign, IL: Stipes.

Corcodilos, N. (2009). Making the liberal arts degree pay off: A headhunter explains how to market your skills in the business world. *The Key Reporter, 74*(3), 10. Retrieved from http://www/montana.edu/wwwpy/AdvisingFolder/PBKarticleCareersLiberalArts.pdf

Crain, S. J., & Ragan, K. P. (2012). Designing a financial literacy course for a liberal arts curriculum. *International of Journal of Consumer Studies, 36*, 515–522.

D'Abate, C. (2010). Developmental interactions for business students: Do they make a difference? *Journal of Leadership & Organizational Studies, 17*(2), 143–155.

Daft, R. L., & Weick, K. E. (1984). Toward a model of organizations as interpretation systems. *Academy of Management, 9*(2), 284–291.

Dean, K. L., & Fornaciari, C. J. (2014). Creating masterpieces: How course structures and routines enable student performance. *Journal of Management Education, 38*(1), 10–42.

Donaldson, L. (2002). Damned by our own theories: Contradictions between theories and management education. *Academy of Management Learning & Education, 1*(1), 96–106.

Duckworth, A. L., Peterson, C., Matthews, M. D., & Kelly, D. R. (2007). Grit: Perseverance and passion for long-term goals. *Journal of Personality and Social Psychology, 92*(6), 1087–1101.

Duckworth, A. L., Quinn, P. D., & Seligman, M. E. P. (2009). Positive predictors of teacher effectiveness. *The Journal of Positive Psychology, 4*(6), 540–547. doi:10.1080/17439760903157232

Evers, F. T., Rush, J. C., & Berdrow, I. (1998). *The bases of competence: Skills for lifelong learning and employability.* San Francisco, CA: Jossey-Bass.

Gentile, M. (2010). *Giving voice to values: How to speak your mind when you know what's right.* New Haven, CT: Yale University Press.

Ghoshal, S. (2005). Bad management theories are destroying good management practices. *Academy of Management Learning and Education, 4*(1), 75–91.

Giacalone, R. (2004). A transcendent business education for the 21st century. *Academy of Management Learning and Education, 3*(4), 415–420.

Gilinsky, A., Jr., & Robinson, R. (2008). A proposed design for the business capstone course with emphasis on improving students' information competency. *Journal of Management Education, 32*(4), 400–419. doi:10.1177/1052562907307633

Glaser, E. M. (1941). *An experiment in the development of critical thinking.* New York: Teacher's College, Columbia University.

Godwin, L. (2015). Examining the impact of moral imagination on organizational decision making. *Business & Society, 54*(2), 254–278. doi:10.1177/0007650312443641

Godwin, L., & Neville, M. G. (2008, Spring). Learning from a whole-system, strength-based approach: A case of collaborative curriculum development. *Journal for Quality and Participation,* 11–14.

Gordon, R. A., & Howell, J. E. (1959). *Higher education for business.* New York: Columbia University Press.

Greenberg, D., McKone-Sweet, K., & Wilson, H. J. (2011). *The new entrepreneurial leader: Developing leaders who shape social and economic opportunity.* San Francisco, CA: Berrett-Koehler Publishers, Inc.

Henninger, E. A., & Hurlbert, J. M. (2007). Using *The seven principles for good practice in undergraduate education:* A framework for teaching cultural diversity in a management course. *Journal of Business & Finance Librarianship, 12*(2), 3–15.

Herrington, J. D., & Arnold, D. R. (2013). Undergraduate business education: It's time to think outside the box. *Journal of Education for Business, 88*(4), 202–209.

Hershatter, A., & Epstein, M. (2010). Millennials and the world of work: An organization and management perspective. *Journal of Business and Psychology, 25*(2), 211–223.

Hibbert, P. (2013). Approaching reflexivity through reflection: Issues for critical management education. *Journal of Management Education, 37*(6), 803–827. doi:10.1177/1052562912467757

Hjorth, D. (2007). Lessons from Iago: Narrating the event of entrepreneurship. *Journal of Business Venturing, 22*(5), 712–732.

Holtzman, D. M., Stockton, R., & Kraft, E. M. (2010). Skills required of business graduates: Evidence form undergraduate alumni and employers. *Business Education and Accreditation, 2*(1), 49–60.

Hunt, D. E. (1999). *Beginning with ourselves: In practice, theory, and human affairs.* Cambridge, MA: Brookline Books.

Johnston, J. S. (1986). *Educating managers: Executive effectiveness through liberal learning.* San Francisco: Jossey-Bass.

Journal of Management Education (2015). Special Issue. *39*(1).

Kassel, K., Rimanoczy, I., & Mitchell, S. (2016). The sustainability mindset: Connecting being, thinking and doing in management education. *Proceedings from 76th Annual Meeting of the Academy of Management,* Anaheim, CA.

Khurana, R. (2007). *From higher aims to hired hands: The social transformation of American business schools and the unfulfilled promise of management as a profession.* Princeton, NJ: Princeton University Press.

Kimball, B. (1996). A historical perspective. In N. H. Farnham and A. Yarmolinsky (Eds.), *Rethinking liberal education.* New York: Oxford University Press.

Kimball, B. (2003, January). Interpreting the liberal arts: Four lectures on the history and historiography of the liberal arts. *Journal of the Institute for the Liberal Arts, 1.*

Knight, M. (1999). Writing and other communication standards in undergraduate business education: A study of current program requirements, practices, and trends. *Business Communication Quarterly, 62*(1), 10–28.

Kohn, J. (2013). Federalists #10 in management #101: What Madison has to teach managers. *Journal of Management Education, 37*(5), 683–703.

Kolb, D. (1984). *Experiential learning: Experience as the source of learning and development.* Englewood Cliffs, NJ: Prentice Hall.

Lampe, M. (1997). Increasing effectiveness in teaching ethics to undergraduate business students. *Teaching Business Ethics, 1*(1), 3–19.

Lechtenberg, S. (2014). Is learning a foreign language really worth it? A new Freakanomics radio podcast. [Podcast] *Freakanomics radio.* Retrieved from http://freakonomics.com/2014/03/06/is-learning-a-foreign-language-really-worth-it-a-new-freakonomics-radio-podcast

Long, C. M., & Shrikhande, M. M. (2007). Improving information-seeking behavior among business majors. *Research Strategies, 20,* 357–369.

MacPherson, K. (2002). Problem-solving ability and cognitive maturity in undergraduate students. *Assessment & Evaluation in Higher Education, 27*(1), 5–22.

Martin, R. L. (2007). *The opposable mind: How successful leaders win through integrative thinking.* Boston: Harvard Business School Press.

Martinez, Z. L., Padmanabhan P., & Toyne, B. (2007). Integrating international business and liberal arts education: The southern cone studies program. *Journal of Teaching in International Business, 18*(4), 37–55.

McInnis-Bowers, C., & Chew, E. B. (2008). The true teamwork model: Blending the liberal arts and international business education. *Liberal Education, 94*(3), 24–29.

Mezirow, J. (1991). *Transformative dimensions of adult learning.* San Francisco: Jossey-Bass.

Mintzberg, H. (2004). *Managers not MBAs.* San Francisco: Barrett-Koehler.

Mitroff, I., & Swanson, D. (2004). An open letter to the deans and the faculties of American business schools: A call for action. *Academy of Management News, 35*(2), 6–8.

Musil, C. M. (2009). Educating students for personal and social responsibility: The civic learning spiral. In B. Jacoby & T. Erlich (Eds.), *Civic engagement in higher education.* San Francisco, CA: John-Wiley & Sons, Inc.

Navarro, P. (2008). The MBA core curricula of top-ranked U.S. business schools: A study in failure? *Academy of Management Learning and Education, 7*(1), 109–123.

Nesteruk, J. (2005). A liberal model for professional education. *Liberal Arts Online, 5*(8). Retrieved from www.liberalarts.wabash.edu/lao-5-8-lae-professional-ed/

Neville, M. G. (2004). *Generating holistic wealth: A framework for positive change leadership at the intersection of business and society* (doctoral dissertation). Weatherhead School of Management, Case Western Reserve University, Cleveland, OH. Dissertation Abstracts International, 64, 12A.

Neville, M. G. (2007). Using appreciative inquiry and dialogical learning to explore dominant paradigms. *Journal of Management Education, 32*(1), 100–117. doi:10.1177/1052562907305558

Neville, M. G. (2015). Opening the floodgates of curiosity: How dialogue can increase the flow of relational space. *Journal for Quality and Participation, 38*(2), 24–31.

Neville, M. G., & Godwin, L. (2011). Returning to a holistic management education and the tradition of liberal education. In C. Wankle & A. Stachowicz-Stanusch (Eds.), *Management education for integrity: Ethically educating tomorrow's business leaders*. Bingley, UK: Emerald Group Publishing Limited.

Neville, M. G., Godwin, L., Senchack, A. J., & Parks, D. (2007). *Re-envisioning business programs in liberal arts worlds: 2006 summit proceedings and outcomes*. Georgetown, TX: Southwestern University.

Pierson, F. (1959). *The education of American businessmen: A study of university-college programmes in business administration. Carnegie series in American education*. New York: McGraw-Hill.

Quinton, S., & Smallbone, T. (2005). The troublesome triplets: Issues in teaching reliability, validity and generalization to business students. *Teaching in Higher Education, 10*(3), 299–311.

Rimanoczy, I. (2014). A matter of being: Developing sustainability-minded leaders. *Journal of Management for Global Sustainability, 2*(1), 95–122.

Rimanoczy, I. (2016). *Stop teaching: Principles and practices for responsible management education*. New York: Business Expert Press.

Rimanoczy, I. B. (2010). *Business leaders committing to and fostering sustainability initiatives*. Doctoral dissertation. Teachers College, Columbia University, New York, Rotman School of Management. Retrieved from www.rotman.utoronto.ca

Short, J., & Ketchen, D. (2005). Teaching timeless truths through classic literature: Aesop's fables and strategic management. *Journal of Management Education, 29*(6), 816.

Stein, M. (2005). The Othello conundrum: The inner contagion of leadership. *Organization Studies, 26*(9), 1405–1419.

Thurston, E. (2000). Enabling systems thinking in the "Mesonic millennium": The need for systemic methodologies for conceptual learning in undergraduate management education. *Journal of Management Education, 24*(1), 1–31.

Useem, M. (1989). *Liberal education and the corporation: The hiring and advancement of college graduates*. New York: Aldine de Gruyter.

Van Maanen, J. (2011). Ethnography as work: Some rules of engagement. *Journal of Management Studies 48*(1), 218–234. doi:10.1111/j.1467–6486.2010.00980.x

Waddock, S. (2007). Leadership integrity in a fractured knowledge world. *Academy of Management Learning & Education, 6*(4), 543–557.

Wells, H. L. (1953). *Higher education is serious business: A study of university business management in relation to higher education*. Harper: Unknown binding.

Wick, M., & Phillips, A. (2008, Winter). Liberal education scorecard. *Liberal Education*, 22–59.

Wilton, N. (2008). Business graduates and management jobs: An employability match made in heaven? *Journal of Education and Work, 21*(2), 143–158. doi:10.1080/13639080802080949

INDEX

Note: Page numbers in italics indicate figures and those in bold indicate tables.

behavior and 116, 117; behaviors towards sustainability and 78–79; being dimension and 115–117; circular motivational continuum of 79; classification of 115–116, **116**; cooperation and 80–81; defined 76, 113, 117; education, and sustainability 83–89, 85, **88**; enacted 115; espoused 115; ethics and, development of 117–123; Indian perspective on 119–123; instrumental 115; introduction to 71–72; management education and 71–90; mobilizing approaches to, and sustainability-oriented teaching 85; motivational types of **77**; norms of culture and 116–117; personal, development of 117–119; pro-sustainability, attitudes and 82–83; sociological social psychology view of 72; for sustainability 72–76, 113–114; terminal 115; term use of 71; theory 76–78, **77**

values dimension, ecological worldview content area: biospheric orientation **15**, 15–16; compassion 23, **23**, 24; interconnectedness, sense of **20**, 20–21; oneness with all that is **26**, 26–27

Values in Action (VIA) classification, character strengths **125**

value system, defined 113

Van Der Kamp, M. 113

Van der Laan, S. 106

Van Lopik, W. 309

Van Maanen, J. 335

Verlanken, B. 79

virtue 121–122

Visva-Bharati university 121

Vivekananda, S. 146

vocation, sense of as spiritual intelligence principle 242

Voss, R. S. 339

Vries, H. J. M. 239

walkabout project 195

Wall Street Journal, The 27

Walmart Sustainability Index 290

Waste Bank network 198–199

Weick, K. E. 335

Wells, H. 349

Wessler, R. 279

Wheeler, D. 25

Whitney, D. 192

whole person, strategic building *325*, 338–339

Why Religion Matters (Smith) 147

Wick, M. 337, 349

Wilber, K. 284–285

Wilson, H. J. 334–335

Winston, A. S. 29

wisdom, defined 291–292

Wong, P. T. P. 25

World Commission for Economic Development 73

worldview, defined 239

writing 329–330

Yeager, D. S. 4, 8

Yin, R. K. 246

Young, S. 22

Zambia dairy value chain study 207–210, *208*, **210**; Appreciative Inquiry results 211–216; sustainability mindset shift in learning 216–217; *see also* agripreneurship, sustainable cross-cultural learning processes for

Zimmerman, S. 311

Zohar, D. 48, 146, 241

PGMO 04/18/2018